# Doing Business with
# Croatia

## CROATIAN CHAMBER OF ECONOMY

The Croatian Chamber of Economy is a modern, professional institution that speaks for and promotes Croatian economic interests in Croatia and abroad.

With its 153 years of tradition, the CCE is a reliable source of information for all Croatian companies and their foreign partners. It offers a wide variety of services, from business information about companies, regulations and laws in the field of economics to business education and professional specialization, quality improvement and environmental protection. The doors of the Croatian Chamber of Economy are wide open for all domestic and foreign business people.

The CCE was first established in Zagreb in 1852, and has been operating ever since. After Croatia gained independence in 1991, it was organized to be the single chamber for all business entities in Croatia in line with European tradition. The changes to the territorial organization and to the organization of business domains in the CCE were followed by corresponding changes in the work of its professional services.

Within its regular activities, the CCE provides business information, services and contacts. The services that the CCE provides are the representation of the interests of its members before government authorities, the coordination of the common interests of its members, the promotion of the Croatian economy abroad, the establishment and development of all types of business relations with foreign countries, the establishment of contacts between domestic and foreign business entities, and similar.

The CCE exercises public authority, which includes the issuance and certification of various documents evidencing the Croatian origin of goods (non-preferential origin of goods; FORM A certificate of Croatian origin of goods, which is used for the implementation of preferences on the basis of the General Scheme of Preferences — GSP). Also other documents are issued or certified that accompany exported/ imported goods, such as export permits and non-preferential certificates for textile products; ATA Carnets; documents that facilitate customs procedures for the temporary import/export of goods intended for personal or professional purposes and, in particular, those that accompany commercial samples, professional equipment, fair exhibits, objects used for exhibitions, and similar.

In addition, The CCE has a member database, which is regularly updated. The database includes a business register, a products and services file, a performance file and an export and import file. The sources of information for updating the register of Croatian companies are the Croatian Bureau of Statistics, the Commercial Court, the State Payment Transactions Bureau and the Customs Administration. The data is classified in accordance with global and European standards.

In conclusion, the Croatian Chamber of Economy was among the first institutions in Croatia that created their own websites. The website, www.hgk.hr, presents the Chamber's structure and activities, as well as the following business services: registering of Croatian companies, business opportunity exchange (offer and demand of goods and services) and waste materials exchange.

GLOBAL MARKET BRIEFINGS

# Doing Business with

# Croatia

SECOND EDITION

Consultant editors:
Marat Terterov
Višnja Bojanić

Associate publisher:
Vanja Ivkovic

Published in association with:

INDUSTRIJA NAFTE, d.d.

GMB

This second edition first published in Great Britain and in the USA in 2005 by GMB Publishing Limited.

GMB Publishing Ltd
120 Pentonville Road
London N1 9JN
UK
www.gmbpublishing.com

Distributed by Kogan Page Ltd
120 Pentonville Road
London N1 9JN
UK

22883 Quicksilver Drive
Sterling VA 20166–2012
USA

© GMB Publishing and Contributors 2005

ISBN 1–905050–03–8

British Library Cataloguing-in-Publication Data
A CIP record for this book is available from the British Library

Typeset by Saxon Graphics Ltd, Derby

Printed in the United Kingdom at the University Press, Cambridge

# Contents

| | | |
|---|---|---|
| Foreword | | xi |
| *Mrs Kolinda Grabar-Kitarović, Minister of Foreign Affairs and European Integration* | | |
| List of contributors | | xiii |
| Map 1 Croatia and its neighbours | | xxiii |
| Map 2 Zagreb and the surrounding area | | xxiv |

**PART ONE: BACKGROUND TO THE MARKET**

| | | |
|---|---|---|
| 1.1 | Croatia: Historical, Geographical and Political Overview | 3 |
| | *Biljana Radonjic, Civilitas Research* | |
| 1.2 | Economic Overview | 11 |
| | *Iva Condic-Jurkic, Institute of Economics, Zagreb* | |
| 1.3 | Croatia and the EU – A Progress Report on Entry | 29 |
| | *Mrs Kolinda Grabar-Kitarović, Minister of Foreign Affairs and European Integration* | |
| 1.4 | Living and Working in Croatia: An Enviable Position | 42 |
| | *Wade Channell, American Chamber of Commerce, Croatia* | |

**PART TWO: THE INVESTMENT ENVIRONMENT**

| | | |
|---|---|---|
| 2.1 | Foreign Direct Investment in Croatia | 49 |
| | *Hrvoje Dolenec and Zrinka Živković, Raiffeisenbank Austria d.d. Zagreb* | |
| 2.2 | The Investment Climate and Future FDI Flows | 58 |
| | *Igor Maričić, Croatian Trade & Investment Promotion Agency* | |
| 2.3 | Formulating an Appropriate Investment Strategy | 62 |
| | *Michael Glazer, Auctor Securities* | |
| 2.4 | The Banking System | 68 |
| | *Hrvoje Dolenec, Raiffeisenbank Austria d.d. Zagreb* | |
| 2.5 | The Securities Market in Croatia | 76 |
| | *Zlatko Gregurić, Raiffeisenbank Austria d.d. Zagreb* | |
| 2.6 | Foreign Exchange Regulations in Croatia | 80 |
| | *Adrian Hammer, Deloitte & Touche* | |
| 2.7 | Corruption: Understanding Risk and Building Stability | 83 |
| | *Josip Kregar, School of Law, Zagreb University* | |

## PART THREE: PROSPECTIVE SECTORS FOR INVESTMENT

3.1  A Protected Environment in the Adriatic Area:                    97
A Key for Sustainable Economic Development
*Dr Anamarija Frankic, University of Massachusetts, Boston*

3.2  Agriculture, Fisheries and Food Production                      102
*Croatian Chamber of Economy*

3.3  The Croatian Construction Industry                              110
*Croatian Chamber of Economy*

3.4  Healthcare and Pharmaceuticals                                  116
*Ivana Blašković and Igor Mataić, Raiffeisenbank Austria d.d. Zagreb*

3.5  Food and Beverages                                             126
*Ivana Blašković, Raiffeisenbank Austria d.o.o Zagreb, and*
*Igor Mataić, Raiffeisen Consulting*

3.6  Textiles and Apparel                                           135
*Croatian Chamber of Economy*

3.7  Small and Medium-sized Enterprises (SMEs) in Croatia           141
*Hayley Alexander, Deloitte Emerging Markets*

3.8  Tourism                                                        146
*Croatian Chamber of Economy*

3.9  The Telecommunications Market                                  157
*VIPnet*

3.10 Mobile Telecommunications                                      164
*VIPnet*

3.11 Telecommunications: The Regulatory Framework                   171
*VIPnet*

3.12 Information and Communication Technology (ICT) in Croatia      179
*Professor Velimir Srića, PhD*

3.13 Real Estate for Foreign Citizens and Enterprises              190
*Višnja Bojanić*

## PART FOUR: CROATIA'S MOST DYNAMIC COMPANIES AND PROSPECTIVE INVESTMENT PROJECTS

4.1  INA Industrija nafte d.d.                                      201
4.2  Konstruktor-Inženjering d.d. Split                            207
4.3  Dalekovod d.d.                                                217
4.4  MTC                                                            228
4.5  Jadranski Pomorski Servis d.o.o., Rijeka                      231
4.6  Piramida d.d.                                                 237
4.7  Koestlin d.o.o.                                               244
4.8  Centrometal d.o.o.                                            249
4.9  Emka d.o.o.                                                   254
4.10 The Zagreb Insurance Company                                  259

## PART FIVE: THE TAXATION AND LEGAL ENVIRONMENT

5.1 The Legal Framework for Doing Business with Croatia    267
*Adrian Hammer, Deloitte & Touche*

5.2 Business Entities in Croatia    273
*Vanja Markovic LLM, Tax and Regulatory Services,
Deloitte & Touche, Zagreb*

5.3 The Taxation System    288
*Helena Schmidt, Tax and Regulatory Services, Deloitte & Touche,
Zagreb*

5.4 Personal Income Tax and Social Security Contributions    302
*Adrian Hammer, Deloitte & Touche*

5.5 Auditing and Accounting    306
*Marina Tonžetić, Deloitte & Touche*

5.6 Employment Law and Work Permits for Foreigners    313
*Adrian Hammer, Deloitte & Touche*

5.7 Legal Regulations on Land/Real Estate Ownership in Croatia    319
*Marinko Mileta, Marković & Plišo Law Firm*

5.8 Arbitration and Dispute Resolution    325
*Ante Glamuzina and Kristijan Galić, Marković & Plišo Law Firm*

5.9 Intellectual Property    329
*Nikolina Staničić and Josip Grošeta, Marković & Plišo Law Firm*

5.10 The Regulation of Investment Funds    335
*Josip Grošeta, Marković & Plišo Law Firm*

## PART SIX: APPENDICES

Appendix I      Business Organizations      343
Appendix II     Useful Websites      346
Appendix III    Contributor Contact Details      350

Index      355

# AMERICAN CHAMBER OF COMMERCE IN CROATIA

AmCham Croatia was established in December 1998 with 20 Founding Members. AmCham is a non-profit, non-governmental, voluntary organization of enterprises and individuals dedicated to promoting mutual cooperation and business networking. AmCham maintains good relations with the US government and its agencies and representatives in the US and abroad, as well as the Croatian government. However, AmCham is and will remain independent of and unaffiliated with any government, including the US government.

AmCham employs a small staff and also operates through committees of its members that address topics that affect their businesses. Each committee is focused on an area of interest or importance to a significant portion of AmCham's membership. AmCham currently has the following committees: Competitiveness, Environmental, EU & Tax/Legal, Health Care, ICT, Investment, Research & Development and Publication. Representatives of AmCham members are invited to join the committees established by AmCham.

## VISION

AmCham Croatia was formed to advance the interests and views of the US and other foreign businesses in Croatia and of Croatian businesses abroad, to assist in improving the business environment in Croatia generally and to promote high standards of commercial practice. In so doing, AmCham helps Croatia attract both the expertise and technology needed to compete on foreign markets and the investment capital required to build new factories, employ Croatian citizens and restore tourism and other industries.

## MISSION

AmCham is to establish and maintain close communication among the foreign investors already present in Croatia, foreigners considering investing in Croatia, Croatian companies and the Croatian government and its ministries and institutions. AmCham organizes a variety of activities at which information can be exchanged: monthly luncheon meetings at which keynote speakers, including government officials, local and foreign business leaders and other experts, address topics of significance to AmCham's members; sponsored cocktails, power breakfasts, seminars and roundtables. In addition, AmCham provides its members with a magazine which contains a broad range of useful information, including business and governmental contacts and specific information about applicable laws, regulations and programmes. AmCham also seeks to identify impediments to business in or with Croatia and, through its close relationship with Croatian and foreign governments and the Croatian and foreign business communities, to make suggestions as to how these problems can be resolved or reduced. AmCham also promotes philanthropic projects benefiting the broader community and encourages and facilitates such philanthropy among its members.

## *MEMBERSHIP AND SERVICES*

Members of AmCham join for different reasons. Although most join mainly to make business contacts, exchange useful information and enhance community goodwill, others join to enjoy the benefits of AmCham's services, which include:

- facilitating business and government contacts;

- organizing regular luncheons featuring Croatian, US and other foreign business leaders and officials as keynote speakers;

- organizing informal monthly cocktails sponsored by AmCham members which have a short presentation of their companies/ products;

- facilitating networking among our members;

- publishing *News & Views* magazine containing relevant information about changes in legislation, regulations in addition to business opportunities, reports on AmCham events, advertising of our members;

- organizing seminars and training sessions on important topics;

- access to our library which contains English translations of some Croatian laws;

- co-operation with the activities of the US Chamber of Commerce and the European Council of American Chambers of Commerce (ECACC) – 'Mutual Services & Benefits Program' participation in AmCham committees.

AmCham members come from many parts of the business community: US companies, Croatian companies, US citizens, Croatian citizens, companies/citizens from other countries and non-profit organizations.

## CONTACT US

AmCham Croatia welcomes feedback from members and non-members, along with their recommendations on how to improve its representation and services. Please write, call or email us at the following contact:

American Chamber of Commerce in Croatia
Mr Damir Vucić, Executive Director
Krsnjavoga 1
10000 Zagreb, Croatia
Tel: +385 (0) 1 4836 777
Fax: +385 (0) 1 4836 776
Email: info@amcham.hr
Please visit us at: www.amcham.hr

# Foreword

The year 2004 bore a great significance for Croatia's European integration path. In that year, Croatia became a candidate country and the date for the commencement of the accession negotiations was set for 17 March 2005.

The Government of the Republic of Croatia is firmly determined to finalize the accession negotiations and to be ready to assume the obligations arising from European Union (EU) membership in 2007. Even though Croatia began the accession process rather late, we have been fortunate to learn from the experiences of the new member states, both the good and the bad negotiating and harmonization experiences. We have also been able to test our potential and capacity since 2001. Therefore, we are quite realistic when stating that we are capable of accomplishing our accession negotiations within the two and a half-year period.

The actual membership will not depend solely on Croatia's determination and preparedness, but also on the willingness and preparedness of the EU to accept new members after the fifth enlargement wave in 2004 and the completion of its internal reforms.

I am confident that the said goal of the Croatian government can be reached, provided that the present dynamics of meeting EU membership criteria are upheld. In this way, we are achieving our goal – to make Croatia a model European democracy and a strong market economy with a powerful social component, all to the benefit of Croatian citizens. Membership of the EU comes as the result of those comprehensive reform activities.

When it comes to the business environment, we have to continue reforming our legislation by bringing it in line with the European *acquis*, as well as to enhance our administrative capacity, thus creating a familiar and reliable legal framework for investors and entrepreneurs. Macroeconomic stability is a long-lasting trend in the Croatian economy. The government's economic and financial policy is being supported and endorsed by the World Bank and IMF arrangements. Additional efforts are being undertaken to boost the sustainable development of the real sector of the economy, especially by improving the investment framework. Croatia's overall economic performance represented a proper basis for the European Commission to evaluate it as a functioning market economy that should be able to cope with competitive pressures and market forces within the EU in the medium term.

In this respect, the business community should start to regard Croatia as a future EU member state. Doing business in Croatia today means that businesses are able to take advantage of liberalized trade and economic relations with the EU. But it also means that they can benefit from the fact that Croatia has become an economic leader and political model in South-East Europe.

By embarking upon the accession path, Croatia also wants to contribute to the stability of the wider region of South-East Europe and to demonstrate to the other Stabilization and Association Process countries the profitability of carrying out the required reforms, making their prospects of EU membership more realistic. With this step, Croatia does not intend to, and cannot, disassociate itself from the region. We have the same, if not higher, interest as the EU in forging a politically and economically stable neighbourhood in the Balkans. We are willing to contribute to that stability by assuming our responsibility as a leader in the region.

Croatia is ready to start the negotiations for accession to the EU and, upon becoming a member, will contribute to the great project of European integration and the building of societies based on peace, freedom, democracy, human rights, rule of law, security, solidarity and economic prosperity. Consequently, our road is only the one leading to the EU.

*Mrs Kolinda Grabar-Kitarović*
*Minister of Foreign Affairs and European Integration*

# List of contributors

**Višnja Bojanić, MA** graduated at the University of Zagreb, Faculty of Philosophy in 1980, and earned her Masters Degree in European Studies at the Faculty of Law, University of Zagreb in 2002.

From 1992 to 1997, she worked as an interpreter/translator with the United Nations mission in Croatia, in the French logistic department. From 1997 to 1999, she worked in the Croatian Helsinki Committee for Human Rights (CHC). She was responsible for drafting annual reports on human rights violations in Croatia, for the International Helsinki Federation and the Organization for Security and Cooperation in Europe (OSCE). She collaborated in the preparation of a final paper 'Military Operation Storm and its aftermath', written by Professor Žarko Puhovski, Ph.D. and published by the CHC in 1999. She took part in the research of the media coverage of 1997 parliamentary and presidential elections, in cooperation with the European Institute for the Media from Düsseldorf, for *Elections in the Media*, published in 1999. She also contributed to the making of *The People, Press and Politics of Croatia*, a book by S Malovic, Professor at the Faculty of Political Sciences in Zagreb and G Selnow, Professor of Communication at the San Francisco State University, USA, about the evolution of the press in Croatia from Tito to Tudjman's era, published in 2001.

Since 1999 Ms Bojanić has worked in the Tax & Legal department of the consulting firm PricewaterhouseCoopers and, since 2001, as a marketing manager in Deloitte, Croatia. She was also editorial consultant for the first edition of *Doing Business with Croatia* sponsored by Deloitte & Touche, Croatia and published in 2003 by Kogan Page, London.

Ms Bojanić is a member of the Executive Board of TI Croatian, the Chapter of Transparency International.

**Wade Channell** is a legal reform and economic development consultant for various international development agencies. He recently completed a one-year term as President of the **American Chamber of Commerce (AmCham) in Croatia**, after completing a one-year consulting assignment involving judicial reform. Prior to living in Croatia, he spent more than two years managing projects there from the United States. During these past four years, he has also visited or worked in all of the countries in the Balkans. He considers himself a firm believer in Croatia's potential for sustained growth and achievement, and an addict to their café culture. Mr Channell can be contacted at wade.channell@earthlink.net.

**Biljana Radonjic** is an assistant director of **Civilitas Research**, an independent policy research centre (think-tank) providing commentary and analysis on politics and society in Southeast Europe and the Eastern Mediterranean. Its primary objective is to contribute to informed international debate on the region. Civilitas Research meets this goal by publishing books and articles, delivering presentations and briefings and by contributing to media coverage on various aspects of regional security, democratization and EU integration.

Located in Cyprus – the historical meeting point between Europe, the Middle East and Africa – Civilitas merges a local, 'on the ground' perspective of the problems facing the countries of the region with the best practices of international academic research and policy analysis. In addition to the core team, Civilitas also draws on the knowledge and expertise of an extended network of 150 leading scholars, analysts and correspondents. As well as freely published research, Civilitas Research has also provided custom research and analysis for a number of public, private, non-profit and international organizations. It was founded in 2001.

**The Croatian Chamber of Economy (HZK)**, which was founded over 150 years ago, is a reliable source of information for all businesses in Croatia, as well as for their international partners. In addition, the Chamber provides a host of services, including business information on specific companies, laws and regulations relating to the economy, business education and skills training, environmental protection and quality control. The door of the Croatian Chamber of Economy is always open to all domestic and foreign business people. The Chamber offers business services, contacts and information within its regular activities.

**The Croatian Trade and Investment Promotion Agency** (Croatian: Agencija za promicanje izvoza i ulaganja – APIU) was established in the first half of 2003. The main goals of the Agency are promotion and support of Croatian exports as well as investments in Croatia. The initiator and founder of the Agency is the government of the Republic of Croatia.

The Agency is an information point as well as project manager and coordinator for investment and trade projects in Croatia. In its investment operations, the Agency provides one-stop-shop concept services for foreign and domestic investors.

**Deloitte Croatia** is a member of Deloitte Touche Tohmatsu, a Swiss Verein. It belongs to an organization of member firms around the world devoted to excellence in providing professional services and advice, focused on client service through a global strategy executed locally in nearly 150 countries. With access to the deep intellectual capital of 120,000 people worldwide, Deloitte delivers services in four professional areas – audit, tax, consulting, and financial advisory services – and serves more than one-half of the world's largest companies, as well as large national enterprises, public institutions, locally important clients, and successful, fast-growing global growth companies. Deloitte Croatia is one of the leading professional services organizations in the country, providing services in audit, tax, consulting, and financial advisory services through over 120 national and specialized expatriate professionals in three cities. Known as an employer of choice for innovative human resources programmes, it is dedicated to helping its clients and its people excel.

**Hayley Alexander** is a senior manager with **Deloitte & Touche Emerging Markets**, based in Washington, DC. The Emerging Markets Group is a specialized part of Deloitte & Touche that deals exclusively with consulting engagements in emerging markets all over the world. Mr Alexander has an undergraduate degree in business (BBA) from Eastern Michigan University and a postgraduate degree (MBA) in marketing from George Washington University in Washington, DC. He spent nine years in marketing, contract administration and financial management for a privately owned Detroit area firm that manufactured and sold specialized vehicles to the US government. Then in 1994, he joined Deloitte & Touche and moved to Russia to join a business development project. Since then he has worked on long-term business consulting and institutional development projects in Egypt, Ukraine, Bosnia and Herzegovina and, presently, Croatia. He has worked both in project management and technical assistance capacities, the latter mainly in marketing and financial management.

**Russell Aycock** is Regional Director of Deloitte & Touche's Tax and Regulatory Practice for the Adriatic Region (Slovenia, Croatia and Bosnia). Prior to joining the Central European and CIS practices in 1997, he was based in Deloitte's New York office, where he served media clients and financial institutions. Russell is a US Certified Public Accountant with extensive experience in international taxation, structuring of inbound and outbound investment, cross-border mergers and acquisitions, financing structures, transfer pricing, Central European corporate taxation and intellectual property taxation.

**Adrian Hammer** is a consultant in the Tax Department at Deloitte & Touche Croatia. Adrian graduated with a law degree at the University of Auckland, New Zealand, in 2002. Following graduation, he worked at the top New Zealand law firm, Russell McVeagh, specializing in corporate law and tax. In 2004, Adrian joined Deloitte in Croatia as a tax consultant and, since then, has been involved with a number of transactions, including legal and tax due diligence, mergers & acquisitions, transfer pricing issues as well as general tax advisory services. Adrian's area of priority is focused on corporate income tax and VAT. In addition to tax expertise, his experience in the corporate legal field enables him to advise on a number of issues related to corporate laws.

**Dr Anamarija Frankic** is a research faculty associate at the Virginia Institute of Marine Science (College of William and Mary), and an assistant professor at the University of Massachusetts, Boston. In 1993, she received the USAID International Fellowship Award to pursue doctorate education in marine science and natural resources management. Consequently, she left Croatia and the National Park Plitvice Lakes where she had worked as an ecologist since 1986. In 1995, Dr Frankic was the first Croatian to receive a prestigious two-year international fellowship award from the American Association of University Women (AAUW). In 1997, she received the US Sea Grant Congressional Fellowship award and worked for the US Senator Daniels Akaka (democrat from Hawaii). During that year Dr Frankic initiated several important environmental bills, two of which became laws: Coral Reef Conservation Act (106/562); National Aquaculture Development, Research and Promotion Act (S. 1080); while the Hawaiian Tropical Forest Products Certification Act received the McArthur Foundation Award for the 'first green bill'.

At the same time, Dr Frankic has been initiating environmental projects in Croatia, and two major ones received the Global Environment Facility (GEF) grants: Karst Ecosystem Conservation project brought US$8.5 million for protection and sustainable development in Lika and Gorski Kotar and their five protected areas; the Coast project will support conservation of natural resources and enhance sustainable development of the Dalmatian coast and islands (estimated US$10 million). In 2002, Dr Frankic received a grant from the US National Science Foundation to initiate the first international environmental management studies in Croatia, Dubrovnik, which is now educating the first generation of students. She also helped prepare guidelines and strategy for integrated coastal area management and sustainable aquaculture development in Croatia (Norway grant).

Dr Frankic has been invited as an expert and speaker to many national and international conferences and working groups to promote applied science and management for coastal and marine ecosystems and protected areas. She has been part of the working groups for

UNESCO's Coastal–Global Ocean Observing System; organized NATO's research workshop on Transatlantic and EU-Mediterranean coastal policies; the EU's coastal management projects in Ireland and Belgium; and UNESCO's Rio (10 conferences).

Dr Frankic lives in Williamsburg, Virginia with her husband and son.

**Michael Glazer** is responsible for merchant banking and corporate finance, international business development and strategic planning at **Auctor Securities**, Croatia's leading independent securities firm. Prior to the establishment of Auctor Securities, Mr Glazer taught finance as a Fulbright Professor at the Zagreb Economics Faculty and worked as a consultant to the Croatian government. Before coming to Croatia in 1994, Mr Glazer worked at Financial Security Assurance, the monoline insurer, where he specialized in cross-border securitization as well as sovereign and quasi-sovereign financings. These included the first credit card securitization in Hong Kong, the refinancing of Barcelona Holding Olímpic S.A., one of the vehicles through which Barcelona financed the 1992 Olympic Games, and receivables securitizations in Italy. Before FSA, Mr Glazer was associated with Cleary, Gottlieb, Steen & Hamilton, the New York-based international law firm, where his practice focused on sophisticated international financial transactions, including sovereign debt restructuring. While at Cleary, Mr Glazer established the first Malaysian American Depository Receipts programme, participated in the creation of the Scudder New Asia Fund and effected the recapitalization of ENDESA, Chile's electric company. Mr Glazer speaks English, Croatian/Serbian/Bosnian, French and some Spanish, Slovene and Macedonian. He is a graduate of Yale Law School (J.D.), Princeton University's Woodrow Wilson School of Public and International Affairs (M.P.A.) and the University of New Hampshire (B.S. Physics). Mr Glazer was founding President of the Board of Governors of the American Chamber of Commerce in Croatia and is Founding President and current Co-President of Junior Achievement in Croatia.

**The Institute of Economics**, Zagreb is a scientific and research institution engaged in scientific and applied research projects in the field of economics. Since its foundation in 1939, the Institute has provided analysis of the Croatian economy and has examined economic development factors, proposing concrete solutions to key economic issues with the aim of serving as guidelines to the national economic policy makers. In the process of accomplishing its developing objectives, the Institute has intensified the scientific cooperation with similar institutions abroad.

**Iva Condic-Jurkic** works as a junior research assistant at the Institute of Economics, Zagreb within the Department of Economic Development and Economic System. In 2003, she graduated from the

Faculty of Economics at the University of Zagreb. At the moment Iva is about to gain her Masters degree in macroeconomics at the same faculty. She participates in research projects with the emphasis on macroeconomic issues, economic policy and the economic system in Croatia.

Since 1982, **Josip Kregar** has been a regular Professor of Law at the Zagreb University School of Law. From 1975–1981, he worked as a researcher on the Institute for Social Researches at the Zagreb School of Law. Since 1998, Professor Kregar has been the Dean of the Department of Sociology at the University of Zagreb, Faculty of Philosophy (the Department of Croatian Studies) and, since 1999, the Director of the Department for Sociology at the Zagreb School of Law.

In 1992 and 1993, Professor Kregar was visiting Professor at the Scholar University of Graz and, in 1995 and 1996, at the School of Law, Yale, USA. Professor Kregar also lectures in Public Administration, Sociology and the Sociology of Law, and on postgraduate studies of public administration at the Universities of Ljubljana and Zagreb and is also the Director of the postgraduate seminar 'Economy and Democracy' at the Inter-University Centre (IUC) in Dubrovnik, Croatia.

As an expert in law, Professor Kregar drafted and strongly lobbied the proposals of the 'Local Government Act' in 1993 and 2001, the Conflict of Interest regulation in 2002, the Law on Political parties (Financing of Political Parties) in 2002, Access to Information in 2003. In 2002, he took part in preparing the National Strategy to Fight Corruption, and was also the editor of the paper 'Strategy for Administrative and Political Development' (Croatia in the 21st century).

He is a member of the NGO project 'Croatia 2020'. He is President of the Foundation 'Centre for Democracy and Law – Miko Tripalo', and, from 2000–2003, he was the President of the Open Society Board. In March 2000, he was appointed the Commissioner for the City of Zagreb.

Professor Kregar is author of more than a hundred published books, articles and studies.

**Zoran Marković** and **Miroslav Plišo** established their respective law offices in 1987. Initially, the offices dealt with cases related to general civil law, but in the following years they started focusing more on advising. During 1989, new legislation allowed the establishment of private enterprises, so their legal practice began offering its services to numerous clients in the field of corporate law, legal consulting, and representation before courts and other legal authorities. This work soon represented 80 per cent of the matters handled by the office and such corporate focus continues today. In the Spring of 1995, they formally founded the law firm **Marković & Plišo** in Zagreb, which currently employs 18 jurists, nine of whom are attorneys at law, two legal advisors, seven legal trainees, six executive secretaries, a translator/court interpreter (for English and German languages) and two paralegals. Their law firm enjoys an ongoing cooperation with Radovan Pavelic, an attorney from New York (licensed to practice law in New York, Washington, DC, and Connecticut), as their special advisor for common law. In addition to their regular work, the law firm is also engaged in privatization proceedings and offers legal advice on securities, construction, taxes, financing, denationalization and similar matters.

**Kristijan Galić** graduated from the Law School, University of Zagreb in 1995. During his practice he worked in Privredna banka Zagreb d.d., and the Law Firm Marković & Plišo. Today he runs his own legal practice.

**Ante Glamuzina** graduated from the Law School, University of Zagreb in 1998. Since graduation, he has performed legal practice as an attorney at law in the Law Firm Marković & Plišo, Zagreb.

**Josip Grošeta** graduated from the Law School, University of Zagreb in 1998. He worked as a legal advisor in Raiffeisenbank Austria d.d. Zagreb and since 2002 he has performed legal practice as an attorney at law in the Law Firm Marković & Plišo, Zagreb.

**Marinko Mileta** graduated from the Law School, University of Zagreb in 1987 and since 1999 has performed legal practice as an attorney at law in the Law Firm Marković & Plišo, Zagreb.

**Nikolina Staničić** worked with Law Firm Marković & Plišo and today she works as legal advisor in HT Hrvatske telekomunikacije d.d. Zagreb.

**The Ministry of European Integration** has been engaged in preparatory activities for the establishment of a system leading to the efficient adjustment of the Croatian institutional, social, legal and economic system to those of the European Union (EU). In this respect, the Ministry is mandated with the coordination of the implementation of the Stabilization and Association Agreement and Interim Agreement, coordination of the process of harmonization of the Croatian legal system with EU law, coordination of EU assistance programmes, analytical support to the process of European Integration, raising public awareness for the process of rapprochement to the EU, the training of civil servants in the field of European Integration, as well as the establishment and coordination of the system for translation of EU legal documents.

The staff of the Ministry of European Integration numbers eight state officials and 161 employees, with an average age of around 31. As far as level of education of the Ministry's personnel is concerned, 44 of them have Master's degrees, while 148 of them are graduates. Women account for 72 per cent of the Ministry's personnel and 28 per cent are men. All of them have received proper training and are very well educated in all relevant fields.

**Mrs Kolinda Grabar-Kitarović** is the Minister of Foreign Affairs and European Integration of Croatia and the Head of Delegation for the negotiations on the accession of Croatia to the EU. She holds various degrees in international relations, security policy and diplomacy, as well as in the English and Spanish languages. She was a Fulbright scholar. Her career so far has been with the Ministry of Foreign Affairs of Croatia, occupying various posts (adviser to the deputy minister, Head of Department for North America, and was posted to the Croatian Embassy to Canada).

Since 1986, **Mr Velimir Srića PhD** has been a regular Professor of Management at the University of Zagreb, Faculty of Economy. He holds an MBA from the Columbia University, New York (Fulbright Scholarship) and MS in Electrical Engineering (Management Information Systems). Mr Srića earned his Doctorate in management information systems at the University of Zagreb, Faculty of Electrical Engineering.

From 1995–1998, Mr Srića was a full visiting professor at UCLA (University of California at Los Angeles), and in 1982 at the Beijing People's University in the People's Republic of China. From 1986–1990, Mr Srića was the Minister of Science, Technology and Computing and an active member of the Croatian government. He was also the President of the City Council of Zagreb from 2001–2002.

Since 1993, Mr Srića has been a Member of the Board of CEEMAN – Central and Eastern European Management Development Association – and is also a member of the Club of Rome. Since 1997, he has been the Director of DELFIN (Developing Effective Leadership for Innovation), a private executive development programme. From 1985–1986, Mr Srića was the Director of the Croatian Information Technology Institute. In 1990 he received Gerald Ford Fellowship and Eisenhower Fellowship awards.

He is a co-author of the *International Encyclopedia of Business and Management*, Thomson Publishing Company, London 2001 and of the *Handbook of IT in Business*, published in 1999. He has published altogether 35 books, some 200 scientific papers and 70 articles in popular magazines.

Mr Srića is also a management consultant to a number of Croatian and international companies (DHL, Coca Cola, Uljanik, Croatian Telecom, FINA, Brodosplit, PBZ, INA, Gorenje, Krka, NLB, SRC.SI etc) and The World Bank expert on Change Management.

Since 1999 he has been an honorary member of the Croatian Helsinki Committee for Human Rights.

In 1994, the 117-year-old Raiffeisen banking group from Austria decided to invest in Croatia and founded **Raiffeisenbank Austria d.d. Zagreb (RBA)**. Now headquartered in Zagreb, Petrinjska 59, it was the first foreign-owned bank in Croatia. Today, RBA holds third place by volume of its assets, employs over 1,100 people and operates through a dense business network covering 15 Croatian towns and cities. RBA's success is based entirely on organic growth and investment in the training of its staff as well as continuous development of the products and services it offers.

In addition to offering retail and corporate customers as well as small businesses a broad range of products and services, RBA is well known for its sophisticated e-banking solutions. An important contribution to RBA becoming a household name has been its macroeconomic and financial research unit. For several years now RBA has been issuing a series of publications that have become an important and often-quoted source of information in both professional circles and the media. The periodicals published in Croatian are *Daily News* (a daily financial report), *RBA Info Spot, Raiffeisen Weekly Report, Raiffeisen Research Report* (published quarterly) and the most recent addition, *Commercial Papers,* while *CEE Weekly Bond Markets Outlook* (published in cooperation with RZB), *RBA Croatia Weekly Report, CEE Equity Weekly* (also published in cooperation with RZB) and *Raiffeisen Research Report* are published in English. All publications are available at RBA's home page, www.rba.hr, or can be obtained via email, while the quarterly reports are available in print.

RBA is a member of the global Raiffeisen Banking Group (RBG), the largest Austrian privately-owned banking group, comprising roughly one-quarter of the Austrian banking industry. The group's central unit is the Vienna-based Raiffeisen Zentralbank Osterreich AG (RZB).

**VIPnet** is the first private GSM operator in Croatia. It is owned by mobilkom austria, and a member of mobilkom austria group, together with Slovenian Si.mobil and mobilkom lichtenstein.

VIPnet is the most successful second GSM entry in Europe. In only five years, VIPnet became one of the most successful Croatian companies, employing over a thousand young experts. With its innovative products and services VIPnet attracted more than 1.2 million customers. Today, VIPnet, as a member of mobilkom austria group, is the exclusive Vodafone partner and one of the few operators in the world who offer two 3G technologies – EDGE and UMTS.

For further details please contact: Nina Kulaš, VIPnet Corporate Communications, Tel: +385 (0) 1 4691 182; Fax: +385 (0) 1 4691 189; GSM: + 385 91 4691 182.

**The Zagreb Insurance Company (Osiguranje Zagreb d.d.)** is the oldest private insurance company in Croatia. In keen market competition, The Zagreb Insurance Company maintains a high place, and its portfolio structure is increasingly similar to that of the same type of company in the European Union. According to these criteria, the Zagreb Insurance Company is a leading Croatian insurance company.

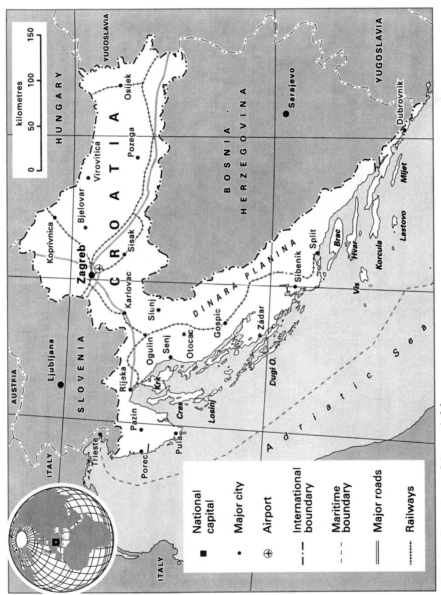

**Map 1** Croatia and its neighbours

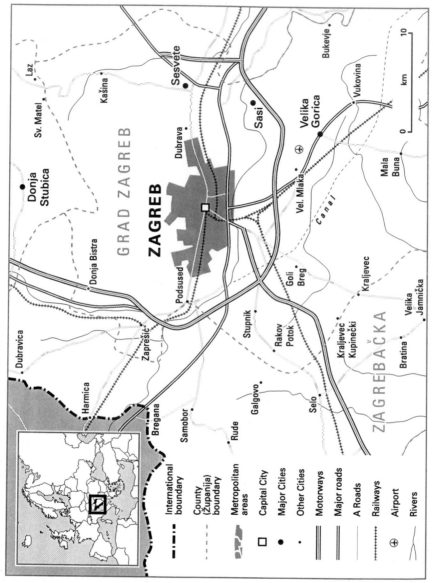

**Map 2** Zagreb and the surrounding area

# Part One

# Background to the Market

# 1.1

# Croatia: Historical, Geographical and Political Overview

*Biljana Radonjic, Civilitas Research*

Croatia, along with Slovenia, was the first constituent republic of the federal Yugoslavia to secede. However, unlike the brief skirmish in Slovenia, Croatia's declaration of independence in June 1991 led to lengthy war, as the Serb minority, supported by the federal army, resisted the move. In large part as a result of the war, the socio-political landscape of Croatia was dominated by the right wing conservative and nationalist policies of the Croatian Democratic Community (HDZ) for most of the rest of the 1990s, until the death of its autocratic leader Franjo Tudjman in late 1999. Croatia started its integration into the European family of nations in 2000, when a centre-left coalition government, led by Ivica Racan, came to power and a new president, Stipe Mesic, took over.

Since 2000, the country, which has five million inhabitants, has made impressive economic and political advances and taken significant steps towards joining various Euro–Atlantic structures. Croatia's fast growing economy, hefty foreign investments and the highest per capita GDP in the Western Balkans, places it on a par with most of the new Eastern European EU member states. Moreover, Croatia has stable democratic institutions, assured rule of law, free elections, independent media and active political opposition. However, some serious democratic deficiencies still persist. The main areas of concern relate to cooperation over war crimes, the treatment of Serbian minority and the return of refugees, as well as persistent corruption and judiciary reforms. Nevertheless, the current Croatian administration, led by Ivo Sanader, appears dedicated to overcoming these difficulties with a view to joining the European Union (EU) in the next five to six years.

Croatia is a southeast European country bordering the Adriatic Sea, Slovenia, Hungary, Serbia and Montenegro and Bosnia and Herzegovina.

# The political structure

Croatia is a constitutional parliamentary democracy. The Croatian Parliament, known as the 'Sabor', is a unicameral legislature that is elected on a four-yearly basis. It currently has 152 seats. Its authority covers virtually all major legislative and policy areas, including constitutional changes, national budget, national security and defence strategy. However, the government has wide-ranging executive powers, including passing decrees, introducing legislation and adopting strategies for economic and social development. The president of Croatia, who is head of state and commander-in-chief of the armed forces, is directly elected for a maximum of two five-year terms. The Constitutional Court has the power to review legislation to ensure its consistency with the Croatian constitution. It also rules on jurisdictional disputes among various branches of government. The Ombudsman – elected by the parliament for a period of eight years – protects the constitutional and legal rights of the citizens in the course of their dealings with governing bodies.

# Political history of Croatia before the collapse of Yugoslavia

Except for a short period of independence in the 10th century under King Tomislav, the different parts of present-day Croatia have long been dominated by foreign powers. In 1089, the central part of Croatia opted to live under Hungarian control but with a considerable degree of autonomy. In 1526, after the Hungarian army was defeated in the battle of Mohac, most of Croatia came under Ottoman rule for more than 150 years until 1699, when Croatia became part of the Habsburg Empire. At the same time, the coastal area of Dalmatia changed hands numerous times and was ruled by the Byzantines, Venice, Napoleon, the Ottomans and, lastly, by the Habsburgs.

In 1918, following the collapse of the Austro-Hungarian Empire at the end of the First World War, Croatia joined a newly formed Kingdom of the Serbs, Croats and Slovenians led by Peter I of Serbia, which later became the Kingdom of Yugoslavia. However, the centralized system of administration set up and dominated by the Kingdom's Serbian elites, soon led to resentment among the Croats. During the years leading to the Second World War, clashes among the constituent national groups destabilized Yugoslavia, which quickly crumbled when the Axis powers invaded and partitioned the country in 1941. A Nazi-sponsored puppet state, the Independent State of Croatia, was set up and led by the Ustase, an extreme right-wing group. This led to the deaths of hundreds of thousands of Serbs, Jews and gypsies. But, at the same time, many Croats joined the communist Partisan movement, which eventually liberated Yugoslavia in 1944. Soon afterwards, a socialist federation was established under the leadership of a popular and charismatic figure, Josip Broz Tito, who was himself half Croat. Within Yugoslavia, Croatia had great autonomy and was the second most prosperous republic after Slovenia.

Despite this, nationalistic sentiments in Croatia, often fuelled by the diaspora, came to the surface several times in the decades that followed. At other times, such feelings were the result of more widespread disillusionment that would affect all constituent parts of Yugoslavia. In one way or another, the Serbs, Croats, Slovenians, Macedonians, Montenegrins, Kosovo Serbs and Albanians all perceived themselves to be economically or politically disadvantaged vis-à-vis the other nations in the federation. In the early 1970s, the activists of a political mass movement, 'Croatian Spring', which included prominent academics, dissidents, students and some members of the Croatian Communist Party, advocated enhanced autonomy for Croatia and eventual secession. Demands such as greater democratization and market economy were also present but to a much lesser extent. The movement was harshly suppressed. Ironically, a few years later in 1974, Yugoslavia changed its constitution to include some major demands of 'Croatian Spring', including recognition of the right of every republic to secede.

After Tito's death in 1980, Yugoslavia's many socio-economic problems stemming from socialist mismanagement started to become painfully obvious. The country owed over US$18 billion to Western creditors. Again, disillusionment grew and nationalist sentiment developed in all the constituent republics. The rise to power of Slobodan Milosevic in Serbia, who had a hegemonic vision of Yugoslavia dominated by the Serbs, acted as a catalyst for strong nationalist tendencies to come to the fore across Yugoslavia. In 1989, Franjo Tudjman, a former communist-turned-nationalist general, established the HDZ in order to bring about Croatian independence.

## Breakaway from Yugoslavia and the war for independence

The first multi-party elections in Croatia were organized in April 1990, at the time when Croatia was still a federal republic of the former Yugoslavia. The HDZ won a massive victory and took almost two-thirds of the seats in the new Croatian Parliament, which was constituted in May 1990. Soon afterwards, Franjo Tudjman was elected president. The new Constitution was adopted in December 1990, which allowed the new government to swiftly organize a referendum on independence, held on 22 May 1991. An overwhelming majority of Croats voted to break away from Yugoslavia. Croatia duly declared independence on 25 June 1991, at the same time as Slovenia.

However, the anti-Serb rhetoric of HDZ, coupled with frequent attacks on individuals and properties, created a climate of fear amongst the country's Serbian community. These feelings were quickly used by the power-hungry Croatian Serb leadership and the opportunist Milosevic regime in Belgrade to justify the creation of independent Serb Autonomous Regions (SARs) in Krajina, Eastern Slavonia and Baranja, Sirmium and Western Slavonia in October 1991. With the help of the Yugoslav army and Serbian paramilitaries, the Serbs, who represented 12 per cent of the population, took control of one-third of the country, expelling the Croat population.

In January 1992, a UN-sponsored truce was put in place and 14,000 peacekeepers were sent to maintain the uneasy ceasefire. However, fighting continued in Krajina and Slavonia. The subsequent decision by the EU and the US to recognize Croat independence, a move prompted by Germany and Austria, led to the intensification of fighting as the Serbs attempted to resist their integration into the new state on the grounds that their civil and political right would not be safeguarded. In August 1992, the first parliamentary elections in an independent Croatia were held. Again, Tudjman's HDZ triumphed.

While most of Croatia did not suffer major material devastation or loss of life during this phase – the fighting was still centred around the rebel areas of Krajina and Slavonia – the country nevertheless suffered from interrupted trade links and lack of foreign investment. At the same time, civil war in neighbouring Bosnia brought about new problems. Croatia remained politically and diplomatically isolated because of the government's support of the separatist aspirations of Bosnian Croats, led by Mate Boban, who proclaimed the independent 'Croatian Community of Herceg-Bosna'. Moreover, by the end of 1993, over 800,000 Bosnian Croats had sought sanctuary in the country, further straining the state's finances.

In 1995 the Croatian army launched a massive offensive to reclaim the Krajina and Western Slavonia. In a whirlwind attack, Croatia retook the regions and expelled around 200,000 Serbs in the course of just a few days. In doing so, Croatian troops committed many atrocities. Many of these are only now being dealt with by the Croatian domestic courts and the International Criminal Tribunal for the Former Yugoslavia (ICTY), which has indicted several high-ranked Croatian officers for their conduct during these and previous operations. Indeed, the issue of war crimes still presents the main obstacle for Croatia's Euro–Atlantic integration. Following the attack on Krajina and Western Slavonia in November 1995, Croatia agreed to peacefully reintegrate Eastern Slavonia, Baranja and Western

Dirmium under the terms of the Erdut Agreement. The war officially ended on 14 December 1995, when Serbian, Croatian and Bosnian leaders signed the Dayton Peace agreement.

## Tudjman's Croatia after the War, 1995–2000

The second parliamentary elections were held in October 1995, immediately after the Croatian army took control of the Serb rebel areas. This helped Tudjman secure yet another overwhelming victory. Although the 1990 Constitution provided President Tudjman with great powers, he nevertheless used this victory to consolidate his control over the state and the control of the HDZ. For example, the party further strengthened its grip on the national state-owned public broadcaster, Croatian Radio–Television (HRT). In the sphere of economics, the process of privatization and the transformation to a market economy was held up by nationalist views. President Tudjman also kept army and police politicized and divided, thereby making control over them easier. This whole process was helped by the relative weakness of the opposition, which proved unable to challenge the HDZ in any meaningful sense. For example, following the opposition victory in the 1995 municipal polls, the opposition parties failed to take action when President Tudjman kept vetoing their candidates for the mayor of Zagreb.

In April 1997 the first nationwide regional and municipal elections took place. The HDZ took a clear majority in 40 per cent of the counties. Later that year, the second presidential elections were held. Mr Tudjman won again, this time with 61.4 per cent of the votes. However, there were deep concerns about the way in which the elections were conducted and the Organization for Security and Cooperation Europe (OSCE) called them 'undemocratic'. This all had a wider impact. Tudjman's authoritarian style, concerns over the country's human rights record and continued failure to work with the war crimes tribunal in The Hague, led the EU to decide against opening membership talks with Croatia for the meantime.

## Post-Tudjman's politics in Croatia after 2000

In December 1999, Franjo Tudjman died. Soon afterwards, the country held a general election. It was a turning point for Croatia. The HDZ suffered a major defeat and a new administration was formed from a coalition of six rather diverse parties. The most dominant was the left-of-centre Social Democratic Party of Croatia (SDP), which was made up of the members of the former reformist part of the Croatian communist party. Their leader, Ivica Racan, became prime minister. The next most important partners were two centre-right parties – the moderately nationalist Croatian Social Liberal Party (HSLS) and traditionalist Croatian Peasant Party (HSS). They were joined by three smaller parties, the Istrian Democratic Assembly (IDS) and two liberal parties, the Liberal Party (LS) and the Croatian People's Party (HNS). Unsurprisingly, the administration was weak. There were considerable tensions within such a diverse coalition and these led to numerous political crises. The IDS was the first to leave the coalition in June 2001.

However, the government did bring about some important changes. The new president, Stipe Mesic, of the Croatian People's Party (HNS), and the new government jointly worked on shifting the country's foreign policy orientation firmly towards Euro–Atlantic integration. In May 2000, Croatia joined the NATO Partnership for Peace Programme. In response to the progress on defence reforms, in May 2002, Croatia was admitted to the NATO Membership Action Plan (MAP), which was an important step on the path towards full NATO membership. Croatia also started the first phase of talks with the EU. As a result, a Stabilization and Association Agreement (SAA) was signed with the EU in October 2001. This came into force in March 2002. A formal application for EU membership was then submitted in February 2003. Just over a year later, in June 2004, the European Council agreed to accept Croatia as an official candidate for membership and formal negotiations are expected to start in early 2005.

In terms of regional relations, there has also been a transformation. While at first the administration attempted to disassociate Croatia from the Balkans, pressure from the EU has forced it play a more active role in regional initiatives, such as the Stability Pact for Southeastern Europe and the Southeast Europe Cooperative Initiative. As a consequence, relations with neighbouring Serbia and Montenegro (SMN) have slowly improved, thereby allowing the UN Observer Mission in Prevlaka Peninsula to be closed in late 2002. Similarly, the government took steps to stabilize the situation in neighbouring Bosnia-Herzegovina by suspending its illegitimate ties with Bosnian Croats and committing itself to supporting the state created in the Dayton Agreement.

Corruption in Croatia was considered to be widespread in Tudjman's era. In 1999, Croatia ranked 74 out of 99 countries examined by Transparency International, a think-tank investigating corruption around the world. Its score was 2.7 on a scale where 0 represents all-pervasive corruption and 10 denotes a clean bill of health. After the new government came to power in 2000, the perception of corruption among businessmen and analysts improved considerably. Croatia jumped up the scale more than 20 places. Its rating for that year was

3.7. In 2001, the government formed the Office for the Prevention of Corruption and Organized Crime (USKOK) and Croatia received an even higher 3.9 rating. However, USKOK was initially understaffed and its ability to function was subsequently obstructed by insufficient funding. Also, despite signing and ratifying several UN and Council of Europe anti-corruption laws and conventions, the government failed to make adequate policies to eliminate bribery and corruption. Unfortunately, Croatia has not been able to improve its record any further. Indeed, in the latest figures released for 2004, it had lost ground. With a rating of 3.5 it was ranked 67 out of 145 countries.

Regarding democratization, the Racan government showed a fairly liberal attitude towards the independent media, relinquishing control over state media. However, it stopped short of making the state-owned television channel, HRT, completely independent. Meanwhile, the freedom of non-governmental organizations (NGOs) was generally respected. The government also took some other important steps. For example, it was during this period that the first attempts to return Serb refugees were made. In other areas, improvement was not quite so marked. Although the government sincerely wished to cooperate with The Hague Tribunal, its efforts were hampered by the strong veterans' organizations, by the HDZ and the conservative wing of the Roman Catholic Church. Indeed, the issue of extraditions was the most sensitive matter facing the government and on several occasions brought the administration to the verge of collapse. In July 2001 and February 2002, several ministers from HSLS resigned from the government in response to the extradition of war crime suspects. The HSLS left the coalition in July 2002, which in turn triggered the resignation of the Prime Minister Racan and the formation of a new government also led by Mr Racan.

Most analysts agree that the backbiting among coalition partners about war crime extraditions, together with public intolerance to painful economic reforms, were main factors in the failure of the government in the November 2003 elections. A considerably reformed HDZ, which now calls itself a traditionally conservative party, led by Ivo Sanader, came to power in December 2003 at the head of a minority coalition government. Contrary to all expectations and the pre-electoral rhetoric, since taking power as prime minister, Mr Sanader has shown a genuine commitment and high level of pragmatism with regards to the question of the repatriation of Croatia's Serbian refugees and the cooperation with the ICTY. For example, the government quickly passed the constitutional Law on National Minorities and extradited an important Bosnian Croat war crime suspect. However, Mr Sanader still faces major problems. Strong internal opposition within hard-line elements of HDZ is hampering attempts to hand over the main Hague suspect, General Ante Gotovina. These same groups, which include radical elements in the military and police, are also unhappy about the government's policies of rapprochement towards ethnic minorities.

## Likely future developments in Croatia

Although it is still early days, the current government seems likely to be able to see out its full term. At the same time, as it had been expected, President Mesic was elected to a second term of office in early 2005. In the medium to long term future, the Croatian political scene will be dominated by the NATO and EU accession talks and all the issues that these processes will entail. Croatia is expecting to be invited to join NATO in 2006. In this regard, the main challenges confronting the government are the continuation of military reforms and improvement of civilian oversight of the armed forces, as well as of the relatively low public support for NATO and EU membership, which currently lingers between 45 and 55 per cent.

Also, as far as the EU membership is concerned, many of the key economic criteria have been satisfied. Instead, the main obstacles are in the political sphere. Further steps need to be taken to improve the justice system. This includes tackling the massive backlog of around 1.5 million court cases. The fight against corruption is also a problem that will need greater attention. More needs to be done to protect minority rights, including steps to speed up the return of Serbian refugees. The United Nations High Commission for Refugees (UNHCR) estimates around 250,000 Croatian Serb refugees are registered in Serbia, Montenegro and Republika Srpska. However, only about 15 per cent have stated that they would like to return to their homes in Croatia. More recently, a border dispute with Slovenia and other issues stemming from the dissolution of the former Yugoslavia are likely to present a serious problem for Croatia. Yet, the major challenge on the road to both NATO and the EU is the continuation of the full cooperation with The Hague Tribunal. In April 2004, Croatia was proclaimed as fully cooperating with the Tribunal. However, the remaining war crime suspects are yet to be located and transferred to ICTY.

Although the government has set itself a target of EU membership by 2008, this may be a little too ambitious – although by no means impossible. Instead, most observers are confident that Croatia will be a part of the European Union by the end of the decade.

# 1.2

# Economic Overview

*Iva Condic-Jurkic, Institute of Economics, Zagreb*

## History and nature of transition

Through the major part of the 20th century, Croatia was a part of Yugoslavia and, in 1991, declared its independence. At the beginning of the transitional process Croatia had to deal with a multitude of challenges derived from the rejection of communist ideology, accompanied by aggression and occupation of its territory, which together had serious implications on the domestic economy as well. Croatia faced a huge downturn in industrial output, unemployment growth and a high inflation rate. Macroeconomic stability was achieved by starting a stabilization programme in late 1993 (the inflation rate fell from 39 per cent monthly to 1.4 per cent just a month after the start of the programme). However, retaining price stability led to a 'trade-off' in terms of even higher unemployment, caused mostly by slow progress in restructuring and modernizing the economy and wage increases above productivity gains. In the period 1994–1997, economic activity started to accelerate and the Croatian economy showed an average above 6 per cent real GDP growth rate. Further deteoriation of the economic situation began in 1997 and was the result of various factors – a tightening of monetary policy, mounting structural problems, a crisis of the banking industry, increases in taxes and administrative prices, the Kosovo crisis etc. Croatia found itself in a recession, which started in the last quarter of 1998 and continued through the first three quarters of 1999.

From the end of 1999, the macroeconomic situation started to improve. A rebound in household consumption, improved exports and the very good performance of the tourism sector in 2000, meant that GDP started to grow again in the last quarter of 1999, albeit at modest levels, with a rate of 3.7 per cent in 2000, while price inflation remained subdued. Industrial output started to recover only moderately in 2000, with an output growth of 5.4 per cent in 2002 and 4.1 per cent in 2003.

Since the mid-1990s, Croatia has recorded satisfactory GDP growth, averaging 4.5 per cent (IMF, 2004), and inflation in the low single digits. These numbers compare well with the EU-15 and Central and Eastern European (CEE) countries. A persistent gap between savings and investment since the mid-1990s has led to a current account deficit of 8.4 per cent (IMF) and a gradual build-up of foreign debt, both of which were particularly fuelled by a credit boom in 2001–2002. Unemployment has grown steadily since Croatia's independence, reaching an average rate of 22.3 per cent in 2002, showing a downward trend with 19.1 per cent on average in 2003.

The first 10 years of democracy in Croatia was determined by the ruling of the conservative Croatian Democratic Union. On 13 January 2000, the coalition of six political parties won the elections and formed a new pro-reform oriented government. That date was a major turning point not only for future political orientation of the country, but also for economic policy questions. Measures introduced by that government showed progress in lowering general government deficit and expenditure ratios. Although some structural reforms were undertaken (privatization and the restructuring of the banking sector, which suffered three severe banking crises in the 1990s), the coalition government did not show enough courage to introduce a wider range of reforms and adjustments (not always welcomed by the general public) that would supplement macroeconomic policies and prepare the economy for EU accession. However, the public debt ratio continued to climb, the labour market remained inflexible and several large public enterprises were a drag on the economy. Against this backdrop, the coalition government programme promised further substantial progress. Parliamentary elections, held on 23 November 2003, brought about a change on the Croatian political scene, through the victory, once again, of the Croatian Democratic Union, which leads the newly formed centre-right government. It has repeatedly stressed its pro-EU and NATO foreign policy orientation. On the internal front Croatia continues to face a number of challenges, and acceleration of structural reforms and reducing further external indebtedness are among the major challenges. The latter includes enhanced efforts to implement a reform of the judiciary, an accelerated privatization of public utilities and the remaining state tourism sector portfolio, restructuring of agriculture and shipbuilding and reforming public administration.

The main economic indicators are given in Table 1.2.1.

**Table 1.2.1** Main economic indicators

| | 1995 | 1996 | 1997 | 1998 | 1999 | 2000 | 2001 | 2002 | 2003 |
|---|---|---|---|---|---|---|---|---|---|
| **Economic activity** | | | | | | | | | |
| Real GDP (% change) | 6.8 | 5.9 | 6.8 | 2.5 | -0.4 | 3.7 | 4.4 | 5.2 | 4.3 |
| Real private consumption (% change) | n/a | n/a | n/a | -0.6 | -2.7 | 4.1 | 4.5 | 6.6 | 4.1 |
| Real government consumption (% change) | n/a | n/a | n/a | 2.3 | 0.8 | -0.7 | -6.2 | -1.8 | -0.3 |
| Real investment (% change) | n/a | n/a | n/a | 2.5 | -1.1 | -3.5 | 7.1 | 10.1 | 16.8 |
| Industrial output (% change) | 0.3 | 3.1 | 6.8 | 3.7 | -1.4 | 1.7 | 6.0 | 5.4 | 4.1 |
| Unemployment rate (registered, %, pa) | 14.5+ | 16.4+ | 17.5+ | 17.2 | 19.4 | 21.3 | 22.0 | 22.3 | 19.1 |
| Nominal GDP, (US$ million) | 18,811 | 19,872 | 20,109 | 21,628 | 20,064 | 19,031 | 19,863 | 22,812 | 28,810 |
| GDP per capita (US$) | 4,029 | 4,422 | 4,398 | 4,805 | 4,371 | 4,153 | 4,476 | 5,141 | 6,493 |
| **Prices, wages and exchange rates** | | | | | | | | | |
| Implicit GDP deflator (% change) | n/a | n/a | n/a | 8.4 | 4.1 | 6.4 | 4.0 | 2.9 | 3.3 |
| Retail prices (% change, pa) | 2.0 | 3.5 | 3.6 | 5.7 | 4.2 | 6.2 | 4.9 | 1.7[i] | 1.8[i] |
| Producer prices (% change, pa) | 0.8 | 1.4 | 2.3 | -1.2 | 2.6 | 9.7 | 3.6 | -0.4 | 1.9 |
| Average gross wage (% change, pa) | n/a | 12.2 | 13.1 | 12.6 | 10.2 | 7.0 | 3.9 | 6.0 | 4.8 |
| Net wage bill (% change, pa) | 42.8 | 7.8 | 16.4 | 11.5 | 7.8 | 8.3 | n.a. | n.a | n.a. |
| Exchange rate, HRK/DM/EUR (pa) | 3.65 | 3.61 | 3.56 | 3.62 | 3.88 | 3.90 | 7.47 | 7.41 | 7.56 |
| Exchange rate, HRK/US$ (pa) | 5.23 | 5.43 | 6.16 | 6.36 | 7.11 | 8.28 | 8.34 | 7.86 | 6.70 |
| **Foreign trade and capital flows** | | | | | | | | | |
| Exports of goods (US$ million) | 4,517 | 4,643 | 3,981 | 4,517 | 4,302 | 4,432 | 4,666 | 4,904 | 6,187 |
| Imports of goods (US$ million) | 7,352 | 7,784 | 9,101 | 8,276 | 7,799 | 7,887 | 9,147 | 10,722 | 14,209 |
| Current account balance (US$ million) | -1,407 | -995 | -2,512 | -1,453 | -1,397 | -549 | -725.0 | -1,918 | -2,085 |
| Current account balance (% of GDP) | -7.5 | -4.8 | -12.5 | -6.7 | -7.0 | -2.4 | -3.7 | -8.4 | -7.1 |
| Gross foreign direct investment (US$ million) | 114 | 511 | 533 | 932 | 1,479 | 852 | 1,561 | 1,124 | 1,998 |
| Foreign exchange reserves (US$ million, eop) | 1,895 | 2,314 | 2,539 | 2,816 | 3,025 | 3,525 | 4,704 | 5,886 | 8,191 |
| Foreign debt (US$ million, eop) | 3,809 | 5,308 | 7,452 | 9,586 | 9,872 | 10,840 | 11,317 | 15,426 | 23,554 |

**Table 1.2.1** Main economic indicators *contd*

| | 1995 | 1996 | 1997 | 1998 | 1999 | 2000 | 2001 | 2002 | 2003 |
|---|---|---|---|---|---|---|---|---|---|
| **Government finance** | | | | | | | | | |
| Conventional central government deficit (HRK million) | -715 | -134 | -1,160 | 1,257 | -2,522 | -6,108 | -4,309 | -3,500 | -2,187 |
| Conventional central government deficit (% of GDP) | -0.7 | -0.1 | -0.9 | 0.9 | -1.8 | -3.9 | -2.6 | -2.0 | -1.1 |
| Primary central government deficit (HRK million) | 677 | 1,084 | 577 | 3,208 | -423 | -3,509 | -1,294 | -240 | 1,400 |
| Primary central government deficit (% of GDP) | 0.7 | 1.0 | 0.5 | 2.3 | -0.3 | -2.2 | -0.8 | -0.1 | 0.7 |
| Privatization proceeds (HRK million) | 594 | 1,123 | 461 | 1,789 | 6,311 | 3,101 | 4,597 | 218 | 3,598 |
| Domestic public debt (US$ million, eop) | 3,337 | 3,116 | 2,465 | 2,409 | 2,191 | 2,617 | 2,981 | 4,023 | 5,239 |
| Foreign public debt (US$ million, eop) | 241 | 2,397 | 2,906 | 3,395 | 3,973 | 4,753 | 5,076 | 6,305 | 8,404 |
| Total public debt (% of GDP) | 19.0 | 27.7 | 26.7 | 26.8 | 30.7 | 38.7 | 41.3 | 41.1 | 43.2 |
| **Monetary indicators** | | | | | | | | | |
| Narrow money, M1 (% change, eop)* | 24.0 | 38.1 | 20.8 | -1.5 | 2.4 | 30.1 | 31.5 | 30.2 | 9.8 |
| Broad money, M4 (% change, eop)* | 39.3 | 49.1 | 38.3 | 13.0 | -1.1 | 29.3 | 45.2 | 9.5 | 11.0 |
| Total domestic credit (% change, eop)* | 18.6 | 3.1 | 44.4 | 22.4 | -6.6 | 9.0 | 23.1 | 30.0 | 14.6 |
| DMBs credit to households (% change, eop)* | 35.4 | 39.5 | 93.5 | 38.4 | 8.6 | 21.0 | 29.3 | 43.0 | 27.7 |
| DMBs credit to enterprises (% change, eop)* | 21.2 | 2.6 | 35.6 | 17.1 | -14.5 | 0.9 | 21.3 | 22.6 | 5.1 |
| Money market interest rate (%, pa) | 21.1 | 19.3 | 10.2 | 14.5 | 13.7 | 8.9 | 3.9 | 1.8 | 3.0 |

+ Non-military; main economic indicators

* Intertemporal comparisons including 1999 are impeded because banks in which bankruptcy procedures have started were excluded from monetary statistics while certain items of Privredna banka Zagreb balance sheet were cleared during its privatization

¹ Consumer prices (% change, yoy, pa)

Conventional abbreviations: n/a: not available; pa: period average; eop: end of period, HRK: Croatian kuna; DM: German Mark, US$: US dollar; EUR: euro, DMB: deposit money bank

*Sources:* Central Bureau of Statistics, Croatian National Bank, Ministry of Finance, Payment Transfer Agency

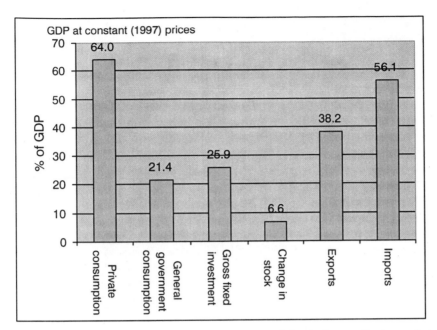

*Source:* Republic of Croatia – Central Bureau of Statistics, preliminary data, June 2004

**Figure 1.2.1** Components of gross domestic product (GDP) for the first quarter of 2004

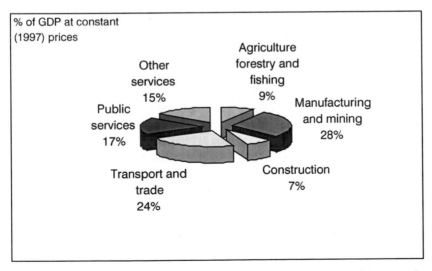

*Source:* Republic of Croatia – Central Bureau of Statistics, preliminary data, June 2004

**Figure 1.2.2** Origins of GDP for the first quarter of 2004

# Overall health and recent performance of the economy[1]

After the rapid expansion of economic activity in 2002, fuelled by rising domestic demand (real GDP grew at an annual rate of 5.2 per cent), figures for 2003 showed signs of a slowdown. Year 2003, as a whole, saw a 4.3 per cent growth of the economy. In the last couple of years, growth was extensively driven by domestic demand and relied strongly on credit expansion. A credit tightening, observed in 2003, probably induced the weakening of demand, which, together with substantially negative net exports, led to decelerating GDP growth. The best performing industries in 2003 were construction (with a 20.2 per cent growth), financial intermediation services, transport and communication, and hotels and restaurants (approximately 10 per cent growth). In the first quarter of 2004, the Croatian economy gained new momentum, recording an expansion by 4.2 per cent year-on-year, followed though by a mild slowdown in the second quarter with a 3.8 per cent growth, driven mainly by the continued upswing of investments and strong personal consumption.

Despite a mild slowdown over the previous quarters, the second quarter's upward trend of personal consumption remained robust, setting the tone for the overall growth. Personal consumption grew 3.8 per cent over the same quarter last year and contributed 2.4 percentage points to the GDP growth, suggesting the high importance of consumer behaviour for overall growth performance.

After a rather long period of gradual reduction, the second quarter of 2004 saw a rise of 0.7 per cent in government consumption over the same period last year, probably caused by stringent conditions on expenditure in the first quarter due to the provisional budget in force at the time.

Intense highway construction and business equipment investment were still supportive of strong investment growth, up to 16.8 per cent in 2003 compared to 2002. In addition, it should be noted that a strong and stable upward trend has characterized overall investment activities for the last three years, suggesting a general improvement in the business environment. Furthermore, investment by private companies accounts for more than half of all investments, indicating widespread recovery and generally improved business confidence. The investment expansion continued in the first quarter of the year at a modest level (with an 8.9 per cent year-on-year growth), as well as in the second quarter with an increase of 7.7 per cent year-on-year. Although

---

[1] This part of the text is based on *Croatian Economic Outlook Quarterly*, Numbers 15–20, issued by the Institute of Economics, Zagreb.

expansion has moderated somewhat compared to the last two years, it has remained strong enough to contribute 2.2 percentage points to GDP growth. Investment strength can probably be attributed to intensive activities in motorway construction, due to tight deadlines for the opening of large sections of the Zagreb-Split highway.

In 2003, exports were strong, mainly thanks to a prolonged tourist season and its beneficial financial effects, while imports showed two-digit growth rates in both goods and services segments. In 2004, according to the national accounts data, external sector developments have shown clear signs of deceleration – the exports of goods and services expressed in constant kuna terms have slowed down, while comparable import values have stagnated since the final quarter of 2003. The second quarter saw an increase of exports by 3.9 per cent compared to 2003 figures, and an increase in imports by 5.4 per cent. The trade deficit in the second quarter was wider than in the previous year.

In July 2004, foreign debt stood at €21.4 billion or US$25.7 billion, representing 76 per cent of the GDP projected for 2004. Although average foreign debt increase was about 1.8 per cent in 2004, based on euro values, month-on-month dynamics suggests a minor slowdown that reflects a partial accomplishment of the government's goals.

After a strong performance in the first quarter, industrial activity has slowed down. Data available up to September 2004 shows that the cumulative industrial activity expanded by 3.5 per cent in the first three quarters compared to 2003, with a most respectable contribution from the manufacturing industry.

Following four months of uninterrupted decline, the registered unemployment rate stood at 17.2 per cent at the end of August 2004, when the number of unemployed people started to rise again and reached 299,500 by the end of September. Unemployment has remained one of the key problems of the Croatian economy since the beginning of the transitional process. However, the ways to resolve it have been seen differently by different partners: the government is trying to introduce more flexibility on the labour market through the introduction of easier dismissal procedures, sponsored education programmes etc, while trade unions believe that the unemployment issue cannot be resolved by reducing workers' rights, on the contrary, they believe this issue can be properly addressed only by creating new jobs.

Turning to monetary developments, a tighter policy stance is suggested by a slower growth of major monetary aggregates throughout 2004. The M1 monetary aggregate grew by 1.0 and 1.2 per cent in July and August respectively, with a year-on-year rate reaching 2.9 per cent at the end of August. After stagnating in the first half of the year, broad money growth recovered in July and August under the impact of seasonal factors, showing 2.7 and 2.9 per cent month-on-month growth rates respectively. Credit activity in the banking sector decelerated, although it still remains strong. Within the aggregate, credits to enterprises stagnated from the beginning of the year, while credits to households continued to grow strongly, showing a 16.0 per cent year-on-year growth rate.

An early July issue of government kuna bonds (€400 million), denominated in euros, put pressure on the money market as well as the foreign exchange market. Built-up appreciation pressures forced the central bank to intervene on two occasions in the money market. During July and August, the central bank intervened four times in the foreign exchange market (buying a total of €116,0 million and supplying additional kuna liquidity to the market in order to prevent any stronger appreciation of kuna, which can be explained partly by seasonal factors), as well as during September, in order to improve kuna liquidity ahead of the ten-year bond issuance on 20 September.

The inflation rate in Croatia has remained stable since the thriving stabilization programme in 1993. In 2003, consumer prices grew by 1.8 per cent on average compared to 2002. Recently, as in the rest of the world, inflation data has been predominantly under the influence of oil price movements. So far, the impact is mostly visible in producer price inflation (5.7 per cent in September year-on-year), while the consumer price index movements has been less volatile recently (1.6 per cent year-on-year in September).

The government debt reached HRK91.4 billion at the end of June, or almost HRK9 billion more than at the end of 2003. More than half of that increment (HRK4.6 billion) refers to the external public debt, which participated in the total external debt with 36.6 per cent at the end of June, or 0.6 percentage points more than at the end of 2003. This trend will probably be reversed in the second half of the year, when the government plans to finance itself predominantly on the domestic market and repay its debt due to foreign creditors.

# Structural reforms and government policy

For every country in transition, there is an urgent need to conduct serious structural reforms. The gradual implementation of crucial reforms is often the toughest challenge for the government of a country in transition, since structural reforms often have great social impact. While reform efforts are being made in Croatia, there are still many areas left unaddressed by reforms. The European Bank for Reconstruction and Development (EBRD), in its Transition Report for 2001, praises notable progress being made in the following areas: the privatization of state-held enterprises and banks, the liberalization of capital account transactions, the reduction of consolidated central government deficit, the reduction of the total number of arrears in the economy, the consolidation of the banking system and social reform (the launching of a privately-managed second pillar pension system in January 2002).

The government prepared a programme, presented in the Memorandum on Economic and Financial Policies, as a part of the stand-by agreement with the IMF approved in August 2004, that determines its policy actions over the next 20 months. The programme focuses on limiting external vulnerability arising from the high current account deficit and foreign indebtedness. It relies on fiscal consolidation with a more restrictive policy mix, aimed at discouraging further foreign borrowing, as well as reducing the budget deficit. Introducing structural reforms still remains the major challenge for the government in order to modernize the economy and prepare it for EU accession. Among them, a key role is played by public finance reform (enhancing transparency and efficiency in public expenditure and debt management, as well as making the tax system more harmonized with the tax systems of the EU member states) and accelerating the privatization process (according to the stand-by agreement the Croatian Privatization Fund should sell all the companies in which the government holds a share of up to 25 per cent by the end of 2004, and all remaining holdings in its portfolio by mid-2005; the government is to sell at least 15 per cent of the oil company INA, and complete the third phase of privatization of the telecommunication company (HT) by the end of 2005; preparing the insurance company Croatia Osiguranje for privatization and disengaging from Croatia Banka by mid-2005). Other reforms include the introduction of more efficiency in public administration, judicial system reform, improving financial sector supervision and statistics.

Four new funds and agencies have been created under the 2003 budget (the environmental protection fund, the agency for small and medium-sized enterprises, the agency for investment and export promotion and the state aid agency). This year the government's emphasis on promoting the growth of small- and medium-sized enterprises (SMEs) was designed to help meeting the government's goal of fostering sustainable development within the framework of the market-oriented, stable and predictable business environment.

In 2003, a new foreign exchange law was created in order to induce reforms in the financial sector. It aimed to be consistent with EU standards and to empower the Croatian National Bank to introduce temporary restrictions on short-term capital inflows. It also required that foreign securities that are eligible for outward portfolio investment by residents satisfy minimum ratings from international rating agencies. The Croatian National Bank also prepared several bylaws (on classification of claims, calculation of capital-asset ratios, supervision methodology, auditing decision, consolidated supervision, management of liquidity risk and operation of subsidiaries) to implement the new banking law.

New company, competition and labour laws were approved in order to enhance the functioning of markets and encourage the growth of employment. A new bankruptcy law, aimed at accelerating bankruptcy procedures and allowing payoffs to creditors before the completion of all procedures, was passed as well.

Within the limits of its tight financial resources, the government plans to develop a more active employment policy to alleviate the acute unemployment problem. Particular emphasis is placed interrelating the re-training and re-employment measures for workers affected by the restructuring privatization of state-owned enterprises and public sector redundancies. Also, measures that aim to rationalize social welfare policies and to establish a new labour rights legislative framework are being conducted. Trade unions are very much opposing the new labour policies, claiming that they leave the workers less protected.

The European Commission, in its Country Strategy Paper for Croatia, 2002–2006, suggests that both the size and the role of the state in Croatia are still very large and there is therefore a need not only to reduce government expenditure, but also to increase the efficiency of public administration. This can be done through decentralization, which would strengthen local administration and self-government units. Therefore, regional development has to be taken more seriously. There are two principal goals in regional development:

- to reduce the development imbalances, in particular promoting the prospects for sustainable development of war affected areas, rural areas and islands, and

- decentralization, territorial reorganization and strengthening of local authorities. The effects of an inefficient state administration have clear economic impacts, since both foreign and domestic investment face a variety of administrative barriers to investment.

The Croatian health system is at a critical and unstable point, with its finances in major deficit. The health sector, therefore, represents a major fiscal problem, but it is also a sensitive social issue that needs to be addressed very carefully. Some reforms have been made, but they were insufficient to induce more effective health spending.

# Foreign trade and the role of foreign direct investments

Foreign trade has traditionally formed a significant portion of Croatia's economy. Exports of goods and services represented 51.8 per cent of GDP in 2003, and imports of goods and services represented 59.7 per cent of GDP in the same year (HNB, 2004).

Foreign trade, in particular commodity export and import, tourism, and especially transport services, were seriously affected by the aggression and the warring activities in the last decade of the previous century. Atypical transition processes, as well as the inadequate privatization concept applied to exports, have had an additional adverse effect on the development of foreign trade relations.

However, foreign trade activities in the Croatian economy have been rapidly recovering. The effects of the processes that have been taking place for the past few years in the various areas of foreign trade are different.

Table 1.2.2 indicates the stagnation of the export performance (caused by several factors, mostly the loss of traditional markets, slow modernization of industry, non-competitive prices, and partly by an extremely rigid foreign exchange rate policy). A large current account deficit can be mostly attributed to a negative balance in the goods account. However, it should be noted that Croatian exports in 2003 were significantly more dynamic in relation to the previous year.

Foreign trade deficits have been covered by boosted revenues in the services sector – tourist trade, transport services, funds remitted from abroad. As a result, the current balance reveals no dramatic deficit, although even this figure worsened in 2002 and 2003. The negative current account balance was 8.4 per cent of GDP in 2002 and 7.1 per cent of GDP in 2003.

Apart from the stagnant export performance, the structure of trade is another weak point in foreign trade. It is dominated by raw material intensive goods (fertilizers and fuels, rubber, etc), and labour intensive goods (textiles, footwear, clothing, etc) rather than capital-intensive goods and research-oriented goods (there are only a few goods based on modern technologies such as transport vehicles, specifically ships). The share of raw material intensive goods and labour intensive goods relative to capital-intensive goods and research-oriented goods is larger in the structure of exports than in the structure of imports. Croatia shows an advantage in the production of products of low value-added, and there is a low level of integration in the international market of goods, of intra-industry trade and of specialization.

Regarding the structure of foreign trade by economic classification of countries (see Table 1.2.3), one should note that in spite of the relatively high participation of the EU countries in total Croatian imports

**Table 1.2.2** Exports, imports and current account balance (in US$ million)

|  | 1995 | 1996 | 1997 | 1998 | 1999 | 2000 | 2001 | 2002 | 2003 |
|---|---|---|---|---|---|---|---|---|---|
| Exports | 4,517.3 | 4,677.4 | 4,020.9 | 4,580.6 | 4,394.7 | 4,567.2 | 4,758.7 | 5,003.6 | 6,307.7 |
| Imports | 7,744.9 | 8,165.5 | 9,404.2 | 8,652.0 | 7,693.3 | 7,790.9 | 8,860.0 | 10,652.2 | 14,216.0 |
| Trade deficit | -3,227.6 | -3,488.1 | -5,383.2 | -4,071.5 | -3,298.6 | -3,203.8 | -4,101.3 | -5,648.6 | -7,908.3 |
| Services balance | 1,047.0 | 1,579.7 | 2,024.2 | 2,076.7 | 1,625.2 | 2,267.9 | 2,927.4 | 3,154.7 | 5,641.4 |
| Current account balance | -1,407.0 | -955.8 | -2,512.1 | -1,452.8 | -1,397.2 | -460.8 | -725.8 | -1,920.1 | -2,084.7 |

*Source:* Croatian National Bank, 2004

and exports, the trend shows a gradual shrinking of the relative share of foreign trade with the EU-15 (the share in imports dropped from 62.1 per cent in 1995 to 56.6 per cent in 2003, and the share in exports declined from 57.6 per cent to 54.7 per cent in the respective years), suggesting gradual decline in the competitiveness of Croatian economy. Croatia's traditional economic partners have remained dominant, with Italy and Germany being the leading ones. Other major foreign trade partners include other countries in the region, those that emerged after the disintegration of the former Yugoslavia.

**Table 1.2.3** Imports and exports by economic classification of countries (in %)

| Exports | 2002 | 2003 | Jan–July 2003 | Jan–July 2004 |
|---|---|---|---|---|
| *Developed countries* | 70.9 | 74.6 | 76.0 | 73.1 |
| EU-25 | 65.5 | 67.6 | 66.7 | 65.8 |
|   Slovenia | 8.7 | 8.3 | 8.1 | 7.3 |
|   Hungary | 1.7 | 1.3 | 1.3 | 1.2 |
| EU-15 | 52.7 | 54.7 | 56.2 | 53.2 |
|   Austria | 7.5 | 7.7 | 8.2 | 9.7 |
|   Italy | 22.7 | 26.7 | 27.0 | 23.7 |
|   Germany | 12.5 | 11.9 | 12.3 | 11.3 |
| EFTA | 0.8 | 0.8 | 0.7 | 1.0 |
| *Developing countries* | 29.1 | 25.4 | 24.0 | 26.9 |
| CEFTA | 0.4 | 0.7 | 0.7 | 0.8 |
|   Bosnia and Herzegovina | 14.4 | 14.4 | 13.8 | 13.2 |
|   Serbia and Montenegro | 3.5 | 3.1 | 2.9 | 3.0 |
|   Russia | 1.7 | 1.2 | 1.2 | 1.3 |
| **Imports** | **2002** | **2003** | **Jan–July 2003** | **Jan–July 2004** |
| *Developed countries* | 80.1 | 80.8 | 81.7 | 79.2 |
| EU-25 | 71.3 | 72.0 | 73.0 | 79.2 |
|   Slovenia | 7.7 | 7.4 | 7.5 | 7.3 |
|   Hungary | 3.0 | 3.0 | 3.0 | 2.9 |
| EU-15 | 55.8 | 56.6 | 57.6 | 55.7 |
|   Austria | 6.6 | 6.6 | 6.5 | 6.8 |
|   Italy | 17.3 | 18.2 | 18.5 | 17.4 |
|   Germany | 16.2 | 15.6 | 15.7 | 15.7 |
| EFTA | 2.0 | 1.8 | 1.7 | 1.5 |
| *Developing countries* | 19.9 | 19.2 | 18.3 | 20.8 |
| CEFTA | 0.6 | 1.2 | 0.9 | 1.2 |
|   Bosnia and Herzegovina | 1.6 | 1.6 | 1.5 | 2.1 |
|   Serbia and Montenegro | 0.5 | 0.5 | 0.5 | 0.7 |
|   Russia | 6.7 | 4.8 | 4.3 | 6.4 |

*Source:* Croatian Bureau of Statistics and Croatian National Bank, 2004

Although the Croatian foreign trade sector has recorded certain unfavourable developments, the overall trend and the perspectives of activities in the sector should not be perceived as discouraging. Recent developments in the exports of goods (see Figure 1.2.3), as well as the growth in revenues from the services sector (especially in tourism), show that difficulties have been gradually overcome. However, imports have been recording their highest levels (mostly due to the ever greater openness of the Croatian economy), so there is an urgent need for Croatia to decelerate this trend by encouraging the production of goods and services that could be competitively produced at home (particularly related to agricultural products).

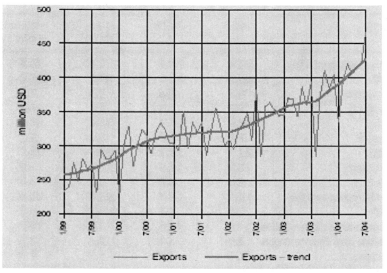

*Source:* Croatian Bureau of Statistics and Croatian National Bank, 2004

**Figure 1.2.3** Merchandise exports (FOB) and trend, other transport equipment excluded, at constant 2002 exchange rate

According to the latest figures from the Croatian National Bank, from 1993 until the end of the second quarter of 2004 foreign direct investments totalled US$10,114.8 million. It is important to note that until 1996, only ownership investments were registered, while from 1997, total investment included reinvested profits and other non-ownership arrangements (see Figure 1.2.4).

The first notable foreign investments in Croatia took place after 1995 and the completion of the successful military liberation operations in the country, while the amount of over US$ billion of FDI was, for the first time, reached in 1999 as a result of a notable privatization

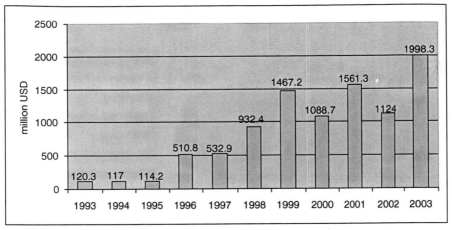

*Source:* Croatian National Bank, 2004

**Figure 1.2.4** Direct foreign investment in Croatia, 1993–2003, per year

of the large state systems and banks. Direct foreign investment in 2001 reached US$1.56 billion (the telecommunications sector participated with 61.7 per cent of total foreign investments), and, in 2003, reached US$1.99 billion, partly due to the privatization of the oil company, INA.

In the period 1993–2003, direct foreign investment in Croatia was realized through a number of sectors. Due to the privatization of Croatian Telecommunications, large Croatian banks and the sale of Pliva shares on European markets, approximately half of total foreign investment was concentrated in the telecommunications, banking and pharmaceutical industry sectors (see Figure 1.2.5). These were followed by investments in cement production, the extraction of crude oil and natural gas, etc.

According to investments by country of origin, the largest single investor in Croatia during the period 1993–2003 was Austria (see Figure 1.2.6). Austrian investments made up more than 25 per cent of total foreign investment during the period. The second largest investor was Germany with almost 20.73 per cent, while the United States was third with 14.74. They were followed by Hungary, Luxembourg, Italy, the Netherlands, Slovenia and the United Kingdom and the EBRD. Over 75 per cent of total foreign investments up to the end of 2003 came from member states of the EU.

The total of direct foreign investments for the period 1993–2003 reached over 30 per cent of GDP or about US$2,174.32 per capita, which places Croatia amongst the more successful transition countries as far as attracting investment is concerned. It is important to emphasize that most investments were directed toward domestic

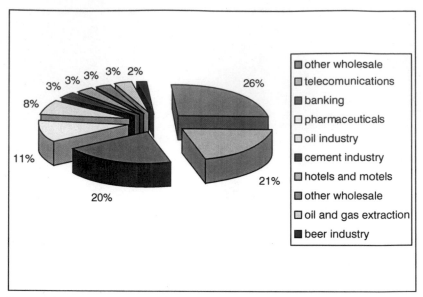

*Source:* Croatian National Bank

**Figure 1.2.5** Direct foreign investment in Croatia, 1993–2003, by sectors

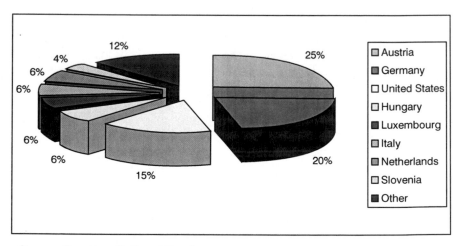

*Source:* Croatian National Bank

**Figure 1.2.6** Direct foreign investment in Croatia, 1993–2001, by country of origin

markets ie monopoly or oligopoly positions. Also, a large portion of investments were directed into the non-tradable sector (banking, telecommunications). FDI flows into the tradable sector were almost completely absent, bringing Croatia into the position of growing imbalances in international trade. Therefore, in the coming period, a very intense effort needs to be made in accelerating structural reforms, which would help create the conditions to attract FDI to the tradable sector, as well as lead to a higher level of competitiveness of the economy.

# Relationship with international institutions and donors

In October 2001, Croatia signed the Stabilization and Association Agreement (SAA) with the EU, which was then ratified by the Croatian Parliament and the European Parliament. Having signed the SAA, Croatia made an important step forward in institutionalizing its relations with the EU, and started a comprehensive process of fulfilling its assumed obligations to bring its political, economic, legal and institutional systems in line with European standards. Further impetus to continued membership negotiations gave Croatia the long-awaited EU candidate status that European Council granted on 18 June 2004 at the meeting in Brussels. The accession negotiations should begin early in 2005. These developments are expected to give a positive push to overall activity and serve as an important signal to boost the confidence of foreign investors.

Croatian CEFTA membership took effect on 1 March 2003. Also, free trade agreements with Macedonia (1997), Bosnia and Herzegovina (2001), Turkey (2003), Albania (2003) and Lithuania (2003) took effect. A free trade agreement with Serbia and Montenegro was concluded in 2002, and with Moldova in 2004.

Croatia has been a member of the IMF since 1992 and has benefited from the IMF's technical assistance in key monetary, fiscal and public administration areas. The arrangement provides the government with a framework of economic policy-making and monitoring. In August 2004, the IMF approved a 20-month Stand-by Arrangement in an amount equivalent to SDR97 million (about US$141,3 million) for Croatia to support the country's economic programme. The Croatian authorities intend to treat the arrangement as precautionary and are not planning to draw funds under the credit. The previous stand-by arrangement, also treated as precautionary, was approved in February 2003 and expired in April 2004.

Also, Croatia has developed relationships with donors such as the World Bank Group (assistance has been shifted from post-war reconstruction to capital market developments, reforms of the financial sector, health, agriculture and forestry), the EBRD (commitment classified as private sector operations), USAID (assistance to local government, political parties, labour unions, media) and CEB (engaged in health, education, refugee return and cultural heritage projects).

## 1.3

# Croatia and the EU – A Progress Report on Entry

*Mrs Kolinder Grabar-Kitarović, Minister of Foreign Affairs and European Integration*

## Introduction

Full membership in the European Union (EU) is one of the most important strategic foreign policy goals of Croatia, and the values underlying the European democracies are principal guidelines in the internal development of Croatia. Hence the tasks to be carried out towards these ultimate objectives occupy a central place in the Croatian government's programme. Upon becoming a candidate country in June 2004, Croatia was both realistic and ambitious when declaring its goal to finalize its accession negotiations in 2007, which are scheduled to begin on 17 March 2005. Croatia is also confident in its abilities to reach the appropriate level of readiness for EU membership in 2007. Substantial evidence of the appropriate individual capacity of Croatia already clearly exists, best reflected in the European Commission's Opinion on Croatia's membership application adopted in April 2004. Furthermore, up to now, Croatia has fulfilled a major part of the obligations stemming from the *Stabilization and Association Agreement (SAA)*.[1] Candidate country status and the prospect for the opening of accession negotiations certainly encourages

---

[1] SAA entered into force on 1 February 2005.

and motivates Croatia to successfully continue the reform processes and meet in full the *Copenhagen and Madrid criteria*.[2]

## Recent development of Croatia – EU relations

Croatia signed a Stabilization and Association Agreement (SAA) in October 2001, a far-reaching framework with mutual rights and obligations. As a signatory Croatia has been gradually taking on board the core obligations of membership, aligning its legal and economic framework with that of the EU, strengthening cooperation with its neighbours and cooperating with the EU on a number of issues.

Until its entry into force, its trade and transport provisions have been applied through the *Interim Agreement on Trade and Trade Related Matters*, which was signed on the same day as the SAA. The Interim Agreement has been applied since 1 January 2002, and entered into force on 1 March 2002. Being aware that only a successful implementation of the SAA is the way to ensure continuous progress towards the negotiations for full membership, the government has adopted the *Implementation Plan for the SAA*.

The Implementation Plan defines measures, deadlines and responsibilities for implementing the SAA for the period 2002–2006, mirroring the goal to become ready for membership in 2007. The Implementation Plan was upgraded by the *National Programme for the Integration of the Republic of Croatia into the European Union*, based on the experience of the National Programmes for the Adoption of the Acquis. Since its introduction in 2003, the National Programmes serve the purpose of an annual roadmap by which the Croatian Government realistically assesses its capacities, and the capacities of Croatian society as a whole, to implement all that is included in the adjustment to the EU criteria.

Croatia submitted the *application for membership in the EU* to the Greek Presidency in Athens on 21 February 2003. On the occasion of his visit to Croatia on 10 July 2003, the President of the European

---

[2] In June 1993, the Copenhagen European Council recognized the right of the countries of central and eastern Europe to join the European Union when they have fulfilled three criteria:

1. political: stable institutions guaranteeing democracy, the rule of law, human rights and respect for minorities;
2. economic: a functioning market economy and the ability to cope with the competitive pressure of the internal market;
3. incorporation of the Community *acquis*: adherence to the various political, economic and monetary aims of the European Union.

These accession criteria were confirmed in December 1995 by the Madrid European Council, which also stressed the importance of adapting the applicant countries' administrative structures to create the conditions for a gradual, harmonious integration.

Commission, Mr Romano Prodi, handed over the *Avis questionnaire* to the Croatian Prime Minister. On the basis of the information provided, the European Commission finalized and adopted its positive *Opinion on Croatia's application (Avis)* on 20 April 2004, recommending the opening of accession negotiations. The exact date for commencement of the negotiations was set by the European Council on 17 December 2004 for 17 March 2005.

The Council of Ministers adopted the *European Partnership for Croatia* on 13 September 2004. It lists short- and medium-term priorities for Croatia's preparations for further integration with the EU, identified in the Commission's Opinion on Croatia's application for membership, and serves as a checklist against which to measure progress. The European Partnership for Croatia reflects its current stage of preparation and is tailored to its needs. The European Partnership priorities form the basis for the programming of the financial resources making up Community assistance.

The European Commission adopted the *Pre-accession strategy for Croatia* on 6 October 2004. The pre-accession strategy contains proposals for a negotiating framework within which negotiations on full membership should be conducted, and makes pre-accession financial instruments PHARE, ISPA and SAPARD available for Croatia as of 1 January 2005.

Croatia is determined to conclude the negotiations by 2007 and to reach the required level of readiness for full membership of the EU. In addition, Croatia's efforts in the next few years will focus on complete harmonization of Croatia's legislation with the *acquis communautaire*, and on strengthening the institutions that will be implementing the adopted regulations. The process shall be accompanied by adjusting the economic system with the aim of establishing an efficient market economy and strengthening domestic competitiveness.

## Economic adjustment

The economic policy measures taken in the Republic of Croatia at the beginning of the transition process, in order to develop a functioning market economy, were primarily related to the liberalization of prices and foreign trade systems, the attainment of currency convertibility, financial stability, acceleration of the privatization process, primarily in small- and medium-sized enterprises, banking and telecommunications systems, upgrading of the labour market with a view to cutting unit labour costs and reducing unemployment, an efficient market competition policy and development of the overall macroeconomic and institutional environment for a market-oriented economy. Accordingly, reducing the difference between domestic savings and investments, which would in turn reduce the external debt share in GDP in the mid-term, represents one of the main economic policy objectives. Although the Government of the Republic of Croatia has already made significant progress in this area in the last year, further progress is required in the implementation of reforms aimed at integration into the European market.

All the planned activities for the implementation of the economic criteria for EU integration are compliant with the priorities contained in the European Partnership for the period until 2007 and the European Commission Opinion on the Application of Croatia for Membership of EU.

At the end of 2004, the Croatian government adopted the Pre-Accession Economic Programme (PEP) for the period 2005–2007. The PEP is a binding document which EU admission candidates submit to the European Commission every year and in which they define their economic policies and the reforms necessary to join the EU. The document focuses on the main economic movements, a macroeconomic programme, public finance, and structural reforms. The structural reforms defined in the PEP refer to privatization, market competition, the energy sector, transport and communications, the agricultural policy, the social security system, measures in the health sector, the judicial reform, and the reforms of the education and science sectors.

Accordingly, the main macroeconomic objectives of the Croatian government for the medium- to long-term period include:

- economic growth and development, along with increased standards of living;

- employment growth;

- improved competitiveness of the economy.

The Republic of Croatia's adjustment concerning the Copenhagen economic and legal criteria, which requires a successful implementation of reforms, should reflect positively, in the mid-term, on strengthening the competitiveness of the Croatian economy.

*Existence of the functioning market economy*
According to the European Commission's Opinion on the application of Croatia for membership of the EU, Croatia can already be regarded as a functioning market economy that should be able to cope with competitive pressures and market forces within the EU in the medium-term.

The Croatian economy has achieved a considerable degree of macroeconomic stability with low inflation and there is an increasing political consensus on the essentials of economic policies. Enhanced economic stability and structural reforms undertaken so far permit the working of market mechanisms. This holds, in particular, for the liberalization of prices and trade as well as for privatization, albeit to a lesser extent. Croatia is characterized by a relatively well-educated labour force and good road transport and telecommunication infrastructure. The country has a well-developed banking sector and a competitive tourism industry. Croatia's economy is already well integrated with that of the EU.

In the Republic of Croatia, the liberalization of foreign trade relations began in 2000, with the WTO accession. Following WTO membership, the process accelerated significantly, both globally and regionally, by concluding the free trade agreements (bilaterally, with EFTA, CEFTA, EU). Croatia has so far liberalized trade with 37 countries, through 10 free trade agreements, which implies that more than 80 per cent of the Croatian foreign trade is based on the free trade principles.

Croatia's market economy is characterized by a traditional satisfactory growth and low inflation. The average real GDP growth stands at 4.5 per cent, single digit inflation has been recorded since the mid-1990s, the economy is open to the world, foreign investments are substantial and structural reform has made progress in the broad area. On the basis of these results, which correspond to the results of the other countries in the region, the European Commission has recently issued a positive opinion, in which a recommendation has been made for the onset of the Republic of Croatia's EU membership negotiations. Following the Commission's recommendations, the economic policy objective of the Republic of Croatia is the following:

- *in the short-term:* to re-establish discipline in public finances in Croatia and restrict vulnerability caused by a large current account deficit and a burdening external debt;

- *in the medium-term:* to modernize and reduce the role of the government, improve private sector activities and prepare Croatia to be competitive in the EU. These objectives are complementary. A stable macroeconomic environment and low fiscal deficit are required for long-term competitiveness and economic growth, and for EU accession in particular.

*Capacity to withstand competitive pressures and market forces within the EU*
In order to have the capacity to withstand competitive pressures and market forces within the EU, as one of the most important strategic objectives of economic policy, the competitiveness of the Croatian economy needs to be strengthened. In view of the fact that Croatia was granted the status of an EU candidate country this year, this objective has become even more important, imposing a need for an even more expeditious and efficient regime of strategic positioning of the Croatian economy as a competitive one.

According to the EBRD's transition indicators (EBRD Transition Report 2004) progress on reform in the transition countries in 2003–04 is continuing to gather pace, and particularly good progress was noted for Croatia.

Since 2002, Croatia has been included in the study of global competitiveness by the World Economic Forum, providing a comprehensive assessment of competitiveness. According to the report for 2004, Croatia ranks 61st out of 104 countries listed with regard to the growth competitiveness index and 59th out of 104 countries listed with regard to the macroeconomic competitiveness index. This study positioned Croatia behind the new member states but in line with candidate countries for membership of the EU.

At present, strengthening of competitiveness must be accompanied by efforts related to the overall development policy, which will allow the Republic of Croatia to respond in due and timely manner to all challenges, requirements and changes that may arise both in the domestic and external markets. It is extremely important that, in addition to economic policy measures implementation, a high quality reform of public administration and judiciary is carried out.

## Mechanisms of legal harmonization

Pursuant to the Programme of the Croatian Government for its Term of Office 2003–2007, which defines Croatia's integration into the EU as a national and foreign policy priority, the government has, in 2004, made significant progress in the adjustment of its legislation to the *acquis communautaire*. This process has been accelerated and emphasized by the positive *avis* of the European Commission on the Croatian application for membership, followed by the positive decisions of the Council of Ministers and European Council. As Croatia intends to conclude the negotiations by 2007 and to reach the required level of readiness for full EU membership, efforts over the next few years will focus on complete harmonization of Croatia's legislation with the *acquis communautaire* and on strengthening the institutions that will be implementing the adopted regulations.

All ministries and state administration organizations have continued to undertake, without delay, preparations to modify the legislation, which the Republic of Croatia will have to harmonize with the *acquis communautaire*, and to take into consideration in the preparation of new acts, to the greatest possible extent, the provisions of *the acquis communautaire*, and to provide information about the level of harmonization in the explanation of the act.

The importance of the harmonization process is stressed by the legislative procedure in which the opinion of the Ministry for European Integration has to be attached, *inter alia*, to the draft proposals on acts and other regulations which harmonize Croatian legislation with the *acquis communitaire*. The same relates to reports, information and similar materials. Through the amendments to the *Rules of Procedure of the Croatian Parliament* (OG no. 117/01), a proposal on an act that is harmonized with EU regulations bears a special mark, namely 'P.Z.E. no...'. At the request of the proposer, an act that is harmonized with the EU regulations may be enacted in an urgent procedure, which combines the first and second readings of the act. The Committee for European Integration of the Croatian Parliament has a key role in this legislative process since, among other things, it monitors the harmonization of the legal system of the Republic of Croatia with the legal system of the EU.

## National Programme for the Integration of the Republic of Croatia into the European Union

As a follow-up to the first National Programme for the Integration of the Republic of Croatia into the EU (NPIEU) 2003, the government of Croatia, on 15 January 2004, adopted the *National Programme for the Integration of the Republic of Croatia into the EU – 2004 (NPIEU 2004)*. The plan for the legal harmonization (Annex A) was also adopted by the Croatian Parliament on 29 January 2004.

The priorities specified in the NPIEU 2004 have been defined on the basis of a number of sources, including the Croatian Government Programme for the Term of Office 2003–2007, the SAA, the SAA Implementation Plan, the assessments of Croatia's progress contained in the European Commission's Report, assessments of its cooperation with the EC Delegation to the Republic of Croatia, etc. Thus, the National Programme reflects Croatia's readiness to reach its short- and mid-term priority goals in the process of approaching the EU, with emphasis on the year 2004. Based on the structure of the European Commission's Report, the NPIEU 2004 focuses on several topics that represent challenges on Croatia's road towards the EU:

- meeting politically-determined criteria;

- economic adjustments;

- harmonization of national legislation;

- strengthening the administrative capacity for carrying out the reforms;

- a communications strategy aimed at informing the Croatian public about the European integration process of the Republic of Croatia.

Due to the analysis of the implementation of the 2003 National Programme and the SAA Implementation Plan, these two strategic and operational documents were combined in the NPIEU 2004. The SAA Implementation Plan has thus made its presence felt in every chapter of the 2004 National Programme, as well as in every chapter of the *acquis* dealt with by the 2004 National Programme's chapter on 'Harmonization of the Croatian Legislation with the *acquis communautaire* in accordance with the Stabilization and Association Agreement'. The SAA Implementation Plan, after being incorporated into the 2004 National Programme, no longer contains any legislative measures; rather, it now contains measures of a different nature, ie analytical, institutional, and the like.

A novelty in defining priorities in the NPIEU 2004 was the inclusion of the priorities set out in the *Council Decision on the principles, priorities and conditions contained in the European Partnership with Croatia*, adopted in September 2004 as an additional impulse for strengthening and accelerating the ongoing European integration process in Croatia. After the adoption of the Decision, additional legal measures proposed by the state administration bodies were included into the Annex A of the NPIEU 2004. Through this process, for some sectors, already defined measures were included in the 2005 National Programme.

The first phase of the harmonization of legislation has encompassed the basic elements of the internal market, trade and trade-related areas and, finally, other elements of the *acquis* referred to in Article 69 of the SAA. This initial phase of the harmonization of legislation, as mentioned above, has been focused on five priority areas, namely: competition and state aid, public procurement, technical legislation, consumer protection and intellectual property, and industrial and commercial property. Significant progress in the NPIEU 2004 has been carried out with the expansion of the process of the harmonization of legislation to the 29 negotiating chapters for accession to the EU.

In 2004, the government adopted 36 acts that were forwarded to the Croatian Parliament, which, by the end of 2004, had adopted 28 of them.

Some of the acts adopted in 2004 were:

- Act on the Amendments to the State Aid Act;
- Media Act;
- Interest Rates Act;
- Savings Deposits Guarantee Scheme Act;
- Air Protection Act;
- Waste Act;
- Maritime Code;
- Criminal Code;
- Act on Transport on Public Roads;

- Road Traffic Safety Act;

- Act on Amendments to the Air Transport Act;

- Act on Gradual Phasing-out of Single-hull Oil Tankers;

- Act on Safety Protection of Merchant Ships and International Ports.

Some of the acts adopted in the First Reading of the Croatian Parliament and that will be adopted in 2005 are:

- Act on Representation in the field of Industrial Property;

- Obligatory Relations Act;

- Act on Genetically Modified Organisms;

- Nature Protection Act.

It is significant that 2004 was the year of implementation for about 180 sub-laws adopted or drafted by state administration bodies that have carried on the legal harmonization process initiated by the adoption of framework acts in previous years.

The government, on 9 December 2004, also adopted the third National Programme for the Integration of the Republic of Croatia into the EU – 2005. In defining priorities in the 2005 National Programme, major emphasis was put on the inclusion of the priorities set out in the European Partnership – the remaining short-term recommendations not included in the 2004 National Programme, as well as the medium-term recommendations stemming from the European Partnership.

NPIEU 2005, apart from foreseeing measures for one year, also foresees measures for the period to 2007 on the basis of the mid-term priorities from the European partnership. These projections are not only the basis for future National Programmes, but also a foundation for running negotiations for membership.

Novelties introduced in the NPIEU 2005 are the Table of Planned Budgetary Funds and the Table of Foreign Assistance Funds. For the first time, significant emphasis is put on the determining of budgetary funds necessary for the implementation of all planned activities. This enables the linking of all planned reforms and activities with budgetary funds and foreign assistance funds. In line with the three-year budgetary projections, these estimates for the necessary budgetary funds are made for a period of three years.

## Institutional mechanisms to support legislative harmonization

In order to enhance cooperation, with an emphasis on the European integration process, the government has entrusted its ministers to appoint persons at the level of assistant ministers as *coordinators responsible for the overall functioning of the Ministries in the process of adjustment to the EU.* In addition to that, all ministries were obliged to establish units dealing exclusively with this segment of their competence of cooperation with the EU. In line with the commitments laid down in the SAA, the Ministry for European Integration was entrusted with the coordination of the activities in the preparation of the National Programme for the integration of the Republic of Croatia into the EU.

In order to exchange experience and knowledge at the level of state administration bodies, the Ministry for European Integration has launched a *national twinning* initiative – an exchange of lawyers from state administration bodies and lawyers employed in the Ministry for European Integration. Given that the Ministry for European Integration is a coordinating body in the process of the harmonization of national legislation with the regulations of the EU and that it assesses in regular government procedures the degree of the harmonization of proposals on regulations with the relevant *acquis* of the EU, this approach allowed for an exchange of knowledge among experts about specific sectors on the one hand, and the European regulations relevant for the harmonization in those sectors on the other.

In 2004, the Republic of Croatia had opportunity of using *TAIEX (Technical Assistance Information Exchange Unit)*, which provides technical assistance by organizing seminars for the representatives of the Croatian state administrative bodies according to the chapters of the *acquis communautaire*, enabling study visits and the exchange of experts.

For the purpose of enhancing the monitoring of the EU accession process, the Ministry of European Integration, according to the *Government Conclusion on 15 July 2004*, holds weekly working meetings with the representatives of all ministries and other state administrative bodies in charge of the coordination of the activities relating to EU accession.

## *EU technical assistance to Croatia*

In order to support the participation of South-East European countries in the Stabilization and Association Process, the Council of the European Union adopted, at the end of 2000, the assistance programme called CARDS – Community Assistance for Reconstruction, Development and Stabilization.[3] Croatia belongs amongst the countries that benefit from the CARDS programme, both its national and regional component.

---

[3] www.europa.eu.int/comm/europeaid/projects/cards/index_en.htm

Since 2001, Croatian state bodies have been actively participating in the preparation and implementation of projects funded by the European Community. Under the national component of the programme, Croatia has received €255 million over the budget period 2001–2004. In addition to national CARDS allocations, Croatia also benefits from the regional component of the programme, under which an additional €94 million has been allocated over the period 2001–2004 to support regional cooperation among the countries of South-East Europe.

The assistance provided to Croatia is in line with priority areas outlined in the European Commission Strategy for Croatia for the period 2002–2006, and the first Multi-Annual Indicative Programme for the period 2002–2004. It focuses on the following sector areas:

- democratic stabilization;

- the return of refugees and internally displaced persons;

- the development of civil society;

- economic and social development;

- the promotion of trade in line with the provisions of the Stabilization and Association Agreement;

- the creation of favourable conditions for foreign investment;

- the promotion of social cohesion;

- justice and home affairs;

- the modernization of justice;

- assistance with policing and the fight against organized crime;

- support for the integrated management of state borders;

- administrative capacity building;

- reform of public administration;

- national, regional and local development;

- reform of public finance sector;

- the environment and natural resources.

In the Conclusions of 17 and 18 June 2004, the European Council entrusted the European Commission with the development of a Pre-accession Strategy for Croatia, which would set the framework of the accession process and Croatia's needs and establish the form of the EU pre-accession aid that would be put at the disposal of the Republic of Croatia. The aim of the Pre-accession Strategy, published by the European Commission on 6 October 2004, is to provide support for

Croatia in its preparation for EU membership, particularly in the field of harmonizing national legislation with the *acquis communautaire*.

The Pre-accession strategy sets the type and amount of assistance to be available to Croatia in the period of the remaining two years of the current Community budgetary period (2005 and 2006) and provides a link with the forthcoming financial perspective (ie the period from 2007 to 2013).

The Republic of Croatia has been allocated an amount of €105 million from the 2005 EU budget (ie €80 million for the Phare programme and €25 million for the ISPA programme), while an amount of €140 million has been allocated to Croatia from the 2006 EU budget (ie €80 million for the Phare programme, €35 million for the ISPA programme and €25 million for the SAPARD programme).

In the budgetary period 2007–2013, a new pre-accession instrument called IPA has been envisaged for all the candidate countries and potential candidate countries. The IPA will succeed the Pre-accession Programmes (Phare, ISPA and SAPARD, as well as the Regulation on the Pre-accession Assistance for Turkey) and the CARDS Programme. The amounts that will be available to the Republic of Croatia will be established within the framework of the forthcoming financial perspective.

In addition, the EU and the Government of the Republic of Croatia, on 22 November 2004, signed the Framework agreement on the general principles for the participation of the Republic of Croatia in Community Programmes. The purpose of the Community programmes is to support the EU's internal policies. They are action programmes designed primarily as means of achieving objectives set by the EU and its Member States, based on the internal budget headings. Consequently, being a candidate country, Croatia will have to pay a financial contribution for a given programme. They will be part-financed by the PHARE Programme.

Croatia is already participating in Community programmes with an external component for the Western Balkans, such as LIFE III (environment protection) – http://www.europa.eu.int/comm/environment/life/life/third_countries.htm; TEMPUS (higher education) – http://www.europa.eu.int/comm/education/programmes/tempus/index_en.html; the 6th Framework Programme for Research and Development (scientific research and technological development) – http://www.europa.eu.int/comm/research/fp6/index_en.html; YOUTH (informal education of young people) – http://www.europa.eu.int/comm/youth/index_en.html; and INTERREG (promotion of cross-border, transnational and interregional cooperation).

The INTERREG III initiative covers the period from 2000–2006 and is designed to strengthen economic and social cohesion throughout the EU by fostering the balanced development of the continent through cross-border (strand A), transnational (strand B) and interregional cooperation (strand C). Croatia is actively participating in the following INTERREG programmes:

- Adriatic Cross-border Programme between Eastern Adriatic Countries and Italy;

- Trilateral Operative Programme Hungary/Slovenia/Croatia;

- INTERREG III B CADSES (http://www.cadses.net);

- INTERREG III C East Zone (http://www.interreg3c.net).

Croatia also benefits from a number of bilateral programmes and is the recipient of loans from international financing institutions such as the European Investment Bank, the European Bank for Reconstruction and Development, the World Bank and others. Recognizing the importance of the coordination of overall foreign assistance in Croatia, the government has established a Permanent Working Group for this purpose. As technical support and a tool for the work this group the Ministry for European Integration has set up the interactive database of foreign assistance in Croatia. (http://www.mei.hr/default.asp?ru =173&akcija=)

# Living and Working in Croatia: An Enviable Position

*Wade Channell, American Chamber of Commerce, Croatia*

Many of us who find our way to Croatia as expats have a hard time finding a reason to leave. Life in Zagreb, with its café culture, proximity to the coast, and feeling of urban community can be addictive. Indeed, this charming land has converted more than a few short-termers into permanent residents. For those re-posted regularly, the next station is often a disappointment after the Illyrian allure that captured their imaginations whilst here.

Whatever the planned term of duration, there are a number of culture factors that newcomers should know in order to enrich both experience and investment.

## A small town feeling

Zagreb is, without a doubt, one of the safest places on earth to live. The levels of random crime, anonymous violence, petty theft and burglary that plague so many urban centres to the north and west are remarkable only in their scarcity. Even pre-teen children safely ride the tram, freely walk into the main square, or play unconcerned outside with their friends. For families, Zagreb is a haven.

Obviously, as long as there are humans in the neighbourhood, there will be some crime. There is even evidence that petty crimes have been increasing, along with an increase in drug use. Even so, the rates are far below those of the US and Northern European cities.

One of the reasons, perhaps, for the level of real and perceived safety is that Zagreb is in many ways still a small town. Although 'a city of a million hearts', Zagreb has a community feeling about it, whether in local neighbourhoods, pedestrian walkways, or sparkling new shopping malls. Running into friends and neighbours around town is a constant. It is difficult to walk the café-lined streets without spotting at least a few acquaintances.

For Croatians, time is more than money – it is also relationships with family and friends. Weekends are marked by people spending time together, at home or on the coast. Holidays are spent year after year in residential retreats, coastal homes and apartments, where entire families move for much of the summer. Cafés sprawl onto the sidewalks and streets in warmer weather, where clusters of colleagues congregate, unhurried by waiters or much else. Anyone sitting alone is likely to be either a foreigner, or a Croatian waiting for a friend to show up.

## Managing in a relational culture

Café culture is an expression of the importance placed on relationships in Croatia. Although many joke that full cafés are a sign of underemployment, many of the tables are actually filled with business people. It is quite common for meetings to take place out of the office over coffee, in a setting where people can get to know each other while working out a business relationship or discussing details of a deal.

This emphasis on relationships has implications for new arrivals. If working directly with Croatian counterparts, it is essential to allow time to establish credibility before expecting impact. Like many other countries in transition, Croatia has had plenty of experience with foreign 'experts' who know little about Croatia but expect Croatians to respond positively on short notice to recommendations, corrections, and critiques. Such efficiency may work in New York – between New Yorkers – but in Croatia this is naïve at best and rude at worst. Trust has to be established first, but once established, it is the foundation for success in working together.

The closeness of a small town can also have a flipside – it can be hard for newcomers to gain entry. Croatia, fortunately, does not suffer heavily from such closed circles, but openings must be earned. This is done through friendship and service. Expertise alone is not enough.

## Understanding legacies

In some ways, Croatia is still searching for its past, while reaching for the future. All cultures deal with merit, awarding respect, honour and privilege to those who have it. Merit can be inherited through birth or association with an institution of merit, or earned through individual effort. In the US, the culture tends to give higher marks for earned merit, with less emphasis put on who your parents are and more on what you have done. Croatia, like many of its neighbours, puts more emphasis on ascribed merit.

This emphasis on pedigree shows up in several ways. First, many Croatians see themselves as the proud heirs of the Austro-Hungarian Empire, the land where Maria Teresa kept houses and where buildings reflect Viennese taste. Historically, Croatia served as a buffer zone against the Ottoman Empire, with its soldiers called to protect Northern Europe and Hungary from Turkish incursions. This history, coupled with the shared religious traditions of Catholicism in Austria and Germany, mean that many Croatians, especially of older generations, see themselves as Germanic rather than Slavic.

This would be little more than an interesting cocktail discussion, except that in a number of areas it has implications for foreign managers of local investments. First, it means that Croatians are often highly sensitive to foreign opinion about them. They expect to receive the respect afforded to Germany, and many honestly do not understand how Romania and Bulgaria – clearly not part of Western Europe – could be considered for EU membership before Croatia. Indeed, some believe that Croatia's first attempt at NATO membership failed because they mistakenly believed membership was awarded on the basis of inherited merit, and did not bother to earn their place by making a number of necessary changes.

On a day-to-day basis, it is wise to show respect for Croatia and its heritage, even if you feel that some local pride is misplaced. You should also be careful about making comparisons, especially ones that put Croatia in a negative light against their southern neighbours. The wounds from the war with Serbia are far from healed, and even the wounds of the 1940s are still fresh. Rather than comparing Croatia to a specific country (unless that country is relevant), talk about international best practices or EU standards when describing the goals your company needs to meet. Also, on a personal level, learn about Croatia's modern successes – for example, in sports (skiing, basketball, waterpolo); science (the invention of ultrasound, advances in pharmaceuticals); and ancient glories, such as the democracy practiced in medieval Dubrovnik. Use these as examples of what Croatia is capable of.

It may be necessary to manage your own expectations and those of the people you work with while identifying their approach to merit. Advancement in Western corporate culture generally comes through personal or team achievement and accomplishment, not on inherited merit. It will be important to communicate this sensitively and recognize that many (particularly older) counterparts may be slow to respond. Historically, state-owned companies did not necessarily connect advancement to productivity. Jobs, once given, used to be permanent with insufficient regard to performance. An achievement-oriented Western style system will inspire some but frighten others. Be ready to help with a period of adjustment.

In some fields, such as law, any reforms or recommendations coming from a German-speaking country will be favoured over other countries. It is commonly thought that those from common law jurisdictions simply cannot understand Croatia's needs in the light of its continental history. While untrue, the perception requires reformers to understand how to draw the best examples from favoured countries, or to show how those models do not apply to Croatian reality today.

## Taking and giving correction

Modern management has introduced the world of performance reviews and structured criticism. Frankly, virtually no one likes these reviews in any part of the world, no matter how much management insists they help us to excel. Criticism and review take on their own peculiar characteristics in Croatia, however, due to its history.

The authoritarian models of government imposed until recently were based on a hierarchical chain of command in which decision-making and initiative came from the top. Subordinates did not take initiative, nor did they openly express disagreement. Direct criticism was dangerous, and when received from a superior, it could be followed by serious consequences. For the past three generations, Croatians have perfected the fine art of indirect communication. They are not used to direct criticism, nor do they normally give it.

For managers, this has several implications. First, your direct reports will need to be acclimatized to expect instructive input for the purpose of improving performance. Whether this is done on an annual or on an as-needed basis, it is not a part of existing business culture. When giving criticism, the same rules apply as anywhere else in the world – emphasize positives as well – if possible, even more than the negatives.

Second, do not expect the kind of direct, even blunt feedback you might be used to back home at headquarters. It is common practice to criticize around the edges: complaining about the format of a report is an indirect way of rejecting the substance. Why such roundabout habits? Not so many years ago, direct disagreement could cost you your job, or worse if your superiors took a different view. Such habits die hard, so you will have to create a climate of trust and security, where your local counterparts can learn new habits to meet the changing demands of the business world.

Third, learn to let others take credit if you want your ideas to succeed, especially if your recommendations are to equals or superiors in your hierarchical structures. Forceful introduction of 'foreign' ideas often results in passive or active resistance until the ideas can be 'localized'. There are a number of examples of consultants whose ideas seemed to be ignored until they left town; at that point, the recipients could implement the ideas without having to give someone else the credit. In some ways, this cultural aspect is similar to Asian concepts of face: if you allow your Croatian colleagues room to save face, even to build it, you will enable them to achieve much more than through direct pressure.

## A sense of humour

Any healthy cross-cultural move requires a sense of humour, as you deal with inevitable misunderstandings and frustrations, as well as the joys of discovery. In addition, it is helpful to know a bit about the local sense of humour as you join in.

Many from the US and other conservative corporate cultures are surprised to find that Croatian jokes are often ribald. Many are suggestive, but just as many are quite explicit. Various ethnic jokes are also quite popular, with Croatians able to accurately roast most nationalities, including their own. Self-effacing humour is common, often serving to take the edge off possible criticism for a perceived weakness.

Of course, the rules of engagement in humour are just as true in Croatia as elsewhere. Unless you are considered to be Croatian, never make jokes with Croatia as the brunt. That is off limits. On the other hand, telling jokes about your own background can serve as an avenue for endearment.

## Pleasant opportunity

Croatia is still one of the best-kept secrets on the European continent: safe, pleasant, blessed with natural beauty in every direction, and only a few hours by car or plane from the capitals of Europe. Are there cultural challenges? Of course! But that is part of the richness of investing here.

For those analyzing the spreadsheets to see if Croatia makes sense as a business location, it is important not to forget to quantify the quality of life for expatriate staff. All else being equal, Croatia is not equal – it is miles ahead of its competitors as a desirable place to live and work.

# Part Two

# The Investment Environment

## 2.1

# Foreign Direct Investment in Croatia

*Hrvoje Dolenec and Zrinka Živković,*
*Raiffeisenbank Austria d.d. Zagreb*

## Methodology

Many Eastern European countries try to comply with the IMF's definitions when processing foreign direct investment (FDI) data. The basic methodological problem is how to cover all investment types. Although all Central and Eastern European (CEE) countries try to comply with the IMF's definitions and methodological guidelines, in reality there are numerous difficulties because national methodologies are often not clearly defined and are prone to changes. Still, the trend is improving both in accuracy and coverage. The central banks of the CEE countries are the main institutions for collecting FDI data.

Table 2.1.1 showing levels of international investments in Croatia is made in accordance with the recommendations of the IMF (*Balance of Payments Manual*, Fifth Edition, 1993). Data sources include reports from banks, enterprises, the Croatian National Bank (CNB) and the Zagreb Stock Exchange. Data on foreign direct and portfolio investments are taken from the CNB's statistical research. Foreign investments in the Republic of Croatia are shown in US dollars.

One of the most important challenges of transition economies, in the medium term, will be to maintain a stable FDI inflow, both to cover the external deficit and to raise competitiveness. A reduction in the growth of the global economy could negatively influence the expansion of multinational companies and consequently of FDI. Over recent years there has been a notable increase in the FDI inflow into the CEE countries, attracted mostly by lower production costs, the proximity of the European Union (EU) and improvements in the business environment. In the beginning, the FDI inflow was connected to mass privatization, especially within the banking and telecommunication sectors. Croatia

**Table 2.1.1** Foreign direct investments in Croatia (in US$ million)

| | Equity investments Claims | Liabilities | Reinvested earnings | Debt securities Claims | Liabilities | Other capital Claims | Liabilities | Total |
|---|---|---|---|---|---|---|---|---|
| 1993 | 0.0 | 120.3 | n/a | n/a | n/a | n/a | n/a | 120.3 |
| 1994 | 0.0 | 117.0 | n/a | n/a | n/a | n/a | n/a | 117.0 |
| 1995 | 0.0 | 114.2 | n/a | n/a | n/a | n/a | n/a | 114.2 |
| 1996 | 0.0 | 510.8 | n/a | n/a | n/a | n/a | n/a | 510.8 |
| 1997 | 0.0 | 359.5 | 40.4 | 0.0 | 0.0 | −8.0 | 141.0 | 532.9 |
| 1998 | 0.0 | 635.6 | 68.3 | 0.0 | 0.0 | −14.6 | 243.2 | 932.5 |
| 1999 | 0.0 | 1283.7 | 47.1 | 0.0 | 0.0 | −0.6 | 137.1 | 1,467.3 |
| 2000 | 0.0 | 711.4 | 93.9 | 0.0 | 0.0 | 0.0 | 283.4 | 1,088.7 |
| 2001 | 0.0 | 815.0 | 153.0 | 0.0 | 0.0 | 0.1 | 593.2 | 1,561.3 |
| 2002 | 0.0 | 664.9 | 151.5 | 0.0 | 0.0 | −0.3 | 307.9 | 1,124.0 |
| 2003 | 0.0 | 870.3 | 657.2 | 0.0 | 0.0 | −1.8 | 472.5 | 1,998.2 |
| 2004 Q1,Q2 | 0.0 | 213.5 | 266.2 | 0.0 | 0.0 | −0.1 | 68.2 | 547.8 |
| Total | 0.0 | 6416.2 | 1477.6 | 0.0 | 0.0 | −25.3 | 2246.5 | 10,115.0 |

has been no exception regarding the privatization process during the last decade.

# FDI by economic activity

Out of the most significant privatization accomplishments in the past few years in Croatia, we can single out the privatization of Croatian telecommunications (HT), (US$859 million for a 35 per cent stake in 1999 and another €500 million for additional 16 per cent stake in 2001).

In the banking sector, we can list numerous privatization examples. According to the last available data from the Croatian National Bank, 91 per cent of domestic banking assets is under foreign ownership. In 2002, the government sold a 25 per cent stake in Privredna banka Zagreb to IntesaBci and the EBRD (in the amount of US$140 million, not including the sale of the first stake in the bank in 2000 for US$300 million). Additionally, Riječka banka was sold to Erste bank. In the same year HVB bought Splitska Banka from Unicredito, and Charlemagne Ltd became the owner of Nova Banka and Dubrovacka Banka.

Ever since 1999, FDIs in Croatia have regularly exceeded one billion dollars. Despite the slowdown in 2002 (compared with 2001), the total amount of FDI, according to the revised data of the Croatian National Bank, reached US$1,124 million. After the release of 2002 data, there has been a correction of results for the previous periods, so 1999, when FDI totalled at US$1.47 billion prompted by the sale of a 35 per cent stake in HT, is no longer considered to be the record year. Although the end of 2002 saw the sale of the remaining state-held stake in one of Croatia's leading banks, FDIs failed to reach their record levels due to a delay in the privatization of the state insurer, Croatia osiguranje, and the state oil and gas company, INA, which was sold to a Hungarian company in the last quarter of 2003.

FDI in 2003 amounted to US$1.956 million, with most of the investment in the last quarter of the year (US$533 billion). With this amount, FDI in Croatia has reached a record amount on a yearly basis. Compared to 2002, when it totalled US$1.12 billion, in 2003 FDI rose by 74 per cent, which was largely a consequence of reinvested profits that rose by US$510.7 million or 337 per cent. The rise in reinvested profits was achieved primarily in the second quarter of 2003, partly based on the transfer of market value of Pliva's patents to its related company abroad.

Analysis broken down by economic activity showed that 2003 was dominated by the item manufacture of refined petroleum products, which accounted for 60.85 per cent of total foreign direct investments. It was followed by 'other retail sale in non-specialized stores' (6.72 per cent) and 'other monetary intermediation' (5.78 per cent), 'business and management consultancy activities' (4.14 per cent), 'extraction of crude petroleum and natural gas' (2.30 per cent), 'buying and selling of own real estate' (1.80 per cent), 'other wholesale' (1.61 per cent), 'retail sale in non-specialized stores with food' (1.39 per cent), 'manufacture of steel tubes' (1.19 per cent), and 'manufacture of corrugated paper and paperboard' (1.03 per cent).

This analysis by economic activity showed that the lion's share of last year's FDI (some 60 per cent) came from the production of oil derivatives, that is, the INA sale. INA was sold for some 500 million dollars. Since the Hungarian company bought INA, the lion's share of last year's FDI (some 30.5 per cent) came from Hungary. This is very important, because from 1993 to 2002 cumulative inflows of FDI from Hungary were not significant for Croatia (in terms of FDI inflows), but with the last year's additional amount, Hungary took the fourth place, behind Austria, Germany and the USA.

In 2003, significant inflows of FDI came from Austria (23.61 per cent) and the US (19.38 per cent). These three countries accumulated almost three quarters (73.47 per cent) of the total FDI in 2003, followed by Germany (8.75 per cent), the Netherlands (6.08 per cent) and Slovenia (4.45 per cent).

According to the CNB's data, foreign direct investment in Croatia in the first half of 2004 totalled US$547.8 million, which represents a decrease compared with the same period last year when FDI totalled US$990.65 million. However, most of FDI was placed in retail and wholesale activities, whereas it would be desirable that FDI comes to manufacturing and exports activities because of their positive impact on economic development. A large part of FDI came from Austria (29 per cent), Germany (22.5 per cent), Italy (10.8 per cent) and the Netherlands (6 per cent). The main characteristics of the H1/2004 FDI are a large portion of retained earnings (US$266 million) and the rest are direct investments in equity capital. But, at the same time this means increase in investor confidence and a positive sign for doing business in Croatia.

Cumulatively, in the period from 1993 to H1/2004 foreign direct investment totalled US$10,115 billion, out of which 'telecommunications' account for roughly one fifth (22.96 per cent), followed by 'other monetary intermediation' (19.61 per cent), 'manufacture of pharmaceutical preparations' (11.27 per cent), 'manufacture of refined petroleum products' (7.86 per cent), 'manufacture of cement' (3.29) 'hotels and motels, with restaurants' (3.05 per cent), 'other retail sale in non-specialized stores' (2.98 per cent) 'extraction of crude petroleum and natural gas' (2.84 per cent), 'manufacture of beer' (2.09 per cent), and 'business and management consultancy activities' (1.12 per cent) (see Table 2.1.2). In 2004, it is expected that FDI will reach the amount of around US$1 billion and US$1.5 billion in 2005, largely from planned privatization income, for example the sale of Croatia osiguranje (an insurance company).

Among the first on the list of countries that invested in Croatia in the period between 1993 and 2003 is Austria, with a share of 25.70 per cent over the period concerned. If combined with FDI from Germany (20.73 per cent), these two countries accounted for almost a half of the FDI in that period. It is important to mention that these two countries are among Croatia's most important trading partners. The US accounted for a 14.74 per cent share in FDI for the period 1993–H1/

**Table 2.1.2** Foreign direct equity investments in Croatia (%)

| Activity | 1993–2004 Q2 |
| --- | --- |
| Telecommunications | 20.96 |
| Other monetary intermediation | 19.61 |
| Manufacture of pharmaceutical preparations | 11.27 |
| Manufacture of refined petroleum products | 7.86 |
| Manufacture of cement | 3.29 |
| Hotels and motels, with restaurant | 3.05 |
| Other retail sale in non-specialized stores | 2.98 |
| Extraction of crude petroleum and natural gas | 2.84 |
| Manufacture of beer | 2.09 |
| Business and management consultancy activities | 1.12 |
| Others | 24.93 |
| **Total** | **100.00** |

2004, Hungary follows with 6 per cent, Luxembourg with 5.86 per cent and Italy with 5.71 per cent.

Italy is one of Croatia's most important trading partners, accounting for 20.6 per cent of the total trade in goods in 2003. In the first half of 2004, Italy's share in Croatian foreign trade remained high (above 19 per cent). The fifth position of Luxembourg on the list of FDI is very interesting but one should bear in mind that foreign companies often use their subsidiaries located in tax havens. Such a case was at hand with Luxembourg, through which an Italian bank paid PBZ, thus resulting in a relatively low recorded FDI percentage from Italy. If we analyse the value of Croatia's foreign trade with developed countries over the last few years, we come to the conclusion that there is a connection between the proximity of the market and the intensity of the FDI. Germany invested the most in telecommunications and other monetary intermediation. Austria placed the majority of its FDI in money business, production of instruments and apparatus for measurement and control, production of bricks, and roofing tiles, etc, while Italy largely specialized in investments in monetary intermediation.

# Economic and political environment

An overview of Croatia's main indicators, which are an integral part of the package reviewed when considering an investment in a country, reflects that, in comparison to the other Central European countries in transition, Croatia shows moderate competitiveness: a small country by the number of its inhabitants, with high unemployment, low inflation and positive GDP growth rates over the last few years.

There are signs of positive movements in trade and product distribution to third markets – tariff protection of Croatia's market was reduced by the country's admission to the WTO, and, at the beginning of March 2004, the Republic of Croatia became the eighth CEFTA member country. However, most of the CEFTA member countries became an integral part of the EU in May 2004. Since then, trade and transport provisions of the Stabilization and Association Agreement that have been applied as of 1 January 2002, through the Interim Agreement on trade and related issues between the EU on one hand and Croatia on the other, also relate to the new EU members. Once the process of ratification in member countries is concluded, the Stabilization and Association Agreement will come into force.

On 21 February 2003, the application for Croatia's membership of the EU was formally submitted in Athens. This was a crucial step on Croatia's path towards EU membership in the second wave of EU enlargement. The EU was expected to give its opinion on Croatia's application for EU membership sometime before the summer, and that expectation was fulfilled – the EU institutions have decided to begin negotiating Croatia's entering the EU. The main findings of the European Commission Opinion on the application of Croatia for membership of the EU are that Croatia is a functioning democracy, with stable institutions guaranteeing the rule of law. According to the Opinion, Croatia can be regarded as a functioning market economy, which should be able to cope with competitive pressure and market forces within the EU in the mid-term, provided that it continues to implement its reform programme to remove the remaining weaknesses. Further efforts will be needed to align legislation with the *acquis communautaire* and ensure implementation and enforcement.

Croatia became an official candidate for EU accession on 18 June 2004. The negotiations are to be scheduled for the beginning of 2005 (probably in March). Such a decision should support Croatia's determination to push further positive reforms towards EU membership and make its economy convergent with the EU. It can also help FDI attraction, especially greenfield investment, which can support production capacity and output. At that time, Standard & Poor's credit ratings agency revised Croatia's credit outlook from stable to positive. In their statement, it is affirmed BBB– long term foreign currency outlook but with a positive outlook in the mid-term. The outlook revision reflects Croatia's strong track record of structural reforms, which are expected to be built on. However, a possible credit rating upgrade is dependent on fiscal consolidation, external debt developments and balance of payments developments.

The positive atmosphere created during Croatia's new steps towards EU membership can help to support the interest of investors in Croatia, contribute to political stability and speed up the necessary reforms of the Croatian economy. It would be desirable if conditions would arise within the framework of these reforms to attract foreign investments, especially the so-called greenfield investments to increase production capacities of the domestic economy, in the light of slackening credit activities under the influence of a restrictive monetary policy in the situation of rising foreign debt and a high trade deficit.

The actual negotiations will follow after official acceptance of the application. Croatia hopes to complete the EU accession talks in 2006 and join the Union in 2007 or soon thereafter. But, in order to make membership by 2007 a realistic goal, negotiations will need to progress fast. Croatia's entry into the EU is a strategic task, for this or any other government, and needs to be pursued seriously, regardless of the fact that the election campaign had unofficially begun. Furthermore, at the end of March 2004, an annual report of the European Commission on the Stabilization and Association Agreement in Croatia, showed that the political situation is stable, the economic situation continues to improve and the overall situation in the country is satisfactory. In this way Croatia has continued increasing its presence in the neighbouring markets and its attractiveness to investors. Furthermore, in October 2004, the European Commission adopted a Strategy Paper on progress in the enlargement process that contains the pre-accession strategy for Croatia, and according to which it would benefit from all three pre-accession financial instruments: PHARE, ISPA and SAPARD.

Among the country's most important natural resources are the Mediterranean climate, combined with 5,800 km of coastline, laced with over 1,100 islands. In such an environment, tourism is a fast-developing branch of the economy because Croatia is the nearest destination for tourists from East European countries, as well as Germany, Austria and Italy.

Motorway construction gained momentum over 2003 and 2004, which created additional optimism regarding further tourism development. Profit driven future investors will most certainly increase the pressure for the prolongation of a currently short tourist season and thus the pressure on the entire economic microenvironment, starting from local government institutions, regional suppliers and small and medium-sized entrepreneurs.

Despite large-scale state investment in road construction, the infrastructure has still not reached the level necessary for complete and normal functioning of the economy. Problems are most pronounced in rail transport. Difficulties are also created by legal complexities and slow bureaucracy in the process of establishing new companies, not to mention the fact that local governments do not have a unified mechanism for regulating land and utility fees.

## The Act on Stimulating Investments

The Act on Stimulating Investments, the guidelines of which can be summarized by the following few points, has been in force since the beginning of 2000:

- A person is considered an investor if he/she invested at least HRK4 million. Investors who invested HRK4–10 million (approximately €0.53–1.33 million) can count on incentives (in the form of incentives for employment or staff retraining, as well as tax-free equipment imports).

- The Act contains fiscal and non-fiscal aspects. The fiscal aspect concerns gradual income tax exemption (partial or overall) and import benefits for the import of new equipment and machinery. Pursuant to this Act, an income tax relief on investment of HRK10 million (€1.33 million) and employment of at least 30 employees would amount to minimum 28 percentage points; on investments exceeding HRK20 million (€1.66 million) and employment of at least 50 employees it would amount to 32 percentage points and on investments of HRK60 million (€8 million) and employment of at least 75 people the relief would amount to 35 per cent, which is the amount equal to total income tax. The tax relief remains valid over a long period of time, 10 years, which ensures continuity but also high costs for the state budget. The non-fiscal aspect, in addition to the aforementioned employment and staff retraining incentives, includes handing over land and real estate to investors.

- The Act stipulates employment as the primary goal of investment stimulation.

- Many provisions of this Act contain the phrase 'may approve', which gives plenty of room for discretionary decisions and thus the increase of administrative costs and decrease in transparency.

These incentives are only part of the package foreign investments depend on, and a superficial comparison with the neighbouring countries shows that Croatia has reacted faster than Slovenia in implementing stimulative financial measures. For instance, in comparison with Hungary, Croatia has defined a lower level of investment capital under which an investor qualifies for state stimulation benefits. The tax benefit duration period of 10 years was probably taken from other countries in transition, in order for Croatia to be competitive with these countries. It is important to point out that a general improvement in investment conditions is a substantially bigger incentive to foreign and domestic investors than immediate subsidies. In this respect, Croatia is trying to push ahead strongly, especially within the framework of European integration.

A shortcoming Croatia must gradually overcome is the lack of knowledge of the ways of the market economy, as well as business management and organization. This problem could be alleviated by foreign investments and the know-how on conducting business in a market economy that foreign investors are expected to bring, thus encouraging competition, as has been the case in the telecommunication and banking sectors. This could, again, lead to the more efficient operation of domestic companies by means of implementing new products and technologies, resulting in a faster restructuring of the country's economy.

# Conclusion

An advantageous territorial structure and friendly legislation, a diverse land attractive to businesses and tourists, a large number of independent commercial entities on the market and a strong transit location at the hub of east-west and north-south routes are all factors that create a favourable environment for investors. The government actively encourages FDI to stimulate the economy with the number of multinationals that are already established in the Croatian market. Croatia has accelerated integration into Western institutions and increased the prospects of regional political stability (it has joined NATO's Partnership for Peace, become a member of the WTO and European Free Trade Association, concluded the Stabilization and Association Agreement with the EU, submitted the application for full EU membership and become a candidate for EU membership). Foreign investors are entitled to special tax exemptions, depending on the nature of the investment and the activities they carry out in Croatia. As regards opportunities for investment, tourism can be singled out, because the rapid re-emergence of tourism provides investors with an opportunity to invest in a dynamic and growing sector.

## 2.2

# The Investment Climate and Future FDI Flows

*Igor Maričić, Croatian Trade & Investment Promotion Agency*

In 2004, Croatia became a candidate country for European Union (EU) membership, and mainly thanks to that fact, among other circumstantial or targeted characteristics of Croatia, a whole new round of investment opportunities suddenly began. Is it only EU accession or is there more to the story? Is it really so sudden and unexpected?

## The Croatian image abroad

There are different points of view regarding Croatia and its image – the one from people who have never set foot there, the one from those people who came to live and/or work in Croatia and, of course, the Croatian side of the story.

So, having established that there are three sides to every story – yours, mine and the truth – we still have to see which one is the true one, especially regarding investments and the investments side of the Croatian image. By analysis made in 2004, the rest of the world (neighbouring countries excluded) usually sees Croatia through a few pictures – CNN's Dubrovnik in flames in 1991, or sports and Croatian sportsmen. The war? What war? Oh, the one in last century...

Croatians today, although remembering the 1990s, are looking to the future in light of growing economy and opening up to the world. I have frequently been asked by investors a number of simple questions about Croatia and its people, local prices, etc. Why is Croatia more expensive than some other transition countries? Why are salaries in Croatia somewhat higher? Why do Croatians speak rather good English? Simple questions, no matter how much taken for granted by Croatians, do not have simple answers. Just showing the fact that the Croatian labour force has a higher productivity rate than many other countries in the region did not seem enough.

Perhaps the easiest way to answer those questions is to explain a few basic historical facts. Croatia was not always a transition country. It was one of the most prosperous ex-Yugoslav republics; and former Yugoslavia, although it was a socialist country, had a somewhat different position than other countries in the region.

Croatians were free to travel abroad and to do their shopping in Trieste, Italy or in Austria for example, and could generally afford to go skiing in the Austrian Alps. Compared to other socialist countries, Croatian stores were usually full of goods for the consumer to buy. The standard of living was much higher than in other socialist countries and Croatian students usually went for their school excursions to other socialist countries because it was incredibly cheap for them to do so.

Small things matter, so by watching American or English films without language synchronization and by listening to the language and reading subtitles, during the socialist period English became a frequently spoken language, especially among the young and highly educated people.

To a large extent, the freedom Croatia enjoyed during the past became one of the structural reasons for what Croatia is today. It influenced our economy and our society. Some Western business standards as well as some Western companies were present in Croatia, even during socialist times.

Expatriates from other countries investing, working and living in Croatia will perhaps give you their side of the story – Croatia as a land of opportunity and unique lifestyle, a transition country with a number of issues still to be resolved and adjusted to full Western standards, but also the place where you can get higher margins and higher growth rates for your business than in Western countries. The proximity of the long Croatian Adriatic coast or Slovenian or Austrian skiing resorts also makes it an attractive place to live.

## Investments and a new FDI policy

Foreign investments in Croatia, after the rather dry early 1990s, picked up in the second half of the 1990s. A number of foreign companies entered the Croatian market in banking, telecoms and other business sectors. But after waves of privatizations and some greenfield investments, it became obvious that the Croatian FDI structure has been lacking certain types of investment.

Croatia will encourage every investment in the country. Companies like Deutsche Telecom (who acquired a majority stake in Croatian Telecom), Siemens and Ericsson (who acquired local ICT companies with significant market influence not only in Croatia but also on other Eastern markets) or banks like Italian BCI Intesa and Unicredito, as well as major Austrian banks, have already entered the Croatian markets. However, while these are clearly positive developments for Croatia's efforts to attract FDI, it is obvious that the Croatian FDI account is lacking greenfield investments in production sectors.

While Croatia commenced the 1990s as an export-oriented economy, the Croatian trade balance turned into deficit during the last decade and Croatia has become an import-oriented economy at present. These were the reasons for the Croatian government to reposition its FDI policy in 2004.

Croatian FDI inflow was never before so strategically and precisely positioned and structured. The FDI account looked more than good. FDI figures were, and still are, among the best in Central and Eastern Europe (CEE), not to mention Southeast Europe (SEE). Croatia is among the top CEE players in FDI per capita terms, just behind the Czech Republic and Hungary. In SEE, out of approximately US$6 billion of FDI in 2003, Croatia attracted almost US$2 billion FDI. However, to continue high GDP growth rates, as well as to restructure its own trade balance, Croatia will need more export-orientated greenfield investments. The Croatian government will welcome and support a wide range of investments in this area.

Numerous steps have been initiated in order to improve absorption capacity of Croatia for more greenfield investments. A one-stop-shop principle was introduced as a way of cutting down the red tape and making investments easier in every step of the investment process. The Investment Promotion Law is undergoing changes in order to make Croatia more competitive and a more investor-friendly environment. The land registry is also going through a restructuring process, with the intention of speeding up real estate transactions.

Two levels of investment are generally preferred – first, manufacturing and services with high export orientation and second, high tech investments and investments that will put Croatia on higher regional or global business competition scale.

This does not mean Croatia will forget its traditional business sectors like processing (wood, textile, metal, etc) or its strong tourist orientation, especially in Government Special Care Areas, where special tax and other incentives are offered.

The future of FDI flows in Croatia will no longer be determined by large privatizations, although the process of privatization will continue. Current greenfield investment in the pipeline for the next two to four year period is definitely more in favour of greenfield investments in the processing sectors or the energy sector, for example.

# Why come to Croatia?

Croatia offers a stable and predictable investment environment, as well as a business environment compatible to Western markets. Its relatively inexpensive but still quality educated and very productive labour force makes a difference to investors. English is commonly spoken, especially among the higher educated population. A well-established industrial and engineering tradition will provide fruitful grounds for investments in high tech and other demanding industrial sectors.

Its geographical position is Croatia's strong point because Croatia is on the crossroads between Western Europe and Southeast Europe, and South and North of Central and Eastern Europe. By capturing the best of both worlds, with its EU borders and future membership oportunities, it has a strong regional business position, supported by infrastructure superior to many other countries in the region.

It is not by chance that tourism is one of Croatia's main industries. Croatian lifestyle itself, a pleasant Mediterranean climate, as well as warm and pleasant people and the proximity of Alpine ski resorts or the Adriatic coast, make Croatia a rather unique place to live and work.

Last but not least, investment incentives (employment, taxes, real estate, etc) and government willingness to attract new and sophisticated industries, as well as investors in traditional Croatian processing sectors, is already a strategic guideline and firm goal of the Croatian Trade & Investment Promotion Agency.

## 2.3

# Formulating an Appropriate Investment Strategy

*Michael Glazer, Auctor Securities*

Strategy depends upon goals and available tools. This is as true for Croatian investments as anything else. Goals, in turn, depend upon the type of investor: portfolio/direct investment, risk-tolerant/risk-averse, short-term/long-term, etc. The intellectual, financial and organizational tools that investors have at their disposal can be even more varied. One size does not fit all in any market, let alone in a transitional economy like Croatia.

Despite the wide variety in investors' aims and capabilities, and the consequent futility of creating the single right investment strategy, it *is* possible to provide insights into the constraints and opportunities an investor will find in Croatia and even to give some guidance as to what might be wise approaches to investing in the country.

Investors need to keep a number of key points in mind. Some may seem self-evident, but unfortunately even sophisticated investors often fail to take into account some of the more obvious ones.

## Key points

### Key point 1

Croatia is its own country. Small, yes; recently formed from a larger entity, true; but still very much a separate, sovereign entity. This bears mentioning since there is a tendency for investors not to spend the time, effort and talent required to understand Croatia in its own right and to assume that techniques that worked elsewhere will *a fortiori* work in Croatia. This is simply not true.

## Key point 2

Despite its relatively small population, Croatia is a varied country. The Dalmatian coast differs from the Pannonian plain not just in geography, but also in business culture, business opportunities, political orientation, etc. Of course, the sophisticated cross-border investor will not need to be told this, but experience shows that the point needs to be made.

## Key point 3

Croatia is a transitioning economy. Most investors know this. In fact, that is often why they have identified Croatia as a promising place to put their money. But frequently they then proceed to forget that the consequence of this is that, although it is definitely making progress, Croatia is still not quite up to EU standards in a number of areas.

Specifically, property ownership issues can be problematic, especially for real (as opposed to personal) property. There is no question of state expropriation or any of the more dire dangers, but an imperfect property record-keeping system, slow data entry and records tangled by years of neglect, often make it difficult to determine who has claims against a piece of land and it can be time-consuming to resolve the question. Even portfolio investors need to be aware of this, as must any investor in an existing firm that has important real estate holdings. Does the company really own free and clear the land and buildings it thinks it does?

In addition, the legal system is a work in progress. Delays, improper influence and inexperience of both adjudicators and counsel are all problems. The good news is the government is quite aware of this, as is the EU. Both have made improvements a priority.

Counterparts may also still be learning the Western ropes, although many are quite competent. Payment may be slow, among other things. Luckily, the stock market has a Payment Against Delivery clearing system that obviates most problems of this sort in security trades.

Croatian corporate governance is also not all it could be. This is, of course, a problem that affects countries with much more developed market economies than Croatia's, including some very prominent EU members. It is likely to improve in Croatia, but slowly.

## Key point 4

Croatia will continue to draw closer to the EU, of course, but the pace depends on many imponderables. Domestic political problems connected to cooperation with the Hague tribunal can likely be resolved relatively soon, speeding Croatia's accession negotiations. In fact, technical issues are likely to be resolved by 2007–8. But admission by those dates is very unlikely and the timing is, in many ways, outside of Croatia's control. If the EU's upcoming referenda on its Constitution go the wrong way, it will have its hands full resolving the status of its current members. Even if the Constitution is adopted without major disputes, the complexities introduced by the EU's recent induction of 10 new members could prove so daunting that current members become allergic to further expansion. The most likely case is that Croatia's present momentum towards EU membership is maintained, and few new obstacles arise: Croatia is important to the EU, if only as an example to Serbia and Bosnia-Herzegovina.

## Key point 5

Tourism is, and always has been, a major economic driver, but tourism cannot carry the economy on its own, and anyway, it continues to require considerable development itself.

## Key point 6

Alternative economic drivers are either having their own problems (eg large state-owned or formerly state-owned companies) or have not yet had a chance to come into their own (eg SMEs). Both the Croatian government and foreign donors are making significant efforts to improve the SME environment and enhance national competitiveness, so improvements can be expected in the future. Just not overnight.

## Key point 7

Given points 4–6, one can expect a rather dramatic restructuring of the Croatian economy in the next few years, as business adapts to the new realities. The state will recognize its inability to continue supporting aged dinosaurs, while nimble and innovative entrepreneurs will prosper. True, this has been prophesied for some time now, but the steadily increasing power of the SME sector and the increasingly clear unsustainability of governmental dinosaur conservation efforts seem likely to speed the process considerably.

## Key point 8

Croatia has a small internal market. Accordingly, businesses other than the very smallest must cater to foreigners. Getting this right is something Croatian firms have, until now, found difficult. More and more, though, SMEs are exporting, and while problems continue to hinder the sector, tourism revenues from foreigners (economically an export) continue to grow.

### Key point 9

Croatian social programmes are unsustainable at present levels without dramatic alterations in taxation or other revenue producing measures. Accordingly, there must be significant readjustments in the expectations of Croatian labour and retirees. These adjustments will not come easily or without significant citizen discontent.

### Key point 10

Croatian labour is expensive and not as productive as it could be, in part because the adjustments mentioned in Key Point 9 above have yet to be made. The competitiveness of Croatian labour will continue to improve, but slowly. On the other hand, Croatian wages are sufficiently high to discourage employees from job swapping regularly or giving up and heading for other countries. This stability brings greater returns on human resource investment.

### Key point 11

As a consequence of the problems identified above, in many areas Croatia is not currently competitive with alternative destinations for capital. The government appears to recognize this and to be considering steps to lower and rationalize the tax structure and to adjust benefits to reflect fiscal realities.

### Key point 12

Croatian companies are small by world standards. This limits opportunities for investors that have large minimum deal requirements or that are required to take minority positions. This is a particularly acute problem in Croatia, since many of Croatia's most dynamic companies are SMEs.

### Key point 13

Croatia's currency is closely tied to the euro and inflation is low. Both are a matter of pride for Croatians, and the Croatian National Bank and the Croatian government are unlikely to permit this to change voluntarily. There is still significant room for policy error, though, as social demands and sound economic policy increasingly clash.

## Strategic principles

Any successful investment strategy must be formulated with the above points in mind and, again, while no single strategy can apply to all investors, some general principles apply.

### *Strategic principle 1*

Do your research. Croatia cannot just be lumped in a 'Central Europe' box. Research includes legal analysis, investigation of the overall economy and the specific economic sectors and geographical regions that interest the investor.

### *Strategic principle 2*

Specifically, invest in individual firms, not sectors. Croatia has too few firms to permit a pure sectoral investment strategy. Often a sector may consist of one or two large firms and, perhaps, a few smaller ones. Pharmaceuticals in Croatia, for example, consist of Pliva and Belupo, at least as far as firms of any size are concerned.

### *Strategic principle 3*

Think small if you can. Small firms are, as previously noted, often the most nimble, best managed and most promising firms in Croatia.

### *Strategic principle 4*

Choose firms that have good corporate governance. This increases your returns by upping the odds of your having a return, of course, but good corporate governance is also a strong indicator of a more modern approach to business.

### *Strategic principle 5*

Plan on legal and social changes. While these will, for the most part, produce positive effects, they will nonetheless inevitably be disruptive. On the other hand, these changes can provide opportunities if correctly anticipated, and indeed form the basis for a convergence strategy.

### *Strategic principle 6*

Choose your investments to minimize your exposure to labour costs and other areas in which Croatia is uncompetitive. Croatia's small internal market makes this more difficult, since it means that, in theory, few sectors are immune to external competition. Although significant portions of the Croatian market are currently at least somewhat insulated from competition due to regulatory and other barriers, this will change, potentially quite rapidly, as Croatia implements EU acquis. Accordingly, the advice holds.

### *Strategic principle 7*

Take a cautious view on inflation and exchange rates. This may seem obvious, but Croatia's excellent track record to date may tempt investors to assume the past will be prologue. This may well be correct, but it is not a certainty, as noted above.

### Strategic principle 8

Plan for EU membership. The timing is uncertain, but the reality of joining the EU eventually is not. Today's investment in Croatia is tomorrow's investment in 'Europe'.

## Conclusion

Principles are not a strategy. The hard work of applying them remains. But for thoughtful investors with a clear vision of their goals and capabilities, they can make the formulation of a strategy easier and the strategy itself more effective. Croatia, despite its small size, has excellent profit potential. It is worth the effort.

# The Banking System

*Hrvoje Dolenec, Raiffeisenbank Austria d.d. Zagreb*

Croatia has a two-tier banking system in which the Croatian National Bank (CNB) acts as a central bank but does not engage in commercial banking. There are 38 banks operating in Croatia. Foreign banks may operate in Croatia and currently there are 16 majority foreign-owned banks in the country, which control around 92 per cent of total banking assets. Most of the foreign owners are from Italy (the two largest banks) and Austria (the next four largest banks). Only two banks are state-owned, with a 3.4 per cent stake in total banking assets. The rest are small, domestic private banks.

## The Croatian National Bank

The CNB became the central bank of Croatia on 23 December 1991, when the Croatian dinar was introduced as legal tender.

Its role as a central bank was defined by the Act on the Croatian National Bank, passed on 4 November 1992 (CNB Act). Article 53 of the Croatian Constitution and CNB Act established the CNB's independence and specified its relations with parliament. The Governor of the CNB and members of its Board of Governors are appointed by parliament for six-year terms and can only be removed by parliament in extraordinary circumstances defined by the CNB Act.

A new law regulating the policies and powers of the CNB was enacted on 5 April 2001 (the 2001 CNB Act). This Act, which is modelled on the rules governing the European Central Bank, grants the CNB further independence and allows it new powers of self-governance. For example, the new CNB Act prohibits the government from borrowing directly from the CNB, and allows the CNB to trade only in the secondary market for government short-term and long-term securities. Also, the new CNB Act specifies that the CNB's main goal is price stability, while retaining the CNB's responsibility for banking supervision and monitoring of the payments system.

# The Croatian banking system

Banks in Croatia are mostly structured as universal banks. They are authorized to carry out wholesale and retail banking activities, with all of them having licences to operate internationally. The five largest banks (Zagrebacka banka, Privredna banka Zagreb, Erste bank, Raiffeisenbank Austria and HVB Splitska banka) accounted for around 72 per cent of all banking assets in 2004. At the end of 2004, the two largest banks held 45 per cent of total capital and the five largest banks held 67 per cent of total capital, while the two largest banks held 45 per cent of total banking assets. The banking system may be described as oligopolistic, with a significant concentration of the power among the largest banks, although it created significant competition among them for increased market shares. Indicators of the business constantly improve after the rehabilitation and consolidation process.

In 1999, four housing saving banks were established, three of which are foreign-owned. After a merger of two saving banks in mid-2002, and the entrance of one additional housing saving bank in the market, four still operate, all in foreign ownership. They are permitted to collect deposits from their customers, who must maintain their deposits for at least two years before they may be granted mortgages. After this period, customers may be granted mortgages proportionate to their savings, which are dependent on the duration of their deposits. Interest rates on such loans are 6 per cent per annum, with 10 to 15 year maturities.

During 1998 and 1999, some of Croatia's small and medium-sized banks encountered severe difficulties. Between January 1999 and February 2001, 10 banks were declared bankrupt and two were rehabilitated through a process of government receivership. In addition, in 2000 and early 2001, there were several mergers and bank liquidations. Further mergers and aquisitions were conducted throughout the later period up to the present time. Such developments reduced the number of banks from 60 in December 1997 to the current 38, and increased the stability of the whole system.

# Bank regulation and prudential standards

Since 1992, the CNB has set prudential guidelines for all Croatian banks. The current system of prudential standards includes a minimum 10 per cent risk-weighted capital adequacy ratio, calculated in accordance with BIS recommendations and international authorities' standards; daily monitoring of liquidity levels; classification of the quality of bank assets; provision of reserves with respect to problem loans; and limits on foreign exchange positions. Individual loans or the total of all loans to a single borrower cannot exceed 25 per cent of liable capital (defined as tier-one capital and a portion of tier-two capital).

Banks must provide security for their operations, and are therefore required to set aside provisions. In addition to general provisions for covering unidentified potential loan losses, banks must set aside specific provisions against identified potential losses from doubtful credits, investments and a portion of off-balance sheet items. Annual reports of banks must be checked and evaluated by an authorized external auditor. Large banks usually have their annual reports audited by internationally recognized auditing firms.

Banks are independent in their business activities from the government and the CNB, and operate as joint stock companies, with management being responsible to the shareholders. Banks may be established by one or more legal or natural persons, resident or non-resident. The minimum equity capital requirement is set at HRK40 million. Both new banks and savings banks must obtain a licence from the CNB. Licence applications must include, among other documents, proof of the capital required, qualified managers and business plans for two years. Under certain conditions the licence can be revoked if the bank does not comply with the regulations.

Major legal changes occurred in 2002 when the Parliament approved the 2002 Banking Act. The new Act has introduced a legal framework for banks' operations during accession to the EU. It has further strengthened the CNB supervisory power and it has introduced consolidated supervision. Under the new Act, all bylaws and regulations were enacted by January 2003, although the Act itself came into effect immediately, except for certain provisions that can only be applied once Croatia joins the EU.

The Act on the State Agency for Deposit Insurance and Bank Rehabilitation (which came into force on 11 June 1994, and was amended in 1998, 1999 and 2000) provides for a scheme of bank-funded deposit insurance for all banks. The Act creates a special account with full coverage for savings deposits of individuals in Kuna or foreign currency up to a level determined by the Minister of Finance. This level is currently HRK100,000. The deposit insurance scheme started functioning in mid-1997, so that depositors who held their money in banks that failed during the 1998–1999 period received payment from the State Agency up to the HRK100,000 limit. These payments were all made by the end of 2000.

# The bank rehabilitation programme

Since achieving independence, Croatian banks have suffered both from high levels of bad debt and from liquidity problems.

Shortly after Croatia's declaration of independence on 25 June 1991, the National Bank of Yugoslavia (NBY) froze all the foreign exchange deposits of Croatian banks that it held. For Croatian banks this amounted to approximately US$3 billion. Frozen foreign exchange deposits on the banks' balance sheets were subsequently converted into government bonds with a maturity of 10 years, with repayment linked to the Deutschmark and bearing interest of five per cent per annum.

In an attempt to recapitalize banks suffering from high levels of bad debt and to aid indebted enterprises, in 1991 and 1992 the government issued bonds under the so-called 'Big Bonds Scheme'. The proportion of claims on the government is declining. At the end of 1993, 40.2 per cent of the total assets of deposit money banks were net claims on the government; this ratio had fallen to 6.8 per cent by September 2004.

# Rehabilitation programme and the privatization of banks

The legislative structure for the new rehabilitation programme was set out in the Act on Bank Rehabilitation and Restructuring, which came into force on 11 June 1994 (the Act on Rehabilitation). The Act was revoked in 2000, after the government privatized most of the restructured banks. In late 1995, the government began implementing this new rehabilitation programme for the banking system. The objectives of the programme included changing bank ownership structures, ensuring additional capitalization of banks that are suitably qualified to operate successfully, and excluding bank debtors from the management of the banks.

Rehabilitation was being implemented on a case-by-case basis. The CNB was responsible for appraisal of the economic feasibility of rehabilitation in particular instances. A new state agency, the State Agency for Deposit Insurance and Bank Rehabilitation (the Agency for Rehabilitation), was established to implement certain aspects of bank rehabilitation.

The bank rehabilitation process had three phases:

1. a financial restructuring designed to recapitalize the bank, restore its liquidity and transfer its non-performing assets to the Agency for Rehabilitation;

2. an institutional reform process, designed to install new governance, controls and policies, and to focus the business strategy and operations of the bank on new and growing markets;

3. as the rehabilitation process was completed, the Agency for Rehabilitation would return the bank to the private sector by selling

its shares to qualified investors (ie investors who are not also major debtors of the bank).

Six banks have entered the rehabilitation process: Slavonska banka and Splitska banka were successfully privatized in 1999 and 2000. Slavonska banka was sold to the European Bank for Reconstruction and Development (EBRD) and Hypo Alpe-Adria-Bank AG. On 17 December 1999, the State Agency for Deposit Insurance and Bank Rehabilitation (the DAB) announced that it signed an agreement to sell 66.3 per cent of the shares in Privredna banka Zagreb d.d. (PBZ) for €300 million to Banca Commerciale Italiana SpA (BCI). The DAB sold the remaining stake of 25 per cent plus two shares in December 2002. In the first quarter of 2000, Rijecka banka was sold to strategic partner Bayerische Landesbank for US$41 million. This was subsequently followed by a strategic sale of Splitska Banka to Unicredito Italiano for €48 million.

In 2001, Unicredito Italiano sought approval from the CNB for the acquisition of a majority shareholding in Zagrebacka banka, Croatia's largest bank. CNB approved the acquisition subject to Unicredito Italiano, selling its interest in Splitska Banka to HVB Bank. Both transactions were completed in April 2002.

In March 2002, Rijecka banka announced heavy losses in foreign exchange trading activities resulting from internal fraud. Due to a successful agreement between its two major shareholders, Bayerische Landesbank and the Croatian government, the crisis was quickly brought under control. Bayerische Landesbank withdrew from the bank by returning its shares to the Croatian government and, in April 2002, the government sold an 85 per cent interest in the bank to Erste Steiermarkische Bank for €55 million, with an obligation to inject a further €100 million into the bank as capital.

In March 2002, Dubrovacka banka was acquired by Dalmatinska banka for €24 million. After a successful merging process in 2004 under the name of Nova banka, which included two additional but rather small banks (Sisacka banka and Istarska banka), it was announced that the established bank is ready to be sold to a strategic investor in early 2005. There have been four official interested parties. Two of them are foreign banks with interest in the Croatian market – OTP Bank from Hungary and Société Generale from France.

Government majority ownership still exists in two Croatian banks, but the official strategy is still to privatize such banks. The privatization of Croatia banka is expected to be completed in 2005. Hrvatska postanska banka is also planned for privatization, with an action plan for this to be produced by the end of June of 2005. Both of these processes are included in the new Stand-by Agreement with the IMF approved in August 2004.

# Current developments

The overall size of the Croatian banking system (total assets in percentage of GDP) surpassed the GDP for the first time in 2003. Total assets reached HRK204.5 billion (€26.7 billion). Despite restrictive measures by the central bank, total assets still grew by 14.3 per cent year-on-year (yoy) in euro terms last year. In December 2004, the Croatian banking system assets reached the level of almost €30 billion.

The market is dominated by six banking groups that cover 84.4 per cent of the market when looking at their respective asset volumes. The growth of the banking system has been realized by decreasing the number of banks through mergers and acquisitions, and there are new up and coming activities that will further decrease the number of banks. Currently there are 38 banks operating in Croatia and the trend is for a further decrease. The largest part of the banking system is owned by foreigners, which is evident in the high share of assets (close to 92 per cent).

New measures to curb credit growth were introduced in 2004 and the continued restrictive monetary policy should further slow down the growth of the banking system. After limiting loan growth to 16 per cent (valid only in 2003) and increasing portion of reserve requirement on foreign currency deposits allocated in domestic currency, new measures in 2004 are: the increased minimum amount of reserve requirement allocated (from 40 per cent to 60 per cent, the rest can be maintained as balance on accounts of liquid claims) and marginal reserve requirement on increased amount of deposits and loans received from abroad (24 per cent).

Commercial banks still account for around 85 per cent of the whole financial system, although competition from other institutions is slowly growing. In 2003, exceptionally high growth was recorded in the leasing industry, as competition to ordinary credits. At the same time, competition in the collection of savings is forming in the shape of investment funds, pension funds and building societies (see Table 2.4.1).

The whole Croatian financial system continued to grow during 2004, with some softening of the bank domination that was present in past years. At the end of 2003, the assets of the financial system reached a volume nearing €33 billion, that is, approximately 125 per cent of the value of realized GDP. Along with the strong rise in pension and investment funds, the influence of leasing companies grew significantly in 2003, whereas second place, as regards assets, is still held by insurance companies. At the end of 2003, the share of the banking system in financial system assets fell slightly below 85 per cent. The biggest leap was from the leasing companies, growing under the influence of the CNB's monetary measures against curbing placements

**Table 2.4.1** Financial institutions, assets at 31 December 2003 (in euro millions)

|                                 | Amount   | %    |
|---------------------------------|----------|------|
| **Banks**                       | 26,743.3 | 84.7 |
| **Non-bank financial institutions** | 4,817.2  | 15.3 |
| Insurance                       | 1,659.3  | 5.3  |
| Leasing                         | 1,418.2  | 4.5  |
| Loans & savings institutions    | 156.9    | 0.5  |
| Building societies              | 453.6    | 1.4  |
| Open-end investment funds       | 385.9    | 1.2  |
| Closed-end investment funds     | 127.8    | 0.4  |
| Obligatory pension funds        | 611.7    | 1.9  |
| Voluntary pension funds         | 3.9      | 0.0  |
| **Total**                       | **31,560.5** | **100** |

*Sources:* CNB, Hagena, MoF

with banks. Although some of the limitations were abolished during 2004, leasing companies continue to grow in comparison to the slow growth of the banking system placements. The share of pension and investment funds are also continuously rising.

Competition among the largest banks has increased over the last couple of years, even though the number of banks operating in the Croatian banking system fell significantly in the course of the consolidation process (rehabilitation in the 1990s, privatization, M&As). The top six banks (and banking groups) accounted for almost 85 per cent of total banking assets in 2003. Currently the top two banks (Zagrebacka and Privredna) are still ahead of the next four banks (including Raiffeisenbank), which are growing strongly and competing for third place.

Bank assets in Croatia have two major characteristics. Almost 70 per cent of liabilities are denominated in foreign currency or indexed to foreign currency (predominantly the euro), which results in loans portfolios also largely indexed to foreign currency. The second characteristic is the high share of retail loans. Credits to households increased to almost 30 per cent of GDP, growing significantly faster than credits to private enterprises. Croatia has the highest ratio of retail loans, as a percentage of GDP, among all CEE countries, but is still well below the EU average. Credit growth has decreased in 2004 due to a restrictive monetary policy and slower growth of deposits and, unlike in the past, both retail and corporate loans have been showing less but still existing disproportional growth in favour of retail loans. One of the characteristics of the Croatian banking system is a large portion of retail loans in the loan portfolio (48 per cent of total loans), and total retail loans have reached the HRK61.3 billion level or approximately 29 per cent of GDP. According to the latest indicators, this is the highest share among CEE countries, although still much below the levels in the eurozone. Total loans have reached the level of nearly 58 per cent of GDP, which is also above the CEE countries' average, but considerably below the 110 per cent level in the eurozone. On the other hand, retail deposits reached the level of around 40 per cent of GDP, which is significantly above the average of the new EU members (approximately 28 per cent), whereas in the eurozone, the level is around 55 per cent of GDP.

Bank profits increased in 2003, but due to continued assets growth, return on average assets recorded a slight decrease, although the return on average equity increased. As credits increased, the quality of assets has improved, which is evident from the declining share of classified loans in the banking system during the past few years (currently below five per cent).

**2.5**

# The Securities Market in Croatia

*Zlatko Gregurić, Raiffeisenbank Austria d.d. Zagreb*

## Overview

The Croatian securities market in 2004 has primarily been marked by Croatia's progress towards EU membership, especially after the EU's formal acceptance of Croatian membership candidature in June 2004. The market responded very positively to these events, as both turnover and prices went up. The debt market, which heavily dominates the Croatian capital market with an 85 per cent share in total turnover (during the first three quarters of 2004), has experienced strong narrowing of the Croatian eurobond spreads, even stronger than expected at the beginning of 2004.

This was also due to agreement on the new IMF Stand-by Arrangement, which also resulted in improving the country's credit rating (Standard & Poor's BBB upgraded one notch in December, Moody's Baa3 with stable outlook was not changed). Spreads went down from 120 basis points with longest maturities in March 2004 to a 40 basis points level in December. The current spread levels are still much wider than spreads of the new members of the EU, and these are the ones that may be reached in the next few years as the negotiations with the EU progress.

The Croatian debt securities market includes government bonds, bonds with government guarantee, corporate bonds and municipal bonds as long-term securities and treasury bills of the Ministry of Finance as well as commercial papers of companies as short-term securities. Croatian eurobonds are also traded in domestic market. A negligible portion of turnover is made up by three existing issues of corporate bonds (US$9 million), which are mostly held until maturity. This is also true for two municipal bonds, issued in 2004 in nominal amount of €24 million.

The year 2004 has, in fact, already been the best year ever, in terms of both number and value of new bond issues. Beside the new municipal bonds, there were also three new corporate issues in nominal amount of €117 million, while the government has issued three bonds tranches with maturity in 2014, totalling €650 million, a bond of €400 million nominal value maturing in 2007, and a bond of €200 million maturing in 2019. That was the highest annual amount of primary government issues ever.

Turnover of government and government guaranteed bonds (total issue of €2,307 million) comprised almost the total bond turnover (99 per cent). There are four banks acting as market makers in the bond market and investors are mainly institutional, such as pension funds, insurance companies and growing investment funds. The domestic capital market is still characterized by the 'plain vanilla' bond issues with a fixed coupon and principal repayment upon maturity. Most of the domestic issues are pegged to foreign currency (the euro), denomination of €1 and semi-annual coupon payment.

The domestic equity market consists of two stock exchanges, the Zagreb Stock Exchange and the Varazdin Stock Exchange. In general, the Croatian equity market is characterized by many small investors who have become shareholders through the process of privatization. There are an estimated 600,000 private shareholders and a few institutional shareholders. The key players in the market are, however, commercial banks, investment funds and private brokerage houses that are members of the exchange. The pension and health funds, which have also received parcels of shares as part of the privatization process, have not yet sought to manage their portfolios. The Croatian Privatization Fund is active on the market, though only as a seller, as it seeks to dispose of its holdings.

## Croatian Stock Exchanges

The Zagreb Stock Exchange (ZSE) was founded in 1918 but was disbanded in 1946 by the communist authorities. In June 1991, the ZSE was incorporated as a joint stock company and reopened by 25 commercial banks and insurance companies. Today, the ZSE has 43 shareholders. Trading at the ZSE may take place either on the official market (the ZSE's principal market) or through the ZSE's second-tier market. There are only three companies that are presently listed on the official market, although approximately 61 companies have a second-tier listing. Companies can be also listed in 'JDD' (public shareholding companies) quotation, with three companies on the ZSE and one on the Varazdin Stock Exchange (VSE). Creating this kind of quotation, the government and the Croatian Securities Commission

(CROSEC) sought to give a stimulus to a greater level of public listings. All trading is now executed through MOST, a new fully electronic distributed trading system, developed in-house by the ZSE.

In July 2002, the over-the-counter market in Varazdin became the Varazdin Stock Exchange. Varazdin OTC started to operate in 1993. Currently, there are 386 different securities listed on VSE in six different quotations, with the first quotation introduced in autumn 2002. VSE has 32 members. In 2002, VSE introduced a new trading system, BTS, which allows networking of regional stock exchanges. In this context, in early 2003 VSE signed a cooperation and data exchange agreement with the Ljubljana Stock Exchange. Both on the ZSE and the VSE, most shares are listed on less demandable quotation. The liquidity of the Croatian equity market has strongly improved, as both domestic institutional and various foreign investors have driven the rising demand. However, the market is still quite illiquid, with only a few stocks accounting for most of the trade.

Even though there are more and more stocks being traded, only a small number of the most active stocks are regularly traded every day. The year 2004 witnessed very strong price growth among almost all traded stocks, especially on the VSE, which has had one the strongest growths in the Central European markets. The Croatian Equity Market Index (CROEMI), which was developed and calculated by Raiffeisen Consulting in Croatia as the only index that combines both stock exchanges in Croatia, rose almost 25 per cent by the end of September 2004. In the same time, the total turnover made by shares was more than US$380 million (out of which US$140 million was traded on the VSE); the total bond turnover was almost US$2,300 million; and the average daily turnover of shares was US$2 million (both stock exchanges combined). Market capitalization at the end of September was around US$9,100 million, which is almost 30 per cent of the GDP projected this year.

All securities in Croatia exist only in electronic form and they are deposited in the Central Depositary Agency (CDA), a state-owned depositary and clearing house, which commenced operations in April 1999. In February 2001, the CDA implemented a new automated clearing and settlement process (NKS), replacing the manual trade-for-trade environment between counter-party brokers. Currently, the settlement date in Croatia is four working days after the transaction (T+4). The new Act on the Securities Market that came into force on July 2002 instituted primary and secondary market procedures and regulations along standard Western lines, and it also set up CROSEC, with supervisory powers over the primary and secondary markets. CROSEC is legally obliged for 'the efficient regulation and supervision of the securities markets in the Republic of Croatia'. It has the authority and the means to prevent, as well as to sanction, any illegal activity and, together with the CDA, it represents the institutional framework and safety network of the market.

All foreign investors are legally allowed to buy Croatian securities. In order to trade, an investor should first either open an investment account at the CDA or a custody account with an authorized Croatian bank. According to the provisions of the Croatian Foreign Exchange Act, non-residents are obliged to hold a security at least for a year once they have purchased it. However, citizens of many countries are excluded from this provision and are able to sell Croatian securities in their ownership at any time because of bilateral agreements between the Republic of Croatia and those countries.

## 2.6

# Foreign Exchange Regulations in Croatia

*Adrian Hammer, Deloitte & Touche*

The legislation governing foreign exchange transactions in Croatia was extensively revised in 2003. Such transactions are now regulated by the Foreign Exchange Transactions Act. This Act has significantly liberalized and simplified the rules governing these transactions.

## Residence

The underlying criterion for the definition of residence under this legislation is the 'economic interest', except for natural persons temporarily residing in Croatia, to which the criterion of 'temporary residence' applies. Thus, natural persons temporarily resident in the Republic of Croatia who, on the basis of a work permit, achieve their economic interest abroad, are classified as residents.

Subsidiaries of foreign companies registered abroad are considered resident, whereas representative offices of foreign founders, whose status has not been defined under the current law, are defined as non-residents.

Residents for the purpose of the Act are:

- legal entities headquartered in the Republic of Croatia, except for their subsidiaries abroad;

- subsidiaries of foreign companies and sole traders entered in the register kept by the competent state authority or administration in the Republic of Croatia;

- sole-traders, craftsmen and other natural persons headquartered or resident in the Republic of Croatia, who carry out, independently, the economic activity they have been registered for;

- natural persons resident in the Republic of Croatia;

- natural persons residing in the Republic of Croatia for minimum 183 days on the basis of a valid work permit;

- diplomatic, consular and other representations of the Republic of Croatia abroad financed from the state budget, and Croatian citizens employed by such representation offices and their family members.

## Direct investments

The Act defines direct investments as a sub-category of capital transactions in accordance with the Directive of the Council of the European Communities No. 88/361/EEC.

Direct investments may be one of the following:

- initial capital investment in a new company, or in the share capital of an existing company fully owned by a foreign investor; establishment of a subsidiary, or acquisition of an existing company fully owned by the investor; or investments in the business of a sole entrepreneur;

- investment in a new or existing company if the investor acquires a 10 per cent or higher share in the share capital of a company, or acquires 10 per cent of votes;

- subordinate or hybrid loans for a period of five years or more to establish permanent economic relations;

- reinvestments of profit, ie a share of a direct investor in the profit of a company not distributable as dividend or similar;

- debt transactions between the direct investor and the investee (the company), including debt securities, commercial loans, untied loans and other creditor/debtor relationships.

Direct investments of residents made abroad are unrestricted.

## Real estate investments

Residents are free to transfer funds abroad to acquire real estate, provided that the obligations ie taxes and other duties payable in Croatia as defined by law have been settled.

## Resident investments in securities abroad

Residents are allowed to make investments in securities abroad. This is a very important change that was introduced in 2003, bearing in mind that the previous foreign exchange regime did not permit Croatian residents any transfers of capital for the purpose of portfolio investments abroad. However, the Act distinguishes several categories of residents in terms of free transfer of capital for the purpose of portfolio investments.

Residents abroad are allowed to make unrestricted investments only in securities issued by the OECD countries or international financial institutions (such as the EBRD, the World Bank, the European Investment Bank). Resident financial institutions, however, are not subject to this restriction.

## Lending activities

The Act allows unrestricted approval of long-term loans (over one year) to non-residents. Liberalization in the area of short-term loans is expected upon the expiry of the four-year period from the effective date of the Stabilization and Association Agreement with the EU. This agreement is expected to be signed sometime during 2005.

## 2.7

# Corruption: Understanding Risk and Building Stability

*Josip Kregar, School of Law, Zagreb University*

## An overview of recent political trends in Croatia

Croatia has recently experienced considerable transformation in its economic and political landscape. The economic structure is moving quickly toward a dynamic, market-based system, while Western-style infrastructure (laws, institutions, etc) are being developed. The political system, between 1990–99, was described as authoritarian. Franjo Tudman, the first president, was re-elected in 1995 and the HDZ, the strongly organized nationalist party, was repeatedly triumphant in elections. The elections were described as 'legal but not fair'. The media freedoms and human rights policy of government was criticized and Croatia was occasionally isolated due to the pro-nationalist leadership of the country. The regime and the period of the HDZ in power was highly and publicly criticized as corrupt, cleptocratic and politically isolated from Europe.

The old regime of the late Franjo Tudman was replaced by elections in the year 2000, however, and not by force or violence. After the parliamentary and presidential elections of that year, the level of expectation and support for political and economic reforms in society was very high. However, the new coalition government led by the Social Democratic Party of Croatia (SDP) was slow to implement the reform process. The reasons for this, as given by the government, were inadequate staffing, fear that the military and police were not under civil control, and the lack of a coherent programme to pursue reform in general. The fact that the government managed to come to power after ten years in opposition within an authoritarian political system was itself seen as a positive achievement. Clearly, the expectations of the people were much above the preparation and willingness of the new government to act on its electoral success.

The new coalition government started to deconstruct the apparatus of the old regime and expose its shady affairs, which led to the discovery of scandals. The main interest of the public was focused on corruption and privatization scandals, and problems related to the independence of the judiciary. The coalition government was confused and unhurried in its political and administrative reforms. It maintained the inherited economic policy based on monetary stabilization, pursued conservative measures to reduce budget costs and maintained economic growth at a relatively healthy four to five per cent. One of the main obstacles for the coalition government was its relations with the ICTY (the international tribunal for war crimes in The Hague). The main perpetrators of war crimes from Croatia had already passed away (F Tuđman, G Šušak and M Boban) and public opposition to the accusation of the notorious 'Croatian generals' (Bobetko, Gotovina) increased rapidly. Organized revolt almost transformed into insurgency, with open support for political opposition and some media. The secret services conducted their activities outside of the sphere of government and it appeared that the coalition was losing its grip on power. The coalition government initiated public works (roads), rebuilding of war-affected areas, re-schedule of some of Croatia's debts, and accepted new credits, but, overall, real economic reforms were perceived by the public as 'too late, too slow'.

The government slowly lost trust and support and local elections showed that the divergences in the coalition were an obstacle to coherent policy. For Prime Minister Račan, it was not easy to maintain the legitimacy of the government. The opposition enjoyed the backing of many social groups appealing to national feelings and the 'dignity of Croatia's war of independence'.

The HDZ-led group of political parties formulated a programme for the parliamentary elections of November 2003, which focused on the fight for Croatian national interests. They did not formulate precise economic or political programmes, but put forth a set of proposals regarding the 'protection of national dignity', 'dignity of homeland and protection of war heroes' (alluding also to the case of Ante Gotovina, who was accused of war crimes by ICTY), protection of family values and Christian traditions. The profile of the party is that of a Christian conservative and nationalist party. This image, however, does not reflect its real policies, as in reality the nationalist language slowly disappeared from official declarations and the speeches of the government leaders. The conservative elements (family, abortion, religion, moral traditionalism) are adjusted by pragmatic political discourse, and, in general, the ideological elements were of secondary importance in the main decisions in preparation for the election, selection of candidates, etc. Nevertheless, the HDZ-led group won the elections.[1]

Two outcomes are important from these elections. First, this was the first time that elections were completed within same electoral models. In previous elections, the governments used gerrymandering – reshaping the counties' borders and changing election rules – thus manipulating the votes to increase the chances for their own candidates, ie the electoral units were very different in size, according to their expectations and benefits. The elections were described as 'free but not fair'. The change of government was peaceful and without scandal or violence. Second, elections caused turbulence within the political parties. The HDZ had its own internal elections before the parliamentary elections, and the party's new direction, symbolized by its leader, Ivo Sanader, successfully eliminated the nationalist radicals (blamed for use of violence and manipulation of party congress), extremists and people discredited in the HDZ under the Tuđman regime. Other parties that achieved results in the elections – from the Social Democratic Party to the Croatian Peasants' Party – experienced internal tensions and there were efforts from their old leaderships to stay in positions of power.

The HDZ experienced problems in forming a majority in parliament. The HDZ formed a government in December 2003 and the new prime minister, Ivo Sanader, decided to form a government with the votes of minority representatives, pensioners and, surprisingly, representatives of Serbian parties. This move appeared to be an excellent political compromise, since the party, perceived as an arduous Croatian nationalist party, accepted the Serbian representatives as partners in the coalition. The language of hate was replaced by a rhetoric of kindness and tolerance. Ivo Sanader made special considerations to pensioners in spite of the recommendations of the IMF, creating a special voucher system, compensating the debt to pensioners (the previous decision of the government from 1996 to reduce pensions was unconstitutional). However, the representatives of minorities (Bosniak, Italian, and Slovak) are not reliable partners in the coalition, and the government is, from time to time, under pressure to accept some particular interests of those partners. The problem of this barely-reached

---

[1] According to the election results, the Croatian parliament, or the Sabor, has 152 seats (140 representatives, four representatives of expatriate community and eight representatives of ethnic minorities). The HDZ won 66 seats, the SDP-led coalition 43 seats, the HNS-led coalition 11 seats, and the HSS nine seats. The surprise of the elections was the performance of the Croatian Party of Rights (eight seats); and the Croatian Pensioners' Party (HSU) with three. Other parties – 15 parties are represented – have one to three seats, while 17.76 per cent of MPs are women. In fact, the parties from prior coalition government won more electoral votes (almost 300.000!) but the gerrymandering of units and characteristics of the electoral model misrepresented the majority.

majority is the reason for the unwillingness of the government to propose some new laws and programmes. The interests of small parties of a new coalition simply prevent essential reforms, for example pensioners are not ready to support the reduction of their social rights. As in a convoy, the speed of all can depend on a slow ship. That was also obvious in the discussion about corruption scandals, and responsibility of ministers for nepotism during the preparation of the Law on Prevention of the Conflict of Interests.

After one year, the political picture has become even more complex. The new Sanader government achieved its main goals in foreign policy, while in its national policy the results are ambiguous. The HDZ calmed the ambitions of Croatian president Mesić to once again regain his powerful position in Croatian politics,[2] and Ivo Sanader increased his personal influence over the party and government. The HDZ fulfilled some of its electoral promises, but primarily to its own supporters. The government was perceived as 'a spoiler', and tactfully replaced many of the former regime's professional functionaries and reduced the requirement for professional posts. Some appointments, even at the lower levels of administration, were obviously politically biased. The government also reduced the number of ministries (as was proposed by European Union (EU) advisors). The number of appointees and functionaries grew rapidly, however, contrary to the electoral motto about 'small and inexpensive government'. The appointments on the board of public companies prepared for future privatizations were suspect, and some privatizations finished in scandal (ie Sunčani Hvar, INA).

In fact, the government discarded its main electoral promises: instead of 'more national independence and pride', it increased cooperation with ICTY; it has not fulfilled promises regarding concern for Croatia's under-developed regions, industry and agriculture; and it will not decrease VAT from 22 to 18 per cent. Organized crime has become more powerful and the institutions fighting corruption remain weak. Contrary to the promises, the government is providing military bases to the US and sending troops to Afghanistan. In spite of certain achievements in public relations activities, general relations with the media have not been well accepted (there has been some direct interventions in editorial policy, even in news and journalist's reports), giving the impression that the government is not respecting the independence of the media.

Contrary to general perception of the government, the role of Prime Minister Ivo Sanader is perceived as positive. Mr Sanader, as a person, holds leadership and authority within the government and has also shown leadership in some significant decisions. For instance, he was the

---

[2] That was only a temporary victory as Stipe Mesić achieved a landslide victory against the HDZ candidate in the presidential elections of 16 January 2005, winning almost 66 per cent of the votes.

first to express sympathy and recognition for the cultural heritage and political role of the Serbian minority. He has a very strong appearance and holds a good public image. He has excellent communication skills and international contacts, is an intelligent, educated and cultured politician, but his weak points are his lack of legal and economic knowledge.

In sum, the common impression is that the prime minister has achieved his goals but that the government is not a homogeneous team, and that numerous members of the political elite in power lack professional credibility and are politically irresponsible and ethically problematic. Indicative of this is the fact that the HDZ has lost some local elections.

## On the road to the EU: Political criteria

As is stated in Opinion on the application of Croatia for membership of the EU on 20 April 2004 (COM (2004) 257 final)

*'Croatia has stable democratic institutions which function properly, respecting the limits of their competences and cooperating with each other. The 2000 and 2003 elections were free and fair. The opposition plays a normal part in the operation of the institutions. There are no major problems over assuring the rule of law and respect for fundamental rights. However, Croatia needs to take measures to ensure that the rights of minorities, in particular of the Serb minority, are fully respected. Croatia should speed up the implementation of the constitutional Law on National Minorities and accelerate efforts to facilitate the return of Serb refugees from Serbia and Bosnia and Herzegovina. Croatia needs to make substantial improvements in the functioning of the judicial system. The effectiveness of the fight against corruption needs further strengthening. Croatia's cooperation with the International Criminal Tribunal for the Former Yugoslavia has improved significantly in the past months. In April 2004, the Prosecutor stated that Croatia is now cooperating fully with ICTY. Croatia needs to maintain full cooperation and take all necessary steps to ensure that the remaining indicted are located and transferred to ICTY in The Hague. Croatia remains committed to regional cooperation; sustained efforts are needed in this area. In particular to resolve border issues with neighbouring countries in line with international standards for dispute settlement, and issues arising from the unilateral declaration of the protected 'Ecological and Fishing Zone' in the Adriatic.'*

## On the road to the EU: The economy

The main emphasis regarding economic criteria from the Opinion on the application of Croatia for membership of the EU on 20 April 2004 (COM (2004) 257 final) are:

*'Croatia can be regarded as a functioning market economy. In Croatia, there is an increasing political consensus on the essentials of economic policies. The Croatian economy has achieved a considerable degree of macroeconomic stability with low inflation. Enhanced economic stability and structural reforms undertaken so far permit the working of market mechanisms. This holds in particular for the liberalization of prices and trade as well as for privatization, albeit to a lesser extent. Croatia is characterized by a relatively well-educated labour force and good road transport and telecommunication infrastructure. The country has a well-developed banking sector and a competitive tourism industry. Croatia's economy is already well integrated with that of the EU. Enterprise restructuring and privatization has been slower than expected and some large state and formerly socially-owned enterprises still play an important role in the economy. The necessary reforms of the fiscal and social security systems as well as the public administration are not yet completed and fiscal consolidation needs to be vigorously pursued.'*

From a political and economic perspective, therefore, it can be said that Croatia is well placed in its negotiations for EU entry.

## Corruption as a barrier to development

The present political and economic situation in the country encourages, to some degree, the risk of corruption, while civil society and the independent media are not powerful enough and therefore cannot bear the full responsibility for fighting corruption. Risks of corruption arise from the economy (mass privatization, denationalization, under-regulation of market rules) but also from general weakness of institutions (nepotism, formalism, primitive bureaucracy) and general instability of social norms (explosions of consumption and aspiration, social anomie, lack of orientation). The phenomenon of corruption reflects the growing pains of a new democracy, a common symptom in the institutional systems of transitional political economies.

Corruption is a real problem in the Republic of Croatia and not just a creation of the media. The fact that we cannot measure exactly[3] how widespread corruption is in the Republic of Croatia does not mean that we do not know for sure that it obstructs business and that the

---

[3] There are various sources of statistics on corruption. The State Attorney issues an annual report with statistics on corruption cases, which is debated in the Croatian Parliament. Furthermore, the Ministry of Interior keeps separate statistics on corruption offences and the Croatian Bureau of Statistics collects relevant data from state administration bodies including the State Attorney's Office and USKOK.

impression of its extensiveness wards off foreign investors and Croatian entrepreneurs. Moreover, every attempt to relativize indeterminate and uncertain governmental policy against corruption is extremely damaging because it creates a potential excuse for the lack of political decisiveness in implementing measures – questions about whether corruption is inherited or created, whether it is an erosion of morals and who is most to blame are not the issue – the important thing is what is being done to eliminate corruption.

We are aware of the burden of traditions and the traces left by previous political regimes, particularly their darker sides: the privileges given to those who are obedient, the opportunity to steal in the name of high ideals, the fact that everything can be done through connections and influence, and that for those in power, loyalty and obedience count for more than hard work and innovation. We know that other countries have similar problems; we know that corruption can never be completely eradicated, but we also know that we cannot just passively sit and wait for it to go away.

ʿInternational surveys reveal Croatia's slow progress in fighting corruption. According to the CPI index of Transparency International, the Republic of Croatia is in 67th place on the list of 146 countries, relatively the same position as in 2003 (see Table 2.7.1). In 2001, it was ranked 47th out of 90 countries. In comparison with the previous 1999 report, the Republic of Croatia showed a significant advance, since it used to be in 74th place on this scale. After 2001, the stagnation has been slow but evident.

**Table 2.7.1** Transparency International – Corruption Perception Index CPI – Croatia

| Year | 2004 | 2003 | 2002 | 2001 | 2000 |
|---|---|---|---|---|---|
| Index | 3.5 | 3.7 | 3.7 | 3.9 | 2.7 |
|  | ▼ | ▼▲ | ▼ | ▲ |  |
|  |  | −0.0 | −0.2 | −0.4 | +0.8 |
| Place/rank | 67 | 58 | 52 | 47 | 77 |
| Number of countries on the list | 146 | 133 | 102 | 91 | 90 |

Compared with neighbouring and other countries in transition, the Republic of Croatia has been, in spite of its positive development, assessed relatively low. Other countries in the same group, such as Slovenia (6.0) or Estonia, are now much better positioned. In 2003, Croatia was placed together with the Czech Republic, Hungary, Bulgaria and Lithuania. Those countries have improved by some measure, while Croatia has moved toward the group of traditionally more corrupt countries. Together with Poland, its rating now averages around 3.5.

The study carried out by the World Bank shows that the Republic of Croatia, according to surveys conducted at the end of 1999 and in 2003 (BEEPS), can be categorized in the intermediate group of transitional countries. The data indicate a relatively low total index, particularly in Administrative Corruption (low), but a high level of corruption at the level of political decision-making (State Capture Index), and the judiciary (Judiciary Capture Index). The study reveals weak social and political responsibility – which is both a sign of, and a condition for, corruption – and also shows the existence of strong social groups that are ready to impede social reforms.

The recent public opinion research (Transparency International Croatia, May 2003) points out that 85.9 per cent of respondents perceive corruption as an existing problem in Croatian society (49.0 per cent 'very much' and 37.9 per cent 'widespread'). In Gallup's research (June 2003) respondents are of the opinion that corruption is present in the economy (69.5 per cent) and politics (65 per cent). According to the Transparency International Global Corruption Barometer, 2003, a new survey of the general public in 47 countries on all continents, some sections of social life in Croatia are particularly affected by corruption: courts and judiciary (22.5 per cent), the medical system (21.6 per cent) and local government (18.6 per cent).

In spite of some methodological controversy, it is axiomatic that the perception of people, as well as economic analysis, indicate the same conclusion, that corruption is a serious threat to economic and political development.

## Legal regulation

In March 2001, the Croatian parliament adopted a National Programme for the Fight against Corruption, with an Action Plan for Fighting Corruption (hereafter the National Strategy). The National Strategy had been developed in broad consultation with non-governmental organizations (which actually initiated the process) and has been supported by a consensus of all political parties. In December 2004, the government made public its intention to adopt a new programme by the end of 2005.

At the national level, Croatia has adopted and implemented various anti-corruption-related laws. National legislation has been partly aligned with the provisions of the 1995 Convention on the Protection of the Communities' Financial Interests and its protocols, although further improvements are still necessary. Various legal acts, in particular the Act on the Prevention of Conflicts of Interest in Performing Public Duties, contain provisions to prevent conflicts of interest between the private and public sectors.

In the National Strategy, corruption is defined as 'every form of abuse of public authority in order to achieve personal benefit'. This is a sociological and political definition, useful for analysis of phenomena such as misuse of public authority, organized and economic crime, and poor governance and its consequences. The elements of definition – and this is a main point – are changeable. This reflects the increase of public sensitivity toward politicians and government. Some incidents – such as conflict of interest, unauthorized use of public property, benefits for functionaries and leaders – ignored and tolerated just a few years ago, are now under strong public condemnation.

The emphasis of the National Strategy is on preventive measures, improvement of good governance, legal reforms of public administration and judiciary, local self-government and decentralization, the active role of a free media and civil society. Respecting the legislative optimism of government, and their (relative) achievements against corruption, what we need most is the realization of existing new legal initiatives, such as conflict of interest, access to information, public procurement or political parties financing legislation.

There is no single definition of 'corruption' in the Croatian legal system. Conventionally, it is regarded as offering and accepting bribes (347, 348 – Criminal Code (hereafter CC), illegal intercession/trading in influence (343 CC), abuse in performing governmental duties (338 CC), abuse of office and official authority (337 CC), concluding a prejudicial contract (294 CC), the disclosure of an official secret (351 CC), and the disclosure and unauthorized procurement of a business secret (295 CC). Corruption is sanctioned regardless of the form of the bribe; it can be a gift or any other benefit, whether pecuniary or non-pecuniary, real or personal, tangible or non-tangible. Bribes given or promised for the purpose of obtaining both commissions and omissions of public officials are covered.

Article 348(3) of the CC provides that a person who promises or gives the bribe who has been solicited by the public official to do so, and has reported the act to the competent law enforcement authority before the crime was detected, can be exempted from the sanction. Sanctions for active bribery range from three months to three years imprisonment, and for passive bribery, from six months to five years imprisonment. Corruption in the private sector (private corruption) is also criminalized. The new legislation also provides for criminal liability of legal entities. Until recently, all corruption offences fell under the jurisdiction of the Municipal Courts (since the prescribed sanctions for all these offences are below 10 years imprisonment). This has changed with the adoption of the Law on USKOK (the State Office for Prevention of Corruption and Organized Crime). The law stipulates that all corruptive criminal offences will be adjudicated by four major County Courts.

In addition it should be emphasized that Croatia ratified various international legal instruments to fight corruption (Criminal

Convention against Corruption, 2001; Civil Convention against Corruption, 2003; Convention on Money Laundering; Search, Seizure and Confiscation of proceeds of Crime). Croatia is a part of the Group of States against Corruption (GRECO) programme. In its Stability Pact, Croatia actively promotes the 'Anti-Corruption Initiative for South East Europe', developing regional leadership for such programmes. The government has publicly declared its willingness to move towards the OECD conventions against bribery.

## *Institutions*

The main institutions combating corruption are repressive state institutions: the police, the state prosecution, and the specialized investigative body – USKOK.

The Croatian police are conducting preliminary investigations regarding corruption crimes. Croatia has a single centralized police service, which is responsible for public order and detection and investigation of criminal offences. The police are organized as a special service (Police Directorate) within the Ministry of the Interior. The police also have a specialized Department for Economic Crime and Corruption. Such an organizational specialization for combating new forms of white-collar crime (and corruption) was established in order to improve the level of expertise of the investigators.

Criminal proceedings against corruption and economic crime are conducted upon the request of the public prosecutor. The state prosecution, as an institution, is perceived as independent – the National Council of Public Prosecutions has the final authority over appointments and dismissals and control over the performance of duties by individual prosecutors – but rather inefficient in proceedings against powerful companies, gangs or corrupted officials. That was the main reason behind the formation of USKOK as a legally authoritative and organizationally competent institution.

USKOK is formally within the system of the Public Prosecutor's Office. The Head holds the position of Deputy Public Prosecutor General and is appointed by the Public Prosecutor General for a period of four years. All personnel of USKOK are subject to security checks, have previous professional experience (a minimum of eight years in the police or judiciary) a state examination, university education, etc. USKOK has intelligence, investigative, prosecutorial and preventive functions. USKOK prosecutors will direct the work of the police and other bodies in detecting and investigating corruption and organized crime offences, cooperate with competent authorities in other countries and with international organizations, and initiate procedures relating to the seizure and confiscation of proceeds from crime. They have the right to use special investigative means, such as covert surveillance and technical recording, use of undercover investigators, simulated offering of bribes, and supervised transport and delivery of goods.

USKOK's structure and competencies are designed for it to become the leading state authority in the prevention and repression of corruption in Croatia. However, as is stated in the European Commission's Opinion on the application of Croatia for membership of the EU (Brussels, 20 April 2004.): 'Various measures are being taken to upgrade staff capacities, improve working conditions and provide adequate facilities and IT equipment for the courts, the State Attorney's offices and USKOK. However, significant further improvement will be required.'

Various measures of financial control are subsidiary to investigations. The Anti-Money Laundering Office was established in 1997. The Office is responsible for gathering and processing reports on suspicious transactions from banks and other institutions that could be indicative of laundering the proceeds of crime, including the proceeds of corruption. If there is suspicion, the Office has to inform USKOK about any such transactions, proceeds or assets. The Office has limited authority for investigations, but a large database and research software for analysis and recording of evidence.

The State Audit Office is responsible for auditing the use of public finances and those of local self-government, including all state-owned companies and funds (such as health and pension funds).

# Concluding remarks

'Society is like the air; necessary to breathe, but insufficient to live on.' (Santayana). The same is true of laws in political life. The anti-corruption laws, programmes and declarations are not sufficient. The political will, intention to devote resources, interest, even zeal and enthusiasm, has to be measured by results, not by words alone. To confess that corruption exists is not only a gesture of political intention – the warning signal to entrepreneurs – but also an instruction to state institutions to act, and society to condemn and mobilize against. Pure confession is not enough; it has to be commonly accepted and acknowledged that corruption in Croatia is systemic and endemic. Corruption is endemic as a part of traditions crystallized in the collective memory and values of people. The concept of its systemic nature implies that corruption is not an individual incident and singular event: it arises from the very nature of economic, political and social elements of society. Corruption has not a single cause and many factors (weak institutions, a hungry market, a conspicuous but not entrepreneurial elite, traditions and values incompatible with open society, expansion of aspiration for consumption) add equally to new recognition, confession and condemnation of corrupt practices. Corruption is not a phenomenon imported with the coming of a market economy. It is likewise not a relic of the communist past or of oriental or Balkan traditions. It derives and is reproduced from the very system.

In Croatia we can identify three distinct phases in efforts to fight against corruption. The first starting from the end of the 1990s, when NGOs (TI–Croatia, UDD, HHO), independent media (television, daily and weekly news) and professionals (lawyers, economists) all mobilized the public to be aware of the problem of corruption. By the year 2000, after the elections and success of the reformist coalition, this phase was over. The second phase began with the partnership of the government and TI in drafting the National Strategy to Fight Corruption, and the draft of two main laws: Access to Information and the Law on Prevention of the Conflict of Interests.

The third phase started with return of HDZ and the new partnership of the EU with Croatia. This is a phase of implementation and enforcement of laws, standards, and institutions. For this reason it is even more important to invest additional efforts to combat corruption. Orthodox measures should be taken: reform of the judiciary; decrease in bureaucratic procedures; serious measures to establish standards in public life, and the abolishment of party/state elements. This phase began well and improvements have been noticeable. In the past, the greatest difficulty was that corruption was ignored and neglected. Maybe the fact that Croatia had bigger problems played a part in society's neglect of corruption, but investments and business will not flourish in a corrupt society and a greedy political environment. Good governance, promoted by an open and honest government, will ultimately lead to a decrease in the risk and level of corruption.

# Part Three

# Prospective Sectors for Investment

3.1

# A Protected Environment in the Adriatic Area: A key for sustainable economic development

*Dr Anamarija Frankic, University of Massachusetts, Boston*

## Unique and pristine natural heritage

National and international scientific communities have identified the Croatian coastal area as one of the most pristine and rich natural resources in the Mediterranean region. According to very rough estimates, between 6,000 and 7,000 plant and animal species have been found in the Adriatic Sea so far, but comprehensive scientific research is still to be done. Special emphasis is to be given to a great number of endemic Adriatic elements present in the flora of the central Adriatic, numbering 64 taxa or 12.1 per cent of its content. The most important and threatened habitats include: karstic estuaries (Krka, Zrmanja), *vrulje* (submerged freshwater springs), marine caves as typical subaerial karstic phenomena with new species recently found: carnivorous sponge *Asbestopluma hypogea* (in a submarine pit on Dugi otok) and hexactinellid sponge *Oopsacas minuta* (in a cave on the southern part of the island Hvar).

Croatia signed the Convention on Biological Diversity in 1992, and ratified it in 1997. Although there are 176 protected areas divided into eight different categories and protecting 10 per cent of the country, Croatia has yet to complete an inventory of biodiversity base line data. Apart from the Global Environment Facility (GEF) grants that assisted the development of the national strategy and action plan for biological and landscape diversity conservation, and implementation of the Karst Ecosystem Conservation (KEC) project, Croatia and the Adriatic area received very little international assistance to protect biodiversity of marine and coastal ecosystems.

---

The Adriatic Sea is one of seven biogeographic subdivisions of the Mediterranean Sea. It is a long canal (about 780 kilometres), surrounded by Italy on the west and by Slovenia, Croatia, Bosnia, Montenegro and Albania on the east. The average width of the Adriatic is 240 km, and the total area is 131,000 km². The Adriatic Sea is mainly shallow, with an average depth of 44.4 metres in the north, and a maximum depth of 1,324 metres at the south of the central area (Jabuka Pit).

The Croatian coast was formed by specific geological processes creating a so-called Dalmatian type of coast, with parallel spreading of coastline, hinterland mountain ranges, and island chains. Croatia has 1,246 islands, which are divided into 79 islands, 526 islets, and 641 reefs and rocks. Only 48 islands are permanently inhabited, and 100 are considered occasionally inhabited. Whilst all together they represent just 5.8 per cent (or 3,300 km²) of the Croatian land, it is important to note they make up 70 per cent of the total Croatian coastline (4,057 km out of 5,835 km). In addition the Croatian government recently established the 'Ecological and fisheries zone', which increases the maritime area by 25,207 km², so the total marine area is now 56,964 km². This whole sea area has almost no protection. There is no marine protected area in Croatia, only national parks and nature parks protecting mainly terrestrial ecosystems and only protecting about 300 km² (0.9 per cent) of marine ecosystems (Coastal PAs: Brijuni, Ucka, Velebit, Paklenica, Vransko jezero, Krka, Kornati, Telascica, Biokovo, Mljet, Lastovo).

---

In 2003, the World Wildlife Fund (WWF) initiated a large-scale conservation-planning project that identified 15 hot spot marine biodiversity areas in the Mediterranean region. One of 15 sites is in Croatia along the Dalmatian coast (see Figure 3.1.1). It specifically recognizes remote islands: Svetac, Brusnik, Bisevo, Vis, Lastovo, Mljet, Susac, Jabuka pit and Palagruza as important for biodiversity conservation. Current preparation of the UNDP/GEF Coast project will establish, for the first time, a strategy for integrated coastal zone management and sustainable uses of the coastal and marine natural resources. However, those few initiatives are not enough to support scientific research and conservation of important and sensitive natural resources in Croatia. It is urgent to establish a network of marine protected areas (PAs) that will connect the current PAs with identified important marine ecosystems.

In general, the major problem is lack of funding for management and conservation efforts of protected areas. PAs are financed by a

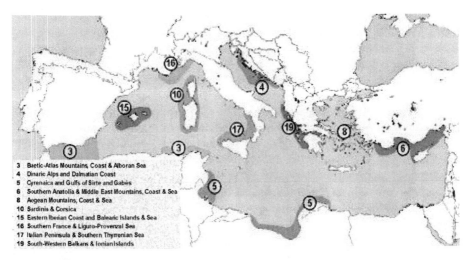

3  Baetic-Atlas Mountains, Coast & Alboran Sea
4  Dinaric Alps and Dalmatian Coast
5  Cyrenaica and Gulfs of Sirte and Gabès
6  Southern Anatolia & Middle East Mountains, Coast & Sea
8  Aegean Mountains, Coast & Sea
10 Sardinia & Corsica
15 Eastern Iberian Coast and Balearic Islands & Sea
16 Southern France & Liguro-Provençal Sea
17 Italian Peninsula & Southern Thyrrenian Sea
19 South-Western Balkans & Ionian Islands

Note: No. 4 is the area in the Adriatic Sea, Croatia

**Figure 3.1.1** The WWF conservation-planning areas in the Mediterranean region

combination of self-generated revenues (visitor fees) and from the government budget, which is not sufficient to render long-term financing of parks. For 2005, the government budget provides only five million kuna (€700,000) for PAs, while in Europe countries with a similar number of protected areas, like Greece, about €100 million is provided for protection annually.

Other PA issues include inefficient tourism management, lack of benefits to local communities, inconsistent legal enforcement, low environmental awareness and education on all the levels, lack of professional capacity and knowledge, and lack of available innovative environmental technologies and scientific solutions. Current initiative to establish the Croatian Conservation Foundation will help provide revenues from different sources (eg yearly memberships, donations, tourism fees, payments for ecosystem services, watershed services, etc).

## PAs and sustainable economic development

Given the importance of the tourism sector to the Croatian economy, sustainable natural resource management is a key factor in the country's future economic growth (US$6 billion from the tourism industry in 2004). Recent analysis by the World Travel & Tourism Council showed that there are three key factors for successful tourism development in Croatia: human potential, price and natural heritage.

PAs have been used effectively throughout the world to conserve biodiversity, manage natural resources, protect endangered species, reduce user conflicts, provide educational and research opportunities, manage humane activities, and enhance sustainable commercial and recreational uses of coastal and marine resources.

Sustainable tourism development represents interconnections of all sectors: protected areas, agriculture, forestry, fisheries and mariculture, transportation and energy, private entrepreneurship, science, technology and education. PAs should and must become ideal polygons and examples for sustainable development in Croatia. Based on the amazing natural beauty and conservation and sustainable use of natural resources, Croatia could become the first Eco-Country in Europe and the Mediterranean.

## *How?*

If responsible coastal tourism is to succeed in a sustainable way, analysis of tourism business decisions must be based not only on estimates of costs and benefits to the entrepreneur, but also must be measured by long-term ecological and socio-cultural costs and benefits for local communities. The basic principle for tourism management strategies is that the decision-making process is based on environmental concerns, and any process and activity must work within the environmental limits of sustainable development.

Today, the tourists want to know what they are eating, drinking, where they are swimming and would opt for the facilities that are providing all this information. Tourists will choose facilities that are supporting conservation of natural and cultural heritage that are within and outside PAs: this could be achieved through tax incentives, such as for environmentally-friendly facilities/infrastructures and organic produce. Therefore, it will be necessary to establish an eco-certification process and create 'competition' among tourism facilities that are providing, conserving and maintaining a better environment (for example, the Ecostar project).

Protected areas not only aim to conserve biodiversity, they also maintain large-scale ecosystem functioning with sustainable human interactions. It is important to understand interactions and relationships between healthy ecosystem function and resource uses. The participation and involvement of the local community is the key to successful protected area management and the base of sustainable economic development. A PA's comprehensive management and business plan should encourage appropriate incentives for biodiversity conservation and linkages between conservation and development. This approach will create more opportunities for development of specific and targeted types of sustainable tourism and broaden a tourism season throughout the year (a good example is Paklenica National Park). Local communities will provide autochthon and organic produce, as well as cultural and folk souvenirs, to PAs and tourism facilities. Local restaurants and hotels can establish special seafood festivals, educating tourists to purchase seafood species that are sustainably managed and grown, and contribute to the greening of fisheries and mariculture industries. If appropriately done, responsible tourism together with PAs can become an important educator of environmental awareness and a positive force in maintaining Croatia's natural and cultural attractiveness toward long-term sustainable economic development.

# Agriculture, Fisheries and Food Production

*Croatian Chamber of Economy*

## Agriculture

### Introduction

Croatia has a total of 3.15 million hectares of agricultural land. About two million hectares of the total are cultivated and the rest consists of pastures, moors, reeds and fish farms. Vineyards cover 58,000 hectares. A total of 81.5 per cent of cultivated land and a little more than 80 per cent of total livestock are privately owned. During the 1990s, agricultural production decreased significantly due to the war and the transition to a market economy. Plant production has been increasing continuously since 1995, but cattle production is still 30 per cent lower than in 1990. There are 1,235 companies registered in agriculture, and they employ a total of 23,700 employees.

### Production

The fundamental advantages of Croatian agriculture are the three different geographical and climatic zones: the lowland zone in the north of the country, influenced by the continental climate; the coastal zone in the south, influenced by the Mediterranean climate; and the mountain zone that occupies the central part of Croatia. Various types of climate, relief and soil are favourable for the production of a wide range of agricultural products, from farm and industrial crops to vineyards; from continental to Mediterranean fruits and vegetables (see Table 3.2.1).

The low level of pollution enables the development of ecological production. Besides agriculture, Croatia has a manifold and well-developed manufacturing and food processing industry. The capacity of this industry is sufficient to satisfy the needs of the domestic market as well as the markets of neighbouring countries. Agriculture is comple-

**Table 3.2.1** Production of selected products, 1998–2003

| Product | Unit of measurement | 1998 | 1999 | 2000 | 2001 | 2002 | 2003 |
|---|---|---|---|---|---|---|---|
| Cereals | '000 tonnes | 3,207 | 2,881 | 2,768 | 3,394 | 3,657 | 2,354 |
| Wheat | '000 tonnes | 1,020 | 558 | 1,032 | 965 | 988 | 609 |
| Corn | '000 tonnes | 1,982 | 2,135 | 1,526 | 2,212 | 2,502 | 1,570 |
| Sugarbeet | '000 tonnes | 1,233 | 1,114 | 482 | 965 | 1,183 | 678 |
| Oil crops | '000 tonnes | 162 | 221 | 149 | 157 | 218 | 152 |
| Potatoes | '000 tonnes | 665 | 729 | 554 | 670 | 736 | 287 |
| Apples | '000 tonnes | 72 | 67 | 81 | 32 | 59 | 58 |
| Plums | '000 tonnes | 83 | 38 | 40 | 39 | 21 | 43 |
| Grapes | '000 tonnes | 421 | 394 | 354 | 359 | 337 | 333 |
| Olives | '000 tonnes | 21 | 35 | 16 | 19 | 33 | 9 |
| Tropical fruits | '000 tonnes | 29 | 25 | 25 | 25 | 22 | 16 |
| Cattle | '000 head | 443 | 438 | 427 | 438 | 417 | 444 |
| Pigs | '000 head | 1,166 | 1,362 | 1,233 | 1,234 | 1,286 | 1,347 |
| Poultry | '000 head | 9,959 | 10,871 | 11,256 | 11,747 | 11,665 | 11,778 |
| Milk | million litres | 633 | 622 | 607 | 653 | 694 | 665 |
| Eggs | million units | 818 | 819 | 774 | 787 | 761 | 873 |

*Source:* Central Bureau of Statistics (CBS)

mented by tourism, which is another important economic sector. In the production of wheat, corn, poultry, eggs and wine, Croatia has reached self-sufficiency. Through a system of subsidies that include a large number of agricultural products, the government is trying to revive production and increase producers' income.

The largest companies in agriculture (by total revenue in 2003) were:

1. Koka d.d., Varaždin (www.vindija.hr);

2. Belje d.d., Darda (www.belje.hr);

3. Agrokor d.d., Zagreb (www.agrokor.hr);

4. Puris d.d., Pazin (www.puris.hr);

5. Agroprerada d.d., Ivanić Grad (www.agrokor.hr);

6. Žitnjak d.d., Zagreb (www.zitnjak.hr);

7. PIK-Vinkovci d.d., Vinkovci (www.pik-vinkovci.hr);

8. Vupik d.d., Vukovar (www.htnet.hr/vupik);

9. Veterinaria d.d., Zagreb (www.vef.hr/rvc);

10. Kutjevo d.d., Kutjevo (www.kutjevo.com).

## Exports and imports

Croatia exports agricultural products mostly to neighbouring countries, in particular to Bosnia and Herzegovina, Italy, Slovenia, and Serbia and Montenegro (see Table 3.2.2). Major agricultural products are tobacco, cereals, seeds, honey, mandarins, medicinal herbs and horses. Apart from tropical and Mediterranean fruits and coffee, Croatia imports significant amounts of soybeans, cocoa, out of season fruit and vegetables, milk, oil crops and breeding cattle.

**Table 3.2.2** Export and import of agricultural products (US$ millions), 1998–2003

|         | 1998 | 1999 | 2000 | 2001 | 2002 | 2003 |
|---------|------|------|------|------|------|------|
| Exports | 57   | 42   | 65   | 63   | 70   | 81   |
| Imports | 274  | 216  | 211  | 252  | 295  | 362  |

*Source:* CBS
Compiled by: CCE Agriculture, Food Industry and Forestry Department

# Fisheries

## Introduction

Croatia's 1000-year-long tradition of fishing testifies to the significance of maritime activities and fisheries, which are traditionally the most important activities in the coastal and island zone of Croatia. Even today, fishing and fish breeding and processing feature strongly in providing sustenance for the local population.

## Marine fish catch

The Adriatic Sea is comparatively thinly populated with fish. However, there is a great diversity of species. The registered catch of sea-fish and other marine organisms is about 24,000 tonnes a year. The catch of small blue fish predominates (73 per cent), primarily for the needs of fish processing plants.

## Aquaculture

Aquaculture (fish and shellfish farming) has great potential in Croatia (see Table 3.2.3). In inland Croatia, fresh-water fish farming has a tradition going back almost 120 years, and mariculture (the farming of marine fish and other marine organisms) has developed over the last two decades. Shellfish farming has been practised for hundreds of years. Several years ago, a new production line was developed – tuna farming for the Japanese market.

Fresh-water fish are grown in about 8,000 hectares of carp ponds located in parts of central Croatia unsuitable for other agricultural production, and also in about 40,000 square metres of trout ponds. Besides farming, the carp ponds are very important in preserving the remaining last habitats of endangered and protected wading birds.

**Table 3.2.3** Marine fish, fresh-water fish and shellfish farming (tonnes), 1998–2003

|                        | 1998  | 1999  | 2000  | 2001  | 2002  | 2003  |
| ---------------------- | ----- | ----- | ----- | ----- | ----- | ----- |
| Carp                   | 2,299 | 1,993 | 2,013 | 2,775 | 1,849 | 1,633 |
| Trout                  | 296   | 471   | 680   | 1,040 | 911   | 791   |
| Sea bass and gilthead  | 1,747 | 1,750 | 2,100 | 2,524 | 2,500 | 2,423 |
| Tuna*                  | 906   | 970   | 1,200 | 3,045 | 3,971 | 3,028 |
| Mussels and oysters**  | 953   | 1,152 | 1,148 | 3,000 | 2,456 | 1,942 |

* figures for catch and additional fattening
** figures for edible and inedible catch

*Source:* CBS

## Fish processing industry

There are 10 fish processing plants that make a variety of fish products. About 15,000 tonnes of products are manufactured annually, 70 per cent of which are canned sardines. The significant decrease in production and shutdowns of manufacturing facilities in the early 1990s have been halted by introducing monetary compensation for canned fish and by providing cheaper fuel for fishermen.

The largest companies in the fish processing industry (by total revenue in 2003) were:

1. Sardina d.d., Postira (www.sardina.biz);

2. Adria d.d., Zadar (www.adria-zadar.hr);

3. SMS d.o.o., Split (www.sms.hr);

4. Marituna d.d., Zadar (www.marituna.hr);

5. Jadranka 1892. d.d., Vela Luka (www.jadranka1892.com);

6. Žuvela d.d., Hvar;

7. Ostrea d.o.o., Benkovac;

8. Irida d.o.o., Daruvar (www.irida.hr);

9. Dajna d.o.o., Murter;

10. Gavros d.o.o., Gračac.

## Export and import of fish and fish products

One of the characteristics of Croatian fisheries is the orientation towards export markets (see Table 3.2.4), which has resulted in a foreign trade surplus for several years now. The export of tuna fish accounts for more than 74 per cent of total fish exports in 2003. The most important markets for canned fish are Bosnia and Herzegovina, Macedonia, Serbia and Montenegro, and Austria. Fresh and chilled fish have been exported to Japan and Italy. In view of its export orientation, Croatian fishery places much importance on further trade liberalization, primarily with EU countries, and on increased export quotas. Imports are shown in Table 3.2.5.

**Table 3.2.4** Exports of fish and fish products (tonnes), 1998–2003

|  | 1998 | 1999 | 2000 | 2001 | 2002 | 2003 |
|---|---|---|---|---|---|---|
| Live fish | 790 | 623 | 456 | 1.361 | 785 | 985 |
| Fresh or chilled fish | 6,134 | 6,260 | 6,076 | 6,020 | 6,740 | 9,613 |
| Frozen fish | 57 | 354 | 611 | 720 | 858 | 1,138 |
| Fish fillets | 13 | 6 | 6 | 71 | 44 | 35 |
| Dried, salted, smoked fish | 20 | 385 | 1,401 | 611 | 1,776 | 2,368 |
| Crustaceans, molluscs | 977 | 1,208 | 1,126 | 1,538 | 1,429 | 1,145 |
| Canned fish | 11,122 | 8,859 | 8,565 | 11,358 | 10,728 | 7,386 |

*Source:* CBS
Compiled by: CCE – Agriculture, Food Industry and Forestry Department

**Table 3.2.5** Imports of fish and fish products (tonnes), 1998–2003

|  | 1998 | 1999 | 2000 | 2001 | 2002 | 2003 |
|---|---|---|---|---|---|---|
| Live fish | 151 | 38 | 341 | 1,108 | 1,772 | 1,219 |
| Fresh or chilled fish | 116 | 93 | 35 | 150 | 273 | 173 |
| Frozen fish | 4,090 | 5,800 | 14,879 | 28,201 | 40,832 | 42,652 |
| Fish fillets | 2,388 | 1,862 | 1,504 | 2,290 | 2,334 | 2,071 |
| Dried, salted, smoked fish | 247 | 236 | 179 | 245 | 304 | 265 |
| Crustaceans, molluscs | 3,795 | 3,727 | 4,474 | 5,965 | 6,421 | 6,406 |
| Canned fish | 2,067 | 2,632 | 3,936 | 4,359 | 4,102 | 4,211 |

*Source:* CBS
Compiled by: CCE – Agriculture, Food Industry and Forestry Department

# Food, beverages and the tobacco industry

## Introduction

The manufacture of food and beverages makes up 17.8 per cent of the gross value added in the Croatian manufacturing industry, while tobacco production accounts for 2.5 per cent. The food, beverages and tobacco industry registers 1,008 companies, which employ about 47,000 people, ie about 20 per cent of the total number of employees in the manufacturing industry. Within the whole Croatian processing industry, this segment generates the largest total income and provides the highest level of employment.

## Production

The output of the food, beverages and tobacco industry dropped with the beginning of the Homeland War. Gradual recovery started after 1993. Within this sector, the branches with largest revenues are the production and processing of tobacco, beer production, processing of milk, tea and coffee and the production of soft drinks. At the same time, these branches have attracted the bulk of foreign investments, and some exceptionally successful companies operate within them. Table 3.2.6 shows recent industrial output of selected products.

The largest companies in the food, beverages and tobacco industry (by total revenue in 2003) were:

1. Vindija d.d., Varaždin (www.vindija.hr);

2. Podravka d.d., Koprivnica (www.podravka.com);

3. Lura d.d., Zagreb (www.lura.hr);

4. Coca-Cola beverages hrvatska d.d., Zagreb;

5. Zagrebačka Pivovara d.d., Zagreb (www.ozujsko.com);

6. Kraš d.d., Zagreb (www.kras.hr);

7. Zvijezda d.d., Zagreb (www.zvijezda.hr);

8. Jamnica d.d. (www.jamnica.hr)

9. Ledo d.d., Zagreb (www.ledo.hr);

10. Franck d.d., Zagreb (www.franck.hr).

**Table 3.2.6** Industrial output of selected products, 1999–2003

|  | 1999 | 2000 | 2001 | 2002 | 2003 |
|---|---|---|---|---|---|
| Wheat flour ('000 tonnes) | 297 | 276 | 279 | 299 | 298 |
| Bread ('000 tonnes) | 125 | 124 | 124 | 124 | 122 |
| Pasta ('000 tonnes) | 6 | 7 | 7 | 8 | 9 |
| Fruit juices ('000 tonnes) | 11 | 26 | 30 | 28 | 49 |
| Canned vegetables ('000 tonnes) | 17 | 16 | 17 | 27 | 21 |
| Condiments ('000 tonnes) | 23 | 17 | 16 | 19 | 19 |
| Fresh meat ('000 tonnes) | 87 | 91 | 100 | 105 | 118 |
| Sausage products ('000 tonnes) | 32 | 35 | 40 | 44 | 45 |
| Canned meat ('000 tonnes) | 17 | 13 | 12 | 15 | 16 |
| Concentrated soups ('000 tonnes) | 4 | 5 | 5 | 6 | 5 |
| Canned fish ('000 tonnes) | 10 | 11 | 11 | 13 | 13 |
| Baby food ('000 tonnes) | 4 | 4 | 4 | 4 | 5 |
| Butter ('000 tonnes) | 2 | 2 | 3 | 3 | 2 |
| Cheese ('000 tonnes) | 18 | 21 | 23 | 22 | 22 |
| Sugar ('000 tonnes) | 114 | 57 | 131 | 172 | 141 |
| Candies, sweets and cocoa products ('000 tonnes) | 20 | 20 | 22 | 24 | 24 |
| Biscuits and related products ('000 tonnes) | 23 | 22 | 25 | 27 | 30 |
| Edible oil ('000 tonnes) | 38 | 35 | 40 | 41 | 51 |
| Margarine ('000 tonnes) | 16 | 16 | 16 | 18 | 18 |
| Fresh yeast ('000 tonnes) | 11 | 11 | 12 | 12 | 11 |
| Refined alcohol, 100% (million litres) | 12 | 13 | 9 | 11 | 10 |
| Beer ('000 hectolitres) | 3,663 | 3,847 | 3,799 | 3,624 | 3,679 |
| Wine ('000 hectolitres) | 426 | 472 | 501 | 450 | 475 |
| Spirits ('000 hectolitres) | 208 | 177 | 163 | 151 | 144 |
| Soft drinks ('000 hectolitres) | 2,499 | 1,471 | 1,657 | 1,949 | 2,238 |
| Livestock feed ('000 tonnes) | 472 | 484 | 524 | 524 | 537 |
| Fermented tobacco ('000 tonnes) | 12 | 8 | 11 | 8 | 8 |
| Cigarettes (million units) | 12,785 | 13,692 | 14,716 | 15,047 | 15,613 |

*Source:* CBS

## Exports and imports

Notwithstanding its significant production potential, Croatia's food imports still exceed exports (see Table 3.2.7). The most important export destinations are the markets of the neighbouring countries: Bosnia and Herzegovina, Italy, Slovenia and Serbia and Montenegro. Major export products are sugar, cigarettes, Vegeta (food seasoning), soups and soup preparations, confectionery, canned fish, canned beef, alcoholic beverages and beer. Imported products include oil cakes, milk, meat, chewing gum, soft beverages, malt and others. Agricultural and food products make up approximately 18 per cent of total exports and imports.

**Table 3.2.7** Export and import of products of the food, beverages and tobacco industry (US$ million), 1998–2003

|          | 1998 | 1999 | 2000 | 2001 | 2002 | 2003 |
|----------|------|------|------|------|------|------|
| Exports  | 450  | 358  | 315  | 366  | 439  | 606  |
| Imports  | 574  | 478  | 473  | 581  | 683  | 874  |

*Source:* CBS

Compiled by: CCE – Agriculture, Food Industry and Forestry Department

Croatia can offer to the world market some distinctive and original high quality products. Products like the *postup* and *dingaĿ* wines, cheese from the Island of Pag, the famous Slavonian salami called *slavonski kulen* and old Slavonian plum brandy (*šljivovica*), have received a geographical origin label. It is to food products that the Croatian Chamber of Economy has given the majority of the quality and originality labels.

**3.3**

# The Croatian Construction Industry

*Croatian Chamber of Economy*

## Introduction

The long-standing tradition of construction in Croatia is characterized by rich experience and workforce skills in using state-of-the-art equipment, materials and organizational schemes. In addition, Croatian construction companies work on building sites all over the world, where, by constructing even the most complex buildings, they have demonstrated the capacity to meet all demands made on them by investors.

Croatian construction companies have earned an enviable reputation by observing deadlines, whilst meeting high standards in performing various tasks and constructing various buildings – geotechnical engineering, industrial plants, power facilities and hydraulic structures, transport infrastructure, residential and commercial buildings, and others. A top achievement at the global level is the well known bridge between the Island of Krk and the mainland, built in 1980, which, until recently (1997), was the largest arch in the world made of reinforced concrete (390m in length).

## Classification

According to the national classification of economic activities, construction includes the following:

- preparatory work on the building site (demolition of buildings and earthwork, test drilling and ground probing);

- full construction of buildings and their parts (building construction, civil engineering, hydraulic engineering, etc);

- installation;

- final construction works;

- lease of machinery and equipment for construction or demolition.

## Legislation

Construction, the professional association of architects and construction engineers, and physical planning are regulated by the following legislation and subordinate legislation:

- Building and Construction Act (NN [Official Gazette] 175/2003, 100/2004;

- Croatian Chamber of Architects and Construction Engineers Act (NN 47/98);

- Articles of Association of the Croatian Chamber of Architects and Construction Engineers (NN 40/99; 112/99);

- Code of Professional Ethics of the Croatian Chamber of Architects and Construction Engineers (NN 40/99);

- Physical Planning Act (NN 30/94, 68/98, 61/00, 32/02, 100/04) and others.

## Industry performance

According to annual figures, the value of construction works in the year 2003 amounted to HRK16,190,009,000 or €2,140,572.890 (according to the CNB's mean exchange rate). This means a growth of 37.8 per cent for that year. The construction industry's share of GDP was 5.6 per cent in 2003, which indicates overall growth when compared to the 4.5 and 4.1 per cent of the two preceding years respectively. The year 2001 marked the beginning of positive trends in construction, which is reflected in the continuous growth of all the three indicators analysed: value of construction works; number of employed persons; and productivity (see Table 3.3.1).

## Residential construction

A total of 18,460 flats, with a total area of 1,529,000 square metres, were built in 2003. This includes residential construction carried out by building companies as well as private construction by individual owners. Laws have been adopted in Croatia that allow the establishment and operation of building societies as an important depository

**Table 3.3.1** Basic indicators for the Croatian construction industry, 1999–2003

| Year | Value of works (euro) | Construction industry's share of GDP (%) | No. of employed persons | Productivity per employee (euro) |
|------|------|------|------|------|
| 1999 | 1,082,947,144 | 4.5 | 71,302 | 15,188 |
| 2000 | 936,438,413 | 3.9 | 65,222 | 14,358 |
| 2001 | 1,178,919,947 | 4.1 | 65,782 | 17,922 |
| 2002 | 1,553,852,670 | 4.5 | 71,788 | 21,645 |
| 2003 | 2,140,572,890 | 5.6 | 78,276 | 27,346 |

*Source:* Central Bureau of Statistics (CBS)

for domestically earmarked long-term savings. Annual budgetary incentives are added to these savings, which, in return, have made mortgages much more accessible and favourable for all citizens. So far, four building societies have been set up under the Housing Savings and Incentives for Housing Savings Act (NN 109/97, NN 76/99, 10/2001).

Table 3.3.2 shows residential construction between 1992 and 2003. With a view to further invigorating residential construction in order to meet the needs of the population, expectations are that, in addition to the already adopted project for socially stimulated housing construction, commercial banks and other long-term assistance programmes will be even more active in the field.

**Table 3.3.2** Residential construction, 1992–2003

| Year | Completed flats | Area in '000m² | Mean size of flats in m² |
|------|------|------|------|
| 1992 | 8,115 | 643 | 79.2 |
| 1993 | 8,820 | 716 | 81.2 |
| 1994 | 10,031 | 840 | 83.7 |
| 1995 | 7,542 | 636 | 84.3 |
| 1996 | 12,910 | 1,063 | 82.3 |
| 1997 | 12,854 | 1,046 | 81.4 |
| 1998 | 12,863 | 1,057 | 82.2 |
| 1999 | 12,522 | 1,061 | 84.7 |
| 2000 | 17,487 | 1,397 | 79.9 |
| 2001 | 12,862 | 1,098 | 85.4 |
| 2002 | 18,047 | 1,438 | 79.7 |
| 2003 | 18,460 | 1,529 | 82.8 |

*Source:* CBS

# Companies by size

The number of active building companies has grown significantly since 1990 – from 819 in 1990 to 8,865 in 1995. Since then, their number has been fluctuating, registering a slight decrease in more recent years. The year 2002 experienced a new increase, 12 per cent on the previous year. There has been a general growing trend in the number of small and medium-sized companies, accompanied by a substantial decrease in the number of large ones. In 2001, the number of large companies dropped by almost 59 per cent in comparison to 1990, with a slight change in their favour in 2002 – a 47.4 per cent decrease compared with 1990.

The current trend towards restructuring in the construction industry corresponds to European trends, where small and medium-sized companies adjust to market demands more easily. Small companies' share of this industry's total revenue in 2002 (HRK28.2 billion) was 28.2 per cent, medium-sized companies accounted for 23.2 per cent, and large companies accounted for 48.6 per cent. The 10 leading building companies (see Table 3.3.3), classified by total revenue in 2003, generated 27.04 per cent of total revenue in the industry.

**Table 3.3.3** The 10 leading building companies by annual financial statement in 2003

| No. | Company name | Headquarters |
| --- | --- | --- |
| 1. | Bechtel International Inc., podružnica u hrvatskoj | Ogulin |
| 2. | Konstruktor-inženjering d.d. | Split |
| 3. | Hrvatske ceste d.o.o. | Zagreb |
| 4. | Viadukt d.d. | Zagreb |
| 5. | Dalekovod d.d. | Zagreb |
| 6. | Strabag d.o.o. | Zagreb |
| 7. | Tehnika d.d. | Zagreb |
| 8. | Industrogradnja d.d. | Zagreb |
| 9. | Hrvatske autoceste d.o.o. | Zagreb |
| 10. | Hidroelektra niskogradnja d.d. | Zagreb |

Note: Hrvatske ceste (*Croatian Roads Ltd.*) and Hrvatske autoceste d.o.o. (*Croatian Motorways Ltd.*) are companies majority-owned by the state. They are in charge of the management, building and maintenance of public roads and motorways. Thus, they are not considered *typical* business entities.

*Source:* Financial Agency – annual financial statements for 2003

## International markets for building services

Croatian building companies have been primarily orientated towards international markets in recent decades, because their experience in the construction of all types of structure has guaranteed a successful completion of even the most complex projects. For example, the construction industry's contracted work in the markets of Europe, Asia and Africa amounted to US$320 million in 1990. In recent years, the export of services has been primarily focused on European, especially German, markets, where the majority of contracts are carried out through quotas. Although this primarily implies subcontracted work, the positive effects come from the application of state-of-the-art equipment and materials, workforce training, etc.

In order to strengthen the export of services, a more active involvement by domestic banks in loan assistance to exports is necessary. Strong diplomatic support is also needed, because stronger export of services associated with investments would also facilitate the export of Croatian products and equipment to the markets made accessible in this way.

Figures for 2003 show a total value of works abroad in the amount of HRK1.24 billion, or approximately US$175.1 billion (see Table 3.3.4) – some 1.9 per cent more than in 2002. Of this sum, construction work performed in Europe amounted to HRK1,190,000,000, or 95.5 per cent of all work carried out abroad.

**Table 3.3.4** Work carried out and mean number of staff employed abroad (1998–2003)

| Year | Work completed abroad in '000 US$ | Average number of staff employed abroad |
|------|------|------|
| 1998 | 174,293 | 2,255 |
| 1999 | 172,895 | 2,787 |
| 2000 | 186,205 | 3,435 |
| 2001 | 190,715 | 3,597 |
| 2002 | 171,897 | 3,402 |
| 2003 | 175,137 | 3,106 |

*Source:* CBS

## Road construction

The most important Croatian transport routes are a part of the European network of main transport corridors (V, X and VII – Danube corridor). Since April 2001, two national companies have been in charge of road management in Croatia: Hrvatske autoceste d.o.o. (Croatian Motorways Ltd – for the management, building and maintenance of motorways) and Hrvatske ceste d.o.o. – for the management, building and maintenance of public roads.

In addition to regular receipts (tolls, charges, etc), revenue is also generated from a surcharge on the price of petroleum products. These companies are also authorized to organize financing for the construction of motorways and roads. If a concession is granted for a period of up to 33 years, it is the government of the Republic of Croatia that decides on the grant. In cases when concessions are given for 33 or more years, such decisions are adopted by the Croatian parliament (NN 180/04). Decisions are reached on the basis of public invitations to bid, prepared and issued by the competent ministry. Preparatory professional work relating to concession granting is performed by Hrvatske autoceste d.o.o.

# 3.4

# Healthcare and Pharmaceuticals

*Ivana Blašković and Igor Mataić,*
*Raiffeisenbank Austria d.d., Zagreb*

## Demographic data

According to the latest population census in 2001, the Republic of Croatia has a population of 4,437,460 (the 2003 mid-year estimate is 4,441,800). The percentage of inhabitants older than 65 years of age reached 16.4 per cent, that is, more than double that on the census conducted in 1961. The percentage of inhabitants under 14 years of age reduced to 16.4. Figure 3.4.1 shows the total percentage of the population over 65.

In 2003, average life expectancy for both men and women in the Republic of Croatia was 74.9 years, 78.4 and 71.4 respectively (source:

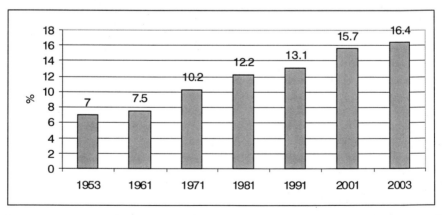

*Source:* Ministry of Health of the Republic of Croatia, Central Bureau of Statistics

**Figure 3.4.1** Percentage of the population over 65

Central Bureau of Statistics). When compared with more developed countries, Croatia is about 4–5 years behind (for example, in Finland life expectancy is 78.17). Croatia still lags two years behind Slovenia, where the average life expectancy is 76.49. However, the situation is 1.5 years better than the average in Central and Eastern Europe of 73.29 in 2001 (see Figure 3.4.2).

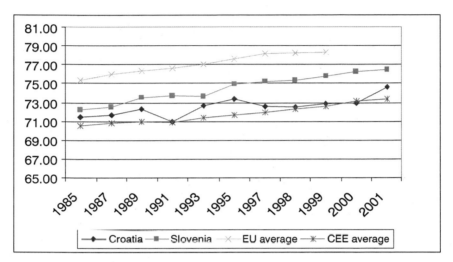

*Source:* Ministry of Health of the Republic of Croatia

**Figure 3.4.2** Life expectancy in Croatia as compared to some other European countries

According to the available data on natural migration of the population, Croatia is counted among countries with a natural decline in the number of its inhabitants. In recent years (2003), the number of deaths (53,650) has exceeded the number of new-borns (41,073) by 12,577. The birth rate totalled 8.9/1,000, whereas the mortality rate 11.8/1,000 (see Figure 3.4.3). Declining birth rates have been registered all over Europe, and a comparison with the average throughout the European Union (EU) and Central and Eastern Europe shows that Croatia has a somewhat lower birth rate.

# Age structure of the population

Similar to other European countries, Croatia is grouped among countries with ageing populations, so we expect an increase in age-related illnesses. In addition, the 'baby-boom' generation, which is more health-conscious, is entering the second half of its life, so combined

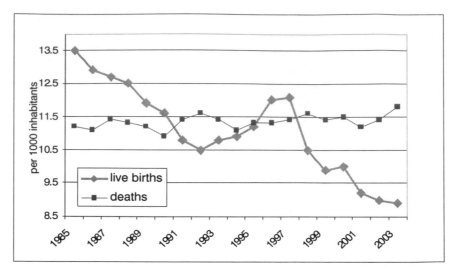

*Source:* Ministry of Health of the Republic of Croatia, Central Bureau of Statistics

**Figure 3.4.3** Birth and mortality rates in Croatia, 1985–2003

with drugs for the treatment of cardiovascular, musculoskeletal and other age-related diseases, we can expect an increase in the sales of so-called 'lifestyle' preparations (regulating weight, help in giving up smoking, etc).

# Pharmaceutical pricing and reimbursement

## Prices of drugs

Cuts in medical costs are to be achieved with new pricing methods, in line with the changes and amendments to the Act on drugs and medical products implemented in 2003 (*Official Gazette* 121/03), as well as the Rulebook on determining wholesale drug prices (*Official Gazette* 84/01, 129/02, 87/04), which regulates prices of drugs under the principle of comparable or benchmark prices.

Furthermore, changes and amendments to the Rulebook on methods of determining wholesale prices (*Official Gazette* 124/97, 53/01, 129/02, 97/04) introduced, for the first time, the generic prices of drugs, which reduce purchasing costs, cutting overall healthcare costs.

Pursuant to this Rulebook, individuals engaged in the production or transport of drugs were obligated to determine wholesale drug prices in comparison with five other countries: Slovenia, Italy, France, Spain and the Czech Republic. After calculating comparable prices in line with the methodology proscribed under the Rulebook, prices were adjusted as follows: those generic drugs prices that were above 70 per cent should be decreased at minimum to 70 per cent of the average comparable price.

After completing the procedure the Croatian Institute for Health Insurance (HZZO) published these new prices as part of the Institute's drug list (*Official Gazette* 127/04, 142/04). The prices of drugs on the list will have to decrease significantly – original drugs by an average of 15 per cent and generics by 30 per cent. On the drug lists there are 1,662 drugs, out of which 709 are generics and 953 original (protected) drugs. On the drug list 60 per cent of the drugs are produced by domestic producers and 40 per cent by foreign producers.

Customs duty on drugs, regulated pursuant to the Regulations on customs duty, was, in 2002, (*Official Gazette* 113/01, 142/02, 183/03) cut from 9.6 per cent to 4.3 per cent for countries outside the EU or to 2.6 per cent for EU member countries. Further, in 2003 the customs duty on drugs was cut to 1.3 per cent for EU member countries, and since the beginning of 2004, the base customs duty on drugs has been 2.4 per cent and there is no customs duty on drugs for EU member countries.

## *Reimbursement*

Pharmacists collect the co-payment off the patient and seek reimbursement of the remainder of their entitlement for the HZZO. The total payment to pharmacists is the drug cost plus a service fee that is determined by a points system. The service fee is negotiated with the HZZO. There are no constraints on the charges that apply to other products (including private prescriptions) sold by pharmacies. To collect their payment from the HZZO, pharmacists need to complete claim forms, which are lodged weekly. The payments to pharmacists from the HZZO usually take around 180–250 days to process. As pharmacists are unable to sustain the cash flow associated with carrying this debt, wholesalers are often asked to bear the burden of this delay in payment.

The governing body of the HZZO established a special fund for drugs for the treatment of chronic diseases such as AIDS, haemophilia, Morbus Gaucher, multiple sclerosis, leukaemia; paklitaksel and cisplatin for the treatment of ovarian cancer; and drugs necessary during heart, kidney, liver, lungs, bone marrow and corneal transplant procedures. Twenty five per cent of the expenses accrued by treatment of the aforementioned diseases are paid by hospitals themselves and 75 per cent is covered by the special fund. Such a procedure has been in force since 1 May 2002.

# Healthcare reform project, July 2000

A major new health reform project was approved by the Croatian parliament in July 2000. Overseen by the Ministry of Health, and supported by various international organizations, the project has the following major objectives: to prolong life expectancy; to improve health-related quality of life; and to reduce inequalities in health and access to healthcare.

These objectives are to be achieved through the following areas of reform:

- restriction of health expenditure growth and establishment of financial stability;

- improved healthcare planning and management;

- reorganization of the system of health service financing and payment;

- improvement in the efficiency and quality of health services;

- strengthening preventive and primary care.

The reform process will maintain the principle of universal access to healthcare, funded principally through the National Insurance (NI) scheme. People will be able to take out supplementary private health insurance to cover areas not included under the NI scheme. Healthcare services will be provided through a mixture of public and private facilities, subject to government capacity planning. This will aim to provide equal access to services and avoid unnecessary duplication of services.

A number of measures have been made a priority and have already been undertaken or begun:

- increased funding for HZZO;

- revision of the NI-funded drug formulary list;

- starting the World Bank-supported project 'New Direction of Health Policy' (see below);

- reorganization of the blood transfusion system.

Following these, a number of reform projects will be undertaken in a wide number of areas:

- institutional reform;

- promotion of the healthcare structural organization (World Bank-assisted);

- reorganization of the healthcare financing system;

- definition of a basic package of services;
- improvement of the healthcare reimbursement system;
- providing capacity planning;
- state hospital reform;
- introduction of clinical guidelines;
- improvement of preventive healthcare services;
- the national drug policy project;
- the health information system project;
- strengthening of international co-operation;
- human rights and ethics in the healthcare system;
- research and development;
- a policy of professional development in medicine and health system reform.

## Distribution channels

Wholesalers must hold a licence, issued by the Ministry of Health, in order to distribute and sell both domestically produced and imported medicines. There are as many as 115 registered drug distributors in Croatia. The four largest, Medika, Oktal farma, Farmacija and medical Intertrade, constitute 76 per cent, while the eight largest constitute as much as 90 per cent of the market. Other smaller distributors specialize in certain areas such as orthopaedic aids, diagnostic equipment, veterinary medicine, dental medicine or only one or two products. Around six distributors cover the whole offer on the pharmaceutical market with their product range. Pursuant to the law, all distributors must purchase products from a local producer directly from the producers, and trading among themselves is forbidden.

## The pharmaceutical market

The Croatian market for pharmaceuticals (drugs on the HZZO list) amounted HRK3.3 million in 2003, which was a 16 per cent year-on-year increase. After a period of accelerated growth (up to 15 per cent annually), a growth rate of around six per cent is expected in the following five years.

The market is dominated by two local producers (Pliva and Belupo), who together hold around 44 per cent of the market (see Table 3.4.1).

**Table 3.4.1** The top Croatian pharma companies

|  | Rank | Sales HRK billion | 2003 | market share % |
| --- | --- | --- | --- | --- |
| Pliva | 1 | 0.9 | | 26.0 |
| Belupo | 2 | 0.5 | | 15.7 |
| **Total market** | | **3.3** | | **100.0** |

*Source:* Pliva, Belupo, Raiffesien research

Krka and Lek are Slovenian-based companies that cover around 13 per cent of the market. Their long presence in the market is still the reason for the high level of prescriptions and sales of their products. All major pharmaceutical companies are present in the market, out of which MSD holds the largest (4.5 per cent) share of the market.

Around 31 million prescriptions are written each year, equal to seven per insured person. The market is dominated by brand generics. The leading therapeutic group in terms of prescription sales is the C (cardiovascular) ATC group with sales of nearly HRK893 million in 2003. Other leading therapeutic areas included J (anti-infectives) and A (gastrointestinal and endocrinological drugs), with sales of approximately HRK501 million and HRK356 million respectively.

## Market Structure

The majority of pharmaceutical companies sell their products exclusively through distributors, apart from Belupo, which sells 50 per cent of its products directly. The pharmacy segment of the industry is larger, although distribution through hospitals is also on the rise from the financial aspect, due to implementation of more expensive, typically hospital drugs, for example citostatic drugs.

## The over-the-counter (OTC) market

The size of OTC market is around HRK48 million a year, which means that around 78 per cent is made up by Rx drugs, and 22 per cent by OTC. OTC market growth rate is around 14 per cent.

## OTC trends

Pharmaceutical companies have realized the advantages of the OTC assortment. First, there is the importance of news being spread by word of mouth and not only by prescription from a doctor. Second, they are paid immediately. Distribution and sale of OTC drugs through consumer channels is gaining importance, and consequently intensifying marketing activities of all OTC companies. So-called lifestyle preparations are becoming increasingly important, such as vitamins and minerals, giving up smoking, hair loss, and 'emergency' contraceptives.

## Rx trends

The market is on the rise but more in financial than actual terms. There is an evident switch towards more expensive, modern drugs. The highest growth rates have been achieved in products connected with the ageing of the population (drugs for treatment of cardio-vascular, musculoskeletal and nervous diseases) and the CNS (central nervous system) group.

# The main domestic producers

## Belupo

Belupo is the second largest producer of drugs in the Republic of Croatia, and 100 per cent owned by Podravka d.d. It develops and produces human pharmaceuticals, herbal medicinal products and dental preparations. Other Belupo products include disinfectants for the skin, surfaces, and instruments, as well as cosmetic and hygiene products.

Belupo has three profit centres:

1. Prescription drugs

- drugs affecting the digestive system;

- drugs affecting the cardio-vascular system;

- drugs affecting the skin;

- drugs affecting the urogenitary system;

- drugs for treating infections;

- drugs affecting the musculoskeletal system;

- drugs affecting the nervous system.

2. Over-the-counter drugs

- over-the-counter drugs;

- herbal products;

- dietary products.

3. Cosmetic products

Belupo has cooperation agreements with a number of business partners – Merck Sharp & Dohme, Solvay Pharmaceuticals, F. Hoffmann-La Roche, GlaxoSmithKline and Janssen Pharmaceutics.

Belupo's principal export markets are Slovenia, Bosnia, Macedonia, the Czech Republic, Slovakia, Russia and other countries of the former

Soviet Union. The company operates a network of representative offices, situated in Moscow, Bratislava, Prague, Skopje and Sarajevo, as well as its Slovenian subsidiary in Ljubljana.

## Pliva

Pliva is the largest pharmaceutical company in Croatia and the largest in Central and Eastern Europe. Pliva became a joint stock company in 1993 and was listed on the London Stock Exchange in 1996. The company manufactures and supplies a wide range of prescription and OTC pharmaceutical products. The company has concentrated on its core business and sold its foodstuff and cosmetic businesses in 2001 and 2002.

The main event in 2002 was the acquisition of the US pharmaceutical company Sidmak. With that acquisition, Pliva gained entry into the world's largest pharmaceutical market. In 2002, Sidmak launched a range of new generic and speciality products. The new products are Ethosux-imide, Fluoxetine, Tramadol, Vitamin D and VoSpire ER (albuterol sulphate). Pliva has expanded in Western Europe primarily via acquisition. AWD is Pliva's largest acquisition in Western Europe. The company was acquired in 2001. The company is focused on the development, manufacture and distribution of generic products in Germany and CEE countries. AWD's leading products in Germany are Katadolon (flupiritine), Quadropril (spirapril), Cordanum (talinolol) and Corinfar (nifedipine). Pliva's other companies located in Western Europe are Pliva Pharma Ltd, and 2K Pharmaceuticals. Pliva Pharma is a UK-based company, while 2K Pharmaceutical is a Danish company with a subsidiary in Scandinavia. Pliva's first acquisition was made in 1997 when Pliva bought Polfa Krakow, one of the biggest Polish companies. Lachema, from the Czech Republic, was the second acquisition in the CEE markets. Through all of these acquisitions, Pliva has transformed from regional company to global pharmaceutical company.

In 2003, Pliva posted a 2003 net profit of HRK984 billion. The company posted total revenues of HRK7.221 billion, up 12.6 per cent in local terms and up 32 per cent in US dollar terms.

From 2004 onwards, Pliva has implemented a new organizational structure. Concurrent with the realization of the new structure will be the reduction of Pliva's workforce of 650 (mainly in Croatia) or 10 per cent of the worldwide total. The key feature of the new Pliva is that it devolves a very significant amount of operational authority to the local (national) operations. One of the reasons for the new structure is to take advantage of research and development tax breaks available in Croatia since last year.

*Research and development (R&D)*

Amongst a range of generics in different stages of development, Pliva obtained the first marketing authorization (MA) approval for carvedilol in Croatia and for citalopram and simvastatin in Germany. Furthermore, Pliva obtained additional MA approvals for five molecules (carbamazepine, clomipramin and isoniazid in two CEE countries and fluconasol and torasemid in one Western European country). Thirteen molecules were submitted for registration in three CEE countries and four molecules in three Western European countries, representing 48 products. Overall, there are currently 361 MA approvals pending in six CEE countries, 149 in six Western European countries and 10 in the United States. Three new chemical entities (NCEs) are currently advancing through clinical studies, and an additional one has been selected as a new candidate for clinical trials. Several NCEs are advancing through different stages of discovery and pre-clinical trials (see Table 3.4.2).

**Table 3.4.2** Status of the most advanced NCE projects

| NCE project | Indication | Status |
|---|---|---|
| PLD-116 | Peptide drug for treatment of inflammatory bowel disease (IBD) | Undergoing Phase II |
| PLD-117 | Thrombocytopenia (TPO) agonist | Phase I completed |
| PLD-118 | Novel oral antifungal | First Phase II completed |
| PLD-147 | Novel oral cytostatic agent | Phase I started in H2 2003 |

*Source:* Pliva

# References

Ministry of Health of the Republic of Croatia
Pliva d.d.
Belupo d.d.

**3.5**

# Food and Beverages

*Ivana Blašković, Raiffeisenbank Austria
d.o.o Zagreb and Igor Mataić, Raiffeisen
Consulting*

This article is divided into three parts:

- the importance of the food and beverages industry in the Republic of Croatia;

- the most important companies in the sector; and

- the latest trends.

## Food industry: production of food and beverages

Output from the food industry went up by 5.1 per cent in 2003 but by only 1.6 per cent during the first eight months of 2004. The production of food and beverages is the most important branch of the processing industry, with a 21.5 per cent contribution to the industry's overall revenue results.

Food and beverage production contributes significantly to the gross added value of the production industry. Its share of the overall industrial results was lower in 2001 and 2002 than a year earlier, dropping from 22.2 per cent in 2000 to 17.1 per cent in 2001 and 10.4 per cent in 2002 (see Table 3.7.1). Its industry share also contracted, while the participation in the overall income of Croatian companies was reduced from 6.0 per cent in 2002 to 5.7 per cent in 2003.

The food and beverages industry employs the highest number of staff of all the sectors in the processing industry; in 2003 it averaged 45,145, which was a small increase on the previous year's total of 43,915.

During the period 2001–2003, the food and beverages production industry made significant improvements, registering a net profit of HRK458.33 million in 2001, compared with a net loss the year before of

**Table 3.7.1** Indicators of the size and importance of the food and beverages industry in the processing industry sector (%)

|  | 1999 | 2000 | 2001 | 2002 | 2003 |
|---|---|---|---|---|---|
| Share of total income of entrepreneurs in the Republic of Croatia | 6.8 | 6.8 | 6.6 | 6.0 | 5.7 |
| Share of total income of the processing industry | 21.1 | 21.1 | 20.9 | 20.5 | 21.5 |
| Share of the total profit of the processing industry | 18.7 | 22.8 | 17.1 | 10.4 | 18.3 |
| Share of the total losses of the processing industry | 14.5 | 25.0 | 14.2 | 13.3 | 20.4 |
| Share of the total number of employees | 4.1 | 4.2 | 4.2 | 4.1 | 4.2 |

*Source:* Central Bureau of Statistics (DZS), FINA

HRK358.14 million (see Table 3.7.2). Costs in this sector started growing significantly faster than income. The consolidated net margin amounted to two per cent, indicating that there is room for further rationalization.

**Table 3.7.2** Profit and loss in the food and beverages industry, 2001–2003 (at year-end in HRK '000)

|  | 2001 | 2002 | 2003 | % change 2002 | % change 2003 |
|---|---|---|---|---|---|
| Total income | 22,425,463 | 23,712,319 | 25,596,825 | 5.7 | 7.9 |
| Total expenditures | 21,731,497 | 23,054,399 | 25,310,907 | 6.1 | 9.8 |
| Profit after tax | 1,115,770 | 1,141,715 | 1,123,090 | 2.3 | -1.6 |
| Loss after tax | 657,439 | 709,913 | 1,055,295 | 8.0 | 48.7 |
| Net profit (+)/loss (–) | 458,331 | 431,802 | 67,796 | -5.8 | -84.3 |
| Profit loss ratio | 0.59 | 0.62 | 0.94 | 5.4 | 51.1 |

*Source:* FINA

During 2003, 1,105 business entities were active in the food and beverages industry, which is a rise of 6.1 per cent on 2002, when 1,041 entities were registered. The income of the 10 largest companies in the sector accounted for a 42 per cent share, while their share of overall profit totalled 29 per cent, which does not fully reflect the strength of the top 10 companies – their share of total profit during the period 2000–2002 averaged 51 per cent. The reduction in this share is the result of 'big bath accounting' carried out by two big food and beverage companies in the year 2003 (see Table 3.7.3).

**Table 3.7.3** Performance of the top ten companies, 2003

| Company name | Rank | Income in HRK '000 | % change | Profit in HRK '000 | % change | ROE* % 2002 | 2003 |
|---|---|---|---|---|---|---|---|
| Vindija d.d., Varaždin | 1 | 2,095,862 | 7 | 44,436 | 18 | 3.2 | 10.93 |
| Podravka d.d., Koprivnica | 2 | 1,805,555 | 5 | 0 | −100 | 2.7 | 0.00 |
| Lura d.d. Zagreb | 3 | 1,699,062 | 11 | 0 | −100 | 3.3 | 0.00 |
| Coca-Cola Beverages d.d. | 4 | 885,211 | 5 | 101,755 | 15 | 13.1 | 17.34 |
| Zagrebačka pivovara, Zagreb | 5 | 869,468 | 6 | 227,242 | −6 | 31.9 | 60.08 |
| Kraš, Zagreb | 6 | 765,066 | −2 | 31,437 | −25 | 4.2 | 4.49 |
| Zvijezda, Zagreb | 7 | 698,395 | 7 | 17,245 | 9 | 2.5 | 3.33 |
| Jamnica, Zagreb | 8 | 660,690 | 29 | 64,912 | 19 | 11.3 | 10.9 |
| Ledo, Zagreb | 9 | 653,208 | 10 | 26,707 | 29 | 4.4 | 9.37 |
| Franck, Zagreb | 10 | 538,311 | −1 | 74,506 | 1 | 12.4 | 13.23 |
| Total food and beverages production | | 25,596,825 | | 1,997,096 | | | |
| Total share of top 10 in the sector | | 42% | | 29% | | | |

*ROE = return on equity

# The most important companies in the sector

## *Agrokor*

Agrokor is a food and beverage producer and retail concern, with a consolidated turnover of HRK9.15 billion (€1.2 billion) in 2003. Agrokor's core businesses are frozen food, beverages, oil, mayonnaise and retail. Ledo, Jamnica, Zvijezda and Konzum are the key companies in the Agrokor portfolio. Ledo produces ice cream, pastry, fruit and vegetables, as well as fish. Despite strong foreign competition, Ledo's domestic market share is around 80 per cent. With a market share of 75 per cent, Ledo is the market leader in neighbouring Bosnia and Herzegovina.

Jamnica is the largest mineral water producer in this part of Europe, with a tradition of over 170 years as market leader in Croatia. In 2000, Jamnica acquired Sarajevski Kiseljak (Bosnia and Herzegovina). Sarajevski Kiseljak is the largest and oldest mineral water producer in Bosnia and Herzegovina, with a tradition of over 110 years and has a leading position on the domestic market. In 2003, Jamnica natural mineral water was awarded the 'EAUSCAR' for the best natural sparkling mineral water.

Zvijezda is the major producer of edible oils and the only producer of margarine, vegetable oil, mayonnaise and delicacy products made with a mayonnaise base. Zvijezda also produces ingredients for other food industries. In just a few years Konzum grew from a local into a countrywide retail chain store, through organic growth as well as acquisition.

### Podravka

The organizational structure of Podravka Group is based on three strategic business units: food and beverages – Vegeta and Podravka dishes (soups, ready-made food and seasonings), desserts, fruit and vegetables, drinks, milling and bakery, Danica (meat industry); the pharmaceutical industry (Belupo); and wholesale. Podravka's most famous product is Vegeta, the universal food seasoning. Vegeta was launched in 1958 and is currently exported to more than 30 countries worldwide.

### Vindija

Vindija's core activity is the production of milk and dairy products, juices, chicken meat, bakery products and other meat and meat products. During the past 40 years, Vindija has been the only producer of blue cheese in the region. Vindija exports 12 per cent of its products, and the company has invested more than €50 million in production facilities.

### Kraš

Kraš began operations in 1911, with the foundation of 'Union' – a chocolate and candy factory. Over the years, Union expanded the range of its activities and merged with Bizjak – a biscuit factory. Kraš emerged from the amalgamation of the two factories. Kraš is Croatia's leading confectionery manufacturer. Its main products are a wide range of chocolate, biscuit and candy products. The current assortment of Kraš chocolate products is known under the name of Dorina. During 60 years of production, Bajadera has become the best-known name of the Kraš assortment and has gained the status of Kraš' ultimate product worldwide. The main export markets are the countries of ex-Yugoslavia and Central and Eastern Europe (CEE).

### Lura

Lura is the leading Croatian producer of dairy products. It was founded in 1999 through the merger of Lura Group d.o.o. and three dairy products producers – Dukat d.d. Zagreb, Sirela d.d. Bjelovar and Zadar Dairy d.d. Today Lura is one of the largest companies in Croatia and employs 1,563 workers. Due to its long-term development of business relations with farmers, Lura d.d. purchases milk from 25,000 milk producers throughout Croatia, using 70 of its own and rented lorries and 2,000 lacto-freezers. The Lura d.d. product range includes more than 120 branded products.

Lura-Pica d.o.o. is a producer of non-alcoholic beverages and also has the exclusive right to bottle, sell and distribute the soft drinks of the Pepsi, Pepsi Max, Mirinda and 7Up brands. Lura d.d. Livno Dairy, situated in Bosnia and Herzegovina, is a company owned by Lura d.d., specializing in cheese production.

### Zagrebacka pivovara

Zagrebacka pivovara was founded in 1892 and has been in the majority ownership of Interbrew Corporation since 1994. Its products consist of Ozujsko pivo, the best-selling lager beer in Croatia, dark Tomislav, Bozicno pivo, and the premium beer, Stella Artois.

## The latest trends

### Modernization

With the modernization of factories and increased effectiveness, accompanied by reduced costs, companies have learnt that if they want to survive they must improve their productivity. The most vivid recent examples have been the construction of Podravka's new Vegeta factories in Croatia and Poland, as well as the construction of a soup factory. Kraš consolidated production at one location, modernized the production line and built a state-of-the art warehouse for its finished products. Vindija invested in a new milk-processing plan and has spent more than €50 million in the modernization of production facilities over the last few years. In the first six months of the year 2003, Agrokor invested more than €60 million in new plants, technology and development. In the last six years, Lura invested over €100 million in production and technology, distribution, and protection of the environment.

### Establishing international standards

International standards of quality have, in recent years, been applied in the largest food companies in the Republic of Croatia. Vindija received an ISO 9001 certificate in 1996, the first food company in Croatia to do so. Koka (a member of the Vindija concern) received the certificate at the beginning of 2000 – the first meat processing company in Croatia to do so. Kraš was issued the certificate in 1997, while Podravka's ISO 9001 certificate encompasses the production of Vegeta, Podravka meals, as well as Lino baby food, Dolcela sweets and Kviki snacks. Lura was awarded the ISO 9001 certificate of quality for its entire production, as well as the ISO 14001 certificate for its environmentally-friendly production system. Several companies within the

Agrokor concern have received certificates for ISO 9001 and the HACCP system (hazard analysis critical control point). Currently the whole sector is preparing for the EU by learning about and licensing the HACCP system.

## Growth through acquisitions

Agrokor registered the most significant growth through acquisitions in more than one segment. The retail chain store Konzum registered a growth rate of 41 per cent in 2003, 58 per cent in 2002 and 72 per cent in 2001. Such rapid growth was based on acquisitions of private companies in Croatia. The second segment where Agrokor registered above-average rates of growth is Ledo, the ice cream maker. It acquired Barpeh in Bosnia and Herzegovina in 2000, which is the market leader with over 75 per cent of the market. In early 2003, it acquired a frozen food and ice-cream factory, Frikom in Yugoslavia. All this enabled Ledo to become the strongest regional company in the frozen food segment.

In 2002, Podravka acquired Ital-Ice, a local food producer, and thus entered into this fast-growing market segment. The company's first acquisition outside Croatia's borders was completed in the Czech Republic in 2002, with the acquisition of the Lagris factory. Lura acquired Sloboda from Osijek, starting its rise from a dairy into a food company.

In the last two years there have been horizontal mergers between food companies. Smaller local producers such as Ital-Ice, Sloboda Osijek and Irida from Daruvar, have been acquired by local market leaders. Although attempts have been made to make the largest companies of the industry targets for multinational companies, to date all offers have been rejected. Lura negotiated a strategic partnership with the French company, Danone, and with the local tobacco producer, Tvornica duhana Rovinj. Kras refused merger offers from Lura and Kraft Food and announced penetration into regional markets through acquisition as well as cooperation with a confectionery producer, Koestlin.

The regions of former Yugoslavia, especially Serbia and Montenegro, are markets where Croatian food companies are well known and where they plan their growth. In our opinion, the main reason why domestic companies rejected the offers from well-known multinationals are that, first, domestic food companies are strong enough to be able to push for acquisitions in the regional markets on their own, and second, their brands (as a foundation for organic growth) are well known. After consolidating the entire market of former Yugoslavia, we believe that the leading domestic food companies will be more open to strategic alliances with big multinational companies for the purpose of further growth and development.

In addition to horizontal consolidation, there have been some vertical moves. The first was the acquisition of the chain store Unikonzum by Agrokor back in 1994. Today, Konzum is the market leader and the main growth driver of the company, with income of HRK5.8 billion and around 25 per cent share of the domestic food and beverages retail market.

Vindija took over the chain store Zagrebcanka with a network of 70 self-service shops. With the entrance of large foreign chain stores to the market such as Billa, Mercatone, Merkator, Kauflan and Metro, other domestic food companies started moving towards vertical consolidation. A consortium of domestic food companies has acquired Diona.

The only segment of the food industry that is almost entirely in the hands of foreign-owned multinational companies is the brewing industry. Out of Croatia's seven breweries, the four largest have foreign owners. The market leader is Zagrebacka pivovara, the Zagreb brewery owned by Interbrew, which holds 46.5 per cent of the market. In 2003, the second largest local producer, Karlovacka pivovara, the Karlovac brewery, was acquired by Heineken. Karlovacka pivovara's market share is 19 per cent (2002). Panonska pivovara is owned by Caltenberg, while Jadranska pivovara was purchased by a Slovenian producer Pivovarna Lasko. These four large breweries cover 80 per cent of the domestic market.

## Creating well-known brands

The food industry in Croatia has concentrated on creating well-known brands. According to a survey by the company Accent, in 2002 the leading brands on the chocolate market were Milka, Kraš and Dorina. Kraš' strongest brands are Dorina (chocolate) and Bajadera (a soft-centre chocolate candy); the company's brands are market leaders. In the mineral water market, the best known are Jamnica from Agrokor and Studena from Podravka. In the ice cream market the uncontested leader is Ledo (Agrokor) with over three-quarters of the market. In the mayonnaise and margarine market, Zvijezda (Agrokor) and Margo hold around 80 per cent, while in the coffee market the company Franck with its brand Frank dominates, with a 59 per cent share, followed by Minas and Nescafé. The relatively low participation of Nestlé in the market could soon change – it has signed a product distribution agreement with Podravka. Dukat (Lura) and Vindija (Vindija) are the two brands holding over 70 per cent of the milk market.

Podravka is working to establish brands such as Dolcela (confection) and Lino (baby food), Podravka soups and Podravka meat. Agokor created the private lebale brand K+ (in its retail segment, Konzum), while Lura launched its Frutisima line (yoghurts). Vindija is pushing its Cekin (meat), and in the smoked and cured meat segment, Gavrilovic and its Gavrilovic brand hold the leading position.

## Growth of imports and exports

According to the preliminary results for 2003, Croatia's exports in this industry segment realized a rise of 40 per cent on the previous year, while imports of food and beverages went up by 27 per cent (see Table 3.7.4). The rise in imports is due to the large foreign chain stores entering the market, improved standards of living of Croatian consumers, and reduced customs duty on agricultural products.

**Table 3.7.4** Trade exchange in the food and beverages segment

| US$ million | 2000 | 2001 | 2002 | 2003* |
|---|---|---|---|---|
| Exports | 264 | 301 | 368 | 515 |
| Imports | 474 | 590 | 701 | 888 |
| Balance | -210 | -289 | -333 | -373 |

* preliminary data

*Source:* Croatian Chamber of Economy (HGK*)*

It is evident from Table 3.7.5 that expenditure on food and drink is contracting, resulting in lower sensitivity to price movements. This generates increased demand for international brands and less dependence and demand for cheaper products. The average share of food and non-alcoholic beverages in the Consumer Price Index (CPI) (introduced at the beginning of 2004) is 32.95 per cent.

**Table 3.7.5** Average share of food and non-alcoholic beverages in CPI

| Year | % |
|---|---|
| 2000 | 38.63 |
| 2001 | 36.81 |
| 2002 | 35.84 |
| 2003 | 35.25 |

The structure of the retail trade also has a substantial influence on the rise in imports. Small privately-owned shops dominated in Croatia and owners are traditionally more inclined to local brands. However, with the change in shopping habits and numerous new foreign chain stores opening, this advantage is expected to disappear soon.

## Domestic vs multinational producers – trends

As can be seen from the data on leading brands in Croatia, domestic companies still hold the dominant position in almost all sub-segments.

This is attributable to long-standing relationships with individual brands. The development of individual brands can be illustrated through the results of a survey showing that young consumers prefer Milka chocolate, while older consumers opt for Kraš.

Domestic producers will probably maintain their position in the mid-term, due to the comparative advantage of being well known and knowing their markets. Longer term, only those that improve the competitiveness of their products will be able to increase their production volumes and be equipped to take on the largest players such as Nestlé, Unilever, Danone and Kraft. The best examples of this are Ledo's acquisition of Frikom, followed by Podravka's acquisition of Lagris. In cases like these, the benefits of synergy are achieved.

The second possibility is cooperation with international companies through distribution agreements, as we have seen from the Podravka example. Podravka signed an agreement with Nestlé on the distribution of its products throughout Croatia, Bosnia and Herzegovina, Serbia, Montenegro and the former Yugoslav Republic of Macedonia. It also signed an agreement with Unilever to distribute its products in Croatia.

**3.6**

# Textiles and Apparel

*Croatian Chamber of Economy*

## Introduction

The manufacture of textiles and apparel in Croatia is traditionally open to international cooperation and trade, adhering to the principles of quality and competitiveness in price and cost. The technological and skills potential of employees in the textile and clothing industry, which also aids its ability to quickly adapt the manufacturing processes to new fashion trends, has won the industry a leading position in the European market. For this reason, the Croatian textile industry has long been a recognized partner to European and international customers.

The main characteristics of the textile and clothing industry are:

- a diversity of processes in the manufacture of textiles and clothing;
- wide distribution of factories, across practically all Croatian counties;
- labour intensiveness;
- strong export orientation;
- manufacture in small, medium and large companies;
- openness to international cooperation;
- readiness to respond quickly to fashion trends;
- observance of delivery deadlines;
- the high quality of work and, to a considerable degree, also design of finished textile products; and ready-to-wear clothing.

Today, the primary production of textiles covers the following activities:

- preparation and spinning of textile fibres;
- manufacture of fabrics;

- textile finishing;

- manufacture of finished textile products (except for fashion apparel) and other textile products;

- manufacture of knitted and crocheted fabrics and knitted and crocheted products.

The clothing industry includes:

- manufacture of leather clothing, other clothing and fashion apparel;

- dressing and dyeing of fur and fur products.

The Croatian textile and clothing industry had some 30,800 employees in December 2003. This is 2.94 per cent of the total number of employees in the Republic of Croatia and 13.05 per cent of the total number of employees in the manufacturing industry.

The textile and clothing industry constitutes 11.32 per cent of total Croatian exports, having registered a foreign trade deficit of US$22.93 million in 2002.

For the major part, exports are generated through contract processing, which accounts for 80 to 95 per cent of total manufacturing capacity. 'Full exports', ie the export of goods of Croatian origin, are associated with the manufacture of clothing for the British, Italian, Slovenian and Bosnian & Herzegovinian markets (mainly of men's suits), whereas the Slovenian, Czech and Bosnian & Herzegovinian markets buy predominantly women's clothes. Germany, Austria and Slovenia buy knitwear, whereas yarn and fabrics are exported mainly to Italy, Germany and Bosnia & Herzegovina.

The textile and clothing industry holds a 4.6 per cent share of the total manufacturing revenue of Croatia, with primary textile production accounting for 31.16 per cent of that amount, and the clothing industry, fur dressing and dyeing for the remaining 68.84 per cent.

In general, new technology equipment holds a 70–90 per cent share of total investment in the textile and clothing industry, while construction (the construction of new manufacturing facilities) accounts for 31 per cent. The clothing industry makes comparatively higher investments because it employs more people, and investment per employee is much lower than in primary industries.

## Current situation

The current position of the Croatian textile and clothing industry is rather complex, both in domestic and foreign markets. The position of this industrial activity in the Republic of Croatia is determined by its high share of total employment and of the manufacturing industry's foreign trade. Exposure to global competition and large manufacturing capacity are a characteristic of this sector, especially in the manufacture of clothes. In the past few years, this industrial sector has faced difficulties in its activity, which is marked by seasonal fluctuations and decrease. Therefore, a special challenge is maintaining the level of manufacturing activity in interim periods. Orders by foreign customers (especially in contract processing) decrease both in quantity and prices. The many free trade agreements between the Republic of Croatia and other countries have not created new export opportunities for this industry. What is more, it has experienced heavier competition and easier inflow of cheaper foreign goods to the domestic market.

Only companies that have made substantial investments and modernized their manufacturing technology earlier during the times of transition (this particularly refers to the purchase of highly-specialized machines intended exclusively for a specific operation in the manufacture of a final product) have good prospects and need not fear extinction.

This sector of industry should also further persist in its own restructuring, in order to reduce labour costs through technological improvements, branding and high manufacturing specializations. To achieve this goal, management should make appropriate decisions leading to larger mutual interconnection.

## Fairs and exhibitions

The textile and clothing industry traditionally participates in the Zagreb Fair's Intertextile annual event. Also, Croatian textile and clothing manufacturers attend specialized fairs and exhibitions throughout Europe. Members of the Primary Textile Industries Group, Tekstil Lio Osijek, Kelteks Karlovac, Čateks Čakovec and Pamučna Industrija Duga Resa, made a successful appearance at Heimtextil in Frankfurt in January 2004.

Four companies participated at the Heimtextil in Frankfurt in April 2004: Regeneracija Zabok, Čateks Čakovec, Kontex Karlovac and TKZ Zagreb. Textile companies also appear at the Belgrade Fashion Fair in spring and autumn.

## Association of the textile and clothing industry within the CCE

The Textile and Clothing Industries Association works within the Industry and Technology Department of the Croatian Chamber of Economy (CCE).

## The top ten companies

There are a total of 721 textile companies registered in Croatia. The top 228 companies generate 94.8 per cent of this industry's total revenue, while employing 92.8 per cent of the workforce. The majority (269) of the remaining 493 companies have up to five employees.

Broken down by total revenue, the top ten companies in the primary industry earn 44.11 per cent of the primary industry's revenue, ie 13.74 per cent of the industry total. Similarly, the top ten clothing industry companies earn 40.22 per cent of the textile and clothing industries' total revenue. Compared to the revenue of the clothing industry alone, fur dressing and dyeing account for 58.43 per cent.

## Appendix

**Table 3.6.1** The top ten textile and apparel manufacturers according to total revenue in 2003

| DB-17<br>Production of textiles<br>Company | DB-18<br>Production of apparel<br>Company |
|---|---|
| 1. Prevent Zlatar d.d., Zlatar | 1. Benetton Croatia d.o.o., Osijek |
| 2. Čateks d.d., Čakovec | 2. Varteks d.d., Varaždin |
| 3. TKZ d.d., Zagreb | 3. Betex, d.o.o., Belica |
| 4. Tubla d.o.o., Čakovec | 4. Heruc Galeria d.o.o., Zagreb |
| 5. Nird d.o.o., Kaštel Lukšić | 5. Kamensko d.d., Zagreb |
| 6. Kelteks d.o.o., Karlovac | 6. Lumik d.d., Rijeka |
| 7. Lola Ribar d.d., Karlovac | 7. Galeb d.d., Omiš |
| 8. Pamučna industrija Duga Resa<br>   d.d., Duga Resa | 8. MTČ Tv. rublja, Čakovec |
| 9. Regeneracija d.d., Zabok | 9. COM-Prom d.o.o. |
| 10. MTČ Tv. čarapa, Čakovec | 10. Kotka d.d., Krapina |

*Source:* Payment Transfer Agency, Zagreb, processed by the Croatian Chamber of Economy

**Table 3.6.2** Main indicators for the total volume of industrial production of textiles, fashion apparel and dressing and dyeing of fur

| | Unit | 1998 | 1999 | 2000 | 2001 | 2002 | 2003 | I–XI 2004 |
|---|---|---|---|---|---|---|---|---|
| **Production of selected industrial products by sections and divisions of NCEA** | | | | | | | | |
| **17. Manufacture of textiles** | | | | | | | | |
| Hemp fibre | tonnes | 0 | 0 | 0 | 0 | 0 | 0 | 0 |
| Cotton yarn | tonnes | 5,088 | 3,946 | 4,238 | 4,919 | 4,126 | 1,483 | 1,954 |
| Wool yarn | tonnes | 468 | 411 | 375 | 257 | 220 | 143 | 138 |
| Hemp yarn | tonnes | 0 | 0 | 0 | 0 | 0 | 0 | 0 |
| Rope, cord and straps | tonnes | 406 | 398 | 370 | 384 | 324 | 298 | 289 |
| Sewing thread | tonnes | 1,056 | 857 | 743 | 616 | 622 | 725 | 50 |
| Cotton fabric and blankets | '000 m² | 16,749 | 13,179 | 13,873 | 14,059 | 13,914 | 12,321 | 9,960 |
| Wool fabric and blankets | '000 m² | 6,550 | 4,018 | 4,155 | 3,583 | 3,645 | 3,150 | 1,742 |
| Manufacture of knitted fabrics except jersey | tonnes | 3,064 | 2,595 | 2,513 | 2,749 | 4,829 | 5,412 | 5,479 |
| Socks | '000 pairs | 21,191 | 18,818 | 18,172 | 21,371 | 22,032 | 20,958 | 18,624 |
| Manufacture of haberdashery | tonnes | 94 | 66 | 75 | 71 | 57 | 30 | 20 |
| Household linen | '000 m² | 8,088 | 6,928 | 7,229 | 6,506 | 6,272 | 6,929 | 5,719 |
| **18. Manufacture of apparel; dressing and dyeing of fur** | | | | | | | | |
| Manufacture of knitted underwear | tonnes | 1,520 | 1,467 | 1,239 | 1,191, | 1,226 | 2,149 | 1,945 |
| Manufacture of knitted clothing | tonnes | 510 | 581 | 559 | 684 | 1,187 | 1,391 | 2,571 |
| Manufacture of linens | '000 m² | 7,123 | 5,940 | 5,945 | 6,038 | 5,784 | 5,950 | 4,242 |
| Ready-to-wear clothing | '000 m² | 26,640 | 24,740 | 24,397 | 24,468 | 19,508 | 17,710 | 15,751 |
| Leather clothing | '000 m² | 286 | 203 | 187 | 0 | 214 | 210 | 149 |
| Ready-to-wear plastic clothing | '000 m² | 0 | 0 | 0 | 0 | 0 | 0 | 0 |

*Source:* CBS, processed by the Croatian Chamber of Economy

**Table 3.6.3** Total investment by branch (in '000 kuna)

| Activity | Total investment by year | | | | | |
|---|---|---|---|---|---|---|
| | 1998 | 1999 | 2000 | 2001 | 2002 | 2003 |
| Textile and apparel industry (DB) | 124,446 | 152,120 | 142,600 | 307,599 | 406,663 | 368,887 |
| Primary textile industry (DB17) | 16,552 | 53,823 | 27,943 | 91,724 | 223,351 | 186,397 |
| Apparel industry (DB18) | 107,924 | 98,297 | 114,657 | 215,875 | 183,312 | 182,490 |

*Source:* CBS, processed by the Croatian Chamber of Economy

**Table 3.6.4** Indices of industrial production and number of employees by divisions of NCEA

2000 = 100

| Branch of industry | Production (index) | | | | | Employees in December '000 | | | | | |
| --- | --- | --- | --- | --- | --- | --- | --- | --- | --- | --- | --- |
| | 1999 | 2001 | 2002 | 2003 | I-XI 2004 | 1999 | 2000 | 2001 | 2002 | 2003 | XI 2004 |
| DB17 Manufacture of textiles | 98.4 | 109.4 | 111.4 | 107.1 | 101.1 | 11.7 | 11.0 | 9.2 | 8.9 | 8.5 | 8.0 |
| DB18 Manufacture of fashion apparel; dressing and dyeing of fur | 101.9 | 101.0 | 87.3 | 95.1 | 62.3 | 29.5 | 28.5 | 28.5 | 24.9 | 24.9 | 24.3 |
| DB total | | | | | | 41.2 | 39.5 | 37.7 | 33.8 | 33.4 | 32.3 |
| Manufacturing industry | 97.4 | 106.4 | 111.9 | 116.8 | 121.6 | 259.4 | 251.0 | 248.7 | 242.2 | 245.4 | 241.8 |

*Source:* CBS; compiled by the Croatian Chamber of Economy, 2003

## 3.7

# Small and Medium-sized Enterprises (SMEs) in Croatia

*Hayley Alexander, Deloitte Emerging Markets*

## Relevance to foreign investors

Individuals and companies considering the Croatian market as a target for potential investment might ask the entirely rational question: Why is the SME sector relevant to me as a potential investor in Croatia? There are at least three answers to this question.

1. While SMEs are less likely targets of foreign direct investment (FDI) than large enterprises, they are nonetheless often just as viable. This is particularly true for mid-sized investors unable to take on the debt and complicated restructuring efforts that are characteristically required for large and/or formerly state-owned enterprises.

2. SMEs tend to lead the economic recovery process in transitional or emerging countries. Their prospects for growth and development thereby serve as a useful barometer to guage the pace of a country's structural reform and its ability to create a business-friendly environment. The more an investor understands about the structural reforms being undertaken in support of SMEs, the better the chance to anticipate structural business and regulatory hazards in the broader sense.

3. SMEs form the basis of second-tier suppliers in any business environment. The strength of a country's enterprises, regardless of size, is at least partially reliant on the availability of a reliable supplier network.

Addressing SMEs as a unified sector is always a risky proposition, due to their diverse nature, widely varying management and technological proficiencies, and disparate markets served. Any attempt to evaluate SMEs at the macro level is, consequently, best focused on aspects common to all. Two of the most important of these are the enabling environment and government policies thereof. Identification of trends among the most rudimentary SME performance indicators is also important. In most countries (Croatia included) the most widely available and relevant SME performance indicators are compiled annually and include: annual sales growth, employment figures, numbers of registered companies and export sales revenues. These are addressed below.

## Croatian SME sector vital statistics

SMEs collectively cannot be ignored in Croatia. They represent well over half, and by some estimates nearly two-thirds, of total employment in the country. In terms of businesses registered, they comprise over 95 per cent of all legally registered concerns and are responsible for approximately half of the gross domestic product. While large enterprises continue to shed employees – losing approximately 30 per cent since the late 1990s – SMEs are maintaining their numbers and making a substantial contribution to keeping the economy on track. The Croatian government has become increasingly aware of the role SMEs play pursuant to economic development, a fact evidenced by the elevation of SME issues on political agendas in recent years.

## The Croatian business enabling environment

Since the creation of the Ministry for Small and Medium Enterprises in 2000, the Croatian business-enabling environment has improved substantially. In their decision to form the Ministry for SMEs, Croatian policy makers correctly assessed the need for special treatment of the one sector of the economy most likely to lead it out of severe recession, which had peaked in 1998. Subsequent to the general elections in 2004, however, the new government conducted an amalgamation of ministries and, once again, merged the functions of the Ministry for SMEs in with the Ministry of Economy. Nevertheless, in so doing, they significantly strengthened the mandate of the small business support agency, known by its Croatian acronym – HAMAG. This agency is responsible for performing two primary functions: 1) to provide loan guarantees to finance business growth and 2) to provide technical assistance mainly in the form of training, quality systems development and business strategy assistance to the country's SMEs. The latter will be done through a network of regional offices in partnership with local administrations.

On the down side, a legacy of overlapping business laws and regulations (promulgated before and since the war) remains to be dealt with. Newly formulated laws and regulations affecting the business climate, when viewed in the context of an already complicated legal framework, are often confusing at best, contradictory at worst. Separate sets of laws exist to address cooperatives, craftspeople and companies, while SMEs in particular have been under the purview of yet another law, the Law on Accountancy. In fact, approximately a dozen individual laws figure prominently in the daily lives of Croatian enterprise managers. Simply put, the process of unravelling the legal and regulatory requirements, for business investments and start-ups alike, can be rather daunting to domestic and foreign concerns.

The existence of a complicated legal structure is not, however, a situation unique to Croatia. Legal and regulatory complexity could be characterized as endemic to post-socialist economies, a consequence that might be expected in the wake of dismantled and partially restructured institutions. In this respect, Croatia is no worse than most other countries in transition and, with appropriate legal assistance, investment decisions can generally be made with a reasonable degree of transparency.

One of the main problems facing Croatia's SMEs and foreign investors is the lack of a centralized property register to establish clear title for due diligence in purchase transactions, and to verify collateral in support of financing proposals. Perhaps more troublesome, especially from the standpoint of foreign investors, is the backlog of claims in the court system and the resulting inability for timely conflict resolution through legal due process.

For those already familiar with the risks of investment in transitional economies, Croatia offers many positive features. The country has for the first time in the wake of the 2000 elections, demonstrated a clear predisposition toward economic reform and tackling corruption. One by one, business constraints are being addressed and dealt with. Business registration, for instance, formerly a key impediment to SME creation, has been greatly simplified; and the measures to create a more friendly business climate, largely in pursuit of increased employment, are beginning to take hold. Foreign direct investment (FDI), led by Germany, Austria, the UK, the US, Italy and Luxemburg, is on the rise and tops the list of its southeastern European neighbours at US$3.8 billion since 2000, much of it in the form of privatization investment. A great opportunity remains for foreign companies looking for strategic partners in Croatia. SMEs should figure prominently in this respect and provide an excellent means with which to establish production and distribution bases. Those in first will gain a foothold into southeastern Europe, a region whose pent-up demand for products and services is expected to yield substantial increases in consumer and industrial markets.

A factor further enhancing Croatia's attractiveness to foreign investors interested in SMEs is the existence of HAMAG and the Chamber of Commerce to aid them in their search. Each are capable and motivated to assist investors to locate enterprises for collaboration or investment. Depending on the nature of the partnership, they may also be able to assist SMEs to finance new technology or acquire know-how.

These are important programmes because the willingness of banks to loan money to SMEs has been evolving at an unacceptably slow pace. Much of the banking sector is now foreign-owned (largely Austrian and Italian), a benefit of which has been the infusion of more sophisticated lending instruments. These notwithstanding, the absence of a fully functioning property register and the difficulty in processing claims through the courts are strong disincentives to financiers to loan on any other basis than heavy collateralization. Even relatively small loans offered to Croatian enterprises typically tie up a disproportionately large amount of their assets with imposed liens, which severely restrict their ability to obtain critical additional financing. Future cash flow is still generally not accepted on its own merit to obtain bank loans. Despite governmental loan and loan guarantee programmes designed to stimulate financing for SMEs, the amount of bank lending is still low in relation to demand. In recent years, typically just one-third of government funding provided to commercial banks for this purpose was actually loaned to SMEs as intended.

The advent of relatively near-term European Accession and the fiscal discipline this implies further reinforces Croatia's need to strengthen its SME sector as a reliable tax base and generator of employment. For these reasons and those already mentioned, a continuation in the positive trends already witnessed in Croatia may be expected; namely, an easing regulatory burden (including tax relief) and further stimulation of the banking sector involvement in SME financing.

## SME key sectors

Croatia's overall economic growth since the mid-1990s has been reasonably strong: real GDP growth has averaged about 4.5 per cent with inflation in the low single digits. A significant portion of this was directly attributable to the tourism sector, which continues to rebound after the devastation caused by the Balkan wars and generates about 20 per cent of GDP. Tourism in Croatia remains largely among the domain of SMEs, with small and medium-sized hotels, restaurants and tour operators at the core of the industry. Such establishments, especially in the medium-sized category, present interesting opportunities for investors. The widely anticipated growth in foreign tourists visiting Croatia, if the sector is sensibly managed and adheres to sustainable development practices, is likely to attract a large amount of investor interest within the next two to three years. Information technology, business services (package delivery, management training, catering, etc) and food processing also offer attractive SME investment possibilities.

Croatia is poised to begin more seriously accommodating foreign investors interested in SMEs. The country's structural impediments have thus far prevented a rapid influx of capital; however, once the flow of investment begins in earnest, available opportunities will be seized. Investors with even marginal interest in Croatia are best advised to begin their research into this intriguing market now.

# 3.8

# Tourism

*Croatian Chamber of Economy*

## Introduction

According to the estimates by the WTO, based on monthly data or preliminary full-year results, in the year 2004 there were more than 760 million international tourist arrivals, corresponding to an increase of 10 per cent.

It has been estimated that tourist turnover in Croatia will increase by three to five per cent in 2005 compared to 2004.

## Tourism figures for Croatia in 2004

The year 2004 recorded six per cent more tourists and two per cent more overnight stays in comparison with the previous year. Thus, in the period under analysis, 9.4 million tourists visited Croatia, with a total of 47.8 million overnight stays.

According to the Croatian National Bank's figures, international tourism revenues in the first nine months of 2004 amounted to US$6.2 billion.

## Tourist regions

Different Croatian tourist regions (Istria, Kvarner, Dalmatia, Dubrovnik and the Dubrovnik region, Zagreb as the capital and interior Croatia) have specific offerings. Further development of their distinctive services is the focus of the country's plan for tourism. The greatest number of tourists and overnight stays in 2004 was recorded in Istria (35 per cent), followed by Kvarner (24 per cent), Dalmatia (30 per cent) and Dubrovnik (8 per cent). Zagreb and interior Croatia accounted for the remaining three per cent.

# Composition of tourists

Foreign tourists account for as much as 89 per cent of total overnight stays, while domestic tourists account for just 11 per cent. In 2004, figures for foreign visitors showed a three per cent increase and for Croatian residents a one per cent decrease in the number of nights compared to the previous year.

In terms of overnight stays, visitors from Germany (26 per cent), Slovenia (12 per cent), Italy (13 per cent), the Czech Republic (10 per cent), and Austria (9 per cent) had a major share. Tourists from these five countries accounted for 70 per cent of nights. There is an evident increase in the number of tourists from all Western European countries.

The average tourist stay in Croatia in 2004 was five days (four days for domestic and five for foreign tourists). The foreign tourist market shows a new trend – demand for shorter holidays, so-called short-breaks, rather than longer, seven- or fourteen-day holiday arrangements.

# Accommodation capacity

In Croatia, tourists prevailingly stay at hotels. Around 35 per cent of them stayed at hotels in 2004, accounting for 28 per cent of overnight stays. Second to hotels are campsites, with 21 per cent of total tourists and 27 per cent of overnight stays, followed by private accommodation (19 per cent and 24 per cent respectively) and marinas (8 per cent and 2 per cent respectively). Croatia has 810,277 beds, 100,080 (12.4 per cent) of which are in hotels, 206,430 (25 per cent) in campsites, 332,240 (41.0 per cent) in private accommodation and 58,905 (7.3 per cent) in marinas.

# Transport used by tourists

In 2004, 35 per cent of tourists chose travel agencies and tour operators to organize their holidays, and 65 per cent made their own arrangements. In comparison with 2003, 2004 shows an eight per cent increase in organized travel and a five per cent increase in private arrangements.

# Tourist motivation

The motivation for most tourists to come to Croatia is still rest and relaxation on the coast, and also entertainment. However, motivation among visitors to Croatia shows a shift that is in line with tourist demand trends towards active holidays in clean environments, with healthy lifestyles and healthy food, which can be addressed through specially tailored tourism services.

# The importance of tourism for the Croatian economy

The Croatian National Bank's preliminary figures for the first nine months of 2004 show that international tourism generated 22.5 per cent of Croatian GDP. International tourism accounted for a 42.8 per cent share of total exports of goods and services, and for 74 per cent of total exported services. The per capita income from tourism in 2003 amounted to US$1,436.

# Investment in tourism

Investment in high quality tourist facilities that provide new jobs are a priority. The trend of rapid development in the tourist industry set by international tourist demand provides opportunities for various entrepreneurial initiatives and investment in a continuously growing sector. The Republic of Croatia holds stakes in 153 companies engaging in tourism and catering. Their total authorized capital is HRK14.1 billion, in which the state share is HRK3.9 billion, or 28 per cent. The government holds stakes above 50 per cent in 42 companies. These companies' total authorized capital amounts to HRK5 billion, and the government holds 72 per cent, which amounts to HRK3.6 billion.

# Tourism policy goals

The main goals for the development of tourism are to profile Croatia as one of the best tourist destinations in the Mediterranean and Europe, and to increase earnings from tourism, as it belongs to the group of most profitable industries, by raising spending in tourism, especially the so-called 'non-room-and-board consumption', and by extending the season.

To implement the tourism development policy in a way to achieve the goals set, it is necessary to create new types of offerings and products in tourism, a distinctive image for Croatian tourist destinations and regions, to raise the quality of accommodation, catering and other services in the tourist industry, while at the same time protecting the environment and cultural and historical heritage.

# Advantages of Croatian tourism

The most important advantages that the Croatian tourist industry can use in the promotion of its tourist destinations and products in foreign markets are the preserved nature and environment, cultural and historical heritage, the mild Mediterranean climate, proximity to European markets and long-established tradition of tourism.

In line with current trends in international tourism demand, the Croatian tourism industry should be further developed through various forms of selective tourism, while taking local peculiarities into account: nautical tourism, dive tourism, cruises on motorized sailing ships, rural tourism, equestrian tourism, sports tourism, day-trip tourism, health tourism, adventure tourism, conference tourism, eco-tourism, hunting tourism, fishing tourism, cultural tourism and religious tourism.

## Value added tax

The VAT rate for all services in tourism is 22 per cent and, since January 2001, a zero rate applies to all organized tourist arrivals from abroad. In order to be competitive with Mediterranean and other international tourist markets, the tourist industry calls for adjusting the VAT rate to rates compatible with competing countries, ie for a differential VAT rate for tourism.

## The hotel industry

Accommodation quality shows an improving trend. Currently, the majority of facilities have three stars (43 per cent), and eight per cent are four- or five-star hotels.

Most beds are in small, family-run hotels and B&Bs, which ensure personalized services and are tailored to guests' needs. They are known in the market as 'boutique hotels'. Trends in the hotel industry are towards specialized services in areas such as sports, health, conferences, and also amenities for gourmets, singles, naturists, etc.

Hotels and restaurants employ 81,000 people, and it is estimated that the whole tourism sector directly employs 140,000 and an additional 175,000 indirectly.

## Travel agencies and tour operators

In the first nine months of 2004, Croatia had 840 registered travel agencies with branch offices (source: CBS). Last year, the Croatian travel industry employed 3,686 people. In the first nine months of 2003, Croatian travel agencies brought 3.3 million tourists (domestic and foreign) into the country, which resulted in 19.2 million overnight stays. The majority of travel agencies in Croatia are registered either as tour operators or agents. Travel agencies are one of the most important channels for marketing Croatian tourism. Their programmes contribute to the promotion of Croatia as a tourist destination all around the world.

# Nautical tourism

Nautical tourism is one of the most attractive and prosperous forms of Croatian tourism. In 2004, the number of tourists in marinas had risen by 13 per cent and the number of overnight stays had risen by 12 per cent compared to the previous year. Nautical tourists accounted for eight per cent of the total number of tourists.

Croatia has 50 marinas, of which 21 are within the system of ACI Marinas. Berths at sea totalled 14,730. In comparison to the year before, 2003 showed an increase in the marina traffic by 10 per cent. At the same time, there were more than 150 charter companies with approximately 2,700 boats, and a 30 per cent increase in turnover was noted.

Strong growth over the previous few years could also be noticed in the field of dive tourism. More than 150 diving centres were registered. There was also an increase in the field of motorized sailing ships, a distinct segment of nautical tourism. Broken down by nations, for the 11,793 vessels using permanent berths, the ranking was as follows: Austria (27 per cent), Germany (23 per cent), Croatia (23 per cent), Slovenia (6 per cent) and Italy (5 per cent). There were a total of 176,527 vessels in transit. It has been estimated that nautical tourism will be on a rising trend, considering Croatia's great potential as a leading Mediterranean country in nautical tourism.

# Health tourism

Health tourism provides various offerings at the seaside (ie thalassotherapy) and in thermal health resorts. Health tourism is based on natural healing factors that combine different kinds of medical, preventive and wellness programmes adapted to the needs of specific tourist groups.

In this sector of tourism, Croatia has 6,000 beds in 18 health establishments. The numbers of tourists and overnight stays are constantly growing. In 2003, health resorts were visited by 22,228 tourists, with a total of 212,729 overnight stays, or 11 per cent more on the previous year. From the total number of tourists in 2003, 9,071 (40.8 per cent) were foreigners, generating a total of 75,583 (35.5 per cent) overnight stays.

According to surveys, domestic tourists account for more than 90 per cent of the guests in continental health resorts. However, depending on the resort, foreign tourists constitute between 30 per cent and 45 per cent of all guests in seaside resorts, and the average stay lasts 15.5 days.

The main potential for the future development of health tourism lies in the diversity of natural resources and ecological quality. Other important advantages are also curative waters and a favourable climate.

# Rural tourism

According to a survey carried out in 2003, there are 70 per cent more registered rural households engaged in tourism, which testifies to the constant progress and continuity in this economic sector. The official tourism policy has recognized the huge potential of rural households as well as the possibility of developing this segment of tourism. Therefore, a number of incentives have been introduced to pave the way for development and investment in this very attractive tourism product. The development and business orientation of every family farm engaged in tourism as an additional activity should be based on the creation of a specific tourist product in accordance with the motto 'tourism as a way of life'. In doing so, we promote all our comparative advantages – a pure and unpolluted environment, diversity of Croatian rural and family cuisine, and the special historical and cultural heritage of Croatian rural regions.

This segment of tourism is best developed in Istria, Dubrovnik-Neretva and Šibenik-Knin counties.

# Adventure tourism

Adventure tourism is a very promising and attractive form of selective tourism, and one which Croatia can offer to domestic and foreign markets. In the foreign market, a constant increase can be noticed in the number of participants in this form of travel.

Croatia has great possibilities for the development of adventure tourism due to its natural resources and all requisite comparative advantages. Primarily, this means a healthy environment and natural resources that could be used in different forms of active holidays.

Adventure excursions consist of different types of active holidays for tourists, for example team building (organizing social activities in order to improve relationships among group members), as well as all adventure events and sports organized as part of adventure products – rafting, free climbing, big wall climbing, trekking, biking, mountain biking, river kayaking, sea kayaking, canyoning, canoeing, cave exploring, horse trekking, adventure diving, balloon flying, paragliding, windsurfing, sky diving, paint ball, jeep safari and adventure races as a new form of extreme sports.

# Campsites

Croatia has 470 campsites along the coast, of which 334 are mini campsites with more than 190,000 camping places. In comparison with

2003, in 2004 the number of overnight stays in campsites increased by five per cent (campsites account for 27 per cent of all overnight stays in Croatia). The most prominent nationalities among campers come from Germany, Slovenia, Austria, Italy and the Netherlands. In terms of European standards of camping tourism, Croatia is in the middle of the rank list, while the biggest improvements in services and facilities can be noticed in Istria and Kvarner, whose campsites got the highest ratings. According to the German ADAC, investment and development in Croatian campsites have an upward tendency. Of the total number of campsites, 73 per cent of them were ranked in the 3rd category, and will be necessary to raise their quality in order to increase income and create a better image. The daily spending in campsites is US$25 (source: TOMAS 2001).

## Conference tourism

Conference tourism is one of the most profitable segments of tourism in the world. The number of conference participants and travel incentives is constantly growing, as is the number of tourist destinations that are being profiled as good conference destinations.

Croatia has started to develop its conference tourism in the last few years (currently, there are 75 convention centres) and Zagreb, Istria, Dubrovnik and Opatija are the leading Croatian destinations in terms of investment in the conference industry and organization of conferences.

Conference tourism in Croatia is expected to grow, and investment in high-category hotels, additional conference infrastructure, high-quality services and overall offerings should distinguish Croatia as a conference destination in demand.

## Croatian tourism in the world tourism industry

International tourism is one of the most expanding fields of the world economy. Europe, and particularly the Mediterranean, still remains the most important tourist destination and a major tourist market. The World Tourism Organization predicts a three per cent annual growth rate for the Mediterranean, where Croatia is emphasized as one of the countries with the highest growth rates in terms of international tourist arrivals (8.4 per cent).

# Tourism figures for Croatia in 2003 and 2004

**Table 3.8.1** Tourist arrivals

| Tourist arrivals | 2003 | 2004 | Index 2004/2003 |
|---|---|---|---|
| Total | 8,877,978 | 9,412,276 | 106 |
| Domestic | 1,469,388 | 1,500,402 | 102 |
| Foreign | 7,408,590 | 7,911,874 | 107 |

*Source:* Central Bureau of Statistics (CBS); compiled by the Croatian Chamber of Economy (CCE)

**Table 3.8.2** Overnight stays

| Tourist overnights | 2003 | 2004 | Index 2004/2003 |
|---|---|---|---|
| Total | 46,635,139 | 47,797,287 | 102 |
| Domestic | 5,311,991 | 5,280,962 | 99 |
| Foreign | 41,323,148 | 42,516,325 | 103 |

*Source*: CBS; compiled by CCE

# Croatian tourism figures from 1994 to 2003

**Table 3.8.3** Tourist arrivals ('000s)

| Year | Total | Domestic | Foreign |
|---|---|---|---|
| 1994 | 3,655 | 1,127 | 2,528 |
| 1995 | 2,610 | 1,125 | 1,485 |
| 1996 | 4,186 | 1,271 | 2,915 |
| 1997 | 5,585 | 1,407 | 4,178 |
| 1998 | 5,852 | 1,353 | 4,499 |
| 1999 | 5,127 | 1,322 | 3,805 |
| 2000 | 7,137 | 1,305 | 5,832 |
| 2001 | 7,860 | 1,316 | 6,544 |
| 2002 | 8,320 | 1,376 | 6,944 |
| 2003 | 8,878 | 1,469 | 7,409 |
| 2004 | 9,412 | 1,500 | 7,912 |

*Source*: CBS, Compiled by CCE

**Table 3.8.4** Overnight stays ('000s)

| Year | Total | Domestic | Foreign |
|------|-------|----------|---------|
| 1994 | 20,377 | 4,450 | 15,927 |
| 1995 | 13,151 | 4,388 | 8,763 |
| 1996 | 21,860 | 4,941 | 16,919 |
| 1997 | 30,775 | 5,661 | 25,114 |
| 1998 | 31,852 | 5,307 | 26,545 |
| 1999 | 27,126 | 5,241 | 21,885 |
| 2000 | 39,183 | 5,138 | 34,045 |
| 2001 | 43,405 | 5,021 | 38,384 |
| 2002 | 44,692 | 4,981 | 39,711 |
| 2003 | 46,635 | 5,312 | 41,323 |
| 2004 | 47,797 | 5,281 | 42,516 |

*Source:* CBS, Compiled by CCE

# The Croatian Chamber of Economy (CCE)

Within the Tourism and Catering Industry Department of the Croatian Chamber of Economy, there operate several associations and their affiliated groups and professional associations. Gathering business entities into appropriate organizations within the CCE creates links between its members that facilitate problem solution as well as the (re)presentation of coordinated views before bodies and institutions. Further, it also facilitates the accomplishment of common interests and the organization of joint promotional activities on a national level for the benefit of Croatian tourism.

Croatian professional associations include the following:

Hoteliers' and Caterers' Association

- Hoteliers Group;

- Caterers Group;

- Campers Group;

- Professional Group – Campsites in Primorje-Gorski Kotar County.

Croatian Association of Travel Agencies (HUPA)

Croatian Nautical Tourism Association

- Croatian Marinas Group;

- Croatian Vessel Chartering Group;

- Croatian Diving Tourism Group;

- Croatian Motor-Sailboat Cruises and Excursions Group.

## Farm Tourism Affiliation

- Professional Tourism Group – Farmers of Primorje-Gorski Kotar County;
- Professional Tourism Group – Farmers of Šibenik-Knin County;
- Professional Tourism Group – Farmers of Split-Dalmatia County;
- Professional Tourism Group – Farmers of Dubrovnik-Neretva County.

## Health Tourism Affiliation

- Professional Group – Croatian Special Hospitals and Health Resorts;
- Professional Group – Croatian Wellness Centres;
- Professional Group – Hotels for Seniors.

## Croatian Adventure Tourism Group

- Professional Group – Providers of Adventure Events and Sports;
- Professional Group – Travel Agencies Organizing Adventure Trips;
- Professional Group for Improving the Safety of Adventure Events;
- Professional Group for Croatian Protected Areas (national and nature parks).

## Croatian Family Accommodation Group

- Professional Group – Family Accommodation Providers of Gorski Kotar County;
- Professional Group – Family Accommodation Providers of Šibenik-Knin County;
- Professionl Group – Family Accommodation Providers of Zadar County;
- Professional Group – Family Accommodation Providers of Split-Dalmatia County.

Croatian Chamber of Economy, Tourism and Catering Industry Department
Managing Director: Ondina Šegvi
Rooseveltov trg 2
HR-10000 Zagreb, Croatia

PO Box 630
Tel: +385 (01) 45 61 570 or (01) 45 61 660
Fax: +385 (01) 48 28 499
Email: turizam@hgk.hr
Details on members and activities are available at: www.hgk.hr,
www.biznet.hr

Croatian Chamber of Economy
Headquarters
Rooseveltov trg 2
HR-10 000 Zagreb, Croatia
PO Box 630
Tel: +385 (01) 45 61 555
Fax: +385 (01) 48 28 380
Email: hgk@hgk.hr

# 3.9

# The Telecommunications Market

*VIPnet*

## Introduction

The telecommunications market has been ranked as the market with greatest potential in 2005 since, in comparison to other sectors, this sector has been constantly adapted to European Union (EU) standards. According to the recommendations of the EU regarding the complete liberalization of the telecommunications market, one mobile and two fixed line services providers were granted licences and concessions, which increased the number of operators from three to six in only two months.

Liberalization of the telecommunications market started in 1999 when the second GSM operator VIPnet began commercial work. In 2000, Croatia became a member of the World Trade Organization (WTO), which resulted in the increase of internet services providers, who were not obliged to use the national operator's infrastructure. Further liberalization of the telecommunications market was conducted in two phases. The first phase started on 1 January 2003 when the market was opened for other operators. The interest of fixed line services providers was expected in the second phase, since the national fixed line operator T-Com is obliged to provide free access to the local loop to all other operators beginning 1 January 2005, thus marking the beginning of the third phase. At the end of 2004, two companies – Optima Telekom and Portus – were granted licences for providing fixed line telecommunications services. They are expected to start commercial business at the end of the first half of 2005.

On the other hand, the mobile communications market saw a new player, consortium *Treća sreća* (Third Time is the Charm), consisting of the Swedish mobile operator Tele2 and nine Croatian companies. The total number of mobile subscribers in Croatia was estimated at 2.54 million at the end of 2004, approximately equally divided between T-Mobile and VIPnet, the current GSM operators in Croatia. As the mobile penetration rate in neighbouring countries is significantly higher (eg Slovenia 90 per cent), it is expected that the increase in penetration rate will expand from the present 60 per cent to 75 per cent by 2006. Looking at the structure of customers, the Croatian mobile communications market is predominantly prepaid, with only 15 per cent of postpaid customers.

The internet penetration rate was rather slow in Croatia due to high interconnection costs for service providers and an inadequate regulatory framework. According to recent public opinion polling, 1.2 million people above the age of 15 uses the internet at least once a month, which is a nine per cent increase on 2003. Approximately 70 per cent of those can be described as regular surfers. The number of surfers is expected to grow in 2005, bearing in mind that 46.6 per cent of Croatian households have a personal computer. The rapid increase in the number of broadband users in 2004 also confirms these expectations.

# Telecommunication companies

## *Fixed telecommunications*

### T-Hrvatski Telekom

The national telecommunications services provider Hrvatske Telekomunikacije (Croatian Telecommunications) was rebranded in 2004 and became T-Hrvatski Telekom, a part of Deutsche Telekom's global T-brand. Fixed line services provider HTtel and internet services provider HTnet were united into T-Com, while the mobile telecommunications services provider HTmobile became T-Mobile. T-Hrvatski Telekom is still the only full spectrum telecommunications service provider in Croatia.

The equity capital of T-Hrvatski Telekom consists of 81,888,535 common shares with the nominal value of HRK100 per share. The majority shareholder is Deutsche Telekom with 51 per cent, while the Croatian government holds the remaining 49 per cent. According to the Law on Privatization of Croatian Telecoms, the government plans to assign seven per cent of its shares to Homeland War veterans, sell another seven per cent to current and former employees of T-Hrvatski Telekom and place the remaining 21 per cent of shares on the stock market.

According to the 2003 Annual Report, fixed line services generated HRK4.9 billion income, which is a drop of 3.1 per cent in relation to 2002. This drop was caused by several factors: Voice over Internet Protocol (VoIP) services providers took over a part of the international voice traffic; calls from fixed to mobile lines and analogue access generated less revenue; and the introduction of new fixed line tariff models decreased revenues a further one per cent. On the other hand, mobile telephony income increased by 16.8 per cent, amounting to HRK2.3 billion and thus creating the greatest contribution to the consolidated income earnings of the group.

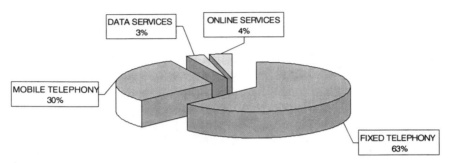

**Figure 3.9.1** Income structure in 2003

**Table 3.9.1** Financial ratios

| Business results in HRK million | 2003 | 2002 |
| --- | --- | --- |
| Total income earnings from core business | 8,051 | 7,690 |
| Consolidated income | 7,840 | 7,479 |
| Corporate earnings from core business | 1,679 | 2,158 |
| Corporate earnings in the financial year | 1,488 | 1,864 |
| Total assets | 16,606 | 15,257 |
| Long-term liabilities | 698 | 726 |
| Total capital and reserves | 14,517 | 13,198 |

*T-Com*
T-Com is a fixed line services and internet provider. T-Com's network consists of 100 per cent digital switching equipment and 15,000 kilometres of fibre optics. T-Com has the capacity to serve 2.3 million subscribers, although the actual number of fixed telephony subscribers at the end of 2003 was 1.7 million, with the penetration rate of 39.6 per cent.

In 2003, the majority owner, Deutsche Telekom, announced its intention to invest most of its resources into the development of broadband internet. This investment resulted in a significant increase in the number of broadband customers, from 4,000 in January 2004 to 20,000 in the closing months of 2004.

*Optima Telekom*
Optima Telekom became the second fixed line services provider in November 2004, after being awarded a 30-year licence by the Croatian

Telecommunications Agency. The company is a part of Optima Group, specializing in building customer call centres in southeastern Europe. Optima Telekom is led by Roland Žuvanić, former Minister of Maritime Affairs, Transport and Communications (today the Ministry of the Sea, Tourism, Transport and Development). The company is expected to begin offering its services in the first half of 2005.

*Portus*

Portus is the third fixed line services provider, which was also granted a 30-year licence in November 2004. Portus is owned by the EM Group, consisting of Mobart (mobile services and applications), EM Service Centre and PINE (transport and logistics), and has been active in the Croatian market for 10 years. The company has already presented its brand H1 and announced the provision of services for the spring of 2005. Portus also plans to build its own telecommunications network consisting of the central communications loop, loops for interconnection with T-Com and mobile operators, and telecommunication fibres leased from the existing operator in fixed line services.

*Other owners of telecommunications infrastructure*

Although they do not provide commercial telecommunication services, the following are the most significant owners of telecommunications infrastructure: Hrvatska elektroprivreda (Croatian Electricity Company), Hrvatske željeznice (Croatian Railways), Jadranski naftovod (Adriatic Pipeline) and Hrvatske autoceste (Croatian Highways).

## Mobile telecommunications

*T-Mobile*

T-Mobile is T-Com's separate legal entity for the provision of mobile communications services. The company is a part of T-Mobile International, which has subsidiaries in seven countries around the world and provides services for more than 60 million customers. Apart from holding the concession for providing GSM services, T-Mobile provides services in the NMT network but this network will cease to exist after March 2005. T-Mobile has also signed a 20-year UMTS agreement. Its market share reached 52.5 per cent at the end of 2003 (more than 1.3 million customers) and is presently the strongest mobile operator in Croatia.

*VIPnet*

VIPnet is the first private GSM operator in Croatia. Its 100 per cent shareholder is Mobilkom Austria. On 7 September 1998, VIPnet won the tender process for a 10-year concession for the construction and operation of the second GSM network in Croatia.

VIPnet is considered to be the best second GSM entry in Europe. After three years of commercial work the company entered the top 10 list of Croatian companies. In only five years of presence on the Croatian market, VIPnet surpassed one million customers, currently serving more than 1,240,000 people. In 2003, VIPnet signed an exclusive partnership agreement with Vodafone, thus enabling Croatian customers to use the benefits of Vodafone services. Several months later, the company presented EDGE, and in December 2004 VIPnet was awarded the UMTS concession for a 20-year period, fulfilling its plans to become the only company offering two types of 3G services, EDGE and UMTS, in 2005. Only one month after the execution of the Concession Agreement, on 18 January, VIPnet had its first commercial UMTS service on offer. Under the Concession Agreement, VIPnet has undertaken to achieve a 25 per cent coverage of the population within two years; such coverage has almost already been achieved. Four major cities – Osijek, Split, Rijeka and Zagreb – are covered by the UMTS network. There are already more than 60 UMTS networks in the world; however, VIPnet is one of the first operators in the world to offer two 3G technologies to its customers on a commercial basis – EDGE and UMTS.

*Treća sreća*

*Treća sreća* (Third time is the Charm) is the consortium consisting of the Swedish operator Tele2 and nine Croatian companies – Dalekovod (construction engineering), Jamnica (beverage industry), FIMA Holding (an investment holding company), Croatia osiguranje (the largest insurance company), Nexe grupa (construction materials company), Konstruktor-inženjering (construction company), Lura (dairy industry), Institut građevinarstva Hrvatske (Institute for Construction) and Privredna banka Zagreb (the second largest Croatian bank).

*Treća sreća* was granted the concession for providing services in the second and third generation mobile networks in December 2004, and is expected to offer services in the first half of 2005. The consortium would most likely not offer 3G services before 2006.

## Major internet providers

The internet market is the least developed of all telecommunications market segments in Croatia. There are only eight active commercial ISPs (AT&T, Europronet, GlobalNet, HTNet, Iskon, Transintercom, Vodatel and VIPonline) and one academic ISP (CARNet), serving the total of 576,000 paying subscribers (mid-2003 data) out of an estimated 935,000 users. The relatively small number of ISPs is the result of strict regulations and market conditions, which do not fully support the development of competition. Namely, T-Com, a subsidiary of T-Hrvatski Telekom, has a major market share with 62 per cent in dial-up access and 45 per cent in the leased line market. The increase in internet penetration rate is slower than expected due to the still unsatisfactory penetration rate of personal computers and rather slow economic growth in the country.

By July 2003, Croatian internet subscribers used 1.4 billion minutes of dial-up connection time. Voice over Internet Protocol (VoIP) in Central and Eastern Europe represents approximately three per cent of total international calls, and, according to some estimates, this could increase to 24 per cent by the year 2007. The most significant providers of VoIP in Croatia are Nexcom, Ceetel and Amis Tel but there are also several other companies that offer VoIP. According to the existing *Rules on fees for rendered telecommunication services*, the provider of the service 'voice over 'internet' will, in the first year, pay the fee of HRK500,000 for the licence and two per cent of the income in subsequent years. Transintercom is the VoIP provider with the largest share on the market. In 2003, VIPnet became a VoIP provider in order to expand the range of services for its business customers. It is estimated that VoIP will grow at the annual rate of 62 per cent in the following four years, while, in 2007, it will reach 24 per cent of total international voice transport.

## Iskon

IskonInternet is the biggest private ISP provider in Croatia with 17.3 per cent share of the market. During 2000 its portfolio was strengthened by significant investments from the United States and Germany (Adriatic Net Investors invested US$5 million and Dresdener Kleinwort Benson Private Equity US$6 million). European and American know-how has contributed to Iskon's development of internet services, and presently it is the strongest in all transition countries. Today it has 150 employees, regional offices and points of internet-connection (so-called POPs) in Zagreb, Rijeka, Split, Osijek, Dubrovnik, Pula, Poreč, Varaždin and Čakovec. IskonInternet is the co-founder of Etours (e-commerce), Eona (the first Croatian safe internet service provider – CASP) and Sanoma Magazines Zagreb. In 2004, IskonInternet offered their customers VoIP and DSL services. Furthermore, IskonInternet maintains a web portal www.klik.hr, which records more than 12 million page views per month, approximately 70 per cent of Croatia's entire internet traffic.

# Globalnet

In July 1999, Globalnet was the first private ISP in Croatia to receive a concession for unlimited line numbers for providing services via the public telephone network. The majority owners of Globalnet are Croatia Capital Partnership (CCP) investment fund and the EBRD. During 2000 and 2001, they increased the capital of Globalnet Group with US$4.2 million. M-San Group, one of the biggest distributors of IT equipment in Croatia, takes part in the ownership structure as well. During 2000, Globalnet provided complete know-how as well as the necessary programme back-up for founding two ISPs in Bosnia and Herzegovina. The first knot of Globalnet Group's Points of Presence (POPs) outside Zagreb, was opened in February 2000 in Rijeka, providing the citizens of Primorsko, Goranska County with access to the internet at a local tariff.

## *Cable TV operators*

Cable TV (CATV) operators in southeastern Europe are oriented towards residential customers, offering TV programmes, voice services and the internet. Unfortunately, such orientation and lack of capital does not make them serious competitors to DSL. Furthermore, most of their potential customers are not with the range of cable networks, which calls for significant additional investment. Even though the price of modems and installation have dropped, the price of subscriptions rose and is higher than the price of DSL. Digital City Media (DCM) and Adriatic-Kabel are the two cable TV market leaders, with 40,000 and 12,000 customers respectively (out of the total of 95,000 customers).

# 3.10

# Mobile Telecommunications

*VIPnet*

## Introduction

Having obtained the candidate status for European Union (EU) accession, Croatia now has to make certain concrete moves towards achieving a fully liberalized telecommunications market. The new Telecommunications Act was the first step towards this, while the recent subordinate regulations additionally support the Ministry of the Sea, Tourism, Transport and Development in its intentions to achieve compliance with EU standards in the shortest possible time.

The value of the Croatian telecommunications market was estimated at €1.5 billion in 2004, according to Croatian business magazines. The penetration rate of mobile telephony is close to 60 per cent, and it is expected to rise to 75 per cent by the end of 2006. Comparing Croatia with the newest EU members, the Croatian telecommunications market is not lagging far behind (except in the number of telecommunications services providers). In its report, the European Commission stated that the most important characteristics of the new EU members are low competition, high prices of interconnection and services, implementation of broadband and the third generation of mobile telecommunications. All these characteristics can be applied to Croatia as well. The mobile telecommunications market is divided between two operators, T-Mobile and VIPnet, which hold almost equal shares of the market consisting of 2.54 million customers.

The third operator, *Treća sreća* (Third Time is the Charm) was granted the combined GSM-UMTS concession in December 2004, and announced its intention to offer voice services in the first half of 2005. The new operator also announced harsher competition by offering lower prices than those of existing operators. On the other hand, both VIPnet and T-Mobile stated that they were prepared for competition and that their goal was not to be the cheapest operators, but to offer high quality products and services at fair prices.

Present operators see their chance in 3G services, announcing the first mobile headsets and services beginning in Spring 2005. Even though there are 75 UMTS operators in Europe, 30 of which provide commercial services and 21 that are still in the test phase, Croatian operators are optimistic because Croatian customers have proved to be very receptive to new technologies. Both operators paid HRK132 million (approximately €17.25 million) for the concession and are obliged to pay an annual fee of one per cent of their total income from UMTS. Moreover, according to subordinate regulations, the operators have to pay HRK20 million annually for the use of radio frequencies. Only one month after the execution of the Concession Agreement, on 18 January, VIPnet introduced first commercial UMTS service in its offer. Under the Concession Agreement, VIPnet has undertaken to achieve a 25 per cent coverage of the population within two years; such coverage has almost already been achieved. Four major cities – Osijek, Split, Rijeka and Zagreb – are covered by the UMTS network. There are already more than 60 UMTS networks in the world; however, VIPnet is one of the first operators in the world to offer two 3G technologies to its customers on a commercial basis – EDGE and UMTS.

T-Mobile and VIPnet work with Siemens and Ericsson on infrastructure development and manufacturing and will expand this cooperation to 3G equipment. They plan to upgrade existing sites and gradually add new locations in order to achieve the proscribed coverage. On the other hand, one of the companies in the *Treća sreća* consortium is Dalekovod, a construction engineering company. Dalekovod also manufactures mobile telephony base stations, so the consortium is expected to use their expertise in the infrastructure sector. However, it is not yet known when *Treća sreća* will offer 3G services.

With the aim of establishing and maintaining better communication with the public, VIPnet and T-Mobile, together with Ericsson Nikola Tesla and Siemens, founded the Mobile Communications Association of Croatia in mid-2004. The Association's primary goal is to provide relevant information to all stakeholders, such as the local community, elected citizens' representatives, interest groups and the general public. Until now, the Association was mainly focused on educating the general public on the electromagnetic radiation of mobile headsets and base stations and their influence on human health.

# The mobile communications market

In 2003, 2.54 million Croatian mobile telecommunications customers spent 1.91 billion minutes talking on their mobile headsets, which is a 27.7 per cent increase on 2002. In the first trimester of 2004, the customers spent 481 million minutes talking, which is a 2.2 per cent drop in relation to the last trimester of 2003. The Croatian mobile communications market is primarily prepaid, and the share of postpaid customers is only 15 per cent. The market has one other specific characteristic – a high percentage of text messaging. Croatian customers on average send more than 70 text messages per month. The total value of mobile messaging worldwide was US$94.5 million, while the value in the entire South East Europe amounted to US$1.2 billion.

# Services

Apart from voice and very popular short message services, VIPnet and T-Mobile offer a wide range of advanced services adjusted to the needs of various types of customer. M-Commerce services are the most popular. M-parking, developed by VIPnet together with Croatian experts, was the first among such services and it immediately generated exceptional interest from operators from various countries. After the success of this service, operators started developing various advanced macro-payment services in cooperation with banks and card companies. Today, mobile telecommunications customers can top up prepaid accounts, buy various types of tickets, pay their mobile bills or even pay off loans in Raiffeisenbank Austria. The latest service allows T-Mobile customers to pay via m-pin in a number of shops around the country, thanks to the m-pay system developed in cooperation with Privredna banka Zagreb, the second largest bank in Croatia.

Both operators offer Location Based Services (LBS), General Packet Radio Service (GPRS), and Multimedia Messaging Service (MMS) designed for various types of prepaid and postpaid customers. LBS-based services are highly developed, enabling foreign visitors to find their desired destinations (monuments, pharmacies, banks, etc), choose the best route, find out the weather forecast and other necessary information. Moreover, in 2004 VIPnet introduced EDGE, high-speed wireless 3G data technology, which enables significantly faster data transfer than GPRS, and now, just recently, VIPnet introduced UMTS.

# Mobile operators

## T-Mobile

Hrvatske Telekomunikacije (HT), the national telecommunications services provider, began to offer analogue mobile telephony services on the NMT network in 1991, while in 1996 the company launched GSM for postpaid users. After the arrival of competition in 1999, HT offered prepaid tariff models to their customers.

In 2002, HT transferred the mobile telecommunication business to its 100 per cent-owned subsidiary, *HT mobilne komunikacije* (HTmobile). HTmobile started its commercial activities on 1 January 2003, until then GSM and NMT services had been provided by HT. In October 2004, HTmobile was rebranded and renamed T-Mobile, thus becoming a part of Deutsche Telekom's global T brand.

T-Mobile has signed a GSM Concession Agreement for a 10-year period, and an NMT Concession Agreement for 30 years, starting from 16 September 1999. However, the NMT network will cease to exist after March 2005, due to a steady drop in the number of customers. In addition to the initial concession fee in amount of HRK100 million, HTmobile currently pays an annual concession fee of HRK4 million for the NMT Concession, and HRK5 million for the GSM Concession. In December 2004, T-Mobile was granted the UMTS concession, for which the company paid HRK132 million. T-Mobile has more than 1.3 million customers and, at the end of 2003, its market share reached 52.5 per cent.

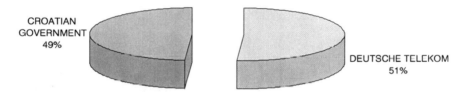

CROATIAN GOVERNMENT 49%

DEUTSCHE TELEKOM 51%

**Figure 3.10.1** Ownership structure of T-Mobile

## *VIPnet*

VIPnet is the first private GSM operator in Croatia, founded in 1998. On 1 January 2005, Mobilkom Austria became the 100 per cent owner of VIPnet.

In September 1998, the company won a 10-year concession for the construction and operation of the second GSM network in Croatia. The concession was granted and the contract was signed on the 30 October 1998. VIPnet's network, established in the record time of only eight months, went 'on air' in July 1999.

VIPnet is the most successful second GSM entry in Europe. They had 50 per cent of market share after only six months of operating and a positive net income on the first full year of operating. The one-million-customer mark was surpassed in the third quarter of 2002 and growth rates, which are among the most important key figures, are constantly rising.

After the launch of the first full-coverage GPRS network in Croatia in May 2001, VIPnet also made M-Commerce a priority. In 2003, VIPnet, as a member of the Mobilkom Austria Group, signed an exclusive partnership agreement with Vodafone. The year after, the company implemented Enhanced Data Rates for Global Evolution (EDGE), 3G technology that delivers broadband-like data speeds to mobile devices, and managed to cover the whole country in record time. In December 2004, VIPnet was granted the UMTS concession, and introduced the first UMTS service in January 2005.

Looking at financial results, the total profits of the company, in 2003, increased by 12.5 per cent to €341.3 million, profit before taxation, interest, depreciation and amortization increased by 41 per cent to €139.2 million, while profit before taxation increased by nearly 20 per cent to €66.6 million. Average revenue per user (ARPU) dropped by two per cent to €19.6. In 2003, VIPnet marked the increase of data services, mainly due to very intensive usage of the short messaging service (on average 73 SMS per user monthly), which recorded a 100 per cent increase to 2.1 million transactions in comparison with 2002.

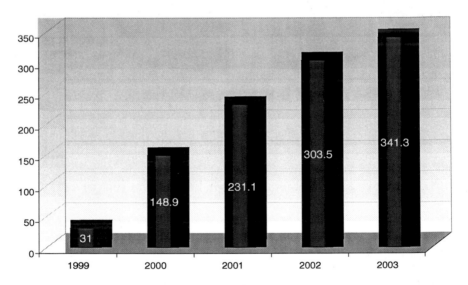

**Figure 3.10.2** Sales growth (in million €)

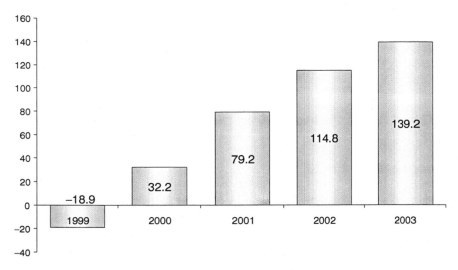

**Figure 3.10.3** Growth of EBITDA (in million €)

## Treća sreća

*Treća sreća* (Third time is the Charm) is the consortium consisting of the Swedish operator Tele2 and nine Croatian companies – Dalekovod (construction engineering), Jamnica (beverage industry), FIMA Holding (investment holding company), Croatia osiguranje (the largest insurance company), Nexe grupa (construction materials company), Konstruktor-inženjering (construction company), Lura (dairy industry), Institut građevinarstva Hrvatske (Institute for Construction) and Privredna banka Zagreb (the second largest Croatian bank). The head of *Treća sreća* consortium is Borislav Škegro, former Minister of Finance, and the director of Questus Investment Fund, who gathered together the aforementioned Croatian companies.

The consortium applied for the first tender for the new mobile operator in July 2004 and was the only company that submitted the offer on time. However, the Council of the Croatian Telecommunications Agency rejected the offer since *Treća sreća* applied only for the GSM concession and the proposed investment would not contribute to the development of the Croatian economy. *Treća sreća* participated in the second tender announced in October 2004, together with Croatia Mobile and Match Telecom. This time the consortium applied for the combined GSM-UMTS concession and offered a significantly improved investment programme. *Treća sreća* was granted the concession for GSM-UMTS in December 2004. It is expected that the new operator will offer voice services in the six-month period after being granted the concession.

CROATIAN COMPANIES
49%

TELE 2
51%

**Figure 3.10.4** Ownership structure of *Treća sreća*

# Prospects for 2005

The telecommunications sector in the EU is recording rapid growth, especially in the sector of mobile telephony and broadband. The penetration of mobile telephony reached 83 per cent or 379 million customers in 2004. The sector is expected to grow by 4.6 per cent, surpassing the growth of GDP and reaching the value of €277 million. Future prospects of the e-communications sector are getting better, intensifying competition on most of the markets.

The year 2005 will bring complete liberalization of the Croatian telecommunications market. The national operator will have to offer carrier pre-select and number portability options to all subscribers from 1 January 2005, while mobile operators are obliged to ensure number portability at the latest by 30 June 2005. The prices of telecommunications services are expected to drop by 20 per cent and the penetration rate of mobile communications is expected to increase to 75 per cent by 2006. On the other hand, ISPs and VoIP providers will also benefit from the liberalization, as they will be able to offer broadband directly to customers.

According to the *Strategy of the Development of Telecommunications and Internet*, operators will be encouraged to implement new and innovative telecommunications services and develop local content. According to the e-Croatia project and the accession of Croatia to the EU, usage of telecommunications services will also be promoted in state institutions and public services.

# 3.11

# Telecommunications: The Regulatory Framework

*VIPnet*

## Introduction

In the light of the newly gained candidate status for EU accession, Croatia is gradually adapting its regulatory framework with the *acquis communitaire*, accompanied by the necessary reforms in order to comply with EU standards. The new Telecommunications Act, passed in 2003, is already fully compliant with EU recommendations, and the government has outlined the following general goals regarding the telecommunications development in the Republic of Croatia:

- creating a legislative framework for more active participation in the new information society, in compliance with the guidance from the *Green Book on Convergence of the Telecommunications, Media, and Information Technology Sectors*;

- active participation in the development of information and communications technology (ICT);

- creating preconditions for a more complete harmonization with the regulations and standards of contemporary European electronic communications, such as the Interchange of Data between Administrations (IDA), ERO Frequency Information System (EFIS), Road Transport and Traffic Telematics (RTTT) etc.

The Republic of Croatia is a member of the International Telecommunications Union (ITU), Conférence Européenne des Administrations des Postes et Télécommunications (CEPT), the European Telecommunications Standards Institute (ETSI), the International Telecommunications Satellite Organization (INTELSAT), the International Mobile Satellite Organization (INMARSAT), the

European Telecommunications Satellite Organization (EUTELSAT), the Regional Agreement concerning the Radiotelephone Service (RAINWAT) and other organizations.

# Government bodies

## Ministry of the Sea, Tourism, Transport and Development

The Ministry of the Sea, Tourism, Transport and Development is responsible for the protection and exploitation of the Adriatic Sea, development of tourism policy and the organization of strategic infrastructure projects, including telecommunications. It participates in making secondary regulations regarding the telecommunications sector and proposes the telecommunication development strategy. The Ministry also performs administrative supervision of Croatian Telecommunications Agency, the telecommunications regulatory body in the Republic of Croatia. The Ministry of Maritime Affairs, Transportation and Communications is the beneficiary of the CARDS 2001 programme, *Further Legal Approximation and Capacity Building in the Telecommunications Sector*, through which it receives technical assistance in the process of drafting the legislative framework and bylaws for this sector.

# The regulatory framework

## The Telecommunications Act and relevant regulations

The new Telecommunications Act (Official Gazette No. 122/03, 158/03, 177/03), passed in July 2003, represents a new legislative framework based on the directives of the EU regulatory framework and the strategic documents of the Republic of Croatia in this area, such as the Strategy *Information and Communications Technology – Croatia in the 21st Century* (Official Gazette No. 109/02), the project *Croatian Telecommunications Market* and the *National Programme of the Republic of Croatia for the Integration into the European Union – 2003* (Official Gazette No. 30/03). The Telecommunications Act regulates the areas of telecommunications and radio communications, the manner and conditions for the provision of telecommunications services and activities, the rights and obligations of providers and users of telecommunications services, the construction, maintenance and use of telecommunications infrastructure and equipment, radio and telecommunications terminal equipment, the management of the radio-frequency spectrum, addressing and numbering space in the Republic of Croatia, electromagnetic compatibility, data protection and inspection and control in telecommunications.

The new Telecommunications Act regulates the telecommunications market, but it is also user-oriented. It ensures a high level of user protection, personal data protection and privacy protection, the optimal quality of telecommunications services and it promotes further development of a free and open telecommunications market.

The Act also consolidated the two regulatory bodies, the Telecommunications Institute and the Telecommunications Council, into the new Telecommunications Agency. The new Agency incorporated regulatory and administrative functions previously distributed between the Institute and the Council.

Other relevant laws and regulations in the field of telecommunications:

- general regulations for telecommunications service providers (Official Gazette No. 84/95);

- regulations regarding concession for performing public telecommunications activities (Official Gazette No. 88/01);

- regulations regarding network access and interconnection (Official Gazette No. 88/01);

- regulations of compensation for attending to telecommunication services and other telecommunication activities and payment (Official Gazette No. 88/01);

- regulations regarding compensation for radio frequency applications and the way of their payment (Official Gazette No. 88/01);

- regulations regarding technical conditions of construction and implementation of the telecommunication infrastructure (Official Gazette No. 88/01);

- Act on the Division of the Croatian Post and Telecommunications to the Croatian Post and the Croatian Telecommunications (Official Gazette No. 101/98);

- Electronic Media Act (Official Gazette No. 122/03);

- Croatian Radio and Television Act (Official Gazette No. 25/03).

## *The Croatian Telecommunications Agency*

The Agency is a national regulatory body in charge of performing regulatory and other activities within the framework and authorities determined by the Telecommunications Act. The Agency is an autonomous, non-profit and independent legal person with public authority, and is listed in the court registry as such. The Agency has to report on its activities to the Croatian Parliament by submitting the annual report to the government and parliament. The report includes the overview of the Agency's work in the past year and the current state and implementation of principles and goals regarding the regulation of the telecommunications market in Croatia.

The Agency passes decisions related to the granting and depriving of licences for telecommunications services (except radio and television), regulates relations between telecommunications services providers and performs other regulatory work proscribed by the Telecommunication Act.

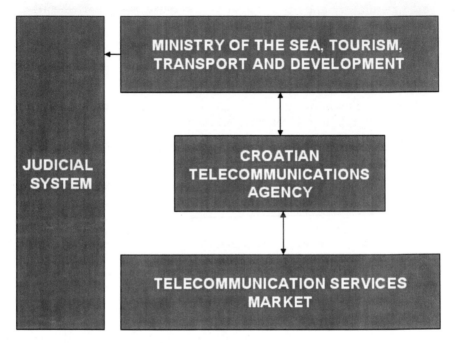

**Figure 3.11.1** The regulatory framework

## *Concession for provision of telecommunications services*

The right to provide telecommunications service is attained by a concession as specified in the Regulations on granting concessions in public telecommunications. A concession is granted in line with the provisions of the Telecommunications Act and, depending on the type of service, the level and size of the area in which the activity is performed. Concessions are given for a limited period not longer than 30 years, and the period is set depending on the type, quality and scope of the service. Technically, concessions of the same type and significance and the same scope of activity are awarded for the same duration, for example UMTS concession is granted for a period of 20 years.

Licences are issued for providing the following services:

- public telephone network at a fixed location;

- mobile communication services – NMT-450i standard;

- mobile communication services – E-GSM and DCS-1800 standard;

- mobile communication services – GSM900 standard;

- mobile communication services – UMTS standard;

- mobile communication services – E-GSM, GSM900 or DCS-1800 with UMTS;

- broadcasting services – TETRA, VSAT, S-PCS, TFTS and other;

- radio;

- TV;

- cable TV.

A company interested in obtaining a concession should submit a request in writing to the Croatian Telecommunications Agency. The request must contain the name and registered office of the company submitting the request, as well as copy of its registration, type and scope of the service for which the concession is requested, evidence on available sources of finance (bank guarantee), construction documents containing the estimated duration of construction, starting date and detailed description of all necessary equipment and facilities.

The price of the concession for voice telephony in the fixed network was lowered in 2004, from HRK40 to HRK8 million, for providing services on the national level, and the request for investment of at least €50 million (in kuna equivalent) into the infrastructure of telecommunication facilities, network or system over four years from the date the concession was granted, was abolished. The second generation mobile network fee amounts to HRK105 million, the price of the UMTS concession is HRK132 million, while the combined GSM-UMTS concession amounts to HRK172 million.

A company holding the concession for providing telecommunications services through the use of the radio spectrum in the system of second generation mobile network (GSM, E-GSM, DCS-1800) must, within two years after the concession was obtained, ensure the following coverage:

- GSM and E-GSM for at least 75 per cent of the population or 60 per cent of the territory of the Republic of Croatia;

- DCS-1800 for at least 40 per cent of the population.

The fee during the first and subsequent years of providing market telecommunications services via the radio spectrum in the second generation mobile network system (GSM, E-GSM, DCS-1800) is regulated by the *Rulebook on fees and charges for providing telecommunication services and other telecommunications activities*.

The concession for providing telecommunication services in the UMTS network includes the right to provide internet access and data transmission services aimed at providing new services, utilizing voice, data, video, multimedia etc, in such a way that it does not coincide with the concession for providing TV and radio services.

The UMTS services provided must meet minimum quality and availability requirements in the sense that they must be available to at least 25 per cent of Croatia's population within two years from the date the concession was obtained, and to at least 50 per cent of the country's population within a period of five years.

The amount of the fee during the first and subsequent years of providing telecommunication services via the radio spectrum in the third generation mobile network system (UMTS) is also regulated by the *Rulebook on fees and charges for providing telecommunication services and other telecommunication activities*.

# Telecommunications service providers in Croatia

According to the contract signed on 22 September 1999 for a period of 30 years, T-Croatian Telecommunications Inc has a concession for providing public voice services and market telecommunications services in the fixed network. Following the Telecommunications Act provisions, another two service providers – Optima Telekom and Portus – were granted licences in 2004.

There are currently two major players on the mobile communications market – T-Mobile Inc. and VIPnet Ltd. VIPnet signed the contract on 30 October 1998 for a period of 10 years, and T-Mobile Inc on 22 September 1999, also for a period of 10 years. The third GSM operator *Treća sreća* consortium, consisting of the Swedish operator Tele2 and nine Croatian companies, was granted the concession in December 2004, and is expected to offer its services in the first half of 2005.

## Operators with significant market power

Telecom services providers and users with significant market power are defined by the Telecommunications Act. An operator has Significant Market Power (SMP) if there is no or only limited competition in the market, resulting in its superior positioning in the market or power to influence market conditions. An operator has SMP measured by its income compared to the market size or control over customer base, as well as access to financial sources or experience in providing products and services.

An operator with SMP on all relevant markets must submit Reference Interconnection Offer (ROI) to the Regulator for approval. Those with SMP on the fixed telecommunication market and on the leased line market have the additional obligation of submitting its retail prices for approval to the Regulator. An operator with SMP must, pursuant to the non-discrimination principle, provide other market participants with equal services under equal conditions as provided for its own purposes or to related companies. An operator with SMP can limit access to the network and linking based only on reasons in line with the EU guidelines and pursuant to other EU regulations.

There are three telecommunications services providers with SMP – T-Mobile and VIPnet in mobile telephony and T-Com in the fixed telephony market and the market of leased line services. All three operators (T-Com, T-Mobile and VIPnet) are designated as SMP on the interconnection market.

# Market liberalization

## *Fixed lines*

Liberalization of the telecommunications sector in Croatia in the area of infrastructure for leased lines is currently in its third phase, and the telecommunications market has been opened for new operators in the fixed telecommunications network since 1 January 2003. The basic optical infrastructure (backbone) of the Republic of Croatia is owned by the national telecommunications operator T-Hrvatske Telekomunikacije, and it includes more than 14,000 km of underground cables laid in plastic tubes, with a total average of installed capacity of approximately 300,000 km of optic cables. The backbone infrastructure is well built throughout the entire territory of the Republic of Croatia.

There is also the option of 'alternative' infrastructure, for instance the project for utilization of optical infrastructure near the roads, railways and electrical lines, owned by several companies (Hrvatske autoceste/Croatian Highways, HEP-Hrvatska elektroprivreda/Croatian Electric Company, JANAF/Adriatic Oil Pipeline, HŽ-Hrvatske željeznice/Croatian Railways), which is currently in the initial phase.

As of 1 January 2005, T-Hrvatske Telekomunikacije is obliged to provide access to its unbundled local loop, as well as the services of number portability and pre-selection of operators. Anticipating those changes, in the last quarter of 2004, two new service providers, Optima Telekom and Portus, have entered the fixed telecommunications market.

## *Mobile telecommunications*

At its 14 July 2004 session, the Croatian Telecommunications Agency passed the decision on the invitation to a Public Tender for granting concessions regarding the use of frequencies for providing public telecommunications services with the use of the radio frequency spectrum in the mobile network system of the second generation GSM/DCS-1800 and of the third generation UMTS mobile network. Two existing operators, T-Mobile and VIPnet, were granted the UMTS concession for 20 years. However, the tender did not result in granting concession to the new GSM operator, the consortium under the name *'Treća sreća'* (Third time is the charm), since the offer, according to the statement of the Telecommunications Agency, did not meet the proscribed criteria regarding the contribution to the development of the national economy and since the candidate requested only the GSM concession. The tender was repeated on 21 October 2004, with new criteria. Three candidates – Match Telecom, Croatia Mobile and *Treća sreća* – requested the combined GSM-UMTS concession and submitted their offers to the Agency. The concession was granted to *Treća sreća* consortium.

## 3.12

# Information and Communication Technology (ICT) in Croatia

*Professor Velimir Srića, PhD*

By the end of 2004, the Croatian ICT environment had been characterized by a high degree of EU-harmonized ICT-related legislation. The government has developed key implementation policies and established regulators. The market is experiencing growth – several ongoing projects and implementations on a national level are preparing the ground for new internet-enabled intelligent e-services.

Also the country faces sound developments in ICT infrastructure and services, and the internet market trends are positive. However, there is stagnation in government computer and communication network implementation, although there has been progress in initiatives for a national smart card, as well as the development of an institutional infrastructure for e-government implementations.

## An overview

The local ICT industry is characterized by a relatively large number of small companies and a small number of large companies. Leading ICT industrial capacities are accommodated at the local branches of the multinational companies, Ericsson and Siemens – Ericsson Nikola Tesla d.d. and Siemens d.d.. World leaders like IBM, Microsoft, Oracle, SAP, as well as many others, have their local representatives in the country, operating relatively successfully. Small satellite companies are also building partnering networks around these foreign principals.

There is a growing tendency towards ICT consortiums and cluster establishments, initiated by large national projects like the National

Health Information System (Ericsson Nikola Tesla Health Consortium – potentially a new Croatian ICT export product). Considering the requirements of information society infrastructure development and respective information society technologies, there is a lot of potential for the new players on the emerging market.

The ICT is recently being established as a new industry sector and there is a growing number of ICT companies among Croatia's 400 largest firms (one ICT company is in the first 100). As a business sector, ICT has been recognized as a branch within the Croatian Entrepreneurs Association.

Croatia is at a relative advantage with respect to its neighbours as far as the existing physical infrastructure to support high-speed networking is concerned (there is a 100 per cent fibre optic backbone network in Croatia). HT-Hrvatske telekomunikacije d.d. (HT) have built a network of more than 14,000 km of underground cables laid in plastic tubes with a total average of installed capacity of 300,000 km of optic cables.

All the switches deployed on HT's backbone are digital. HT is connected to Deutsche Telekom's extensive European backbone network. This connectivity, coupled with connections to Austria, Italy, Hungary, Slovenia, and the US, provides Croatia with international connectivity to 35 countries. As of the beginning of 2005, HT will be obliged to provide access to its unbundled local loop, as well as to secure services for number portability and pre-selection of operators.

Another characteristic of the local ICT infrastructure was a significant increase in ISDN (42.1 per cent in 2003) and ADSL connections and services being built during 2003.

The national telecommunications infrastructure is well developed and characterized by a competitive environment and many modern and well-implemented services.

As far as mobile operators are concerned, Croatia is a classical prepaid market; the share of contract customers is only 15.4 per cent. HTmobile, the big traditional national telecommunications company, reported 1,300,000 customers in 2003. Along with mobile telephony, the following services have been implemented: SMS, WAP, MMS, GPRS, Java support, WLAN, and mobile internet.

Its main competitor, VIPnet, one of the most successful start-up companies in its field, had obtained a share of 55.0 per cent of mobile phone services in the Croatian market by the end of the year 2004, and continues to grow. VIPnet managed to gain 113,000 additional customers in 2003, thus more than 1.2 million customers utilizing the VIPnet network for their mobile phone services. VIPnet's implemented services are: SMS, WAP, MMS, GPRS, Java support, WLAN, and mobile internet.

The growth in the data segment is particularly influenced by high SMS usage (73 SMS per customer and month) and the successful m-commerce service VIP.parking, the predecessor of the Austrian m-parking (2.1 million transactions were made using VIP.parking in 2003, which is a 100 per cent increase on the year 2002). Preparations for 3rd GSM operators and concessions for UMTS had been finalized by the end of 2003.

As far as internet is concerned, there is still a dominance of dial-up connection. HT reported 479,422 dial-up connections (71.3 per cent of the dial-up market) and 506 subscribed permanent connections in 2003 (36.9 per cent of the permanent connections market with an increase of 34.2 per cent). In Croatia, there are around 950,000 active internet users, and access to the internet is available to 35 per cent of country's population (about 1.4 million people).

One of the major ICT implementation fields in Croatia concerns banks and financial institutions. According to the latest reports, 26 banks and two card houses issued, in total, 5,149,902 credit and debt cards. The share of credit cards is 21.5 per cent and debits 78.5 per cent. In relation to the same period in 2003, the number of cards increased in 2004 by 26.3 per cent. The total number of cash dispensers is 1,422 (compared to the same period of last year, it represents a growth of 29.7 per cent). The number of EFT POS terminals amounts to 27,055, representing an annual growth of 40.9 per cent.

There have been several unique and original ICT application solutions developed by Croatian companies in recent years. A good example is Zagrebparking, which has implemented a new system of payments using VIPnet and Tmobile services. This successful m-commerce service, called VIP.parking, was characterized by 2.1 million transactions in 2003, which is a 100 per cent increase on 2002. This innovative solution has attracted the attention of major cities in the world, such as Vienna and London.

In 2003, Croatia's largest online travel agency, adriatica.net, reported the figure of 33,788 customers who have booked their holiday accommodation via its web pages, an increase of 30 per cent on 2002. During the high season, adriatica.net's website was visited by over 15,000 new users per day. Besides the regular quality control of accommodation, in 2004 adriatica.net began offering its customers an extensive range of skiing holidays, cruises, and other tourist products. Guests will have at their disposal a customer service in 12 languages, 365 days per year.

## International ranking of Croatia's information society readiness

The most recent World Economic Forum Report on information technology has shown a relative advancement in Croatia's readiness for the information society and its economy. Let us examine the relative position of Croatia, compared with other 101 countries analyzed in the *Global Information Technology Report 2003–2004*.[1] The overall rank for Croatia in this analysis was 48. Table 3.12.1 exhibits the detailed ranks in the respective categories.

**Table 3.12.1** Croatia's ranking according to the *Global Information Technology Report*

| Overall rank | 48 of 102 |
| --- | --- |
| ICT infrastructure environment | 59 |
| Venture capital availability | 65 |
| Subsidies for company-level R&D | 52 |
| Quality of scientific research institutions | 42 |
| Brain drain | 71 |
| Patents granted (per million inhabitants) | 32 |
| ICT manufactured exports (per capita) | 39 |
| ICT service exports | 31 |
| Telephone lines (per 1,000 inhabitants) | 33 |
| Public pay phones (per 1,000 inhabitants) | 13 |
| Internet servers (per million inhabitants) | 34 |
| Individual readiness | 43 |
| Business readiness | 53 |
| Government readiness | 41 |
| Public expenditure on education (per capita) | 43 |
| Households online | 37 |
| Internet affordability (fees) | 41 |
| Personal computers (per 1,000 inhabitants) | 32 |
| ISDN subscribers (per 1,000 inhabitants) | 49 |
| Internet users (per 1,000 inhabitants) | 49 |
| Computers in businesses (per 1,000 inhabitants) | 35 |

# Legislative and infrastructural environment

Croatia's overall ICT environment is characterized by growing harmonization with EU legislation.

The main focus of the ICT-related legislative and regulatory activities in Croatia is to harmonize the legal environment and all corresponding institutions to the EU's Legal Framework. The list of harmonized ICT-related legislation by the end of 2004 includes all key

---

[1] The International Bank for Reconstruction and Development/The World Bank, World Economic Forum, and INSEAD, 2004.

pieces of legislation (Telecommunication Act, Electronic Signature Act, Electronic Commerce Act, Dana Protection Act, Right to Information Access Act, Laws on Intellectual Property and Consumer Protection etc.)

## Internet service providers

The Croatian telecommunications market consists of seven internet service providers (ISPs): HTnet, Iskon Internet, Globalnet, VIP Online, Vodatel, Net4U, VM mreže, europroNET. A short description of some players on the market follows.

### HTnet / Hinet

HThinet launched commercial operations in 1996. The firm operates as an ISP arm of incumbent telecommunications operator, Croatian Telecom (Hrvatski Telekom). Besides general ISP services, HThinet provides virtual private networking, web-hosting a domain name registration service, and web advertising (banners), etc. Recently, the firm's business users can access roaming services for 23 countries. Its official web portal (at moj.hinet.hr) receives, on average, more than 300,000 visits a day. In mid-2004, it became the first Croatian web portal to make content available to hand-held PC and PDA users. HThinet had more than 350,000 dial-up and 950 leased line users by the end of 2002. In comparison with the previous year, the numbers had increased by 46.7 per cent and 25.9 per cent respectively. The majority of dial-up users have accessed the internet using subscription-free packages. In June 2002, HThinet introduced a pilot version of the DSL service. Since November 2002, the service has been offered commercially, available in eight major cities throughout the country. At the end of that year, the company reported more than 1,000 users of DSL service packages.

### VIPNet

In 1998, VIPNet, a consortium of Western Wireless (US) and Mobilcom (Austria), won the second concession to provide GSM services in Croatia. Their operations, as the first private competitor to HT, began in July 1999. Since then they have developed rapidly, with 170,000 subscribers in January 2000, and strong acquisition of market share following the monopoly breakup. By the end of 2003, more than 1,200,000 subscribers were reported. VIPNet offers a WAP as well as an internet portal and internet services in conjunction with their mobile cellular service. The company provides a complete schedule of internet-related services including email, dial-up connectivity, leased lines, wireless technology, server collocation, web design and web hosting, as well as Virtual Private Networking (VPN). They also offer consulting services to business on web content and development, as well as internet and intranet strategy development.

## CARNet – Zagreb University

The Croatian Academic and Research Network (CARNet), a regional leader in bringing the internet to Eastern Europe, began in 1992. CARNet is a non-commercial, academic ISP, owned and funded by the government. The CARNet nationwide backbone, using leased lines and the wide area network (WAN) backbone of HT, has managed to connect all academic and research institutions in Croatia. Staff of the Zagreb University Computing Centre (SRCE) served as the technical and engineering support for the network.

Since December 2001, CARNet has been connected to GEANT, a pan-European academic network, connecting some 3,000 research and educational institutions in 30 European countries. In February 2002, it launched a new application for user authorization within a system of modem access nodes (called CMU). CARNet's WAN connects 193 locations in 23 major cities in Croatia. It is based on ATM technology and allows internal traffic at the bandwidth of 155Mbps. By the end of 2002, the number of access modems had doubled year on year to 2,160 and CARNet had more than 87,000 dial-up users. Compared to the previous year, the number had increased by more than 50 per cent. Since September 2000, CARNet has managed the Croatian Internet Exchange (CIX), a non-profit service providing more efficient inter-country internet traffic (without encumbering international networks). Besides CARNet, other founders of CIX are Croatian Telecom, Iskon, AT&T Hrvatska, VIPnet GSM and Croatian Radio Television.

CARNet holds the exclusive right to administer and assign internet domains within Croatia. Other services provided by the ISP include CCERTComputer Emergency Response, helpdesk, education programmes, and internet-related publishing (Edupoint, an electronic magazine, designed to increase IT usage in the education sector). Carnet is also a successful organizer of educational seminars and conferences.

## Iskon Internet

Founded in 1997, Iskon Internet was one of the first private challengers to the HThinet's (Croatian Telecom's) monopoly in the ISP area. The company paved the way for internet connections from any part of the country. The company is 30 per cent owned by local individuals and businesses and 70 per cent owned by foreign investors. In 2002, the total number of connections provided by Iskon surpassed 74,500. In comparison with the previous year, the number has increased by 28.5 per cent. The number of leased line users reached

316. In September 2002, Iskon began covering the Zagreb area with a fixed wireless network. The project was based on a feasibility study financed by the US Trade Development Agency. By the end of the year, the ISP served 22 FWA users. The company provides a complete schedule of internet-related services including email, dial-up connectivity, leased lines, wireless technology, server collocation, web design and web hosting, and VPN. It also offers consulting services to business on web content and development, as well as internet and intranet strategy and development.

*Globalnet*
The first private ISP in Croatia, Globalnet launched operations in 1996. Originally, it was a department of BBM, an SME accounting software vendor. Globalnet has been a commercial ISP since the end of 1997 and, in early 1999, became an independent company. In June 2000, a venture capital fund, Croatia Capital Partnership, invested US$5.3 million in the company to acquire a majority ownership stake. Other shareholders include the European Bank for Reconstruction and Development (ERBD) and a number of individuals with minor stock shares.

## The online market

The Croatian financial sector (banks, business card providers etc), with more than 5,100,000 banking cards, is leading the implementation of secure internet payments. The Inter-banking Services Institute (MBU), rather than the banks themselves, has developed technology and support for secure internet payments. New secure internet payment services are implemented by HT, an ISP leader in Croatia, through 'HTnet Pay Way' and 'HTnet Shopping center'.

Due to the respective developments of the electronic card business in Croatia, along with the first implementations of smart cards, connected with electronic payments, the B2C (Business to Customers) e-commerce component is experiencing strong economic and professional growth. An IDC survey of the 2002 B2C market indicated that the aggregate revenue in the Croatian market amounted to US$9 million. Various tourist agencies generated most of that revenue in 2002 (around U$$3.03 million), which is about 60 per cent of the total B2C market revenue in that year. This sum was generated by 32,000 transactions, with the customer base consisting mostly of foreign tourists. Online computer shops generated about US$1.1 million in 2002, about 25 per cent of the total 2002 B2C market revenue. Online bookstores in 2002 made up around seven per cent of the B2C market, generating revenue of around US$0.4 million from 17,560 transactions. Online shops for electronic and electric household appliances and accessories made up about four per cent of the 2002 B2C market. They have generated revenue of around US$0.2 million from 6,000 transactions. However, the sales of consumer goods online did not prove successful, acquiring only four per cent of the total 2002 B2C market share.

The Croatian B2B market segment still remains quite underdeveloped in comparison to other Central European countries. Major initiatives are needed to drive the market forward in future years. However, there are several exceptions in the B2B market segment. The results for the year 2003 have exhibited rather progressive growth rates.

## Telecoms, cable and satellite

The telecommunications market opened for new operators and service providers in the fixed network after the expiration of HT's (Croatian Telecommunications) rights on 1 January 2003. Deutsche Telekom AG owns 51 per cent of HT and the remaining 49 per cent is owned by the Republic of Croatia. As of the beginning of 2005, HT will be obliged to provide access to its unbundled local loop, as well as to the services of number portability and pre-selection of operators.

At the beginning of 2005, the telecommunications sector will be completely privatized, and the new Telecommunications Act does not allow for any limitations to the share of foreign ownership in the telecommunications sector. Hence, there will be no limitations to the entry of new investors (domestic or foreign) to the telecommunications market.

The basic optical infrastructure (backbone) of the Republic of Croatia is owned by the national telecommunications operator, HT, and its total installed capacity consists of 300,000 km of optic cables. The backbone infrastructure is well spread throughout the whole territory of Croatia. As far as alternative infrastructures are concerned, a project has been initiated for the utilization of optical infrastructure near roads, railways and electrical lines, owned by several companies (Hrvatske autoceste/Croatian Highways, HEP-Hrvatska elektroprivreda/Croatian Electric Company, JANAF/Adriatic Oil Pipeline, HŽ-Hrvatske željeznice/Croatian Railways).

The cable television sector is completely liberalized. There are 25 concessions allocated for cable television and two of them are on national level. The cable service providers may provide other telecommunication services (internet, telephony etc) based on the licence obtained from the Telecommunications Agency.

As far as satellite communications are concerned, a local company Oda  iljači i veze d.o.o. owns two BSS land stations for connections with EBU and for broadcasting Croatian programmes via satellites HB-3 and HB-5. There is more than one VSAT network. There are several INMARSAT maritime and land mobile terminals. World infrastructures such as INTELSAT, INMARSAT, EUTELSAT etc, as well as new business entities and competition are emerging in the national telecoms market.

Concerning the data communication services, HT (VPN data) offers users private networks for data transfer based on MPLS (Multiprotocol Label Switching) technology, which encompasses the best features of classical private networks (privacy and quality of service), and of IP protocols (flexibility and stability). The Croatian Electric Company, Croatian Railways, and Croatian Waters have their own networks for data communication.

## Research and development (R&D)

There are a few very strong local R&D units, as well as infrastructural industrial companies, providing the ICT field with a constant flow of new products and services. An example is Ericsson Nikola Tesla d.d. – research, development and design of integral communicational solutions and services in the area of multi-service and mobile networks of the newest generation, including mobile internet. Another example is Siemens d.d. – intelligent information and telecommunication solutions (mobile phones, wireless phones, computers, implementation of IT solutions). Still other examples are Elka d.d., Eurocable Group d.o.o. and Volex d.o.o. – manufacturers of cables, including optical cables, and RIZ-Odašiljači d.d. – the production of radio and TV transmitters, antennas, and production of network installation equipment.

The institutional framework for technology development includes a number of institutions defined by the government HITRA programme, for example The Research and Development Technology Institute, several research and development centres, technology innovation centres, as well as the Business and Innovation Center of Croatia (BICRO).

BICRO was established in 1998 as a state agency and an umbrella institution responsible for creating an overall technology infrastructure. After launching the HITRA Programme, BICRO has been entrusted with the implementation and coordination of the programme for supporting knowledge-based companies in cooperation with the technology centres. Now the whole system has matured and developed, BICRO has been redesigned into an institution investing in technology-based companies. Its role is the introduction and development of new technologies, support of the technology capabilities of companies, and attraction of venture capital.

# Education in the ICT Field

There are five universities in Croatia (the University of Zagreb, the University of Rijeka, the University of Osijek, the University of Split, and the University of Zadar) with eighty faculties, art academies, four-year colleges, university departments and degree programmes. There are also seven two-year colleges (Zagreb, Karlovac, Rijeka, Split, Dubrovnik, and Požega), six independent four-year colleges, thirteen private accredited four-year colleges and one private accredited two-year college.

In the school year 2002/2003, there were a total of 47,225 students enrolled in university education. There were a total of 120,000 students and 8,200 teachers by the end of 2004.

University education for ICT on graduate and postgraduate levels is concentrated around several institutions, the key players all being members of the University of Zagreb: FER – the Faculty of Electrotechnics and Computing, FOI – the Faculty of Organization and Management, and the Faculty of Business and Economics. There are also well-developed accredited company programmes for professional degrees in the ICT field, from companies such as Microsoft and Cisco Systems.

All higher education institutions are connected to the internet through CARNet. CARNet is fully funded by the budget of the Ministry of Science and Technology. The speed of connection ranges from 2 to 622 Mbps. The full cost of connection is covered by CARNet. In 2003, CARNet increased the throughput of the national backbone to 2Gbps.

In 2000, supported by Ministry of Health and initiated by the Croatian Medical Academy, the telemedicine project for Croatian islands was started. The first step, involving four islands in the Krk-Cres-Losinj archipelago, was considered to be a great success. The virtual polyclinic network, established in 2001, now involves the following islands: Cres, Lošinj, Krk, Šolta, Brač, Vis, Lastovo, Mljet; connected to 5 consulting units in Rijeka and 5 consulting units in Zagreb.

# References

*Study of Telecommunication and Internet Development in the period 2003–2005*, Faculty of Electrical Engineering and Computing, Croatia, 2003.
*eSSE ICT Sector Country Status Report*, Croatia, 2004.
*Policy Recommendations for Raising Croatia's Competitiveness*, National Competitiveness Council, Croatia, 2004.
*The Internet Market in Croatia 2002–2007*, IDC, July 2003.

*National Programme for the Integration of the Republic of Croatia into the European Union – 2004*, Ministry of European Integrations, Croatia.

*Global Information Technology Report 2003–2004*, The International Bank for Reconstruction and Development/The World Bank, World Economic Forum, and INSEAD, 2004.

*National Report on Strategy Implementation – Information and Communication Technology – Croatia in the 21st Century*, Ministry of Science and Technology, Croatia, 2003.

*Information and Communication Technology in the Strategy of Development of the Republic of Croatia*, Executive Summary and Recommendations, Croatia, 2002.

## 3.13

# Real Estate for Foreign Citizens and Enterprises

*Višnja Bojanić*

## Introduction

Since signing Stabilization and Association Agreement in 2001, Croatia has experienced strong economic growth, which has placed the country a step ahead of other Balkan countries and the two regional contenders for joining the European Union (EU) – Bulgaria and Romania.

In June 2004, Croatia was granted official EU candidate status and membership negotiations are expected to start in March 2005. Bright prospects for EU membership not later than 2009–2010, a stable political climate created by the current government and a developing economy have all made Croatia a good place in Europe for great deals on holiday property, easy retirement living and affordable real estate for private investors.

Strong demand from overseas buyers and investors is creating a very buoyant market, showing growth in property prices in excess of 20–30 per cent per annum. Between December 2003 and December 2004, prices of building plots have increased by 105 per cent on average; prices for houses at the national level showed an increase of about 24 per cent and in the city of Zagreb, 18 per cent; prices for apartments at the national level showed an 11 per cent increase, 10 per cent in the city of Zagreb and 16 per cent on the Adriatic cost. Only office premise prices, for purchase or rent, are showing slow stagnation, due to excessive building in 2004.

In spite of this property-buying 'boom', Croatia still remains an unspoiled destination. The new Bill of Law on Nature Protection, created in line with the EU standards for the protection of nature, proposes an embargo for foreign nationals and foreign companies on buying property in regions declared protected landscapes, park-woods and monuments of park architecture. The adoption of this law will raise the percentage of protected areas from a current 9.5 per cent to 14 per cent of the whole territory. The current Croatian government is determined to maintain a balance between its policy of encouraging overseas investors in the field of real estate investment and preservation of country's beauty, its natural resources and indigenous cultural heritage.

# Outline of the procedure for acquiring real property ownership

According to Croatian Law on Property Ownership and other Real Rights, foreign citizens and enterprises who want to become owners of real estate in the Republic of Croatia need to obtain consent from the Minister of Foreign Affairs of the Republic of Croatia, issued on the basis of a prior opinion of the Minister of Justice of the Republic of Croatia.

Although the purchase of real estate is straightforward, it is nevertheless advisable to seek professional advice from a real estate agency or an attorney. The selected agency or attorney reviews and analyzes the documents regarding the title of the proprietor to the chosen real estate, and identifies potential legal risks and exposures in respect of the transfer of ownership, for example checks that your future property is free of any debts or mortgage.

Paying the reservation deposit, which is legally 10 per cent of the agreed price, guarantees that the property you have chosen is taken off the market and is reserved for you at the agreed fixed price. After the reservation deposit has been paid, you have up to 30 days to exchange a private purchase contract, ie to pay the remainder of the deposit required. After the agency or attorney has prepared a contract, the parties sign the contract and have it certified by public notary. Only then can the potential buyer initiate the procedure for obtaining consent from the Ministry of Foreign Affairs. The procedure may be initiated by the applicant or through an attorney by sending a request in writing to the Ministry of Foreign Affairs in Zagreb. The request for obtaining consent should be in the form of a brief letter and must contain the following enclosures:

- the legal basis for the acquisition of the property (purchase agreement, gift agreement, support agreement etc), in the original or a duly legalized copy;

- seller's proof of title, ie land registry certificate, in the original or a duly legalized copy, not older than six months;

- original certificate (not older than six months) issued by the authorities of the local administration responsible for urban planning (county departments), confirming that the property is within the construction zone envisaged by the zoning plan;

- proof of citizenship for the Buyer (legalized copy of a passport), or proof of the status of a foreign legal entity (certificate from the register of companies);

- proof of citizenship for the Seller (a copy of his ID or passport will do);

- if an attorney is involved, it is necessary to submit the Power of Attorney, in the original or a duly legalized copy.

In addition to these documents, it is also necessary to enclose proof of payment for the administrative fee. Pursuant to the Law on the Amendments to the Administrative Charges, the following amounts are charged: HRK50 for the application; HRK100 for deciding on property acquisition, and HRK20 for any subsequent supplement to the application (in case of missing documents). Note: administrative fees up to HRK100 are paid in the form of appropriate stamp duty, while the amounts exceeding HRK100 must be paid by means of a general payment order to the account of the National Budget of the Republic of Croatia.

Before even submitting the application to the Ministry of Foreign Affairs, it is necessary to check if there is a reciprocity agreement between the Republic of Croatia and the applicant's country of origin. So far, Croatia has signed reciprocity agreements with all countries members of EU, the United States, Canada and Australia. The reciprocity with the Republic of Slovenia, Italy, Switzerland, Slovakia, Bosnia and Herzegovina, Bulgaria, and Macedonia is conditioned by the status of permanent residence of the foreign citizens of that particular country or, as in the case of Austria and the Russian Federation, reciprocity depends on the regulation of real estate issues of a particular country. There is no reciprocity agreement between Croatia and Serbia and Montenegro.

According to the provisions of the Stabilization and Association Agreement (SAA), the reciprocity principle shall be abolished four years from the entry into force of SAA, ie from 1 February 2005.

After the Ministry issues the respective approval, the buyer can register the real estate in his/her name in the Land Registry as the ultimate evidence of his/her title to that specific property. The buyer must register the purchase at the competent tax authority within 30 days from the day of conclusion of the contract and to pay, within 15 days from the day of receipt of the decision from the tax authorities, five per cent of the transaction value. The tax is calculated based on the price of the real estate as per the sales contract and the value as estimated by the authorized tax authority in charge of the area in which the real estate is located.

All foreign natural and legal persons can sell their real estate in Croatia without restriction. However, if they decide to sell the acquired property at a higher price within three years from acquisition, they are subject to income tax on the price difference at the rate of 35 per cent, plus surtax, depending on the taxpayer's place of residence in Croatia.

It is also worth mentioning that there are no restrictions on the acquisition of ownership of real estate by foreign persons with respect to the number and the size of real estate holdings. Finally, if the consent for the acquisition of ownership of the real estate has been refused by the Ministry of Foreign Affairs, a foreign person cannot repeat the request with respect to the same real estate within five years from the day the request was submitted.

A potential buyer of real estate in Croatia can conclude a sales contract and have it authenticated abroad in the Croatian embassy or consulate, provided that that the notary's authentication is translated to the Croatian language by a certified court interpreter.

Foreign citizens and enterprises cannot acquire ownership of agricultural land, pursuant to the Law on Agricultural Land, but can be granted concession rights depending on the results of a public tender for a maximum of 99 years, or 40 years in the case of agricultural land. The decision on whether or not to grant a concession is made by the Croatian Parliament, which can transfer the decision-making procedure to the government. A concession cannot be granted for the exploitation of forests or other assets regulated by special laws if they are state-owned. Foreign citizens and enterprises also cannot acquire ownership of forests and forest land, pursuant to the Law on Forests.

Limitations on acquiring ownership rights over natural resources, agricultural land, forests and forestry land as well as real estate in national parks and areas of national security interest will remain until Croatia becomes member of EU.

For updated information in relation to consent granting procedure, see the website of the Ministry of Foreign Affairs (http://www.mvp.hr/index-en.htm).

# Old or new property?

For a foreign entity, there is no difference between buying an old house or a new apartment, ie the buyer is equally subject to the five per cent real estate tax. However, value added tax (VAT) of 22 per cent is imposed on transactions involving new structures, and is paid either by the seller or, as is usually the case, is already included in the price of the new real estate. When buying old real estate, it is necessary to verify whether the object of acquisition is a protected cultural monument, as in this case, it must be offered first to the authorities

(Republic of Croatia, Municipality, City, County). If they decline to exercise their pre-emptive right, the property may be offered to foreign citizens and enterprises (Law on Protecting and Preserving Cultural Monuments).

## Buying through a company

Those who cannot obtain approval from Ministry of Foreign Affairs for various reasons, or do not have time to wait for the completion of the purchase formalities (the process of getting approval from the Ministry of Foreign Affairs can last from several months to a year) may effect the purchase by establishing a company in Croatia. Foreign citizens can form either a limited liability company (d.o.o.), whereby the minimum share capital is HRK20,000 (approximately €2,700) or a joint stock company (d.d.) whereby the minimum share capital is HRK200,000 (approximately €27,000). All necessary procedures for establishing a company in Croatia can be completed within approximately one month. A company owned by a foreign person in the Republic of Croatia is considered to be a Croatian legal entity and, as such, may acquire real estate ownership rights without any restrictions and irrespective of whether the real estate is acquired for business or for other purposes.

## Other ways to acquire ownership rights

### Inheritance

A foreign person – both private and legal – can acquire ownership of real estate on the basis of an inheritance document, providing there is a reciprocity agreement with the person's country of residence. If this is the case, the foreign person becomes the owner at the moment of testament, ie on the death of the testator. A foreign person may request, on the basis of a legally valid testament, the registration of ownership in the cadastre.

There are no quantitative restrictions with regard to ownership rights on real estate. However, there are some qualitative limitations; for instance, a foreign person cannot acquire certain real estate on an area that has been declared of a special importance to the state. In that case, a foreign person is entitled to compensation for the inherited real estate in such an area, as provided by the dispossession provisions.

### Legal transaction

When a foreign person acquires ownership on the basis of a legal transaction (eg on the basis of law, or decree of competent authorities), two conditions are to be met in accordance with the Ownership Law: reciprocity and consent by the Minister of Foreign Affairs of the Republic of Croatia. The Minister decides, at his discretion, based on the opinion of the Ministry of Justice. Foreign persons may, if they are not satisfied with the decision, institute administrative proceedings at the competent court. The requirements of reciprocity and the consent by the Minister of Foreign Affairs do not apply to those foreign persons who were Croatian citizens at the effective date of the Law on Amendments to the Law on Compensation for Property Expropriated during the Yugoslav Communist Regime (1996). According to the Law, such persons are fully entitled to ownership.

# Current situation with regard to foreign ownership

According to the records of the Consular Department of the Ministry of Foreign Affairs, up to October 2004, there were 3,120 Croatian real estate sales to foreign natural persons and some 4,000 requests are waiting to be granted the MFA consent. German nationals own most of such titles in Croatia, or as many as 1,869, Austrian nationals own 683 properties, US citizens own 67 houses on the Adriatic coast, Hungary (86), the Netherlands (58), Finland (5), Bosnia and Herzegovina (25), Switzerland (21), France (27), Great Britain (52), Italy (9), Sweden (29), Canada (5), China (2), Russian Federation nationals (12), Macedonia (5), Chinese citizens (2), Ukrainian nationals (2), Czech Republic (1) Venezuela (1) and Belize (1).

There are no accurate data with regard to the number of foreigners who purchased property in Croatia through a company, irrespective of whether their country of origin has signed the reciprocity agreements with Croatia, nor about those foreigners who bought property through a third person (a relative or a friend).

# Major obstacles to buying property

The biggest obstacles to the smooth functioning of the real estate market are the unfinished privatization process and outdated cadastre and land registry. Recognizing the discrepancy between the land and cadastral registers and the actual situation as a major obstacle for investors in economic activities, in February 2003 the government of the Republic of Croatia launched a €37.5 million project financed with the support of the World Bank and the EU (CARDS) for adjustment of data in land and cadastral registers and for necessary normalization of the system. It takes, on average, 120 weeks to complete a registration using the current administration system and Croatia is expecting to cut this time down to just five days. A transparent, expedient and market-oriented system of land and building registration will certainly benefit both domestic and foreign investors.

Another issue is Croatia's emigration problems. In particularly, old stone houses on the coast and on the islands have been family property for generations and many owners with fractional shares disappeared or emigrated long ago. Such ownership remains uncertain as those living abroad can suddenly appear and claim a particular piece of property.

The return of Serb refugees and the restitution of their property is another problem any investor should pay attention to when choosing a property, no matter what its size, location or price, because the seller could turn out not to be the legitimate owner. By the end of 2004, Croatia had returned some 40 per cent of Serb private property used for temporary accommodation and 20 per cent of forcibly occupied property has been retrieved by its owners.

# The real estate market in the city of Zagreb

Taking into account the number of companies, generated revenues and the number of employed people, the City of Zagreb is by far the strongest economic centre in Croatia. Of the 400 largest Croatian companies, according to revenue, 186 of them are located in Zagreb and generate 60 per cent of the revenue. More than one third (35.6 per cent) of all Croatian companies are present in Zagreb, as well as 38 per cent of the labour force. Zagreb is accountable for 40–50 per cent of all trade in Croatia and this share continues to grow. This is particularly so in the case of electricity, gas and water provision, transport and communication and financial services. Consequently, 48.2 per cent of the country's revenue is generated in Zagreb. The Zagreb economy is up to 10 per cent more lucrative than the Croatian average, has a two per cent higher growth rate and a 40 per cent more productive labour force, according to gross wage per employee. Growth in the Zagreb economy is primarily in the services and non-trading sector, whereas the manufacturing sector is declining.

## Office space

Demand for office space has generally grown in Zagreb in recent years due to the stabilization of the local economy in the post-war period. In the mid-1990s, considerable demand was generated by foreign embassies and international aid organizations. As the political situation has become more stable over the last two years, demand from these groups has dropped in favour of new international, as well as growing domestic, companies. Modern office stock (new build and refurbished space) now totals approximately 500,000 m², of which only approximately 50 per cent is considered class A. Average rent for a modern office is €15 per m² per month.

The building boom continues, with more than 150,000m² of modern office space under construction or due to be developed in the next 12 months. A new central business district has emerged in an area one kilometre to the south east of the city centre, in Salsa Street, Vukovar Avenue and Heinzelova Street. There are also some modern offices in the city centre, Novi Zagreb and Buzin (where the American Embassy is located).

### Retail sector

The retail sector is still very much behind in terms of modern supply and demand, despite the increase in business activities over the last two years. Presently there is only 200,000m². of existing shopping centre space in Zagreb and a further 100,000m² for hypermarkets. In order to meet the growing interest from foreign retailers, an additional 500,000m² of quality retail space needs to be built in Zagreb and its suburbs. Average rent for retail space is €7 per m² per month.

### Warehouse sector

The modern warehouse sector is greatly underdeveloped in Zagreb. During 2004, only 20,000m² of new warehouse and light industrial space was completed. There are a number of small modern warehouses and light industrial schemes in newly built and refurbished properties, which in total amount to no more than 80,000m² of built space. Modern industrial buildings are mainly located in Jankomir and in Zitnjak.

# Apartments and houses/villas

Many expatriates attached to a company, diplomatic mission or other organization stay in Zagreb for a period from a few weeks to several years. Unlike on the coast, where foreigners mostly decide to buy property, in Zagreb they opt for renting. The monthly rent for high-quality apartments ranges from €300 for a studio, €500 for a two-room apartment to €900 for a three-room flat.

However, buying an apartment in this fast-developing business centre is always a good investment; in the centre an average price for an old apartment is €1600/m², whereas for a brand new apartment the price is €2,500/m². As the city is following the trend of moving away from the centre towards suburban areas, buying a flat there is a much better solution; an average price for an old flat is €1,350/m² and €1,500/m² for the new flat. Buying a house depends very much on the area; one can buy a house in an excellent condition for €500,000 but for a residential villa one might spend up to €3,000,000.

*Note: * Average prices are valid for the year 2005, courtesy of the Agency for real estate, Brzo d.o.o. Zagreb.*

# Part Four

# Croatia's Most Dynamic Companies and Prospective Investment Projects

INDUSTRIJA NAFTE, d.d.

INA is a modern, socially responsible and transparent company in continuous dialogue with its environment, directed toward sustainable development and care for the health and safety of its employees and community at large.

## INA's Mission

To remain a vertically-integrated oil corporation and an influential player in the oil and gas market in Croatia and neighbouring countries. INA is committed to working toward continuous upgrading of our businesses and quality of our products and services, with the aim of creating increasing value for its stakeholders.

## INA's Vision

To be a recognized and desirable partner, known for the excellence of its products and services, good and fair relations with customers, and committed to safeguarding the interests of our key stakeholders.

For further information contact:

**INA-Industrija nafte, d.d. Zagreb**
Avenija V. Holjevca 10, 10002 ZAGREB
p.p. 555
Switchboard: +385 (0) 1 6450 000
Email: ina@ina.hr
Website: www.ina.hr
INA toll free information telephone 0800-1112

# 4.1

# INA Industrija nafte d.d.

INA is a vertically-integrated oil and gas company. It is the largest Croatian company but also a significant regional energy player.

## Core businesses

### 1. Exploration and production of oil and gas

The upstream division of INA, previously called Naftaplin, is engaged in the exploration, development and production of oil and natural gas in Croatia and internationally. INA commenced upstream operations in 1952 with exploration in Croatia. Since then the division has been active in 20 countries and is currently active in Angola, Egypt, Syria and Namibia.

The majority of production comes from onshore Croatia, where INA owns 100 per cent of all 50 producing oil and gas fields. Offshore production began in 1999 from the Ivana gas field, in which INA and Italian ENI have a joint interest, based on a commercial contract between the two companies. The development of other satellite discoveries in the area south of Ivana is well under way. Production from the Marica gas field started in November 2004. Currently, daily production from the two offshore gas fields (Ivana and Marica) is 2.5 million cubic metres. Total gas reserves in the Adriatic offshore are estimated at 20 billion cubic metres.

In 2003, INA produced a total of 1.21 million tonnes of crude oil and condensate and 1.85 billion cubic metres of natural gas.

In Syria, INA is carrying out intensive exploration operations on the Hayan block, where two gas/condensate fields and one gas field have been discovered. A comprehensive development study is under preparation.

### 2. Refining and wholesale

INA d.d. owns and operates refineries and lubricant plants in Croatia, and supports crude oil and product distribution networks. Crude oil is delivered to refineries by pipeline and products are distributed by ship, road and rail through a number of product depots. Product sales are made on a wholesale basis and also through a retail network.

The two fuels refineries are located in Rijeka (Urinj) and Sisak. The Rijeka refinery is a medium-sized refinery located on the Adriatic coast with access to a deep-sea port and the JANAF pipeline system. The refinery typically runs 3–3.5 million tonnes per year of crude oil, producing a range of petroleum products for the domestic and export markets. The refinery has seven crude oil storage tanks with a total storage capacity of 356,000 m³.

The Sisak Refinery is located 50 km from Zagreb, the main consumption area in Croatia. It is also well located to serve other local markets in Croatia and north-western parts of Bosnia and Herzegovina, the north-eastern part of Slovenia and western and northern Serbia.

The refinery processes local crude oils (produced by INA) plus Russian crude oil imported via connections to the Druzba 1 and Druzba 2 pipelines. It is also possible to supply crude oil from the Mediterranean through the JANAF pipeline.

The refinery typically runs 2.0–2.2 million tonnes per year of crude oil, producing a range of petroleum products for the domestic and near export markets.

In 2005, INA will commence a larger scale programme of refinery modernization in order to upgrade the quality of products in compliance with EU specifications.

*Lubricant plants*
The Mlaka lubricants plant is located within the Mlaka district in the town of Rijeka. It is also known as 'Maziva Rijeka'.

Operations started at the site in 1883, with one of the first refinery operations in Europe. The refinery has been substantially rebuilt, with major investments being made throughout the last century. Today, the plant is focused on the production of base oils, lubricants and bitumen and is the key supplier of these products in Croatia.

The Zagreb lubricant plant is now a fully owned subsidiary company of INA d.d., known as Maziva Zagreb d.o.o.

The plant is located in the industrial zone of Zagreb and close to the markets with the strongest demand, namely the Zagreb area and its industry. Its main activities are production and trade of lubricants, tailor-made lubricants and greases for industry, additives and related products.

*Wholesale and distribution*
Wholesale and distribution operations are managed within the Wholesale Department within the combined Refining and Wholesale division

of INA. The main aim of this part of the division is to manage efficiently the link between refinery production and INA's retail network and wholesale customers.

The Wholesale Department organizes the export of INA's products (gasoline, virgin naphtha, LPG, lubricants, bitumen and other) to the neighbouring markets (Slovenia, Bosnia and Herzegovia, Serbia, Montenegro) and other markets (Hungary, Austria, Germany and others).

## 3. Retail operations

The principal business activity of this division is the retail of fuels and other goods through a network of petrol stations. INA's retail network covers the whole of Croatia, with 405 operating petrol stations plus 31 other specialized sales sites that include warehouses, marine terminals and retail shops.

In 2003, the Retail Services Division sold on the Croatian market 1.18 million tonnes of oil products. In addition to fuel sales, INA's petrol stations offer other services like shops with consumer goods, cafés, etc.

The petrol station network gives INA the leading position in the Croatian fuels retail sector. The sector is open to competition, with a number of other companies owning and operating sites (mostly, in turn, still supplied by INA's refineries).

INA's retail operations in neighbouring countries are managed through subsidiary companies in these countries. The operations include 43 petrol stations in Bosnia and Herzegovina and six petrol stations in Slovenia. Parts of INA's sites in Bosnia and Herzegovina (in the Serb-held regions) are not accessible.

INA also claims ownership of certain assets in Serbia comprising 194 petrol stations, seven terminals and other facilities. It has undertaken legal action in order to regain title to the Beopetrol assets (the company that currently runs INA's petrol stations).

Prices of oil products are deregulated. They are based on CIF Med prices of derivatives and the exchange rate US$ and HRK, including some other parameters included in the formulae.

*Management*
INA's management structure follows the German model and comprises the General Assembly, Supervisory Board and a Management Board.

The Management Board manages the business of the company. It has direct control of commercial decisions and is empowered to enact the company's business. The Management Board is ultimately responsible to the Supervisory Board. INA's Management Board comprises seven members and is headed by the chairman. The company has in place a corporate governance system in line with best practice.

The Management Board, chaired by Dr Tomislav Dragičević, was appointed in January 2000 (with several changes of the members of the Board, but not the chairman). Since then INA has carried out a comprehensive restructuring programme and significantly improved its operational and financial performance.

During the restructuring process, INA reorganized itself as a vertically-integrated oil and gas company with clearly defined key businesses. All other activities are being spun off as independent companies that still operate under the umbrella of INA Group. However, this new independence gives INA's individual operations much greater flexibility and market adaptability.

# Key subsidiaries

**Crosco Integrated Drilling & Well Services Ltd** is a wholly-owned subsidiary of INA. The principal activities of Crosco comprise services in connection with the extraction of crude oil and natural gas, drilling, workover and well completion, well testing, coil tubing and nitrogen cementing, stimulation and well logging. The company has a fleet of 48 modern drilling, workover and geoservices rigs, as well as three offshore platforms (one semi-submersible and two jackups). Crosco has over 40 years of international service experience and has conducted operations in 23 countries throughout Europe, Africa and Asia. (www.crosco.hr)

**Proplin Ltd** comprises the wholesale and retail LPG business of INA. Effective from January 2002, Proplin operates as a separate legal entity within the INA Group.

The distribution of LPG in bottles to households and tanks to industry started more than 30 years ago. Over the years, the business has grown as the number of customers has increased and the LPG consumption has diversified (bottles, small bulks, automotive gas, city gas, industrial consumers, etc)

Proplin operations consist of eight distribution centres in Croatia, geographically well positioned to serve the customers all across the country. It has an estimated market share in Croatia of 98 per cent in wholesale and 35 per cent in retail.

**STSI – Integrirani tehnički servisi d.o.o.** In December 2001, INA was spun off into a wholly-owned subsidiary, the assets used in the performance of preventive and corrective maintenance services. Prior to establishment of STSI, the maintenance services were performed as an operating division within INA.

STSI's mission is to ensure safe, efficient and quality maintenance services for the properties and technical systems of INA's companies at prices that reflect those on the open market. STSI will focus on the development of the maintenance business to become a leader in the domestic and surrounding areas. In addition to maintenance services, STSI also provide the organization of specialized transport services, machining and manufacturing of spare parts, overhaul repairs of processing equipment and other equipment to INA and other customers.

**INA's overseas trade companies** act as distributors of INA Group products and as purchasers of raw materials. These companies also assist INA in the trading of crude oil and obtaining foreign sources of financing for INA. Material trading subsidiaries are InterINA Limited London and InterINA (Guernsey) Limited.

INA has a 16.63 per cent shareholding in the JANAF oil pipeline system. JANAF has signed certain agreements for the implementation of the Družba Adria project that involves the export of Russian crude oil to the world market via the existing pipelines of the Družba and JANAF systems, which extend from Russia, via Belarus, Ukraine, Slovakia, Hungary and Croatia to the Omišalj tanker port and terminal. Realization of this project can be made possible by modifying the Omišalj–Sisak sections so as to allow for the reversal of flow of crude oil.

However, the project has aroused considerable public concern because of its impact on the environment and, specifically, the Croatian coastline.

INA d.d. (a parent company of INA Group) is a joint stock company. Until 2003, it was fully owned by the Republic of Croatia. In July 2003, the transaction agreements were signed between MOL (the Hungarian national oil company), the Croatian government and INA for the sale of 25 per cent plus one share in INA d.d. The transaction was concluded in November 2003. In accordance with the contract, MOL has nominated two members both to the Supervisory Board and the Management Board. These positions enable MOL to participate actively in business activities and the decision-making process. However, the Republic of Croatia still remains the majority owner.

By signing the transaction agreements, MOL has committed to support INA's strategy including the modernization of INA's refineries.

As partners, INA and MOL have a unique position in the fast growing Central European oil product market. Further development of the partnership will enable both companies to exploit synergies in all businesses, and enable better utilization of each company's special-ization and the implementation of joint projects.

INA operates in a transparent business environment. The Republic of Croatia has the status of EU accession candidate and the negotiations for full membership are about to start in March 2005. The Croatian energy legislation is fairly harmonized with the EU regulations and further adjustments will be carried out during the preparations for full membership.

In 2003, INA d.d., the parent company, generated profits of US$121 million, while the profit of the INA Group was US$135 million. In 2002, the INA parent company posted a profit of US$109 million and the INA Group US$125 million. According to current projections, the 2004 profit will be higher than in 2003.

For further details visit our website www.ina.hr

INA-Industrija nafte, d.d. Zagreb
Avenija V. Holjevca 10, 10002 Zagreb
p.p. 555
Switchboard: +385 (0) 1 6450 000
Email: ina@ina.hr
Website: www.ina.hr
INA toll free information telephone 0800-1112

# 4.2

# Konstruktor-Inženjering d.d. Split

## Introduction

KONSTRUKTOR-INŽENJERING d.d. is a company organized for the procurement of works and services as a General Contractor. Its activities in the past covered many different fields: construction of power plants (embankment and concrete dams), varied types of underground structures (tunnels, underground machine houses, transformer chambers and other below-ground premises), pressure pipelines (horizontal, vertical and battered types), water chambers, channels, etc.

In addition to hydro-technical tunnels, the Company built road tunnels and other types of tunnels, highways, roads, bridges, viaducts and other road-related structures. Included in the works that have accounted for the major employment of its available capacity are large-scale infrastructure facilities (water supply and sewerage systems) and marine structures.

Besides civil engineering works, the Company has been permanently engaged in the construction of high-rises intended for varied purposes: residential, business and industrial facilities, health and social care, cultural and education-related buildings, sports and sacral structures, etc.

KONSTRUKTOR was established in 1945, primarily for the needs of reconstruction for the town of Split and the broader area of Dalmatia, which were widely damaged in World War II. It was a period marked by intensive works in the high-rise construction segment, while civil engineering works accounted for a minor share.

Since 1954 the Company has specialized in the construction of high complexity engineering structures, which were undertaken in the territory of former Yugoslavia (Bosnia and Herzegovina, Macedonia, Serbia and Montenegro).

In 1965, KONSTRUKTOR was awarded its first contract abroad (Sri Lanka) and since that time, it has been continuously engaged in the construction of varied projects on the international market (eg Zambia, Colombia, Tanzania, Iraq, Czech Republic, Russia, Germany, Luxembourg).

## KONSTRUKTOR today

In 1992, when Croatia's political and economic system was completely reconstructed, KONSTRUKTOR underwent a privatization process and restructured into a share-holding company, specialized in building construction. It continued its operations under the name of KONSTRUKTOR-INŽENJERING d.d., undertaking projects at home and abroad.

The development of KONSTRUKTOR has been adapted to prevailing investment trends in Croatia, among which the most prominent has been the construction of roads. Therefore, the Company undertook construction of a great number of road infrastructure projects (highways, bridges, viaducts and tunnels), large water supply and sewerage projects and marine structures.

It participated in the construction of a great number of residential, business and industrial facilities, projects related to medical and social care, culture and education, sacral buildings, etc.

During the last few years, KONSTRUKTOR realized earnings of more than €150 million per year. Out of the company's 2,000 employees, some 250 hold university degrees, as engineers (civil and mechanical engineers), economists and legal professionals. The composition of the qualified engineering staff and the labour-side workers has been adapted to the type of projects the company has been developing.

The Company has, at its disposal, building machinery and equipment to the value of €34 million (after depreciation value), the major share of which accounts for modern and high-performance machinery.

It is the aim of KONSTRUKTOR to expand its activities both at home and abroad. Today it has shares in 15 affiliated companies, including branch offices in Zagreb, Frankfurt/Main (Germany) and Mostar (Bosnia and Herzegovina). Intensive market research in south-eastern Europe and Africa is aimed at employing its spare capacity.

KONSTRUKTOR is, at present, one of the most successful construction companies in Croatia and the broader region of this part of Europe, and according to its business results and market size, the company can be ranked amongst the several dozen leading Croatian companies.

# Organization

The company's main organ is the Meeting of Shareholders, at which the shareholders decide, among other things, on appointing the Supervisory Committee, which itself appoints the Board and controls all business activities. Mr Željko Žderiæ is the General Manager, having been employed with the Company since 1979. He holds the office in which he manages the day-to-day affairs of the Company within the realm of his authority.

The divisions of the Company are Technical, Legal and Financial/Commercial Divisions. The Technical Division coordinates all operations via Chief Project Engineers. Included in this division are the Technical Preparation Department (market research, preparation of bids, control of the results and analyses), the Catering Service and the Mechanical Department, as well as all permanent and temporary production plants. Three stationary production plants support the building activities (provide necessary aggregate and concrete). They are organized in a manner where the range of products and output meets the needs of the work sites, as well as sales to third persons. Within this division is also quality control of used materials and built-in works components. These services are carried out in the company's own laboratories, or provisions are made for the use of other testing institutions. The Technical Division also has the Safety at Work Unit, which plays an important role because safety measures related to the physical wellbeing of staff and a pollution-free environment must be adequately provided at all times. All relevant requirements and guidelines are contained in the applicable regulations and the Company's by-laws.

# Road infrastructure

The Republic of Croatia's government has made a very ambitious plan for the construction of the national road network and the reconstruction of existing state roads. KONSTRUKTOR-INŽENJERING is one of the most successful contractors participating in the realization of this programme. A summary of works completed under this segment is given herein below.

## Zagreb–Split (Dubrovnik) Highway

The works completed by KONSTRUKTOR under this project are the sections SV.ROK–ZADAR II, PRGOMET–DUGOPOLJE and VRPOLJE–PRGOMET, and those presently under way are the sections SKRADIN–ŠIBENIK, ŠIBENIK–VRPOLJE, PIROVAC–SKRADIN and DUGOPOLJE–BISKO.

Included in the road structures built under this project are the following road tunnels: SV. ROK, LEDENIK, KONJSKO, OSMAKOVAC, DUBRAVE, KRPANI and ÈELINKA, and the BISKO Tunnel, presently under construction.

The bridges and viaducts constructed under this project are: DOBRA Bridge, viaducts MODRUŠ II and III, ROVANJSKA, CRNA DRAGA, BEJIÆI, FRADIVINA, RODINE GLAVICE, PODGREDE and GARIŠTA, and the KRKA Bridge, which has been completed most recently. The GUDUÆA Bridge is currently under construction, while the MASLENIÈKI Bridge, completed several years ago, is the key structure for connecting southern Croatia with its main landmass in continental Europe. The DRAGA Viaduct on the Skradin-Šibenik section is presently under construction.

### Rijeka–Zagreb Highway

KONSTRUKTOR-INŽENJERING d.d. executed works for the KARLOVAC–VUKOVA GORICA and KUPJAK–VRBOVSKO sections. These sections were provided with the following road tunnels: POD VUGLEŠ, JAVOROVA KOSA, ROŽMAN BRDO and VELIKI GLOŽAC, as well as the JAVOROVA KOSA Framed Cover. The important facilities constructed on this Highway are also the viaducts DREŽNIK, KATUŠIN and STARA SUŠICA, and the KAMAÈNIK Bridge.

### Zagreb–Gorièan (Hungarian Border) Highway

In the period from 1998 to 2000, the Company constructed three sections of this Highway, and the BREZNIÈKOG HUM–NOVI MAROF section in 2003. Also completed in 2003 were the VRTLINOVEC Tunnel and DUGI VRH and ŽUKCI Viaducts.

### Zagreb–Macelj (Slovenian Border) Highway

The Company participated in the works for the KRAPINA–MACELJ section by construction of the KRAPINÈICA, JURIÈKI and TKALCI Viaducts.

### Reconstruction of state roads

Provided under this programme are the works for the BAŠKA VODA–SVETIŠTE VEPRIC section, while works for the MAKARSKA Bypass Road and the RUSKAMEN–DUBCI section are currently underway.

### Split Bypass Road

Included in the completed works are several road subsections under Phase III from Split to Stobreè, and the works underway are subsections under Phase V and the ŽRNOVNICA Bridge.

## Rijeka Gateway Project

Included under this project are road works, the BOBOVA Tunnel and BOBOVA and DRAGA II Viaducts, while the VEŽICE Viaduct has already been completed.

## Other roads and related structures

Included under other roads are the ÈARA–ZAVALATICA, BLATO–PRIGRADICA and ÈARA–PUPNAT roads and the local heliport on the Island of Korèula, as well as the DREŽNIK Bridge in Karlovac and the DUBROVNIK Bridge (2002).

# Power supply structures

At the end of 2004, KONSTRUKTOR completed works for the PEÆ-MLINI Hydro-Power Plant in Bosnia and Herzegovina, and a series of rehabilitation works for the hydro-power plants in Croatia.

# Utilities and marine structures

The Company has been engaged in the realization of one of the largest environmental projects in Europe, works for which started several years ago. Proposed under the project is the construction of the water supply and sewerage systems Split–Solin–Kaštela–Trogir, ordered by the Agencija EKO-Kaštelanski zaljev (the Project Implementation Agency). KONSTRUKTOR-INŽENJERING d.d. has participated in the contracting of its major components. Therefore, included in the completed works under the project are STUPE Hydro-Technical Tunnel, the DUJMOVAÈA Sewerage Network, the KUNÈEVA GREDA Water Supply Network, STUPE Wastewater Discharge, the SV. KAJO Subsystem and a series of other facilities.

At present, new works under this project are likely to be contracted soon. The project of VELA LUKA Hydrotechnical Tunnel on the Island of Korèula is presently under way.

KONSTRUKTOR executed a series of rehabilitation works for the quayside areas on the Dalmatian islands, eg Vela Luka on the Island of Korèula, Sumartin and Povlja on the Island of Braè, Suæurje, the Island of Hvar and the ports of Prviæ Luka and Prviæ Šepurine.

Also completed are the reconstruction and extension works for the Pier No. 3 in the Port of Ploèe, and the rehabilitation and construction works for the VIKTOR LENAC Shipyard in Rijeka.

# High-rises

Included under this segment are residential developments in Split, Rijeka, Dubrovnik and Zagreb, the GORAN IVANIŠEVIÆ Residential/Business Centre in Split and shopping malls for MERCATOR and AUTOCOMMERCE, Split.

Also procured in the city of Split are the reconstruction and extension works for the Brewery and Apartments MAZZUCHELLI within the Diocletian's Palace walls. Projects underway are KERUM Shopping Centre in Zadar, and IGH and NIVA business buildings in Zagreb.

The projects under way in Split are two residential developments and a large transformer substation in the location of Dobri.

Under the projects intended for medical and social care, mention should be made of the RETIRED PEOPLE'S HOME, Blato, on the Island of Korèula, PUBLIC HEALTH CENTRES in Ploèe and Korèula, while extensive works for the extension and reconstruction of the REBRO Hospital in Zagreb (€50 million) are currently underway.

In the last few years, KONSTRUKTOR constructed a number of churches and pastoral centres in Kašatel Stari, Ploèe and Solin and a few minor projects of a similar kind in Split. Included in the projects completed are the reconstruction and extension of the ARCHBISHOP'S ORDINARIATE, Split and the ARCHBISHOP'S RESIDENCE and its ANNEX for the RETIRED CLERGYMAN'S HOME in Zagreb.

# KONSTRUKTOR tomorrow

As reported by Mr Željko Žderiæ, General Director, KONSTRUKTOR-INŽENJERING, Split can expect major employment of its capacities over the next few years in the field of road construction in Croatia (highways and road facilities), and the reconstruction and development of road structures under the Programme of Reconstructing the State Roads.

Also important is the construction for water supply and sewerage facilities proposed under the Split–Solin–Kaštela–Trogir Environmental Project, as well as development of port facilities and other infrastructure in the Republic of Croatia.

KONSTRUKTOR carefully traces trends in the consumer investment business of neighbouring countries (Bosnia and Herzegovina, Serbia and Montenegro, Albania, etc) to maintain its satisfactory performance in the international environment, which features tough competition. Added to this is also the trend of the international financing institutions that are willing to invest substantial funds in the development of these countries.

In the last few years, KONSTRUKTOR confirmed its continuous growth under all business indices. Its total income in 2002 compared to the previous year more than doubled (107 per cent), and in 2003 compared to 2002, it grew by 56.5 per cent.

As for employment, this was also marked by constant growth, with a tendency to balance the share of administrative and operating personnel.

Under the investment policy for the supply of modern and sophisticated building machinery and equipment, more than HRK135 million (or €18 million) has been invested for such purchases in the last two years.

KONSTRUKTOR-INŽENJERING d.d. Split is a company with stable business operation and successful performance that punctually fulfils all its liabilities towards investors and other business partners, owing to which it has earned a sound reputation among those seeking the procurement of works and services in the construction field.

According to information obtained from the General Manager, it is the commitment of the Company to continue to intensively research the market at home and abroad in order to provide new jobs. This trend is well justified by the results from the previous year: the value of quoted works amounted to approximately HRK4.3 billion, and the value of contracted works was approximately HRK1 billion (€130 million), which gives 23 per cent acquisition and which is quite a high percentage. According to market expectations, the company is likely to maintain these business results over the next few years.

Such expectations are firmly supported by KONSTRUKTOR's ability to meet the challenges of the construction market by selecting the optimum solution in order to strike out in the right direction.

# KONSTRUKTOR-INŽENJERING d.d. SPLIT
21 000 Split, Svačićeva 4

**Company Corporate Message: A Distinct Trace in Time and Space**

KONSTRUKTOR – INŽENJERING d.d.
Kralja Petra Svacica 4
21 000 Split
Croatia
Website: www.konstruktor-split.hr
Contacts:
*Zeljko Zderiæ B.C.E.*
*General Manager – President of the Board*
Tel: +385 (0) 21 487044
Fax: +385 (0) 21 487 044
Email: zeljko.zderic@konstruktor-split.hr
*Vice Dodig B.C.E.*
*Director, Technical Division*
Tel: +385 (0) 21 409 297
Fax: +385 (0) 21 486 843
Email: vice.dodig@konstruktor-split.hr
*Meri Soko B.L.*
*Director, Legal Division*
Tel: +385 (0) 21 409 204
Fax: +385 (0) 21 487 186
Email: meri.soko@konstruktor-split.hr
*Frane Galzina B.Econ.*
*Director, Financial Division*
Tel: +385 (0) 21 409 227
Fax: +385 (0) 21 486 856
Email: frane.galzina@konstruktor-split.hr
*Sasa Dukan B.C.E.*
*Director, Branch Office Zagreb*
Tel: +385 (01) 6040 355
Fax: +385 (01) 6040374
Email: sasa.djukan@zg

# 4.3

# Dalekovod d.d.

## Introduction

Dalekovod is a Croatian company engaged in the design, production, and assembling of electric power, traffic and telecommunication facilities, as well as consultancy services for the domestic (Croatian) and international markets. It is a fully customer-oriented company, which insists on the quality of its products and services, based on specific know-how and qualifications of its labour force, as well as the ability to promptly adjust to the impacts of the environment by developing competitive capacities.

The company's mission is to provide a complete service to the infrastructure industry (electric power, road and railway traffic, telecommunications) based on the principles of professional excellence and top quality. Its base is the company's human resources, who possess specific knowledge and skills, which are highly appreciated by Dalekovod's customers. The company is a learning organization with the ability to adapt quickly to turbulent environmental influences. Dalekovod's operation is characterized by a stakeholder approach, reflected particularly in the fact that the company is majority owned by its current and former employees. Dalekovod shall always be a responsible member of society, making sure that its sustainable development will be harmonized with the interests of the wider community and requirements of environmental protection.

## History in brief

Dalekovod was founded in 1949 as a publicly-owned company and it kept this status until 1989, when the transformation of publicly-owned companies into government-owned companies began. This transformation was completed successfully in 1992, when Dalekovod became a joint stock company, fully owned by the government. Between 1992 and 2000, the Croatian government offered a small portion of Dalekovod's shares to the company's employees, which were to be bought on credit.

The rest of the shares were given to other Croatian companies as compensation for trade receivables for the public works contracts those companies had with the government. Dalekovod bought those shares and offered them again to Dalekovod's employees in two Employee Stock Ownership Plans (ESOPs).

Dalekovod, today, is a fully privately-owned company, with 85 per cent of the company's shares being owned by small shareholders (mostly former and present company employees). Two ESOPs (ESOP 2000 and ESOP 2001) have been carried out so far at Dalekovod and 60 per cent of the company employees have taken part in these.

A major difference can be detected in management's policies towards the company from the time Dalekovod was government-owned to the present time, when it is governed by the private sector. When the state was the owner of the company, it was not solely interested in profitability and the company was focused more on corporate social responsibility and its public role. The present day privately-owned Dalekovod has kept its legacy of social responsibility (such as its environmental policies, regard for the welfare of its employees and re-investment of surplus capital back into the Croatian economy, for example) but also introduced new strategies geared towards profitability, company growth and long-term enterprise sustainability.

# Core products and services

Since its foundation in 1949, Dalekovod has developed into a modern organization with over 1,750 employees, offering the following core services:

- design;

- production; and

- erection;

in the following fields of engineering services, in which Dalekovod specializes:

- design and production of suspension and jointing equipment for all types of transmission lines and substations from 0.4 up to 500 kV;

- design, production and erection of steel lattice and lighting towers and other metal structures;

- design, production and erection of electroenergetic facilities, especially transmission lines from 0.4 up to 500 kV;

- design and erection of substations of all types and voltage levels up to 500 kV;

- mounting and laying of aerial, underground and submarine cables up to 110 kV;

- erection of telecommunication facilities, all types of networks and antennas;

- production and mounting of all metal parts for roads, especially for lighting of roads, road shock barriers and traffic signalling, lighting of tunnels and traffic regulation;

- electrification of railways and tram lines in the cities.

Dalekovod's highly-educated personnel can solve each challenge related to the design, production and construction technology relating to the company's line of business. By developing fundamental competencies and skills that are important to this industry, the company tries to add new values to its core products and services.

It should be noted that along with Dalekovod's already traditional business efficiency, the company has also implemented the ISO 9001:1994 system, certificated by the Lloyd's Register Quality Assurance in 1995, which has contributed significantly to the improvement of Dalekovod's business operations. In order to ensure constant quality monitoring, Dalekovod has also carried out an adjustment of ISO 9001:1994 to ISO 9001:2000. Furthermore, Dalekovod's efforts to promote a clean and healthy environment is ensured by the application of the International ISO 14001 standard, whereby the company gives its full contribution to environmental protection. Besides the above-mentioned standards, Dalekovod has also been awarded with following: EN 729–2, BSI OHSAS 18000, ISO/IEC 17025.

By fostering the principles of the engineering profession and by applying acknowledged world quality and environmental protection standards, Dalekovod is continuously seeking to improve its customer satisfaction. Dalekovod, today, is a reliable, renowned and acknowledged partner throughout the world in its wide-ranging area of products and services. The results of Dalekovod's business policy and its cooperation with domestic and international partners is high-quality equipment and services, which, along with acceptable prices, are highly appreciated and accepted by Dalekovod's customers worldwide.

# Organizational structure

Dalekovod belongs to a group of very powerful and influential Croatian companies with regard to manufacturing, sales and service resources in the area of electrical engineering, design and production. The

Company employs 1,750 people, divided into four basic divisions: Design Division (100), Production Division (650), Construction and Erection Division (650), and Support Activities (350) (see Figure 4.3.1).

In the development of its business, Dalekovod has co-founded or acquired several affiliates in different countries:

- Dalcom Ltd in Freilassing (Germany) – limited liability company, engineering office, founded by Dalekovod d.d. Zagreb;

- Dalen Ltd in Ljubljana (Slovenia) – limited liability company, engineering office, founded by Dalekovod d.d. Zagreb;

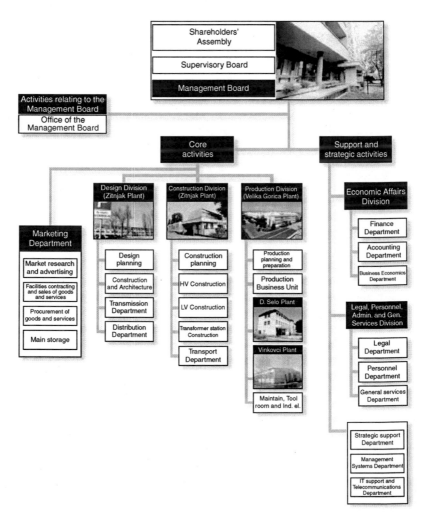

**Figure 4.3.1** Organization chart

- Dalekovod Ltd in Mostar (Bosnia and Herzegovina) – limited liability company, engineering office, founded by Dalekovod d.d. Zagreb;

- Dalekovod Poland S.A. in Warsaw (Poland) – joined stock company, engineering office, co-founded by Dalekovod d.d. Zagreb and partners from Poland;

- Dalekovod-Projekt Ltd in Zagreb (Croatia) – limited liability company, a design office for electric power utilities, founded by Dalekovod d.d. Zagreb;

- Dalekovod-Cinčaonica Ltd in Dugo Selo (Croatia) – limited liability company, a production factory for hot-dip galvanizing, founded by Dalekovod d.d. Zagreb;

- Dalekovod TKS A.D. in Doboj (Bosnia and Herzegovina) – joined stock company, a production factory for steel structures, acquired and 57 per cent owned by Dalekovod d.d. Zagreb.

# Product design

Dalekovod's design department utilizes up-to-date software (Catia V) for 3D modelling and generating software for the machining of tool components, which are fabricated on the CNC processing machines. Thus, Dalekovod's design department is able to respond swiftly to either new customers or market demands. Accumulated experience, references, extensive database and specialized know-how, are, today, coupled with the most sophisticated CAD/CAE technology.

Products from Dalekovod's production programme have been manufactured in its production workshops by means of technologies for forging, casting, mechanical processing, welding, sand blasting, hot-dip galvanizing, mounting etc. The company has its own special tool workshop capacity for the production of all the tools, devices and facilities that are necessary for the quoted technologies.

The galvanizing plant, Dalekovod-Cinčaonica d.o.o., was founded as a limited liability company, is under 100 per cent ownership of Dalekovod d.d. and is located some 20 km from Zagreb. This plant is the biggest hot-dip galvanizing plant in the region. The capacity of this plant is 31,000 tonnes of steel per year. It has two production shops. The first one is for polygonal poles and high masts, guard-rails and accessories, transmission towers and other products up to 12.5 metres long. The dimension of the zinc kettle is $13.00 \times 1.80 \times 2.80$ (h) m. The second shop is for nuts and bolts, suspension and jointing equipment, hollowware, anchor bolts and other small materials. It is equipped with automatic suspended spinning equipment. This galvanizing plant will satisfy the following quality and environment standards: EN ISO 1461, ASTM-A 123, ISO 9001 and 14001.

Dalekovod has arguably the best-equipped laboratory for vibrations in South East Europe. Dalekovod's present laboratory is mostly oriented towards testing Dalekovod's new or improved products and quality control. After the new vibrations laboratory was commissioned, Dalekovod's laboratories have subsequently been able to offer their services to its market.

Also at Dalekovod's disposal are specially equipped teams of experts who can execute the company's work under all climatic conditions and in any terrain, with the benefit of special machines and tools. Apart from the application of special derricks for lifting up loads during the erection process, Dalekovod's experts take pride in having wide experience and knowledge in the use of special work helicopters employed for erection projects.

Dalekovod's expert teams are specially prepared and trained in order to measure up to the requirements of the construction of particular projects. Reference to the following erection projects carried out by the company clearly suggests that Dalekovod is a safe and reliable business partner: erection of 0.4–500 kV electric power transmission projects, 0.4–500 kV substations, laying of underground and submarine power and telecommunication cables, lighting of roads, sports grounds and industrial facilities, railroad contact networks, installation of aerial and TV towers and mobile telephone towers (GSM), guard-rails on motorways, and traffic signpost portals.

The majority of Dalekovod's employees are individuals from Croatia and the company seeks to promote the continuous education of its staff by developing and monitoring annual education plans for each of its employees.

## Business development

Taking a long-term view, Dalekovod d.d. intends to position itself in the markets of Central and South East Europe as a strong and reliable business partner. The company's long-term experience on the world market, whether as a winner of awards for large infrastructure projects, or as a supplier of equipment or subcontractor, shall likewise be extended to the regional markets. Thus, Dalekovod is seeking to appear on these markets both as a local manufacturer and contractor, and as a member of international consortiums for the execution of infrastructure projects as well.

Hence Dalekovod is planning to extend its activities to markets that the company considers promising in the long term, by acquiring local companies operating in Dalekovod's sphere of business. For example, in Bosnia and Herzegovina, Dalekovod d.d. has become the owner of two companies – Dalekovod Mostar d.o.o., 100 per cent owned and TDSK Doboj, 57 per cent owned – after a recent successful takeover of majority stakes in these companies. At the moment, Dalekovod is also screening companies in Serbia and Montenegro.

Dalekovod is a vertically-integrated company, offering various services ranging from infrastructure project engineering, to design and manufacture of products, and invests continuously in the most sophisticated production and environmental technology. The company's development department uses the most up-to-date software 3D design tools, which are connected to CNC machines by a network system.

Due to all of the factors mentioned above, Dalekovod finds itself in a position to react promptly to all customers' demands, and to design and manufacture new products within a very short period of time. We can therefore say that Dalekovod can easily adjust to its industrial environment and market competition, as well as new technologies.

Under the present market conditions, where it is very difficult to anticipate future events, Dalekovod management points out its strategic goal of maintaining a high level of adjustability to new market conditions, which is one of the company's strengths in fulfilling market opportunities.

## Experience with foreign markets

During the near half-century of its existence, Dalekovod d.d. has been exporting products to over 80 countries worldwide. In some countries of Western Europe (eg Norway, Switzerland and Germany), Dalekovod has been present for a number of years with its programme of steel structures and line hardware in the electric power industry, while in Germany it has also been providing challenging civil engineering services for high voltage electric power projects. There has been no continuous export of Dalekovod's products and services to other European countries, although the company has maintained a continuous presence in those markets. Dalekovod imports raw materials mostly from Central European countries, and equipment for power utilities from Western Europe.

In the countries where Dalekovod is seeking to break into the market, the company initially seeks to obtain all of the necessary certificates for its products in order to fulfil the requirements of operating in those markets. Dalekovod will typically search for a local partner in order to present a joint appearance in that market. In the UK, for example, Dalekovod has certificated the equipment for an overhead contact system for the British railways, while in Poland it certificated almost all of its production programme, including steel lattice towers, antenna masts, lighting poles and suspension and jointing equipment for transmission lines ranging from 0.4 to 400 kV. Having fulfilled all the required regulatory prerequisites, Dalekovod is expecting to successfully enter into both the UK and Polish markets in 2005.

## Joint ventures

On 8 September 2004, Dalekovod d.d. concluded a contract on joint investment into forging technology with the company UNIOR d.d. from Zreče, Slovenia. UNIOR d.d. is a company specialized in the forging industry and is one of the highest ranked companies within that line of business worldwide. The contract shall be supplemented by two agreements on business cooperation between the companies' founders and the new joint venture company, whereupon a new company UNIDAL d.o.o. shall be founded in place of the former forging unit of Dalekovod in Vinkovci.

The joint venture between Dalekovod and UNIOR was founded mainly for the mutual benefit of both founders. UNIOR, as the leading company within its line of business in Europe, intends to increase its production capacities, along with maintaining the existing high quality level and production prices. Dalekovod's existing forging line can easily fulfil market demand, provided that fresh capital is injected in order to ensure modernization of the plant and improvement of production, along with the application of state-of-the-art know-how provided by UNIOR. Given that both founders will be obliged (under the terms of the agreement) to manufacture 3,000 tonnes of forgings annually, the investment made into the modernization of the plant will be justified from an economic perspective.

The forge is anticipated to start operating at the beginning of 2005. UNIDAL d.o.o. will produce forged products for the needs of the industries with the greatest demand: the automobile and electric power industries. As a result of this investment, Dalekovod intends to improve the existing forging technology, reduce production costs and enter into new markets by reducing the costs of producing forgings, along with maintaining traditional high quality.

## Financial strategies

Dalekovod employs international accounting standards. In order to ensure independent auditory control of the company, Pricewaterhouse-Coopers has been engaged by the Supervisory Board and the Management Board of the Company. Dalekovod's shares have been listed on the Zagreb Stock Exchange since March 2001, under the stock exchange symbol DLKV-R-A. Financial statements can be downloaded from the company's website: www.dalekovod.com.

Due to its particular growth strategy, Dalekovod does not have a typical annual investment budget. However, the company conducts evaluations of mutually exclusive investment projects, both within Dalekovod or through investment in acquisitions (steel structures factory Dalekovod TKS a.d., Bosnia and Herzegovina), joint ventures (forging factory UNIDAL d.o.o., Croatia) or greenfield projects (hot-dip galvanizing plant, Dalekovod cinčaonica d.o.o., Croatia).

# Croatia and the European Union (EU)

The membership of Croatia to the EU is anticipated for 2007. However, Dalekovod considers that the act itself shall not, unfortunately, ensure an easier access of Dalekovod products to the EU market.

Although the borders have been open since the admission of Croatia to the WTO, the national infrastructure companies of the EU member states have used their lobbying abilities to protect local production by special requirements in the tender documentation for large infrastructure projects. Croatia already has a negative trade balance with many EU member states. Numerous European and global companies have been bidding on the Croatian market for infrastructure projects, with its inexpensive imported labour force and imported low quality products, while at the same time the Republic of Croatia has not ensured any (infrastructure) export contracts for any local manufacturer for the above mentioned countries. This is the most significant challenge that the Croatian companies in Dalekovod's sector are facing today.

# Doing business with Croatia

Dalekovod finds long-term industry profitability, its premiere position on the market and enterprise sustainability to be the main benefits of operating its business in Croatia. Furthermore, Dalekovod management suggests that the Croatian legislative environment is clear, predictable and transparent but adds that there is always room for further improvements. However, the main problem for any construction company operating in Croatia (as well as in other countries of South-East Europe), remains unfair competition, since few companies besides Dalekovod employ vigorous accounting standards. Unfair competition avoids paying taxes and contributions on wages, and does not give much regard for the environment. This results in such companies putting forward cheaper bids in both public and private tenders, thus forcing law-abiding companies to lower their prices.

The main advantage Dalekovod can exercise against such competition is its ability to bid for large projects with financing power, quality and speed, and provide an industry-wide guarantee for its performance.

## Dalekovod: a strategic vision

Dalekovod d.d. is a company engaged in the design, production, construction and erection of electric power transmission and distribution projects, road and railroad traffic infrastructure projects on the domestic and international market. It is a fully customer-oriented company, which insists on the high quality of its products and services under conditions of significant market competition. Its vision is to become the leading company in its line of business in Central and South-Eastern Europe. Dalekovod's objectives are reflected in the increase of its market share in Croatia and abroad, and sales income growth, along with increased volume of production. As for its internal objectives, Dalekovod's efforts are focused on the following objectives:

- investments in development;

- reduction of manufacturing costs;

- constant care in the quality of the company's products and services;

- an increase of the minimum yield per share of 12 per cent;

- customer satisfaction;

- fostering corporate loyalty;

- investment in employees motivation;

- revitalization and reconstruction of existing production.

Dalekovod d.d. has been granted numerous prestigious awards for its business results, including the 'Golden Marten'. This award was granted to Dalekovod by the Croatian Chamber of Commerce for being the top-ranked large-sized company in the Republic of Croatia for the year 2003. Moreover, Dalekovod was given a prestigious award for being 'The best ranking construction company in South-East Europe' by the *Finance Central Europe* magazine from London, two years in succession, for 2003 and 2004. These awards confirm Dalekovod's efforts at self-improvement in the achievement of its strategic vision.

Dalekovod d.d. joint stock company for engineering, production and construction
Ulica grada Vukovara
3710000 Zagreb
Croatia
p.p. 128
Tel: (+385) (01) 6170 447
Fax: (+385) (01) 6170 450
Email: dalekovod@dalekovod.hr
Website: www.dalekovod.com

# 4.4

# MTC

## Introduction

MTC is Croatia's leading producer of socks, tights and other similar clothing items, primarily for children but also for adults. Based in the town of Cakovec, some 90 km to the north of Zagreb and close to the border with Hungary, MTC is a clothing brand known to many people in Croatia and other new republics of the former Yugoslavia. Furthermore, the company is well known in its region of Europe, since it has been operating as a manufacturer of socks and other clothing garments for much of the 20th century and has been through the experience of having been a private company, then a state (socially) owned enterprise, before, once again, becoming a private company during the 1990s.

## Company history in brief

MTC was founded as a private company in 1923 by a family of entrepreneurs from the Cakovec area, and the company's brand of socks and tights became a well-known brand amongst Balkan consumers during the ensuing decades. The company operated as a socially (state) owned enterprise for many of the years after World War II, and the company primarily belonged to workers and management. Like many of the other companies we have presented in this section of the book, MTC was privatized (through a management buy-out) in the early 1990s and became a joint stock company whose shares could be bought and sold by different individuals.

## Organizational structure

It was not until 2002, however, that a private strategic investor, Mrs Darinka Kricka, acquired a 75 per cent stake in MTC, effectively taking control of the company. Mrs Kricka subsequently became the president of the Board of Directors of MTC.

The equity structure of the company is now one with relatively few shareholders, and corporate level decision-making is quite centralized, as is often the case in family-owned firms. In fact, the present owner has expressed an interest in acquiring an even greater equity stake in MTC than the 75 per cent currently held. Therefore, while MTC today is a modern, profitable and well-managed Croatian manufacturing enterprise, as was the case upon the foundation of the company in the 1920s, it still has the flavour of a private, family-owned Central European company.

## Core business

MTC's core business is the production of socks and tights, and the company currently produces some seven million units of socks per year. MTC supplies both the domestic Croatian market, the new states of the former Yugoslavia, as well as exporting to Europe and further afield. MTC is a medium-sized Croatian manufacturing enterprise, employing several hundred individuals.

MTC's production facilities consist of two main production units: a knitting factory and a sewing factory, both of which are located in the main territorial block of the company in Cakovec and both of which are manned mostly by women.

## Business philosophy

The central business philosophy of MTC under its current ownership is competitive pricing, quality of product and reliable means of delivering orders. The new owners hope to double the size of MTC's current business within the next five years and then to possibly prepare for a public flotation of the company on the Croatian stock exchange.

## Business development and the search for new partners

Although much of the company's current business is still based on long-term business contacts, MTC is actively trying to expand into markets further afield and has been seeking to make contacts with agents in North America and the UK. Company marketing representatives have been actively travelling abroad in recent times, attending clothing industry exhibitions and making contacts with agents as well as suppliers internationally, with the objective of winning new business.

More information is available from the company website: www.mtc.hr

MTC
Neumannova 2
40000 Cakovec
Republic of Croatia
Tel +385 (0) 40 328 055
Fax +385 (0) 40 328 051

# 4.5

# Jadranski Pomorski Servis d.o.o., Rijeka

## Introduction

Jadranski Pomorski Servis (JPS) is a leading Croatian maritime services company, performing tugboat operations and various other sea-borne, port-related functions for almost half a century. Based in the port city of Rijeka, JPS was originally a public enterprise owned by the Croatian government's majors in the oil and gas industries and port authorities sectors, but, like many of the other companies we have presented in this section of the book, it was privatized in 1994 and subsequently became a closed joint stock company. Today, JPS provides several tiers of maritime services to its various clients, including tugboat services to all vessels entering Croatian waters in the region of Rijeka, tanker transportation services to INA oil company, as well as general cargo services via the one cargo ship that operates under the company's flag. JPS is a medium-sized company, employing some 147 individuals and 115 ships crew, and having an annual financial turnover of HRK80 million (€10.5 million) in 2003.

## Organizational history and corporate structure

JPS was founded by the government of Yugoslavia in 1956 under the name of 'Floating Objects' and, operating its small fleet of tugboats and ancillary craft, performed some basic port authority and maritime services duties in its early years of business. However, as the company's operations expanded in Croatia's northern Adriatic waters, JPS' fleet became well known regionally and carried out many significant sea-borne operations. Most notably, the company carried out more than 40 salvage operations from 1966 to 1996, where its expanding fleet of tugboats extinguished fires on ships, towed disabled ships to safety, and prevented ships from either sinking or running aground. Although the company, as a public enterprise not obsessed with profit-making, was highly overstaffed and sometimes not perceived to be operating with the greatest levels of efficiency, JPS obtained a good reputation in Rijeka and the North Adriatic as a reliable provider of important maritime and port authority services.

In 1989, the company's name was changed to that of its present title and business started to both diversify and develop significantly during the 1990s. JPS, which was at the time 46 per cent owned by INA, Croatia's national oil company, began to provide tanker transport services, as well as expanding its activities within the realm of Rijeka port. As was the case with Konstruktor company in Split, JPS was privatized in 1994 through a management buyout and became a fully private company. Company management acquired the majority of the equity in JPS as a result of the privatization, and presently owns 96 per cent of the company, with the employees holding the remaining four per cent stake.

A management turnaround did not take place after the privatization and most of the senior people at the company remained after the privatization. The General Manager of the company is Mr Ante Maras, who has had a long-term association with JPS. The company has pursued a strategy of appointing people from inside the JPS ranks to managerial positions at the company and although JPS today is a modern, well-run corporation, the company still retains a strong hint of a family-run enterprise. JPS is a closed joint stock company, and despite the impressive list of maritime assets that the company has come to own over the decades, it is unlikely to become a public (listed) company in the foreseeable future.

## Provision of maritime services

JPS is highly experienced in the field of harbour and terminal towing and related services, maritime transporting, floating cranes suitable for lifting heavy cargo, trading in oil products, preventing and collecting the spread of oil liquids into regional waters, collecting and preventing the spread of liquid waste, as well as mooring and shipping agency services. The level of maritime services that the company provides could be categorized into three different levels of services:

- **Tanker services.** JPS owns and operates a fleet of four oil tankers and has been employing these for some time to transport oil for INA, Croatia's national oil company. This highly-profitable aspect of the company's business was developed by the current General Manager back in the 1990s, as a result of the greater commercial freedom allowed him by the privatization (ie JPS was now operating in a more liberalized business environment which allowed it to diversify its business into more profitable areas of economic endeavour). JPS is looking to expand its tanker services business beyond the waters of the Adriatic, into the Mediterranean and Black Seas, in search of even greater business potential.

- **Tugboat services.** This has long been the breadbasket of the company's core business. JPS has 10 tugboats in its fleet servicing Rijeka's port. These include one recently acquired state-of-the-art craft, specifically built for JPS by Damon of Holland to service supertankers expected to enter the port of Rijeka's Omisalj Terminal, as part of the Druzhba Adriatic oil pipeline project driven by Russian and US oil companies (JPS has already won a concession from the Rijeka port authority to provide tugboat services for these supertankers).

- **General cargo services.** JPS has also been developing general sea freight and cargo transport services in international waters in recent years, acquiring two cargo vessels to develop this aspect of its business. This is seen as a pilot project by JPS management, with possible room for expansion.

Apart from its fleet of ships and the crews that operate them, JPS also owns and operates two floating cranes and three barges. While the company's operations are based out of Rijeka harbour, JPS also serves the following maritime facilities around Croatia:

- Bakar bulk terminal;

- Rasa timber and livestock terminal, Urinj and Omisalk crude oil terminals;

- INA's oil terminal and refinery in Rijeka (and in the ports of Urinj, Bakar, Mlaka and Srscica);

- LPG terminals in the Rijeka refinery and petrochemical refinery in Sepan;

- several Croatian shipyards;

- the ports of Pula and Ploce.

JPS has developed a marine ecology department in order to safeguard the environment and is always in the front line when required to fight environmental threats at sea.

# Business development

Tanker services account for the majority (some 55 per cent) of JPS' present business and the company continues to provide transport services for INA's petroleum products and oil industry operations. INA had a major ownership stake in JPS until recently, when the latter bought its shares from INA, and JPS, to some degree, functioned in part as a subsidiary company of INA – transporting oil and carrying out other sea-borne operations for the oil company.

However, a substantial degree of expectation presently exists amongst JPS management about the business prospects coming from the Druzhba Adria oil pipeline consortium project, which has chosen the port of Rijeka through which to transport Russian Caspian oil onto the European markets. The Omisalj Terminal of the port of Rijeka was awarded the contract – ahead of a number of regional rivals including Italy's port of Trieste – due to its deep sea loading facilities, which are suitable for the type of supertankers that will be used to ship the oil through the Adriatic. As mentioned earlier, JPS has won a concession from Rijeka port to provide tugboat services for this project and the company has already commissioned an ultra-modern, US$6 million tug, *David Prvi*, in anticipation of forthcoming business.

JPS has only one major competitor operating in Croatian waters, the maritime services company, Brodospas, from the port of Split. In fact Brodospas competed in the Druzhba Adratica supertanker tugboat services tender won by JPS. JPS, however, arguably remains the leading company of its type operating in Croatian waters and has been both expanding and diversifying its business impressively since the time of its privatization.

## Labour

JPS was a highly-overstaffed company during its days as a public enterprise (ie employing over 300 individuals in administrative functions alone) and management has tried to rationalize its workforce since it became a private company. Management has employed early (voluntary) redundancy packages as an incentive mechanism for early worker retirement, and worker numbers have been reduced noticeably. JPS employs less than 150 individuals at present, including those individuals serving as ships crew either on the tugs or on JPS' other vessels.

## Doing business with Croatia

Contemplations of Croatia's possible entry into the European Union (EU) is likely to have some positive as well as negative repercussions for the business of Jadranski Pomorski Servis. As the industry stands at present, JPS has only one major competitor operating in Croatian waters and EU entry is likely to bring with it greater levels of competition, which may result in some loss of (JPS') volume of business in Croatia. However, it is likely that JPS will still have the edge over some of the new competition, as it knows Croatia's waters well and has a strong reputation in the country's maritime services industry. JPS has established ongoing business with some of Croatia's major clients (ie INA, the Rijeka Port Authority, and JANAF, the Croatian pipeline operator), all of whom are very close to JPS either on the basis of ongoing business, or due to the fact that they previously held a direct equity stake in the company.

This has also resulted in numerous individuals moving in and out of management and positions on the board of directors between these companies, and many personal contacts at senior levels of the companies remain. Furthermore, the Croatian maritime industry may not be large enough for some of the larger players in the EU, meaning that they may not get into a position to compete with JPS at all. On the flip side of this, is the fact that EU entry may give JPS greater access to various forms of finance available in the EU, which may assist an already rapidly growing company to grow even more rapidly.

Jadranski Pomorski Servic (Rijeka)
Tel +385 (0) 51 214 887
Fax +385 (0) 51 313161
Email: jps@jps.hr
Website: www.jps.hr

ZA PROIZVODNJU STAKLENE
FARMACEUTSKE AMBALAŽE

MANUFACTURER OF GLASS
PHARMACEUTICAL PACKAGING

# PIRAMIDA

Hrvatska, 10360 Sesvete - Zagreb, Resnička 10
Tel.: ++ 385 (0) 1 200 08 84, Fax: ++385 (0) 1 200 06 28
www.piramida.hr

# 4.6

# Piramida d.d.

## Introduction

Piramida is a specialized Croatian manufacturer of glass pharmaceutical packaging, produced from high-quality glass tubing obtained from the most well-known European dealers in this particular industry. Its clients are major pharmaceuticals companies, in Croatia and abroad, whom Piramida supplies with glass packaging products. The company has over 50 years' of tradition in operating in its line of business in the ex-Yugoslav and greater European market, initially as a public enterprise and now as a private (joint stock) company. After some lean years during the 1990s, Piramida was sold off through a privatization to strategic investors in 2001 and a major turnaround in the company's business commenced. Piramida's market position increased and the company has been realizing impressive financial results each year since the privatization. It currently exports 85 per cent of its production, maintains steady relations with a number of major clients in European markets as well as in the former Yugoslavia and has a proactive approach to business – a managerial ingredient absent prior to the company's privatization.

## Organizational history

Piramida was established as a public (state-owned) company on 1 October 1950, as a city association of glassware merchants for the production of Christmas ornaments, with its headquarters in the Zagreb city centre. Piramida changed its location twice prior to arriving at its present location in 1979 and during this time the company gradually acquired new equipment; new contemporary ampoules production lines of the type Moderne Mecanique, as well as new vials production lines for vials type 3 BS and BZ 16. In September 1992, when Croatia embarked upon its transition to a market economy, Piramida was re-incorporated as a joint stock company on the basis of a Resolution approved by the Restructuring and Development Agency of the Republic of Croatia. However, despite the fact that Piramida was reorganized into a joint stock company, little change took place in the company's approach to business, with the same team of senior managers retaining their position at the head of the enterprise.

When Piramida was finally privatized in 2001, the level of investment in the company was increased and further technological modernization was carried out. A Quality Management System was certified in 2002 in accordance with ISO 9001:2000 and a year later the company became integrated with the Environmental Management System in accordance with ISO 14001:1996. In 2003, Piramida invested in the construction of clean rooms class 100.000 (ISO 8) for product packaging and a 100 per cent optical quality control system. Finally, Piramida also designed a production line for dropping pipettes in 2004 and reconstructed its vial and ampoules production lines. As a result, the company was able to compete in the entire European market and a noticeable growth in sales was recorded.

Piramida is currently a private limited shareholding company, where three chief shareholders control 98 per cent of the enterprise. The other two per cent of the enterprise is owned by former employees. The General Manager of the company since 2001 has been Mr Vedran Vilovic.

## Business turnaround after the privatization

Piramida has undergone a substantial business turnaround since the time of its privatization. As a state-owned firm, the company employed 128 individuals, suffered from little capital investment, bad equipment maintenance and little technological upgrading. During the 1990s, some traditional markets were lost and were not replaced by new ones. The main concern of company management was maintaining social harmony within the enterprise, and not so much with profit maximization, product marketing, business development etc. However, the company's accounts remained in balance and Piramida was not reported to have developed any significant debts.

The privatization brought with it a complete change of management and a new business philosophy. Initially, the new owners tried to keep the same management team to develop the company's business, including its leading director, who, by that stage, had been with the company for 18 years. However, the new owners soon realized that the company's management team would not be able to help them realize their vision for Piramida, and some new individuals at the senior management level, including the present General Manager of the company, Mr Vilovic, were appointed.

The firm's main objective was now to make a financial profit and the company's new owners made significant new investments. Piramida's production lines were completely overhauled by changing all vital areas of the company's technologies; quality control laboratories were completely renewed and restructured and an integrated information programme was installed. Piramida acquired ISO certificates and its products underwent international regulatory approval. The number of employees was reduced to the more or less optimum number of 77, with the excess labour that was at the company prior to the privatization taking early retirement packages and other forms of legal redundancy. The company's production started to pick up notably after the privatization.

These steps improved the volume of production and generally had the effect of transforming Piramida from an 'exhausted' former government enterprise into a new, modern, highly-flexible smaller factory, which is viewed as a respectable market player amongst the top European manufacturers of glass pharmaceutical packaging.

## Location and facilities

Piramida is located in the eastern industrial zone of Zagreb, in the outer suburb of Sesvete. The company's offices and production lines are located on 48,370m² of land with very good infrastructure. Buildings occupy 6,353 m², while roads and parking lots occupy 6,474m². The rest of the company's territory is made up of green fields and vegetation.

## Product lines

Piramida produces a range of different glass pharmaceutical packaging items, including ampoules, vials, dropping pipettes, test tubes and flacons. Employing its modern technology and high-quality raw materials, the company's annual production volumes include 170 million (units of) ampoules, 25 million vials, 20 million glass dropping pipettes, 12 million test tubes and flacons. These present volumes of production represent two-thirds of Piramida's full production capacity. In 2002, Piramida acquired ISO 9001 certification and ISO 14 001 in 2003. In 2003, Piramida introduced clean rooms class 100.000 (ISO 8) for product packaging and a 100 per cent optical quality control system. Piramida produces according to GMP guidelines.

## Business development

Piramida operates in both the domestic and international market for glass pharmaceutical packaging. In Croatia, it has a number of large as well as smaller clients, and has recently expanded its presence in Macedonia, Bosnia and Herzegovina, Serbia and Montenegro, and has stable clients in Slovenia and Poland. It is also exploring the Russian market (with which it had substantial contact prior to the collapse of the USSR) and exports its production to France and Italy.

Piramida's main export markets are Slovenia, Poland, Serbia and Montenegro, Russia, France, Macedonia, Italy and Bosnia and Herzegovina. Exports comprise 85 to 90 per cent of the company's sales, with roughly 50 per cent going to the former Yugoslavia and 35 per cent further afield. Some 15 per cent of the company's production is reserved for the Croatian market, all of which goes to the domestic pharmaceuticals giant, Pliva. It should be emphasized that the market for glass pharmaceutical packaging products in Croatia has shrunk significantly during the last decade or so. This is largely the result of the decline of the markets in the former Soviet Union, for whom Yugoslavia was a major supplier.

Piramida imports raw materials (mostly glass) from Italy and Germany and operational equipment from Italy and France. The glass that Piramida imports has to uphold the scrutiny of the major quality controls demanded by the international pharmaceuticals industry, which limits Piramida's ability to source its glass from just a few, well-known international suppliers. This also means that Piramida's products are increasingly geared for the Western, as opposed to Eastern markets due to the higher per unit price that Piramida subsequently levies on its production units. Producers of similar glass pharmaceuticals packaging items in Russia, for example, which source cheaper Russian produced glass, for the most part would not be able to certify their production in the Western markets (as a result of the high levels of quality control and intensive laboratory testing of the glass contained in the packaging products) and therefore mainly produce for the Eastern markets. Piramida's higher priced products and proven quality of the glass they employ does not allow the company to compete in price terms on the Eastern markets, meaning that the company has to naturally look West for new market opportunities. Piramida does not produce packaging items made from moulded glass.

Piramida's main competitor in Croatia is the Croatian firm Tlos. In the international market the major competitors are Alfamatic in Italy, Birgim Avrupa Ilac Ham in Turkey, Medical Glass Bratislawa in the Czech Republic, Ompi in Italy, Pofa S.A. Boleslawa–Gerresheimer Group, Schott from Germany (plant in Hungary). There are less than 20 companies in Europe engaged in the production of glass pharmaceutical packaging, and out of these, industry sources suggest that Piramida is ranked in the top five or six.

Piramida d.d. operates accordingly to its customer satisfaction-driven policy. As an outcome, Piramida's main strengths compared to foreign competitors are excellent quality at a reasonable price, just-in-time (JIT) delivery strategies, good knowledge and understanding of the domestic market in Croatia, and the excellent service that it provides to all its customers.

Weaknesses come from the fact that Piramida is relatively small and although this implies independence from the multinationals, Piramida is in the situation that it has to import raw glass tubes from the companies with whom it is in competition (ie manufacturers of the same products as Piramida who are part of global business conglomerates). Furthermore, Piramida, as a company exporting the majority of its production, currently faces an unfavourable national currency exchange rate, due to the strength of the kuna, and relatively expensive labour compared to other transitional economies.

Piramida employs international accounting standards. It has an annual financial turnover of around €4 million and the company's annual investment budget has been almost €800,000 during the last two years. However, this should not be considered typical since the last two years have been a period of change and developing business from a new starting point as a result of the privatization. Piramida has about 10 major customers at present, four of whom have been won over to the company since the new management took over after the 2001 privatization. This should be considered an impressive effort on the part of Piramida's new management, as it usually takes between 18–24 months to confirm an order from a new client (ie to test sample products in the client's laboratories, to register the packaging form with the government authorities, to fix prices etc), and the new management has had just on three years to bring the four new clients to the company.

Management's strategic vision for the company is to maintain its market position among the top Croatian and international manufacturers of glass pharmaceutical packaging made of the best high-quality glass, whilst maintaining continuous environmental care and protection. In fact, the general manager is aiming to increase the company's annual turnover by 15 per cent year on year for the next five years, and believes that this objective is possible if the company succeeds in a greater degree of penetration of the European markets. However, this may be more challenging than expected, since global demand for Piramida's production is, at best, remaining constant and may even shrink in the future due to the anticipated growth in the use of syringes.

## Labour

Piramida has 82 employees, whose average age is 42 and who have, on average, been with the company for around 15 years. Regarding the education of the company's employees, nine have a university background, four have college education, 30 have completed high school and the rest have production school qualifications. Out of the individuals employed at the company, 60 workers are engaged in production, five in quality control and one in quality assurance. The others are engaged in administration. All workers are from the domestic Croatian labour force and Piramida, for now, does not employ any foreign expatriates.

Human resource development in the company is primarily targeted to achieving excellence as designed in the Quality and Environmental Management System in accordance with ISO 9001 and ISO 14001. Further to this, Piramida has a yearly schedule of internal and external educational programmes for both staff and managers.

New staff or managers arriving at the company are put through both specific and general educational programmes. Specific education is tailored to the specific requirements of the workplace, whilst general education consists of different information about the company profile, position and internal and external operating guidelines.

## Doing business with Croatia

According to company management, the government of Croatia has not created the most favourable business environment for Piramida. Although the bulk of Croatian commercial law is taken from the European Union (EU), and is theoretically adequate for business development, there is some concern with its implementation, the lack of stability that this creates, as well as the lack of stability of the taxation system. However, given that Piramida is primarily an export-oriented company, the main problems faced by the company come from an unfavourable exchange rate (the strong kuna, which works to the advantage of importers and traders), as well as high tax liabilities, diverse obligations and wage contributions.

The core benefit of doing business in Croatia for the company is more than 50 years' of tradition in this market, and excellent, quality-driven and highly-trained employees, who are highly suitable to this very specific production business. Their derived experience cannot be learned in conventional educational institutions but only in direct production, resulting in a relatively small number of such specialized manufacturers as Piramida.

From a purely business perspective, Piramida's management looks to Croatia's likely future membership of the EU with positive expectations. Piramida already operates in a free market environment and looks forward to extending its products and services to as many new customers in the EU as possible. Management is monitoring developments relating to the EU directives and is already preparing the

company for the technical requirements as set out in the EU guidelines. Management also notes the fact that it would be far simpler to
carry out all of its financial operations in euros, as opposed to working
with both the euro and the kuna, and have concerns about fluctuations
in exchange rates, particularly in the case of the latter.

---

Pyramida d.d.
Resnicka 10
10360 Sesvete
Croatia
Tel: +385 (0) 1 200 0884/0756
Fax: +385 (0) 1 200 0628
Website: www.piramida.hr
Contact: Dr Hrvojka Krpan
Head of Commercial Department
Email: hrvojka.krpan@piramida.hr

# 4.7

# Koestlin d.o.o.

## Introduction

Koestlin is a leading Croatian producer of biscuits and other confectionery, located in the city of Bjelovar, to the east of Zagreb. It is a relatively large company, employing almost 600 people in 2004, and turning over 950 tonnes per month in confectionery production and 160 million kuna (€21 million) in revenues during the same year. Koestlin biscuits are a well-known brand in the former Yugoslavia, as well as the neighbouring European countries, where they have been widely distributed for several generations. Previously a state-owned enterprise, the company was sold off to strategic investors in 2002 and has been expanding aggressively since that time, both in terms of volume of production and financial turnover, as well as in its efforts to recapture markets in the neighbouring European countries, which it lost during a flat period in its business during the 1990s.

## Organizational history

Koestlin is a factory with almost a century-long tradition of top quality confectionery manufacture. It was founded in 1905, and since that time the company has grown from a small confectionery manufacturing workshop to a large-scale producer of biscuits and wafer products, famous and highly-renowned in many of the world's countries. The founder of the factory was Dragutin Wolf, and the company carried the founder's name until 1932.

The period 1919–27 was vital in Koestlin's development, as the company's production was diversified, new licences for biscuits and wafer production were obtained and the factory itself was significantly mechanized. At the time, the company employed around 50 people and produced 500 kg of products a day. It was also during this period that the company merged with the Koestlin company from Gyor, Hungary, and from that point on the company carried its present name.

After World War II, production volumes increased further and in 1960 the factory was relocated from the old city centre (of Bjelovar) to a new location in the industrial city zone. During 1979, new large workshops were added to the enterprise and in 1989 regional stocks with 3,300 palette places were built. Production duly increased to 15,000 tonnes per year.

At the end of 1992, Koestlin became a joint stock company through an initial privatization to a Croatian government privatization fund, though the company's business suffered during the rest of the 1990s due to war and commensurate fluctuations in production, resulting in the loss of market share. However, in December 2001, Koestlin was sold off by the Croatian government to a strategic investor, Mepas company (Mirko Grbesic) from Široki Brijeg in Bosnia and Herzegovina. The latter bought an 87 per cent stake in the historical biscuit manufacturer and a major turnaround in the company's business began. A new general manager was appointed to run the company's business, and with an influx of new ideas and significant capital injection during 2003–2004, Koestlin expanded its markets, has taken on many new employees and both sales and production have increased impressively. Koestlin is currently a private, limited shareholder company, and Mr Kresimir Pajic has been the general manager of the company since the Mepas Group became its new owner.

## Product lines

Koestlin produces biscuits, wafers, salted sticks, extruded products and other similar lines of flour-based confectionery products – around 40 different products in total in about 80 different forms of packaging. Since the new management took over the company in 2002, production has recently increased up to an impressive 950 tonnes per month during some months of 2004 (compared to the 1990s, when it was averaging at around 150 tonnes per month). The company's motto is 'good biscuits at a decent price', and while packaging has been changing over the years and the volume of business has been expanding, the methods of production have remained largely the same for the better part of a century. In fact, some of the original recipes from more than 50 years ago, and some of the secret ingredients used to make a biscuit special, are still employed in the Koestlin factories today (Mr Wolf bought his first recipe from a Dutch company back in 1905, which gave him the licence to produce a biscuit subsequently called *speculate*).

In order to carry out its production, Koestlin's factory employs nine technological lines, with a production capacity of between 12,000 to 12,500 tonnes of biscuits and confectionery a year, which is achieved by working in shifts. At the moment, the factory works at a capacity of 7,500 tonnes with the trend towards increasing production capacity.

During the last year, three new lines of production technology have been installed, including the production line of the Austrian company Hecron-Haas for the production of biscuits, the Werner & Pfleider line for the production of salted products and the Schaf line for the production of extruded products. Furthermore, Koestlin has also installed eight automatic lines for packaging (ie horizontal and vertical flow-pack packaging machines), enabling Koestlin to bring its packaging standards in line with the level of quality of the most famous international brands.

Koestlin's new management invests substantial energies into the development of new products and technologies. The company is now seeking to continuously introduce new products and develop and improve the quality of the existing ones. It redesigns the product packaging in order to keep pace with the demands of the market and the consumers, which has always been the company's business motto.

## Business development

Koestlin is presently the second largest producer of biscuits and wafers in Croatia, with a 25 per cent market share. This is a substantial enhancement on the company's market position from the 1990s, when it lost much of its previously held market share and only commanded a miserly three per cent of the Croatian market for biscuits and confectionery. There are presently four major biscuit producers in Croatia and the market is very competitive, with both domestic production and imports featuring prominently amongst the choice available to the consumer in the country.

Prior to the privatization in 2002, Koestlin was only making some HRK46 million (€6 million) in annual financial turnover, which has since risen to nearly HRK160 million (€21 million) in 2004. Although it is not clear as to how the company's business has expanded so significantly since the new owners took over less than two years ago, the new management has emphasized that 'the heart of the biscuit is in the packaging' as well as in the right production technique (ie those age-old recipes and secret ingredients that give a particular biscuit the edge over others). Koestlin's new general manager is not becoming complacent despite the spectacular financial results, and is seeking to build up the company's business to an annual turnover of some €50–60 million.

Around half of the company's production, at present, is for export and Koestlin's production capacity can hardly fulfil its expanding orders at present. The Koestlin brand is said to be the No.1 imported biscuit in Slovenia, No 2 in Bosnia and No 3 in Macedonia. In fact, Koestlin was recently rated by 'Kondin', the Croatian Association of Confectionery, as the 'greatest exporter of biscuits and similar products to the former Yugoslavia with a market share of just over 35 per cent'. While the company is clearly a market leader in the former Yugoslavia, it also sells its products throughout Europe, as well as in North America. Koestlin has done business with all the major companies in Croatia, retailers, traders, suppliers and the like.

## Labour

Koestlin currently employs nearly 600 people, which is almost double the size of the company's labour force during the 1990s. Company management places significant attention into the harmony and welfare of the workforce and employs only qualified workers in the production process. Many of the company's employees were, in fact, trained on the Koestlin work sites, which have nearly a century-old tradition, as well as at the Confectionery School of Bjelovar.

The company's management has promoted a policy of social responsibility towards the workers, a tradition inherited from the industrial relations culture of the former Yugoslavia, paying attention to workers' needs and always paying the wages on time. The composition of Koestlin's workforce has been changing during the last two years or so, with employees nearing retirement age leaving the company on the basis of attractive voluntary redundancy packages, while younger employees have been attracted to the company.

## Industry recognition

In June 2002, Koestlin was awarded the ISO 9001:2000 certificate, which confirmed the company's standards of quality that were recently introduced and are subsequently applied to all of its production and business procedures. Furthermore, in August 2004, Koestlin's management introduced the Hazard Analysis and Critical Control Points system in order to comply with the standards of the international markets.

## Doing business with Croatia

Mr Pajić, Koestlin's new general manager, is extremely optimistic about the business prospects of his company. Having overseen a spectacular increase in the company's annual turnover and production levels during the last 18 months, and having maintained a good working relationship with Koestlin's owners, the new management suggests that Croatia currently provides a very suitable business climate. The country has an abundance of skilled labour and very qualified middle level (technical) management, highly suitable for a production enterprise. Management at the very top level of a modern business, required to raise a company's performance to global levels, is sometimes lacking in the country, however.

Unlike other export-oriented manufacturers, Koestlin does not seem to be negatively affected by (what some perceive to be) high taxation levels and a strong kuna, and is of the opinion that Croatia, at present, offers a very stable business and political environment. Under the company's new management, Koestlin's new philosophy seems to be 'just do business', which is exactly what the company has been doing since the beginning of 2003.

---

Koestlin d.d.
Slavonska cesta 2a
43000 Bjelovar
Croatia
Tel: 00385 43 242 888
Website: www.koestlin.hr

*Member of the Management Board*
Director: Krešimir Pajić
Tel: +385 (0) 43 241 097
Fax: +385 (0) 43 243 371
Email: uprava@koestlin.hr

# 4.8

# Centrometal d.o.o.

## Introduction

Centrometal is a leading Croatian producer of hot water boilers, as well as a full range of central heating and water supply appliances. The company emerged from its humble beginnings in the mid 1960s, when it commenced operations as little more than a garage workshop, to expand its operations significantly during the 1990s. At the time of writing, Centrometal employs some 130 employees and has carried out business with 16 countries. Centrometal is, and has always been, a private company and, unlike many of the other companies we have presented in this section of the book, has never taken the corporate form of a state-owned enterprise, nor was ever privatized. It is a medium-sized, export-oriented manufacturing enterprise, selling around 60 per cent of its production outside of Croatia, with a financial turnover of €10 million in 2003.

## Organizational history

Centrometal company was founded by Mr Karlo Zidaric, in the city of Macinec, north of Zagreb, in 1965. At the time, the company was little more than a small workshop, founded by an individual with an entrepreneurial mind, who came from a region with a significant tradition in craftsmanship and excellence in the production of small-scale manufactured goods. Within two years of the foundation of his company, Mr Zidaric had designed and manufactured his first hot water boiler for central heating purposes, which still, interestingly enough, is produced today under the name *Feroterm*.

However, prior to 1990, the business legislation of the former Yugoslavia did not allow for private companies to employ more than 12 individuals, meaning that strictly private – particularly manufac-turing – enterprises were significantly restricted in the volume of business that they could develop. Only government-owned enterprises (ie companies either nationalized or established by state capital) were capable of engaging in large-scale manufacturing and production. Hence, the promising enterprise that Mr Zidaric founded in the mid-1960s would have to wait some 25 years before it could start realizing its true commercial potential.

By the start of the 1990s, however, the newly independent Republic of Croatia was embarking upon the road to transition from a socialist economy to one operating on the basis of market principles, and laws, such as the ones restricting the number of individuals that could be employed in private companies, were annulled. In fact, it was in 1990 that the company adopted its present name, Centrometal, and business expanded rapidly during the ensuing decade. Centrometal built additional manufacturing and storage space, acquired new machinery enhancing its production line for automatic welding of vessels and a boiler welding robot, thus enabling the company to diversify its range of products. During the 1990s, the company went from being a limited supplier of boilers and associated products for the domestic market, to an export-oriented enterprise supplying both the former Yugoslav republics and the international market proper.

## Corporate form

Centrometal started out as a family-run enterprise, and although it has developed into a modern, well-managed export-oriented corporation, it still retains strong hints of a family enterprise at present. The company is a closed, limited shareholding (joint stock) enterprise, with just one shareholder at present. Centrometal is still 100 per cent owned by the Zidaric family, and company employees, especially management, hold the expectation of career-long employment at the company. There does not seem to be much separation of mentality, or a corporate governance culture, between the company's owners and management, and the latter suggest that the company is likely to retain its corporate form and that the owners are unlikely to release any of their controlling interest in the company in the medium-term future. The Croatian circumstance, however, is rather unique and the war of independence of the early 1990s has seemingly created a culture where (corporate) individuals want to hold on to what they have built, particularly in the present day situation, where they see themselves somewhat like the pioneers of the new, independent Croatia. The company is operating under the quality system ISO 9001:2000 and own research and development teams, as well as a modern research and school centre.

# Product lines

Centrometal produces the following types of manufactured goods for central heating and water-supply appliances:

- gas or oil fired boilers;
- solid fuel fired boilers;
- partment contained heating boilers;
- electric rapid water heaters;
- sanitary hot water accumulators;
- solar accumulators;
- water pressure vessels;
- flue gas elbows and tubes;
- boiler and heating control units.

The company plans to introduce five new products into the market during 2004–2005 and is constantly seeking to expand and diversify its product range. An indepth technical description of all of Centrometal's diverse product range is available for inspection in the company's catalogues, in Croatian, English and German languages, or via the company website (www.centrometal.hr).

In addition, the company also acts as the local agent for the Croatian (ex-Yugoslav) market for some major European suppliers of accessories and equipment for boilers and water supply appliances, including mixing valves, expansion vessels and other similar equipment. All of Centrometal's production is patented and certified in Croatia. The production that is designated for foreign markets is also certified in Slovenia and Germany, while the company has also recently received an ecology certificate GZ:312 R 16/1 for solid fuels boilers in Austria. Company management gives special care to the quality and design of all of Centrometal's products, with customer satisfaction being management's ultimate objective.

# Business development

In 2003, Centrometal's production stood at some 20,000 units of boilers and accumulators, which equated to around 60 per cent of production capacity. Some 80 per cent of the company's business comes from the sale of its mainstream production of boilers and associated products, with the rest coming from the agency business and ancillary activities. Around 60 per cent of the company's boiler production is for the export market, with

Austria, Slovenia and Bosnia and Herzegovina being the prime target countries at present. Of this share of 60 per cent, the majority (some 90 per cent) is distributed in the new countries of the former Yugoslavia, while just 10 per cent is sold in the broader European markets. Management is seeking to increase the figure by the end of 2004.

Out of the ex-Yugoslav Republics, Centrometal has had a particularly positive business relationship with Bosnia and Herzegovina, where the company has been the market leader in the sale of boilers and associated products since 1998. Similarly, Centrometal is also a market leader in Kosovo. At the time of writing, the Centrometal was on the verge of signing a major new contract for the export of its production to new clients in Poland, France and Belgium, expanding the company's business further in Europe's markets.

Much of this market share and aggressive business expansion was built up at the start of this century, when Centrometal opened a branch office in Zagreb to accelerate the company's business, particularly into the Western markets, after some of the restrictive business legislation from the socialist period was removed. Centrometal's business has been expanding annually in each successive year, roughly since the mid-1990s, and the financial turnover of the company stood at around €10 million in 2003.

The remaining 40 per cent of Centrometal's boiler production is earmarked for the Croatian domestic market, where the company is the market leader and commands between 30–40 per cent of the market share. Some 35 per cent of Croatian homes have central heating of the type that require boilers and other water supply appliances such as those produced by Centrometal. The company faces very little domestic competition in its industry and, in fact, much of the company's competition comes from imported (mostly German) boilers entering the domestic market. Although it is much easier said with the benefit of hindsight, in all probability Centrometal would already have been a market leader in Croatia during the 1980s, had the business climate in Yugoslavia's quasi-socialist economy been liberalized earlier and the laws restricting the number of employees that private companies could employ had not been in force. Furthermore, the company's business also expanded in Croatia during the 1990s due to the entry of new foreign banks into the country, such as Austria's Raiffeisen bank, which resulted in companies like Centrometal having greater access to a more diversified set of corporate financial products available for business development.

## Labour

Centrometal employs around 130 employees at its main production headquarters and other facilities in Macinec, and its business development office in central Zagreb. Average monthly wages at the company, for the bulk of the workforce engaged in production, equates to around HRK5000 (€700), which also roughly equates to the Croatian national average wage. Wage contributions are drawn from roughly one-third of the company's annual profits that are disbursed to cover business overheads, with the remaining two-thirds of profits being re-invested back into the company.

## Doing business with Croatia

Centrometal's business has been expanding in a very positive manner during the last decade or so, with seemingly little animosity from the company management towards Croatia's investment environment. In fact, Centrometal looks forward to Croatia's possible membership in the EU with much enthusiasm, since some brand recognition of the company's core products already exists in EU countries; and, undoubtedly, operating within the framework of the dynamic and rapidly expanding EU markets will allow the company to expand its already fast-growing business even further.

TEHNIKA GRIJANJA

**Centrometal corporate message: Quality, Ecology and Satisfied Customers**

Centrometal d.o.o.
Glavna 12
40 306 Macinec
*Technical Department:*
Tel: +385 (0) 40 372 620
Fax: +385 (0) 40 372 621
*Commercial Department:*
Tel: +385 (0) 40 372 610
Fax: +385 (0) 40 372 611
Email: centrometal@ck.htnet.hr
Website: www.centrometal.hr

Centrometal d.o.o.
Branch Office Zagreb
Baboniɸeva 53
10 000 Zagreb
Tel: +385 (0) 1 46 33 762
Fax: +385 (0) 1 46 33 763

# 4.9

# Emka d.o.o.

## Introduction

Emka plc is a leading Croatian company engaged in the production of quality women's fashion, primarily shirts, blouses, trousers, skirts and similar garments. It is a medium-sized company employing just under 200 people, and is a well-known manufacturing enterprise in the Croatian textiles and garments industry. The company is export-oriented, selling well over half of its annual production on the broader European market, as well as focusing its product line into a niche market that the company has created within Croatia. Emka's garments have developed a reputation amongst some of Europe's best-known fashion-makers, with whom the company has developed a business relationship spanning more than two decades. Emka has been functioning as a private company since it was privatized during the early 1990s, is owned and operated by the Sutina family and is located in the town of Pregrada, which is less than 100 km outside the Croatian capital, Zagreb.

## Organizational history

Emka was established as a state-owned manufacturing enterprise in the late 1970s and, when its business was guided by the government of Yugoslavia, the company developed a good reputation as a reliable producer of women's garments amongst some of Europe's best-known fashion designers. However, with the privatization programme of the newly-independent Republic of Croatia underway during the early 1990s, Emka was privatized through a management buyout, and a group of the company's senior managers took control of the newly privatized enterprise.

As it was 'insiders' who took control of the company in the privatization, there was initially little change to the company's business model after it was privatized. Just over 4,000 shares were issued in the newly-privatized Emka, with a market value of some HRK7,717,800, although the bulk of the shares and hence a controlling stake in the company was acquired by the Sutina family, which was closely involved with the company prior to the privatization. Hence the company established the corporate form that it holds to the present day, a limited private enterprise, and essentially, a family-run company. The current director of the company is Maria Sutina, the daughter of the founder of the present-day company. There are currently just three shareholders in the company.

Emka's business developed very positively during the 1990s, despite the fact that Croatia was at war with its neighbour, Serbia, and the country's economy was still in a relatively early phase of transition from a planned economy to one based on market principles. Emka was able to generate significant revenues from its export business during the early-to-mid-1990s, and earn hard currency at a time when foreign exchange was generally scarce in Croatia. The company was even sewing uniforms for the Croatian army, which it was donating to aid the national cause. The company was, likewise, active in various charitable projects in the local communities in the Pregrada region.

The company's business has been going through leaner periods in more recent years, and the main objective of the shareholders is to maintain its current business and fight competition, rather than expand its market position in Croatia or build new markets for the export business.

## Product lines

As already mentioned, Emka produces a range of quality lines in clothing and garments for women, with production currently running at some 120,000 units per year. The company's market niche is to produce high-quality garments in relatively small volumes for established clients at good profit margins, which are sewn to order in Emka's factories from pieces of raw cotton yarn. Orders in the range of 500 units are considered 'good business' by the company's management. Emka also makes collections for its clients and prepares working orders for production placed with other companies. In 2004, Emka's factories were producing garments on the basis of three production lines but during 2005 this will be reorganized into six smaller production lines, which will give greater flexibility and be more optimal for smaller working orders (as little as 20 units per order).

The company's business model and production facilities are not geared to competing with major textiles industry producers from countries such as Romania or China, which produce garments in huge volumes at low prices and are essentially not designed for the niche garments market. Emka tends to produce to confirmed orders, while the bulk producers tend to bring out much higher annual unit numbers, most of which are of different quality standards to that of the Pregrada-based Emka and are ready for the market even before the actual demand is generated. During the mid-1990s, Emka's main competition came from producers in Slovenia, but with the advent of greater market liberalization since year 2000, the company's main competitors have become some of the leading brands in the international textiles industry.

Around 70 per cent of Emka's product is made for export, with revenues generated from exports totalling €920,000 in 2003. Most of Emka's export market is located in the EU (predominantly Germany and Austria), as well as in the former Yugoslavia. The remaining 30 per cent of Emka's production is for the Croatian market, where Emka's revenues are generated primarily through the distribution of its leading brand in women's fashion – the recently released La Divina range. The Croatian market and the La Divina range of women's fashion has brought Emka some €1.4 million in revenues in 2003 (with some 10 per cent of the production for the La Devina range going to Bosnia and Herzegovina).

## Business development

Ever since the company was established (prior to its privatization in 1993), Emka has been cooperating with some of the household names in Europe's fashion industry, including fashion-makers such as Escada, Laurel, Jobis, Rena, Lange, Alexander, Montana and Schneiders, to name a few. Having established a long-standing business relationship with these leading fashion-makers, Emka has been able to develop the know-how required to supply quality garments for some of the world's leading fashion trade marks. Season after season, new and fresh designs, innovative business strategies and constant evaluation of market trends have helped Emka to establish itself as a leading producer of top quality women's fashion wear that suits the needs of the busy, contemporary woman.

Emka's leading product at the moment is its La Divina range of quality women's fashion wear, which is presently establishing itself as a leading brand in Croatia. According to Emka's management, La Devina was created by:

'*experience achieved through successful cooperation with the leading European fashion-makers as well as the careful choice of top quality fabrics and our original idea of the modern woman. La Divina stands for quality, exclusivity and creativity in design. It is a brand created for the modern woman – successful both in her career and in the home. La Divina dresses self-confident women, who are aware of their femininity – the clothes for the divine, perfect woman.'*

Emka is presently widening the range of its La Divina collections. There are plans to introduce jackets and knitted garments that should be combined together with the base collection, which consists of blazers, skirts, trousers, blouses and coats. Emka intends to engage the capabilities and know-how of other Croatian companies to offer jackets and knitted garments.

On the management side, Emka is seeking to achieve a more efficient internal organization of its business and to improve its competitiveness in its core business. Emka's annual income for 2003 reached €2,320,000, and the company spent just €360,000 on imported equipment and other inputs/raw materials required for the business. Most of the source countries for Emka's imports came from the EU (especially France, Germany, Italy) and from Switzerland. The bulk of the company's expenses were spent on raw materials, wages, upgrade of existing equipment and technologies, as well as payment of interest on outstanding loans.

## Labour and HRM issues

Wages in the Croatian textiles industry tend to be below the national average (ie around HRK2,000–3,000 per month, compared to the Croatian national average of around HRK4,000) and Emka management often finds it difficult to recruit new workers. In an effort to improve worker motivation and make the firm more attractive for new employees, Emka has become a benefactor of a Croatian government technical assistance programmme, promoted by the Croatian Ministry of Economy and the international consulting firm Deloitte & Touche.

Emka management has implemented '7 keys' out of the total '20 keys' during the first year of the programme. Emka's workforce has so far accepted the programme quite well; communication within the company has improved and the workers have started to think about how to make their job tasks more effective on the one hand, and easier to perform on the other. The information system in the company has improved and an 'open-door' style management strategy has been adopted. Under the programme, workers have primarily been organized into small working teams but have also been appointed as members to special project teams (particularly during the last four months of the programme, when five special project teams have been established). The main goal of appointing the project teams has been to solve special problems or suggest better production processes, which have subsequently been implemented in the development of new management solutions at the company.

 d.d. PREGRADA

**Company Corporate Message: 'Emka stands for quality, La Divina for excellence'**

Emka d.d.
Dragutina Kunovica 2
49218 Pregrada
Croatia
Tel: +385 (0) 49 376 555
fax: +385 (0) 49 376 144
Email: ladivina@emka.hr
Website: www.emka.hr

# 4.10

# The Zagreb Insurance Company

*Petra Tarle, Zagreb Insurance Company, Zagreb*

The Zagreb Insurance Company was established in 1991 as the first private insurance company in the Republic of Croatia. The company is headed by Mrs Petra Tarle, LLB.

With the enthusiasm and devoted work of its employees, the company has become one of the leading insurance companies in Croatia.

The company headquarters are in Zagreb, and the company operates throughout Croatia via a developed network of branch offices and agencies, and successfully covers the entire Croatian market. The branch offices of the Zagreb Insurance Company are in Zagreb, Split, Rijeka, Pula, Zadar, Karlovac, Čakovec, Koprivnica, Osijek, Dubrovnik and Vukovar.

In 2004, an average of 188 employees were employed by the Zagreb Insurance Company. Among the employees, most of whom had many years' experience in the insurance industry, 56 per cent were highly-educated professionals. In the company, four certified actuaries are employed, who are also full members of the Croatian Association of Actuaries.

All the business processes are supported by a quality integral informatics system, which has been developed using modern informatics technologies with online access to a relational database. Using online technologies provides timely and complete data to all the decision-making structures.

The Zagreb Insurance Company currently has over 500,000 insured clients. It contracts all types of insurance:

- life insurance;

- accident insurance;

- health insurance;
- comprehensive motor vehicle insurance;
- comprehensive marine, river and lake hull insurance;
- insurance of goods in transport;
- property insurance from fire and other hazards;
- other property insurance;
- automobile liability insurance;
- shipping liability insurance;
- other liability insurance;
- insurance of tourism services.

In the company's portfolio, life and non-life types of insurance are equally represented.

The shares of life and non-life insurance within the total portfolios of the European Union, Republic of Croatia and the Zagreb Insurance Company are shown in Figure 3.14.1

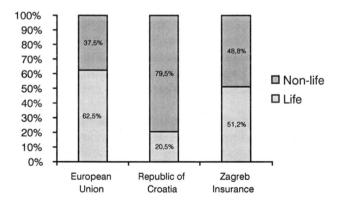

**Figure 3.14.1** Shares of life and non-life portfolios

The basic approach of the Zagreb Insurance Company in settling claims is the rapid, equitable and uniform payment of damages, which is summarized by the company slogan: 'confidence for a reason!'

The portfolio of the company is protected by underwriting contracts with leading world underwriters: Münich Re, Swiss Re, Scor Deutschland and Lloyd's.

# Performance in 2003 and in the first nine months of 2004

The performance of the company in 2003 shows a balance of HRK840 million, which is 20.2 per cent higher than in 2002, and a balance of HRK908 million in the first nine months of 2004, which is 8.2 per cent higher than in 2003.

The premium revenues in 2003 recorded a growth of 9.62 per cent and a total of HRK334.5 million. In the first nine months of 2004, premium revenues were 8.4 per cent higher than in the same period in 2003.

In 2003, the company recorded a growth of 42 per cent in gross profits of HRK20.1 million, with 14.4 per cent higher income than during 2002, while investments grew by 23.4 per cent. In the first nine months of 2004, gross profit was HRK12.3 million, which is 27 per cent higher than in the same period in 2003. In the first nine months of 2004, investments grew by 8.3 per cent.

According to the level of premium revenues in the first nine months of 2004, the company occupies fifth place among 24 Croatian insurance companies – with a market share of 5.2 per cent. In terms of the volume of life insurance operations, it is in fourth place and in terms of non-life insurance operations, it is in sixth place.

# Insurance products in the company's portfolio

The structure of insurance in the Zagreb Insurance Company is illustrated in Figure 3.14.2.

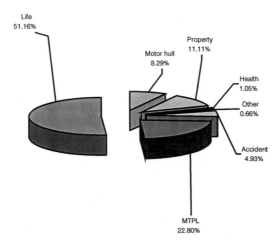

**Figure 3.14.2** The company's insurance structure

## Life insurance

The strategic product of the Zagreb Insurance Company is life insurance. In the life insurance portfolio of the company, there are three basic products:

- life insurance in the event of survival or death;
- risk life insurance; and
- life insurance for children.

In 2004, the share of life insurance in the portfolio of the company was 51.2 per cent. The profit for life insurance customers was HRK20.7 million. A nearly 29.6 per cent increase in the number of newly-contracted life insurance policies in 2004 indicates that life insurance is becoming accepted as a prerequisite for financial security, quality savings and creating additional retirement pension assets.

In 2001, with the beginning of retirement reform and the introduction of individual capitalized savings, an opening was created for more significant life insurance growth in the Republic of Croatia. Since the share of life insurance in the total portfolio in the Republic of Croatia is only approximately 22.3 per cent, the trend in the growth of the number of life insurance policies is certain, and life insurance will continue to remain a strategic product of the company.

Starting in the year 2003, supplementary insurance for critical illness and conditions in addition to life insurance were offered. This new product insures payment in the event of the occurrence of a serious illness or condition, so that the insured person is paid an additional amount, while his or her life insurance continues.

## Non-life insurance

Within the total portfolio of the company, in 2004 non-life insurance had a nearly 50 per cent share.

The level of development and profitability of the non-life insurance is based on the adaptation of our product offerings to the demands and specific needs of the market. For example, we are the only ones on the insurance market in the Republic of Croatia to offer all-risk insurance to objects under construction or assembly and some types of insurance concerning professional liability.

The company devotes particular attention to the development of new products. In 1994, it was the first insurance company to offer compulsory insurance for compensatory damages in the event of injuries at work and professional diseases, and, in 2001, when such insurance was terminated, it was one of the first to offer a new type of insurance for compensatory wages.

In 2003, we expanded our product offerings with several new types of insurance, such as crop insurance, animal insurance, liability insurance, and the most significant new product is private health insurance. In introducing private health insurance products on the market, the company has started with a project of building a health institutions network to provide insured persons with the highest level of healthcare. The first two polyclinics in that system are Poliklinika Osiguranje Zagreb Nemetova in Zagreb and Poliklinika Medico Osiguranje Zagreb in Rijeka.

## Plans

Taking into account the anticipated growth of the insurance market, the strength of the competition and the entry of foreign insurers on the Croatian market, the Zagreb Insurance Company anticipates growth in its share of the Croatian insurance market.

In 2005, the company plans continued development of the sales network, a 20 per cent growth in premiums and achieving second place in the Croatian life insurance market during the next two years. By the year 2010, the company will attempt to obtain a 10 per cent share of the Croatian insurance market with an annual increase in its share of approximately 0.8 per cent.

In establishing company policy, the company administration is guided by goals and respect for the following values:

- confidence for a reason;

- insurance in which the insured person is the centre of interest;

- insurance that operates expressly according to market criteria throughout the territory of the Republic of Croatia;

- insurance that offers security, commercial excellence and the best coverage.

# Part Five

# The Taxation and Legal Environment

# 5.1

# The Legal Framework for Doing Business with Croatia

*Adrian Hammer, Deloitte & Touche*

## Introduction to the Croatian legal system

The legal system of the Republic of Croatia is, by its nature, a part of the legal system of the countries of Continental Europe. The sources of the Croatian legal system are regulations, legal customs, court practice and jurisprudence. Regulations represent a substantive legal source in the Republic of Croatia, as they contain written legal rules applied on a day-to-day basis. Those are, in hierarchical order, The Constitution of the Republic of Croatia, laws and regulations.

The Constitution, being the fundamental and organic act, governs the basic framework of the legal, political and economic systems of the Republic of Croatia as a modern European democracy. Thus, the basic provisions declare the inviolability of ownership as the highest value of the constitutional order of the Republic of Croatia. The ownership right and the right of succession are guaranteed; however, the ownership right is binding for its holders and beneficiaries in terms of their contribution to the general welfare.

Further, entrepreneurial and market freedoms are guaranteed, and monopolies are forbidden. Exceptionally, entrepreneurial freedom and right of ownership may be legally restricted to protect the interests and security of the state, nature, human environment and public health. As regards the protection of foreign investments, the Constitution specifies that rights acquired based on the investment of foreign capital cannot be diminished by law, or by any other legal act. Repatriation of profits and the capital invested are guaranteed.

Constitutional provisions are further explicated by appropriate laws, which represent the foundation of individual legal institutes.

The legal system of the Republic of Croatia is based on the codification of legal institutes in the tradition of Continental Europe. The legal rules of contractual, ownership and commercial relations are codified by the Act on Property and Other Proprietary Rights, the Obligations Act and the Companies Act.

By signing the Stabilization and Association Agreement with the European Union (EU) in 2001, the Republic of Croatia assumed, among others, the obligation to reconcile its legislation with EU laws. In 2004, Croatia received the official EU candidate status. Thus, in the following two or three years, Croatian legislation should be complemented by 50 new acts governing various areas, such as interest rates, savings deposit insurance, copyright and other related rights, and e-commerce.

Regulations govern the implementation of laws; however, certain regulations may exceptionally override the legal force of laws. These are primarily the directives issued by the Croatian prime minister, which govern individual legal issues on an exceptional basis.

Reference to legal customs as a source of law is made only if the customs are based on a legal right. In the law of obligations, legal customs serve as a supplementary source of law, in particular of the commercial and contract law, the so-called commercial customs.

Commercial customs are also codified, thus forming commercial practice. One can distinguish between general and specific commercial practice, by whether they apply to trade in all kinds of goods or services, or only to certain goods and services.

The governing principle underlying the Croatian law of obligations is that commercial practices apply only if the parties have agreed to apply them, or if the circumstances imply that they actually wanted to apply them.

As the legal system of the Republic of Croatia is based on legal right, the court practice in Croatia represents an indirect rather than a direct source of law. In Croatia, court judgments do not have a precedent status; a decision of a higher court, therefore, does not have a binding effect on lower courts. Judgements have a persuasive effect only and may be used when making a legal argument in that context.

The courts in the Republic of Croatia are the Constitutional Court, the Supreme Court, county courts and municipal courts. The Constitutional Court is not a part of the judiciary but rather a separate court, whose activities are aimed at protecting the constitutionality and legality of Croatia's judicial system. The Supreme Court of the Republic of Croatia is the highest judiciary body, issuing final rulings in appellate court proceedings. County courts judge in appellate proceedings in civil matters and represent a first-instance court in criminal proceedings. Municipal courts are first-instance courts in first-instance civil proceedings.

# Regulatory incentives to promote investments in Croatia

## *Investment incentives*

The Investment Promotion Law, enacted in 2000, provides an institutional framework for incentives to domestic and foreign investors, legal persons and individuals, to promote economic growth, development and a more intense participation of Croatia in international trade by enhancing exports and the competitiveness of the Croatian economy.

The Investment Promotion Law has been conceived as a system of incentives, tax and customs benefits to investors under the following prerequisites:

- investors are entitled to incentives when they form new companies in the Republic of Croatia, whose registered activities fall within the scope of those to which the incentives, tax and customs benefits apply (except for investments in tourist trade, where the Croatian government may accept an already existing company to become the incentive and benefits user, on the basis of the proposal of the Ministry of Finance, to which the incentives application has been filed);

- investments comprise the value of items, rights and obligations as defined according to International Accounting Standards, which have to be invested in the initial capital of the incentives beneficiary. Investments in land, buildings older than one year and previously-used equipment are not recognized as investments;

- to be able to exercise the right on incentives, the investor has to make an investment of at least HRK4 million.

Incentives comprise co-financing of new jobs, professional training and retraining of workers, as well as other specific benefits, such as lease, use, purchase and sale of properties or other infrastructural facilities under commercial or favourable terms and conditions, with or without a consideration.

The existing legislation emphasises the role of tax benefits to investors, consisting of a lowered corporate income tax rate, or even tax exemption during a certain period, depending on the amount of investment and the number of new employees at the incentives beneficiary.

Depending on the level of investment and the extent of new staff employed, the reduced corporate income tax rate ranges from 13 per cent to zero rate, ie full tax relief.

For example, for an investment of a minimum of HRK10 million, corporate income tax will be paid at a 7 per cent rate over a period of

10 years from the beginning of investment, provided that a minimum of 30 new staff are employed during the period.

An investment of over HRK200 million will result in a corporate income tax rate of 3 per cent over a period of 10 years from the beginning of investment, if a minimum of 50 new staff are employed during the period.

The incentives beneficiaries who make a minimum investment of HRK60 million will be given the benefit of a 0 per cent corporate income tax rate over 10 years from the beginning of investment, provided that a minimum of 75 new employees are taken on during the period.

Customs benefits are in the form of customs duty exemptions on imports of equipment for the purposes of the business for which customs benefits otherwise apply.

To be able to obtain incentives, tax and customs benefits, the incentives procedure has to be initiated first. However, there is also the obligation of regular annual reporting to the Ministry of Economy and the Ministry of Finance of the Republic of Croatia. The procedure for obtaining incentives, tax and customs benefits is initiated by submitting the application to the Croatian Ministry of Economy and the Ministry of Finance.

## Concessions

The legal framework for concessions in Croatia is defined by the Concessions Act, in effect from December 1992. A foreign and/or a domestic legal person or individual may acquire the following on the basis of a concession:

- the legal right to economic use of natural and other resources that are designated as objects of interest for the Republic of Croatia by a separate legal act;

- the right to carry out a business activity of interest to the Republic of Croatia and to construct and use facilities and plants necessary for this purpose.

Concessions cannot be granted for forests and forest land in Croatia.

The Act has enabled a transparent procedure for granting concessions in Croatia based on public tender. Participants in granting concessions are, in addition to executive bodies (the Croatian government) and legislative bodies (the Croatian Parliament – Sabor), and the executive bodies of the units of local administration and local self-government (towns, cities, municipalities or counties) in whose territory the subject of concession is located. They give a first opinion to the Croatian government, which then forwards the final proposal to the Croatian Parliament as the final decision-making body.

Concessions are granted once the procedure above is completed and once an assessment of bidders is made by the Croatian government based on the following criteria:

- business reputation of the bidder;

- ability of the bidder to qualify for the concession;

- attractiveness of the bid (technical and financial);

- environmental impact of the concession.

The rights and obligations between the government authorities (ie local authorities) and the bidders are governed by a concession contract, which may last for a maximum period of 99 years, except for a concession contract for agricultural land, which is to be concluded for a maximum period of 40 years.

The concession contract, as a legal transaction, should provide appropriate guarantees that the granted concession will meet the economic purpose of the concession, in line with the interests of the Republic of Croatia. Concession contracts are entered in the register of concessions, which is maintained by the Croatian Ministry of Finance.

As there are frequent conflicts of interest represented by local authorities on the one hand and those of the government authorities on the other, the application of this Act has created problems in practice. For this reason, a new legal solution is expected in the near future that would provide an efficient solution of any potential collision between the interested parties, along with the measures to ensure efficiency of the very process of granting concessions.

## Free zones

Free zone regulations represent a major portion of the Croatian legislation, aimed at promoting investments and economic development. The Free Zones Act, in force from June 1996, defines free zones as separate, distinctly marked parts of the Croatian territory in which economic activities are carried out under favourable conditions. Free zones may be established in seaports, airports, river ports, along international roads, or in other areas suitable for their operations.

Free zone users may be the founders of a particular free zone, but also other domestic and foreign persons who carry out their businesses in the zone, based on an adequate agreement concluded with the zone founder. The following activities may be performed in duty free zones:

- manufacturing of goods;

- finishing works;

- wholesale trade and trade mediation;

- services;

- bank and other monetary transactions, if connected with the manu-facturing of goods or provision of services;

- property and personal insurance and reinsurance, if connected with the manufacturing of goods or provision of services.

A special benefit for the free zone users is that they pay corporate income tax at half the normal rate (the normal rate currently standing at 20 per cent). The free zone users involved, directly or indirectly, in infrastructure construction valued over HRK1 million in the free zone, are exempt from paying corporate income tax in the first five years of operating the business in the zone.

The following free zones currently exist in Croatia:

- Krapinsko-Zagorska County Free Zone;

- Free Zone Kukuljanovo, Rijeka;

- Free Zone Osijek;

- Free Zone Podi, Šibenik;

- Port of Rijeka Free Zone;

- Free Zone Zagreb;

- Free Zone Obrovac;

- Port of Split Free Zone;

- Splitsko-Dalmatinska County Free Zone;

- Free Zone Ploče;

- Port of Pula Free Zone;

- Free Zone Buje;

- Free Zone Đuro Đaković, Slavonski Brod;

- Free Zone Ribnik; and

- Free Zone Vukovar.

# 5.2

# Business Entities in Croatia

*Vanja Markovic LLM, Tax and Regulatory Services, Deloitte & Touche, Zagreb*

## Introduction

The basic statute regulating business organizations in Croatia is the Companies Act (*Zakon o trgovačkim društvima*, Narodne novine no. 111/93), which came into force on 1 January 1995.

Croatian company law is modelled on laws and legal practice of the Central European countries, specifically German company law. From 1995, when the Companies Act entered in force, the law was first significantly amended by a Constitutional Court judgement in 2001, which abolished the prerequisite that at least one member of a company management board has to be employed by the company. It was further amended in 2003 by the Amendments to the Companies Act.

Several reasons were given for the adoption of these amendments:

- correcting the mistakes of the Act currently in force;

- introducing changes in the Croatian legal system based on the developments in corporate law of other countries adopted since 1993, eg closely held corporations, abolition of par value shares, restrictions regarding acquisitions of treasury shares, strengthening the position of minority shareholders, information flow in corporations, supervision of companies' operations, more protection for the stakeholders, giving more responsibility to managers and supervisory boards, etc;

- harmonization of the provisions of the Act with other statutes that took effect after the Act entered in force, eg Enforcement Act, Bankruptcy Act, Securities Act and Takeover of Joint Stock Companies Act;

- continuing harmonization of the Act with the provisions on the European Business Interest Grouping in accordance with the EU Directives; and

- making certain provisions of the Act clearer and providing legal solutions necessary to ascertain a uniform application of company law by the courts, which are in accordance with the common practice in the member states of the EU.

# Foreign investments

The equal treatment of domestic and foreign entrepreneurs is proclaimed in the Croatian Constitution. The Constitution also grants foreign entrepreneurs with a right of free movement (transfer) of profit and invested capital. The Act defines the term 'foreign company' and grants equal treatment to foreign investors in Croatia. Pursuant to the Act, foreign investors are deemed to be those legal persons whose principal place of business is not registered in Croatia, and every natural person that is a foreign citizen, refugee or apatride, or Croatian citizen having its permanent residency out of Croatia, that acquires a stake or shares or invests in a company on a contractual basis. From the notion of the foreign investor it derives that investments are limited to corporations, eg joint stock companies and limited liability companies, while partnerships are partially excluded: the Act prescribes that foreign entrepreneurs investing in partnerships should have a legal form of a corporation (joint stock company or limited liability company) and at least one Croatian partner (natural or legal person) personally responsible for the obligations of the partnership.

In accordance with the Act, foreign persons are allowed to organize their business activities in the following manner:

- open a representative office;

- establish a branch office;

- form a company with domestic, or other foreign partners, or to acquire shares or stakes in an existing company;

- enter into entrepreneurial agreements.

## Representative office

Provisions of the Decree on Conditions for Formation and Operation of Foreign Representative Offices in Croatia (*Uredba o uvjetima za osnivanje i rad predstavništva stranih osoba u Republici Hrvatskoj, Narodne Novine no. 7/1997*) apply if there is a legislative reciprocity between Croatia and the country where the founder of a representative office has a registered principal place of business. A representative office is defined as a non-profit organization, and which is not allowed to carry out any commercial activity of its founder or to enter contracts on the founder's behalf. An exception applies to the representative offices of foreign air carriers in accordance with international treaties signed by Croatia. Foreign companies and national or international business organizations are allowed to open representative offices in Croatia. Pursuant to the applicable regulations, a foreign representative office in the Republic of Croatia can be engaged in the following activities only:

- advertising;

- local market investigating activities; and

- carrying on promotion and information gathering activities and marketing.

Such activities might consist of the following:

- developing possibilities for the founder's future activity in Croatia;

- communication with customers;

- procuring business partners in Croatia;

- providing consultancy services and imparting instructions to customers in Croatia on a free of charge basis; or

- collecting and analysing market data and information for the purpose of business planning etc.

Under Croatian law, a representative office does not have a separate legal personality. A representative office is considered a part of the founder, and therefore it is deemed to carry out activities on behalf of the founder and in the founder's name, though commercial activities are excluded. For the latter reason, representative offices are not corporate income tax payers and are not VAT registered. However, for personal income tax purposes, the representative office is considered a separate legal entity in Croatia. In accordance with the personal income tax laws, the representative office is required to pay income tax on behalf of the employees in the office pursuant to Croatian legislation. The representative office is also required to pay all applicable social contributions such as health, pension and other contributions.

From the accounting point of view, the representative office does not have to keep complete and formal accounts. The assets of the representative office are kept in the books of the founder. However, the representative office should keep evidence regarding expenses that occur in the course of its operations and have evidence of payroll taxes.

It is important to emphasize that all payments to and from the founder and the representative office in Croatia are made through a non-resident account. The account can be opened with any commercial bank in Croatia that is licensed to perform foreign transactions. In addition, these accounts can be used by the representative office for receipt of payments from which it can cover the costs of its business operations, for example employees' wages, rent, advertisements, etc.

A representative office starts to exist once it is registered with the Registry of Representative Offices of Foreign Entities at the Ministry of Economy. In order to register a representative office in Croatia, the founder needs to provide the following documents:

- excerpt from the founder's company registry;

- copy of the latest balance sheet of the founder;

- application to the Ministry of Economy of the Republic of Croatia for a formation of a representative office;

- resolution on the appointment of the representative office manager (person responsible for operations of the office in Croatia);

- copy of the payment slip proving the payment of taxes amounting to HRK1,000;

- statement of the founder taking responsibility for all the obligations incurred by the representative office; and

- resolution of the founder on the establishment of the representative office in Croatia.

The Ministry has to decide on the registration within 30 days from the submission of the application.

In the course of its business operations, the representative office is obliged to act in accordance with applicable Croatian labour legislation, ie with respect to its Croatian employees, the rules of the Croatian Labour Act are applicable, and foreign employees must obtain Croatian work permits.

## Branch office

A branch office is not a separate legal entity and is deemed a part of the foreign founder. Consequently, its rights and obligations pertain to the parent company or to the individual merchant and not to the branch office itself. The business operations of a branch office are not limited to a definite list of activities, as is the case with representative offices.

The formation of a branch office in Croatia is regulated by the Companies Act. The first prerequisite for foreign companies or individual merchants to open a branch office in Croatia is the reciprocity with their country of origin. The founder will be able to start business operations through its Croatian branch once it is registered in the commercial court registry with the authority in the area where the branch office will have a seat.

When submitting the request for the registration of a branch office, the founder should include the following documents, translated into Croatian by the certified court translator:

- excerpt from the company registry of the founder (evidence of its business form and the date of incorporation);

- resolution to open a branch office;

- certified copy of the articles of association of the founder;

- certified copy of the latest balance sheet of the founder; and

- resolution on the appointment of the person authorised to represent the branch office.

Employment relations are regulated in the same manner as for representative offices.

From the accounting and tax point of view, a branch office is treated as a separate legal entity. Based on its financial statements, which have to be prepared and kept in accordance with the Croatian laws, a branch is required to calculate and pay corporate income tax in Croatia for the income earned in Croatia.

## *Business organizations*

Pursuant to the Companies Act, where a foreign investor decides to conduct business in Croatia through a legal entity independent from the parent company (ie obligations incurred by a Croatian company are not the responsibility of the founder, as is the case with a representative office or branch), that can be accomplished in two ways:

- by acquisition of shares in existing Croatian companies or other contractual basis;

- by the foreign founder forming a partnership or a company in Croatia.

The Companies Act is not the only source that regulates the formation and legal structure of business organizations in Croatia. There are several specialist laws that regulate particular fields of business such as banking, insurance, brokerage, the labour market or similar that have to be taken into consideration when investing in Croatia. However, the basic provisions on structure and organization of business organizations are included in the Companies Act.

*Partnerships*

The Companies Act provides for the general rules applying to different types of partnerships and leaves ample room for autonomous regulation of relationships within the organization. Foreign investors can participate in the following partnership types that are allowed by Croatian law:

- general partnership (*javno trgovačko društvo*);

- limited partnership (*komanditno društvo*);

- economic interest grouping (*gospodarsko interesno udruženje*);

- silent partnership (*tajno društvo*);

- joint venture (*zajednički pothvat, ortaštvo*).

GENERAL PARTNERSHIPS

A general partnership is a business organization formed by at least two persons for the purpose of permanently performing business activities under a joint name, where the partners are jointly liable for obligations of the partnership with all their assets. Partners in the general partnership may be domestic legal and natural persons, or domestic and foreign legal persons. For foreign companies wishing to form a general partnership in Croatia, the law prescribes the condition that the partnership should have at least one Croatian partner (natural or legal person). A partner can dispose of his or her interest in the partnership only with the consent of all the other partners.

Every partner is authorised to manage the ordinary work of a partnership, but partners are free to determine a different structure in the memorandum of association, which is the basic document required for the formation. For actions that go beyond the normal course of business, it is necessary to obtain the consent of all partners.

The memorandum of association should include the following information for the purpose of registration at the Commercial Court Registry:

- names and seats of the companies participating in the partnership;

- partnership name and registered address in Croatia;

- scope of business; and

- obligations of the companies participating in the partnership, and other information relevant for the operation of the partnership.

LIMITED PARTNERSHIPS

A limited partnership is a business organization consisting of at least two persons, formed for the purpose of permanently performing business activities under a joint name, where at least one of the partners is liable without limitations and jointly and severally with all of his or her assets for the obligations of the partnership (general partner or *komplementar*). The other partner(s) may be limited partners (*komanditori*). Limited partners are those partners whose liability is limited only to the amount of their capital contribution to the limited partnership. As to foreign investors, the same limitation applies as for the rest of partnerships business forms. There should be at least one domestic legal or natural person personally liable with all of its assets for the partnership obligations. The name of the firm must include the name of one or more general partners and letters '*i dr.*' ('and others').

The limited partnership has a legal personality and should be registered at the Commercial Court Registry.

### EUROPEAN INTEREST GROUPINGS

The provisions on the European Interest Groupings (EIG) have been taken from the EU legislation. The Companies Act defines the EIG as a legal person set up by two or more individuals or legal persons, for the purpose of facilitating and promoting their business activities and of promoting or increasing the effect of these activities, with a specific limitation that a grouping may not earn profits for itself.

The law provides that members of the EIG may be natural or legal business persons, ie a person has to carry on business activities or belong to an independent profession, for example lawyers, dentists, etc. Members of an EIG are personally liable for the obligations of the grouping. The law does not provide for any kind of a limitation based on the country of registration for members of an EIG, as is the case in the EU, where the form is available to the persons registered in the EU countries only.

A member may transfer its interest only with the approval of all members. Consent of all the members is also required for accession of a new member.

Formation of an EIG is based on a memorandum of association and has to be registered at the Commercial Court Registry.

### SILENT PARTNERSHIPS

A partnership contract is usually formed on the basis of a person investing certain assets in the enterprise of another person (entrepreneur) and thereby it acquires the right to participate in sharing profits and the obligation to share losses of the undertaking. However, the parties can also provide for a silent partner to be excluded from covering the losses of the partnership.

A silent partnership is founded on mere contractual relationship and is not considered a separate legal person, ie it does not have a name and it is not registered at the Commercial Court Registry. It follows that such a contract does not have effect towards third parties and does not have its own property.

## JOINT VENTURES

A joint venture is a particular type of partnership, which is internationally accepted as a type of direct investment of capital in international business operations. Croatian provisions on joint ventures are included in the partnerships chapter (*ortaštvo*) of the Law on Contracts.

In joint ventures, parties to the contract agree on contributing capital and participating in profits earned or losses incurred in the undertaking of a common interest.

The business operations of the partnership are based on the agreement, for example a joint venture agreement, shareholder agreement etc, concluded between parties. Usually, the agreement is very detailed and includes provisions on common interests, project development, participation and transfer of profit, capital contributions of the parties, management of the partnership, transfer of know-how etc. Pursuant to Croatian law, a joint venture is not deemed a separate legal person, and therefore partners are held personally liable for obligations of the partnership. In fact, if the shareholder agreement does not provide for a specific arrangement to represent the partnership, each partner will have the obligation to represent the partnership towards third parties.

Under Croatian law, a joint venture may operate under two legal structures:

- a contractual joint venture; or

- an equity joint venture.

In the case of a contractual joint venture, the undertaking is limited to the contractual relationship between the parties, excluding the incorporation of a new business entity for the purpose of management of the venture. Conversely, in the equity joint venture, partners to the venture form a company (usually a limited liability company or joint stock company) for the accomplishment of the undertaking. Anti-trust provisions apply to joint ventures.

### Corporations

Pursuant to the Croatian law, a limited liability company and a joint stock company are two types of business organizations whose main feature is that the capital of the company is divided, respectively, in stakes and shares. Accordingly, the rights of a stakeholder in the company will derive from the value of his or her contribution to the share capital. The other key difference from other business entities is that the company members are not held personally liable for the entity's actions.

The transfer of stakes in corporations is free, except for the limitations made in the association agreement. In that respect, Croatian law allows the so-called *vinkulacija,* the term used when the articles of association of a joint stock company, or a limited liability company, provide that shares may not be transferred without the consent of the corporation.

## LIMITED LIABILITY COMPANY

A limited liability company (*društvo sa ograničenom odgovornošću*) is defined as a company in which one or more individuals or legal persons (members of the company) invest their property and thereby participate in the previously agreed capital. The corporate name must include the letters 'd.o.o.', which indicate that the company is structured as a limited liability company in Croatia.

Members of the limited liability company are not held personally liable for obligations incurred by the company. The capital of a limited liability company is divided into stakes, whereby a single investor may not hold more than one stake when the company is formed, although this can be changed later. If the founder of the company is a single investor, the basic document required for registration is the founder's statement (*izjava osnivača*), or in the case of more founders, the basic document will be in the form of articles of association (*društveni ugovor*), both of them in the form of a notarized document.

Pursuant to the Companies Act, a limited liability company is composed of the management board and the general assembly. Investors are free to determine whether they wish to have a supervisory board as well. A supervisory board is mandatory for companies with more than 300 employees and in other situations envisaged by the Act. In the latter case, the supervisory board has to consist of at least three members. Members of the supervisory board are elected by a decision of the members at a general meeting of the company.

All the stakeholders of the company are represented in the company's assembly. Members of the company have votes in proportion to their contribution in the share capital.

The management board is composed of one or more members. There are no restrictions with respect to the appointment of a foreign national as a director. Members of the board have the authority to represent and manage the company. Members of the assembly may recall the management board of the company at any time. From that perspective, the position of the members of the management board is less independent than that of the directors in joint stock companies. The idea of the limited liability company is to have a close relationship between partners who are actively involved in the management of the company.

**Formation**    The fundamental document required for incorporation of a limited liability company is the articles of association, or a statement of the founder in the case where the incorporation is made by a single founder. This agreement must be signed by all the stakeholders and certified by a notary public.

The law provides for a minimum share capital that can be executed in cash or in kind, amounting to HRK20,000 (approximately €2,700 at the time of writing). If contributions are made in cash, the investor should make a transfer into a temporary account of any financial institution in Croatia. If the contribution is in kind, then it needs to be fully rendered.

In addition, investors need to agree on the members of the management board. Investors are free to determine in the memorandum of association if they want to have a supervisory board as well, unless the supervisory board is mandatory by virtue of a specific statute. It is mandatory for companies managing investment funds, and for companies with more than 300 employees. In the latter case, the supervisory board has to consist of at least three members.

**Documentation required**    Under Croatian law, a company will acquire its legal personality once it has been registered at the Commercial Court Registry in the district where the company is going to have its permanent place of business.

A foreign investor has to provide the following documents with the application to the Commercial Court Registry for incorporation purposes:

- original excerpt from the company registry of the founder;

- resolution of the founder forming a company, including the name of the company and the address in Croatia, scope of business and the share capital; and

- statement issued by the Tax Authority to the effect that the founder does not have any outstanding liabilities towards the Tax Authority.

The application for the registration at the Commercial Court Registry will be submitted after the company agreement has been signed, the shares have been paid in compliance with the company agreement and one or more members of the company management board have been appointed.

The application for the registration shall include the following items:

- company name, seat and scope of business;

- share capital;

- statement of the management board members on their obligation to provide all the required information to the court; and

- names of the company members and, if company members are physical persons, their personal identification numbers.

Furthermore, the following documents have to be enclosed with the application:

- copy of the memorandum of association;

- list of members/founders, with a certificate issued by a relevant financial institution

- that it has received the payment of the share capital;

- initial capital guarantee, where the company is being founded by one founder only:

- audit report on the company's incorporation, when the share capital consists of contributions in kind;

- list of persons authorized to conduct business operations, scope of authorizations and statements on acceptance of the given assignments before the notary public;

- approval of the state body; and

- certified signatures of members of the management board.

### JOINT STOCK COMPANIES

A joint stock company is a business organization whose share capital is divided into shares, and shareholders are not personally liable for the obligations of the company. The name of a joint stock company should include the letters 'd.d.'.

The law provides that there is a minimum share capital of HRK200,000 (approximately €15,000) for setting up the company. It is no longer compulsory to issue shares with a par value. If par value is specified, it should be at least HRK10, or a multiple of HRK10.

There can be two types of shares, registered name-shares and bearer shares. Share issues before payment of full par value have to be name-shares. In principle, shares are freely transferable, but shareholders may stipulate restrictions in the articles of association with respect to registered shares requiring the consent of the management board for their transfer (or to be defined in the articles of association).

Joint stock companies are allowed to have treasury shares in cases strictly determined by the law.

**Legal structure of joint stock company**    Pursuant to the Companies Act, a joint stock company is composed of a management board, a supervisory board and a general assembly.

A management board consists of one or more directors. It is appointed by the supervisory board for a maximum period of five years and may be re-elected. Members of the board may be discharged from their duty by the supervisory board if there is an important reason for this. The management is in charge of the management of the corporation. Members of the management board cannot be influenced by the supervisory board in taking business decisions. However, the articles of association may include provisions on mandatory consent of the supervisory board for certain decisions.

A supervisory board consists of at least three members that cannot be members of the management board of the same company at the same time. They are elected by the general assembly of shareholders for a term of four years and can be re-elected. Shareholders may stipulate in the articles of association that no more than one third of the members are nominated by shareholders. The supervisory board has a duty to supervise the management of the corporation.

The general shareholders meeting of a joint stock company is the principal forum through which shareholders exercise their rights.

**Formation**    A joint stock company can be formed by simultaneous incorporation and by incorporation in stages.

A simultaneous incorporation consists of:

- adopting and signing the articles of association by the founders;

- founders giving the statement to a notary public on setting up the company;

- adopting all the outstanding shares;

- payment of adopted shares;

- appointment of the supervisory board and the auditor, and supervisory board

- appointing the management board; and

- reporting on the formation of the company.

A joint stock company must be registered at the Commercial Court Registry.

However, if the company is set up by incorporation in stages, the founders of the company must adopt the articles of association, subscribe a part of the shares and issue a prospectus for subscription to the remaining shares (to be subscribed in the following three months).

## Acquisition of shares and the Takeovers Act

A company may decide to invest in Croatia by acquiring shares in an existing joint stock company. There are two main statutes to be observed in this case: The Companies Act and the Act on Takeovers of Joint Stock Companies (*Zakon o preuzimanju dioničkih društava, Narodne Novine 84/02*). The Securities Act (*Zakon o tržištu vrijednosnih papira, Narodne Novine 84/02*) contains provisions on the Croatian Securities Commission, Central Depository Agency and provisions concerning protection of investors, issue and transfer of securities etc.

Pursuant to the Takeovers Act, an investor is required to publish a tender offer for the remaining outstanding shares in a company in the following situations:

- when a person procures more than 25 per cent of the total number of votes in the main assembly of the issuer, it shall be obliged to report the acquisition to the Securities Commission of Croatia, the issuer and the public, and to publish the tender offer following the procedure prescribed by the Act;

- when a person, by means of a tender offer, achieves less than 75 per cent ownership of voting shares, it is obliged to publish a tender offer in case of any further procurement of shares from the same issuer; or

- when a person, by means of a tender offer, procures itself the ownership of 75 per cent or more of all voting shares, it is obliged to publish a tender offer when procuring additional voting shares of the same issuers in the following situations:

  - when, after the tender offer has been accomplished, it acquires an additional five per cent of voting shares; or
  - after 18 months following the acquisition of shares at the completion of the previous tender offer.

The price for tendered shares cannot be lower than the highest price of shares paid by the tender for shares acquired in the period following the previous tender offer.

Before the publication of the tender offer for the takeover, the offeror must separate, in a special account, the monetary assets necessary to pay for all shares that are the subject of the tender offer for the takeover, or enter into an agreement with the bank about the approved credit for that purpose or originate a bank guarantee for first rights in favour of the shareholder, and for the amount necessary to pay for all shares that the tender offer concerns.

In addition, before the publication of the tender offer for the takeover, the offeror must enter into an agreement with a depositary institution on deposit of the shares due to the acceptance of the tender offer for the takeover.

Within 30 days from the date the obligation for the mandatory tender offer has arisen, the offeror is required to submit the request for the approval of the Croatian Securities Commission to publish the takeover, and the offer and documentation as stated in Article 12 of the Takeovers Act. If all the requirements prescribed by the law have been observed, the Securities Commission is obliged to give its approval within 14 days from the date of receipt of the submitted request.

The offeror is obliged to publish the tender offer in the Croatian National Gazette and in one of the daily newspapers that are regularly distributed throughout the Croatian territory.

The offer is binding for 30 days starting from the day it was rendered public. In the case of a hostile bid, another term of 30 days will start. The law does not provide for the maximum number or duration of extensions.

After expiration of the above term, the offeror has the obligation to acquire all deposited (tendered) shares.

## Mergers and acquisitions

It has become a frequent practice in the business world to concentrate capital, technologies, finance and labour force in order to strengthen the position of a company in the market. These events should be even more evident in Croatia or in other Central and Eastern European countries, which are aware of the significant impact the European Common Market will have on their business operations.

The most common procedure provided by the Companies Act to effect this aim is a procedure of a merger by acquisition. Under the provisions of the Companies Act, a merger by acquisition is defined as a procedure by which one or more legal entities transfer all their assets to another company against shares (or stakes) of the other company. Acquired entities cease to exist without affecting the liquidation procedure.

A merger stands for a procedure where two or more entities form a third company to which all of their assets will be transferred. To perform a merger, Croatian law prescribes a two-year existence for all the merging companies (to be ascertained in the appropriate Commercial Court Registry) if they are joint stock companies. In the case where a merger is effected between a joint stock company and a limited liability company, the restrictions do not apply. Provisions on merger and merger by acquisition apply to limited liability companies and joint stock companies only.

The Companies Act provides for several provisions related to the protection of rights and interests of shareholders/stakeholders participating in the merger. Namely, the Act prescribes the minimal content of the merger agreement; management boards have a duty to prepare a comprehensive report on the merger and inform the shareholders; there has to be an audit of the merger; all companies participating in the merger have to approve the merger with a majority of three quarters of members of the assembly etc. Special attention has to be given to the share exchange ratio of merging companies. The ratio must be related to the net asset value of the respective companies.

*Minority shareholders freeze-outs*
A shareholder of a joint stock company that owns at least 95 per cent of all shares in the company may acquire the remaining shares of the company by a decision to make a minority shareholders payout by giving them an adequate price for their shares.

## Entrepreneurial contracts

The relationship between the subsidiary and the parent can be of different intensity. The entrepreneurial agreements represent a type of relationship between two companies where one of them (the subsidiary) renounces in favour of the other company (the parent) one of the main characteristics of a company, which is to make profit and to act in the interest of its stakeholders. There are two types of entrepreneurial contracts:

- agreement on conducting business operations; and

- agreement on transfer of profit.

An agreement on conducting business operations is the contract by which a company agrees to transfer the conduct of its business operations to another company, while in the agreement on transfer of profit, a company agrees to transfer all its profit to another company. Due to the importance of such a decision, the law prescribes a compulsory majority of three quarters of the votes present at the shareholders assembly of both parties to such an agreement.

The controlling company will be responsible for debts of the subsidiary and has to provide for the severance payment of the minority shareholders in the amount of the estimated annual dividend.

## Dividend payments

Before dividends can be paid out to shareholders, a joint stock company should cover the losses from previous years and should cover the legal reserves. The remaining profits may be used for treasury shares, and finally to cover statutory reserves, if any. It will be impossible to pay dividends if, pursuant to the latest financial statement, the income of a company is lower than the legal share capital increased by the reserves that cannot be paid to the shareholders.

# 5.3

# The Taxation System

*Helena Schmidt, Tax and Regulatory
Services, Deloitte & Touche, Zagreb*

## Taxes in Croatia

A new Corporate Income Tax was introduced on 1 January 2005. The new Corporate Profit Act, as well as the Value Added Tax Act were introduced to create a transparent and modern tax system in Croatia that is comparable with European standards.

The Croatian tax system is based on taxation of income and sales rather than capital. Business income is generally subject to corporate income tax, while income earned by individuals is subject to personal income tax. Most domestic sales and imports are subject to value added tax (VAT) and this is augmented by a number of excise and other taxes and fees levied on specific transactions.

The taxation system is based on a set of direct and indirect taxes, as shown below:

- basic direct taxes;
- Corporate Income Tax (CIT);
- Personal Income Tax (PIT);
- surtax (levied on personal income tax);
- basic indirect taxes;
- VAT;
- excise taxes;
- real estate sales tax.

The taxation system is uniform across the country and only small differences may occur in local taxes. Generally, foreign companies and individuals pay the same taxes as Croatian legal or natural persons. The exception to this rule applies where taxation is regulated by international treaties honoured by Croatia. Croatia honours all the double taxation agreements made between the former Yugoslavia and other countries, and has already signed new agreements on avoiding double taxation with numerous other countries.

# The tax system and administration

## Tax authority

Croatian tax administration is regulated by the Tax Administration located within the Ministry of Finance. The central Tax Administration office is located in Zagreb, and there are 20 regional offices with 120 branches throughout Croatia. The central office of Tax Administration is responsible for monitoring and implementing uniform compliance with tax obligations throughout the country and plays an important role in the formulation of tax policy and tax related regulations.

## General Tax Act

The General Tax Act systematically, integrally and uniformly regulates the legal relations of taxpayers and tax authorities that are common to all taxes. The General Tax Act deals with the broad issues relating to taxation procedure and application of tax provisions, payment, reimbursement, forced payment, evidencing and dispute resolution. Furthermore, this Act defines the main taxation principles. The new provisions of this law extend the rights of taxpayers, clearly defining the relationship between debtors, creditors and successors in the payment, disbursement, guarantee, and compensation and compounding of tax obligations or claims proceedings. It also clearly defines the relationship in proceedings of pledging, ceding and impounding of assets or rights.

## Returns and assessments

In most cases, taxes are levied by self-assessments. As a result, the taxpayer must file a return and make any payment by the due date stipulated by the Act without waiting for a formal assessment from the tax administration.

If the tax is not paid on time, interest is charged at a rate of 15 per cent per annum. The period for the calculation of interest starts from the day when the tax should have been paid and continues to the day when it is actually paid.

## Group registration

There are no group registration provisions in Croatia for tax purposes.

# Corporate income tax

## Taxpayers

Persons liable to pay profit tax are companies or other legal entities engaged in an economic activity for the purpose of making profits. The resident business branch of a non-resident entrepreneur is also a taxpayer. A non-resident entrepreneur is one that does not have headquarters or management in Croatia. A representative office does not fall within the ambit of the corporate profit tax law unless it is engaged in an agency capacity in the airline or other travel industries on income from tickets sold in Croatia.

## Tax rates

Corporate tax is levied at a single rate of 20 per cent on taxable income.

## Taxable base

The taxable base is the profit (difference between revenue and expenditures of the firm) defined as profit increased and decreased according to the accounting regulations. The tax base for resident taxpayers is the total profit made in Croatia and abroad. The tax base for non-resident taxpayers is the profit earned in Croatia. Any profit made during a liquidation procedure is also included in taxable base.

## Tax calculation

The law defines separately all items that increase or reduce profit. The corporate profit tax base is increased for any depreciation charged in excess of the highest tax-deductible amount. It is also increased for 70 per cent of entertainment costs and the costs of fines and penalties, 30 per cent of expenses related to personal transportation, gifts and donations greater than two per cent of revenues made in the previous year, and hidden profits payments or transfer pricing.

The corporate profit tax base can be reduced by the earnings from dividends and shares in profit, depreciation charges that were not allowed in earlier periods and by employment incentives (the amount of the gross salary cost of newly engaged labour).

## Transfer pricing

If through business between a resident branch of a non-resident entrepreneur and founding company or between a resident subsidiary company and a non-resident parent company the expenditures of the resident taxpayer are increased because of expenses for the procurement of goods and services, management services, intellectual services, trade marks, patents, licenses, loans, various fees and the tax base of the resident taxpayer is decreased in other ways and if a hidden profit transfer is made, the said transactions are calculated at market prices that would be achieved for a comparable transaction on the comparable market in the same or similar circumstances among persons that are not connected. The same applies to a hidden payment of profit via reduction in the revenue of the resident taxpayer.

For differences determined in the manner described above, the profit tax base of the resident taxpayer is increased accordingly.

## Relief, exemptions and incentives

The Corporate Income Tax Act provides financial incentives to companies in the form of reductions in the corporate tax rate or additional reductions in the tax base itself.

In order to claim a tax incentive, a company must prove that it is involved in an incentive measure as defined by the Investment Promotion Act. An incentive measure includes the introduction of new equipment/modern technologies, employment and education of employees and modernization and improvement of business.

### Corporate tax rate reductions

Corporate tax reductions are available where new employees are employed and funds are invested in Croatia. The tax rate reduction itself is contingent on both the amount invested (in Croatian kunas) and the number of employees.

Benefits may be given only to newly established companies for a period of 10 years from the beginning of the investment. However, if an investment in tourism is concerned, the already existing company may be the beneficiary of tax benefits.

The incentives presently available in Croatia are as follows:

- the corporate tax rate will be reduced to seven per cent for a 10-year period, beginning in the year of investment, where a company invests at least HRK10 million in the business and employs a minimum of 30 new employees;

- the corporate tax rate will be reduced to three per cent for a 10-year period, beginning in the year of investment, where a company invests at least HRK20 million in the business and employs a minimum of 50 new employees;

- the corporate tax rate will be reduced to zero per cent for a 10-year period, beginning in the year of investment, where a company invests at least HRK60 million in the business and employs a minimum of 75 new employees.

*Employment incentives*
Employment incentives exist that effectively allow a double deduction to be claimed in respect of wages paid to new employees. A new employee is perceived to be an employee with whom an indefinite employment contract has been drawn up, and who has secured employment after being registered as unemployed for a minimum period of a month or who has given up the right to retire or who is being employed for the first time.

The additional reduction in the tax base can only be claimed for one year from the date that the employee was employed, or for a three-year period if the employee is disabled.

*Creation of new employment positions*
If an entrepreneur creates new jobs or employment positions, they may be granted up to HRK15,000 for each employee to cover the cost of job creation. However, it should be noted that when calculating the number of newly created jobs, the number of other job terminations will be taken into consideration.

*Retraining*
The retraining costs can be reduced by virtue of the incentives and assistance available. For instance, when the employer invests in vocational training or retraining of employees, the Fund for the Stimulation of New Job Creation and Retraining of Employees may contribute funds to cover 50 per cent of the costs involved.

*Relief for taxpayers in areas of special national concern*
Taxpayers who carry on their business in an area of special national concern and employ more than five employees, with more than 50 per cent of the employees having their domicile and being resident in the area of special national concern, will pay profit tax at the rate of between 25 per cent to 75 per cent of the prescribed tax rate, depending on the area classification.

*Relief and exemptions for taxpayers in the area of the city of Vukovar*
Taxpayers that carry on their business in the area of the city of Vukovar and employ more than five employees, with more than 50 per cent of the employees having their domicile and residing in the area of the city of Vukovar, are exempted from paying profit tax in the years 2000–2005, and, after that, will pay profit tax in the amount of 25 per cent of the prescribed rate.

*Relief and exemptions for taxpayers who do business in free zones*
Users of free zones as defined by the Free Zones Act will pay profit tax in the amount of 50 per cent of the prescribed rate (10 per cent).

## Tax losses

Tax losses can be carried forward for five years from the year the tax loss was incurred. If losses are not utilized within this time, the loss will expire. Accordingly, losses should be utilized on a 'first in first out' basis. Until 1 January 2001, tax losses were multiplied by an applicable protective interest rate. On 1 January 2001, protective interest was abolished.

## Statute of limitations

The relative period for the statute of limitations is three years. The absolute period for the statute of limitations for establishment of tax debt and interest, the filing of offence procedures, the collection of taxes, interest, costs of execution and fines and the right of the taxpayer to a refund of taxation, interest, costs of execution and fines, is six years, starting from the date when the statute of limitations for tax purposes starts to come into effect. Both relative and absolute periods begin with the elapse of the year in which the tax return was due.

## Assessment

Corporate profit tax in Croatia is assessed for the business year and the business year corresponds to the calendar year. The tax return must be submitted to the tax administration within four months after the end of the tax period for which the profit tax is being assessed, which is normally by the end of April for the preceding business year. The annual profit tax return submitted to the Tax Authority should be accompanied by the following:

- annual financial statements with notes attached;

- review of unused carry-forward fiscal losses; and

- other documentation, depending on each taxpayer's specific status (eg mergers during the fiscal year).

The Croatian corporate profit tax stipulates that the corporate taxpayer pay monthly advance payments, based on the previous year's corporate profit tax return. Shortfall at the year-end must be self-assessed and paid by the corporate profit taxpayer. If corporate profit taxes have been overpaid during the business year, the surplus tax paid shall be returned upon request or it can be brought forward into the next taxable period.

## Withholding tax

Taxpayers who pay compensation to foreign legal entities for the use of intellectual ownership rights, market research services, tax consulting, auditing services, dividends, profit shares and interest rates, are obliged to calculate and pay profit tax at the rate of 15 per cent. Withholding tax is not paid on interest rates for selling equipment on credit, tied loans and loans granted by a foreign bank. However, if Croatia has a double tax treaty avoidance agreement with the country where the compensation beneficiary is resident, then the provisions of such a treaty will apply.

# VAT

VAT was introduced in Croatia on 1 January 1998, replacing the previous sales tax on goods and services. The VAT system is harmonized with the Croatian direct tax laws (ie the Profit Tax Act) and is modelled on the EU Sixth Directive.

## The scope and rates of VAT

*Scope*
The following transactions are subject to VAT unless they are exempt from VAT or 'VAT free' (which is equivalent to being zero-rated or exempt with credits for related costs):

- goods or services provided for consideration;

- imports of goods;

- entertainment and use of personal vehicles and other means of personal transport that are not tax deductible; and

- supplies made to company owners (this refers to supplies for the benefit of shareholders and members of their immediate families, if the recipients of these supplies are not required to provide any consideration or if a personal discount is provided).

*Rates*
The current VAT rate is 22 per cent (applying to most deliveries of goods and services) and 0 per cent on deliveries of some products such as bread, milk, books, certain medicines and medical products. Certain supplies are exempt, including exports. Other exemptions include housing rentals, services provided by health, financial, insurance and educational institutions and similar.

## Place of supply

*Goods*
Where goods are not transported, the place of supply is taken to be the location of the goods at the time of supply. Where goods are trans-

ported, the place of supply is taken to be the location of the goods at the time transportation begins. If goods are installed or assembled by or on behalf of a supplier, the place of supply is deemed to be the place where the goods are installed or assembled for use.

*Services*

As a general rule, the place of supply for services is taken to be the registered office of the person performing the service. If a particular business unit performs services, the place of performance is considered to be the headquarters of that business unit. Where this cannot be determined, the place of performance is taken to be the temporary or permanent residence of the person performing the service.

The following exceptions to the above general rule exist and are similar to those listed in the EU Sixth Directive.

The place of supply is taken to be the place where the recipient is located for the following services:

- the transfer, cession and use of copyrights, patents, licences, trade marks and similar rights, and renunciation of such rights;

- promotional services, including intermediation in such services;

- services performed by engineers, lawyers, auditors, accountants, interpreters, translators, and other providers of consultancy services;

- automated data processing services;

- cession of information, including information on business procedures and know-how;

- banking, insurance and re-insurance services; and

- cession of employees.

The place of supply is taken to be the place where the services are supplied for the following services:

- transport services and services ancillary to transport;

- artistic, scientific, sporting, entertainment or educational services; and

- services (repairs, maintenance and valuation) on movable property.

The place of supply for services relating to land (such as leasing, construction and real estate) is taken to be where the land is located.

## Time of supply

*Goods*

Goods are taken to be supplied at the time the goods are placed at the disposal of the buyer or end user.

The VAT liability on imports of goods arises on the day customs duties are due and payable.

*Services*
Services are supplied at the time of performance. Where a service is performed over two successive accounting periods, the service is taken to be supplied and VAT is charged in the second accounting period. Where services are performed over more than two successive accounting periods, VAT must be charged and accounted for in each accounting period, regardless of when the final invoice is issued.

## Value of supply

The taxable value of a supply is the consideration provided for the good or service, exclusive of VAT.

Where no consideration is provided or where the parties are not dealing with each other on an 'arms length' basis (which includes supplies to employees), the value of a product for VAT purposes is taken to be its fair market value.

The taxable value of an import is its customs value increased by the amount of any customs duties and any other taxes or charges payable.

## Registration

Every resident or non-resident company conducting business operations in Croatia must register its legal entity (eg a branch office or limited liability company) in the Croatian Company Register at the Commercial Court before it commences business operations. This means that a non-resident company must establish a Croatian registered legal entity before it can register for VAT.

The Croatian VAT Act provides that a taxable person is any person or entity supplying goods or services that are subject to VAT. This includes entrepreneurs delivering goods or performing services, issuers of invoices and non-profit organizations that make taxable supplies with the intention of deriving profit.

*Compulsory registration*
A taxable person must register for VAT if their turnover in any calendar year exceeds the compulsory registration threshold of HRK85,000 (approximately €11,350). Turnover, for this purpose, is defined as the total value of delivered goods and services including VAT, which includes the value of zero rated supplies but not exempt supplies.

A person whose turnover does not exceed the compulsory registration threshold can apply to be registered voluntarily.

## Export transactions

As exports are VAT exempt, there is no requirement to issue a VAT invoice in respect of them. However, an invoice issued in respect of an export should clearly state that VAT has not been included.

## VAT returns

The VAT year is the calendar year. A taxable person with an annual turnover (inclusive of VAT) exceeding HRK300,000 (approximately €40,360) is required to file monthly VAT returns. Where a taxable person's annual turnover is below this amount, the taxable person can choose to adopt either a monthly or quarterly VAT period. VAT returns are due by the end of the month following the VAT period.

A taxable person must also file an annual VAT return. The taxable person is required to disclose their annual turnover when completing their annual VAT return. It is also the final adjustment period for any partial exemption calculation and all other adjustments relating to the tax period. Where a taxable person submits monthly VAT returns, the annual VAT return must be submitted by the end of April of the following year. Where a company submits quarterly returns, the annual VAT return must be submitted by the end of February of the following year. The annual VAT period is always the calendar year.

## Payments

VAT is payable when lodging a VAT return and must be made by bank transfer or cheque to an account stipulated by the Minister of Finance.

## Refunds

Where a taxable person's input tax credits exceed its VAT liability, the taxable person is entitled to a VAT refund. The person can either ask to receive an actual cash refund or can elect to treat the excess as a VAT prepayment. The tax refund is indicated on the usual VAT return and the tax authority must pay the refund within 15 days after the tax return is filed.

## Exemptions

*Exemptions without credit*
In Croatia, supplies that are exempt from VAT without credit are similar to those contained in the EU Sixth Directive and include:

- rental of residential property;
- goods and services rendered by banks, savings institutions, savings and loan institutions and insurance institutions;

- medical services, including services conducted by doctors, dentists, nurses, physiotherapists, and biochemistry laboratories engaged in private practices;

- services of medical care performed in healthcare institutions (primary healthcare institutions, casualty medical care institutions, policlinics, general and specialized hospitals and clinics, end services of medical care performed by institutions specializing in healthcare at home and deliveries of goods made by the above institutions);

- services and deliveries of goods by social care institutions;

- services and deliveries of goods by institutions of child and adolescent care;

- services and deliveries of goods by nursery, primary and secondary schools, universities and student catering and boarding institutions;

- services and deliveries of goods by religious communities and institutions;

- services and deliveries of goods by public institutions in the field of culture, such as museums, galleries, archives, libraries, theatres;

- winnings from special games of chance in casinos, slot machine clubs and other gambling means;

- supplies of gold by the central bank;

- supplies of domestic and foreign legal tender;

- company securities and shares;

- supplies of real estate (land, buildings, parts of buildings, housing premises, and other structures), with the exception of newly built buildings; and

- temporary imports of goods that are exempt from customs duty.

*Exempt supplies with credit*
The following supplies are zero-rated or VAT-free under Croatian VAT legislation:

- bread and milk;

- books of a scholarly, scientific, artistic, cultural and educational character, as well as school textbooks (primary, secondary and tertiary education, including materials printed on paper and other media, such as CDs, video cassettes and audio tapes);

- certain medicines and surgical implants;

- scientific journals;

- services rendered by cinemas; and

- holiday packages paid for from abroad (accommodation or accommodation with breakfast, full or half board in all kinds of commercial hospitality facilities).

Exports of goods and services are exempt with credit.

## VAT recovery

Generally, a taxable person has the right to recover VAT costs incurred in the course of conducting their ordinary business activities. This includes making taxable supplies and VAT-free supplies. Input VAT cannot be recovered in respect of purchases made in the process of providing VAT exempt supplies, supplies made abroad which would be exempt if in Croatia and supplies made free of charge, which would be exempt if paid for.

VAT cannot be claimed on the following expenses, as these expenses are taken to be private in nature and are not deductible for Croatian profit tax purposes:

- 70 per cent of entertainment expenditures; and

- 30 per cent of expenses incurred in connection with a person's own or rented personal motor vehicles and other means of personal transport for entrepreneurs, management and other staff.

Expenditure relating partly to exempt or non-business activities must be distinguished and input tax may be partially deducted.

## VAT recovery adjustment

If the tax treatment governing tax exemption of certain goods that was effective in a certain year is changed within five years from the beginning of the use of the assets, then the tax credit adjustment must be effected for the period after the change became effective. In the case of real estate, the period of adjustment of initial VAT recovery is 10 years. The initial deduction is adjusted on a one-off basis upon the change of taxable status. Where the value of VAT does not exceed HRK2,000 (approximately €270) per item, the adjustment is not affected.

## Imports of goods and services

Only a registered Croatian entity (eg a branch or company) is entitled to make a customs declaration in respect of imported goods. A non-resident must, therefore, appoint a Croatian resident agent to complete the customs declaration on its behalf.

*Goods*
VAT is calculated on the total value of imported goods, inclusive of customs and excise duties. VAT is payable at the time the goods are imported and VAT is collected by the Customs Authority.

*Services*
The Croatian VAT legislation contains a 'reverse charge' rule, which requires resident taxable persons to account for VAT at a rate of 22 per cent for certain supplies received from abroad.

The reverse charge rule applies to those services that are taxed according to the place where the registered office of the service recipient is located (see the 'Place of supply' section).

## Exports of goods and services

Only a registered Croatian entity (eg a branch or company) is entitled to make a customs declaration in respect of exported goods. A non-resident making exports from Croatia must, therefore, appoint a Croatian resident agent to complete the customs declaration on its behalf.

*Goods*
Exports (including transport and forwarding service costs) are exempt from VAT and the supplier is entitled to claim input tax credits for the VAT paid in the process of providing the goods.

*Services*
Where a Croatian business provides services and the place of supply is outside Croatia, the supplies are treated as exempt from Croatian VAT, rather than being outside of its scope. However, the supplier is generally entitled to recover input tax credits in relation to these supplies of services, unless a domestic supply of the service would be exempt.

Notwithstanding that a supply is made in Croatia, the supply may be deemed to have been made abroad (ie considered to be an export) in the following cases:

- deliveries of goods to a customs free zone, customs free and bonded warehouses and deliveries of goods within a customs free zone;

- deliveries of goods to diplomatic and consular missions, providing that reciprocal arrangements exist with the appropriate country;

- deliveries of goods to humanitarian organizations, healthcare, educational, cultural, scholarly and scientific, religious and welfare institutions, amateur sports clubs and bodies of national and local government and self-government that are paid for from foreign monetary donations; and

- services provided by a Croatian taxable person in Croatia to a non-resident person that provide air, river and/or sea transport.

## Property

The sale of real estate, including buildings, parts of buildings, housing premises and other structures and parts of structures, is exempt from VAT with the exception of the first supply of a 'new' building. A building is deemed to be 'new' if it was built after 31 December 1997.

The leasing and letting of residential property is exempt from VAT, except for the letting of temporary accommodation to non-permanent guests (ie hotel accommodation). The leasing of commercial property is always subject to VAT.

It is not possible to opt to waive exemption from VAT in relation to exempt supplies (both sales and leases) of real estate.

## Refunds to tourists

Tourists are entitled to reclaim VAT on goods purchased and taken out of Croatia. This is on the condition that the goods have not been used and that their invoiced value exceeds HRK500. A PDV-P form has to be provided by the supplier and stamped at the border. The tourist must claim the VAT refund within six months of the day the invoice was issued. VAT refunds are not available for oil derivatives.

## Refunds to foreign entities

A foreign entity is generally not entitled to a VAT refund unless it has a permanent establishment in Croatia and is registered for VAT.

A foreign entity participating in Croatian Trade Fairs may be entitled to claim a VAT refund in respect of costs incurred in Croatia. This is on the condition that they do not have a residence, business management, branch or any other form of business entity in Croatia. A refund is also available to foreign entities who exhibit at Trade Fairs and who do not have a representative office in Croatia and who would not otherwise be eligible to claim a VAT refund in Croatia.

Foreign exhibitors may be entitled to a VAT refund for the following goods and services: rental of the exhibited area; the costs associated with the exhibited area (electricity, water, gas, heating and cooling facilities and telecommunication services); the construction and maintenance (including materials) of the exhibited area and parking expenses.

An application for a VAT refund can be lodged in the name of the foreign entity by a Croatian tax resident that has authorization from the foreign entity.

An application for a VAT refund must be submitted as part of the ZP-PDV form (VAT application on the tax return) and must be lodged within six months of the end of the calendar year in which the conditions for a VAT refund have been met. VAT refunds are only relevant for amounts in total value above HRK1,000.

**5.4**

# Personal Income Tax and Social Security Contributions

*Adrian Hammer, Deloitte & Touche*

Resident individuals are taxed in Croatia on their worldwide income. Non-residents are taxed on their Croatian-sourced income only. An individual is considered a resident if he/she maintains a permanent or temporary residence in Croatia for at least 183 days a year. Other individuals are considered non-resident.

## Taxable income

Taxable income includes employment income, business or self-employment income, income from property and property rights, income from capital and income from insurance.

Salary and wage income, pensions, benefits (whether in cash or in kind, paid to the employee in relation to current, previous or future work, in various forms such as private use of cars, favourable interest on loans to the employee and the like) and employment-related awards are included in employment income. The taxable base of benefits in kind is based on their market value.

The tax base for business or self-employment income is total revenue less expenses. Losses may be carried forward for five years. Certain individuals pay profits tax instead of personal income tax on their business or self-employment income.

Income from property and property rights includes rental income from real estate and moveable property, copyright royalties and income from industrial property rights. Gains from disposals of property and property rights are also included, unless the property or rights have been held for at least three years. Taxpayers are allowed to deduct 30 per cent of real estate rental income, or 50 per cent in certain circumstances.

Income from capital includes dividends, shares in the profits according to the share in capital and interests. In addition, withdrawals of assets and use of services by the owners of companies for private purposes shall be deemed dividends and shares in the profits.

## Tax return, personal assessments and payments

The tax year is the calendar year. Tax on employment income is withheld at source by the (local) employer.

Self-employed individuals should make monthly advance payments, which are based on the amount of income tax payable in the previous year.

Advance payments must be made in the case of rental income, income from capital and income from insurance. On income from capital, income from insurance and, in certain situations, on rental income, advance payments are made by the employer/persons paying out the income.

A taxpayer who is employed or performs jobs under contract with a non-resident entity in Croatia shall be liable to calculate tax on his salary and pay it within eight days from the date of salary payment. Calculation and payment of tax within eight days from the payment day may, instead, be carried out by a non-resident (employer) salary payer.

An annual tax return is due by the end of February for the previous tax year. The tax authorities will review the return and issue an assessment/resolution for any tax still due after advance payments and employer withholdings. Overpayments will be refunded.

## Tax rates

Currently applicable personal income tax rates (since 1 January 2003) are as follows:

| Income tax rates | Income tax bands / per month |
| --- | --- |
| 15% | up to HRK3,200 |
| 25% | HRK3,200–8,000 |
| 35% | HRK 8,000–22,400 |
| 45% | above HRK22,400 |

Personal income tax is further increased by surtax, ie city tax, which can vary from town to town, the highest rate being 18 per cent (in Zagreb).

Rates for advance tax payment on rental income, income from capital and income from insurance vary from 15 to 35 per cent.

The monthly personal allowance is set at HRK1,600. Additional allowances are available for dependent spouses and children, aid received from legal and natural persons for health purposes (ie operations, medical treatment, drugs and orthopaedic aids), expenses incurred for the purchase or building of a flat or house and investment maintenance on the existing flat or house up to HRK1,000, and gifts in cash and kind for cultural, educational, scientific, health, humanitarian, sport and religious purposes to special organizations up to two per cent per annum of the income earned in the previous year etc.

Reimbursement of expenses, *per diem* allowances, and certain other allowances are not subject to income tax, provided that they are properly documented and that the legal thresholds are observed.

There are certain additional benefits not subject to personal income tax that can be granted to employees, for example:

- gifts for the employees' children under the age of 15 (up to the non-taxable prescribed maximum of HRK400 per annum per child);

- bonuses, eg Christmas bonus (up to the non-taxable prescribed maximum of HRK2,000 per annum per employee);

- monthly commuting allowance equalling the public transportation costs in the employee's city of residence;

- special long service awards (ie for 10 years of service with the employer up to HRK1,500, or for 40 years of service up to HRK5,000);

- severance payments preceding retirement (up to HRK8,000);

- severance payments in case of termination of the employment contract, caused by business or personal reasons (up to four times the base personal allowance, currently HRK1,600 × 4 = HRK4,000, for each year of employment with that employer);

- severance payments in case of work-related injuries or professional illness (up to five times the base personal allowance for each year of service with that employer).

If the company has a supervisory board, the amounts that the supervisory board members receive are considered to be self-employment income for taxation purposes. Such income is taxed at a flat rate of 35 per cent and does not qualify for the personal allowances and benefits listed above.

Foreign taxes paid abroad on foreign-sourced income may be offset from the Croatian tax liability in the form of a tax credit. However, Croatian personal income tax law gives advantage to rules of the applicable treaties on avoidance of double taxation, which Croatia has signed, or honours those signed by the former Yugoslavia. Currently, Croatia applies treaties on avoidance of double taxation with 35 countries.

# Social security contributions

For employees working under Croatian terms and conditions, the employer is required to pay all applicable employer's social contributions, including health and pension contributions, and to remit employees' social contributions to the appropriate authorities, on a monthly basis. Social security contribution rates are shown in Table 5.4.1.

**Table 5.4.1** Social security contribution rates (applicable from 1 January 2003)

| Type of contribution | Employer (%) | Employee (%) |
|---|---|---|
| Pension insurance | – | 20 |
| Health insurance | 15 | – |
| Additional health insurance | 0.5 | – |
| Unemployment insurance | 1.7 | – |

For individuals aged below 40, pension insurance is paid on two levels: 15 per cent to the general savings fund and five per cent to the special fund chosen by the individual.

Entities paying compensation to self-employed individuals based on special 'service contracts' are obliged to withhold social contributions as follows:

- on compensation: pension insurance – Level I at 15 per cent and Level II at five per cent;

- on compensation: health insurance at 15 per cent.

Generally, the treaties on social contributions, which Croatia has signed with 30 countries, define the liabilities on social contributions of foreigners working in Croatia.

# 5.5

# Auditing and Accounting

*Marina Tonžetić, Deloitte & Touche*

## Legal framework

The Accounting Law and the Law on Auditing, published in the *Official Gazette* No 90, 1992, constitute the legal framework for audits and accounting issues applicable to companies. These laws have been in effect as of 1 January 2003, without any subsequent modifications.

Under the law, companies (entrepreneurs) with their registered seat in the Republic of Croatia are to maintain their accounting records and prepare their financial statements in accordance with the fundamental principles of bookkeeping (ie so as to enable insight into the transactions and assets of a company).

Parent companies and their domestic or foreign-related and/or associated companies prepare consolidated financial statements, presenting the group as a single entity.

The financial statements are prepared in accordance with International Accounting Standards (IAS), as published in the *Official Gazette*.

## Definition of an entrepreneur

For the purposes of the Accounting Law, an entrepreneur is a legal person carrying out an economic activity to generate profit. An entrepreneur may also be a natural person carrying out a business activity independently for the purpose of earning profit if such a person has been defined as a corporate income taxpayer under specific regulations.

The Law also applies to foreign organizational units of an entrepreneur, unless the foreign regulations impose the obligation to such a unit to maintain accounting records and prepare the financial statements. Finally, the Law is obligatory for organizational units of foreign entrepreneurs whose seat is registered abroad and who carry out a business activity in the Republic of Croatia (not applicable to representative offices).

# Classification of entrepreneurs

Under the Law, the entrepreneurs that have the obligation to maintain accounting records and prepare the financial statements are classified into three categories: small entrepreneurs, medium-sized entrepreneurs and large-sized entrepreneurs.

## *Small entrepreneurs*

Small entrepreneurs are those who do not exceed the limits set by two of the following three criteria:

- the balance sheet total after deduction of loss presented in assets is equivalent to DEM2 million (the Audit Law was enacted at the time when DEMs were used and has not amended since then);

- income for the 12 months prior to the balance sheet date is equivalent to DEM4 million;

- the annual average number of employees is 50.

## *Medium-sized entrepreneurs*

Medium-sized entrepreneurs are those who do not exceed two of the three criteria applicable to small entrepreneurs and never exceed two of the following three criteria:

- the balance sheet total after deduction of loss presented in assets is equivalent to DEM8 million;

- income for the twelve months prior to the balance sheet date is equivalent to DEM16 million;

- the annual average number of employees is 250.

## *Large entrepreneurs*

Large entrepreneurs are those who do not exceed two of the three criteria applicable to medium-sized entrepreneurs.

For the purposes of the Accounting Law, banks, financial institutions, insurance and reinsurance companies are classified as large entrepreneurs.

# Accounting records

Accounting records have to be kept in accordance with the double-entry bookkeeping principles, and consist of the following:

- journal – a business record serving to enter transactions in chronological order, classified into balance sheet and off balance sheet items;

- general ledger – represents a systematic accounting evidence of changes in assets, liabilities, capital, expenses, income and operating result; consists of balance sheet and off balance sheet entries;

- subsidiary ledgers – they are, as a rule, set up separately.

# Keeping and filing of accounting records

Accounting records are maintained for a business year, which is equal to the calendar year. The general ledger and the journal are to be filed for a minimum of 10 years, and the auxiliary ledgers for at least five years.

# Chart of accounts

Transactions are classified as per a pre-defined chart of accounts (which includes the account description/number), based on the prescribed structure of the balance sheet, the income statement and off balance sheet items.

Accounts in the chart of accounts are further itemized according to the specific needs of the entrepreneur, taking into account that balance sheet and income statement items as specified by the Law are included. The content of the chart of accounts for banks is defined by the first six digits of individual items as provided by law.

# Applicable accounting standards

IAS as published in the *Official Gazette* represent the accounting standards applicable in the Republic of Croatia. The Accounting Law (as well as IAS) additionally defines the fundamental accounting assumptions used in the preparation of the financial statements, which are as follows:

- going concern;
- consistence;
- accrual basis;

When preparing the financial statements, the following fundamental principles of measuring individual positions in the financial statements are to be observed:

- prudence;
- substance over form;
- materiality;
- individual measurement;
- time connection of balance sheet items.

# Statutory financial statements

The statutory financial statements comprise:

- balance sheet;
- income statement (profit and loss account);
- statement of changes in financial position;
- notes to the financial statements.

The statutory financial statements have to give a true, reliable and fair view of the assets, liabilities, capital, cash flows, profit or loss for the period, and should be signed by a legal representative of the enterprise concerned.

# Preparation and disclosure of financial statements

The statutory financial statements are prepared for a financial year. Accounting records and financial statements are kept, prepared in the Croatian language, using the Croatian national currency.

All large and medium-sized enterprises have the obligation to publish their financial statements if they are incorporated as joint stock companies. A report of an auditor is published together with the financial statements.

# Audit of the financial statements

Once a year, the financial statements of all large enterprises are subject to an audit, as well as those of medium-sized enterprises if they are set up as joint stock companies.

Small enterprises incorporated as joint stock companies are subject to a statutory review of operations every three years.

## Presentation of the financial statements and of the annual report to the shareholders

Large enterprises have the obligation to present the financial statements and the annual report to their owners within six months following the expiry of a business year.

Medium-sized enterprises and small enterprises have to present to their owners the financial statements and the annual report within four months from the expiry of a business year.

A group of entities preparing consolidated financial statements has to present the consolidated financial statements and the annual report to its owners within nine months from the expiry of a business year.

## Audit firms

An audit firm is a legal entity registered to carry out audits. An audit firm may, in addition to audits, perform other services from the area of accounting, tax consultancy, financial analysis and controls.

Audits may be performed by a foreign audit firm registered in the Republic of Croatia, or jointly by an audit firm registered in Croatia and a foreign audit firm.

An audit is carried out in accordance with the procedures established by International Standards on Auditing.

## Responsibilities of company management and of auditors

The objective and the fundamental principles governing an audit of the financial statements are to enable the auditor to express an opinion whether the financial statements, in all material respects, comply with IAS, in accordance with the Croatian Accounting Law.

The auditor is responsible for forming and expressing an opinion on the financial statements, and the management of the entity concerned is responsible for the preparation and disclosure of the financial statements. An audit of the financial statements does not reduce the responsibility of the management.

# Availability of information to the auditor

The auditor has a legal right to access the reports, accounts, evidence and other information as required for the purpose of audit and issuing the audit report.

If an enterprise limits the scope of investigation, or disables application of certain audit procedures, the certified auditor is to draw attention to these matters in the audit report according to the Audit Guidelines.

# Content of an audit report

An audit report contains the following:

- the report of the certified auditor; and

- the financial statements subject to audit and notes to the financial statements.

The auditor's report is signed by a certified auditor.

# Indemnification

An audit firm that has deliberately or negligently incurred damage as a result of the audit carried out is to indemnify the enterprise concerned. The indemnification per audit is limited to DEM50,000, to which extent an audit firm has the obligation to provide professional liability insurance coverage.

# Corporate management trends and resulting audit implications

Large-scale bankruptcies among companies are, lately, often brought in relation with the financial reporting issues and have resulted in legal actions, criminal charges and loss of reputation, affecting the management, auditors and employees involved in the company management.

These trends inspired the promulgation of new regulations on a global level, such as:

- Sarbanes – Oxley Act in the United States;

- Reform of the Companies Act and Higgs Review (UK);

- Winter Report (EU).

The new regulations propose a greater responsibility on the part of the management and staff involved in the corporate governance, including the responsibilities for the financial statements and control over the audit as defined by law, as well as higher penalties or more rigid sentences for non-compliance.

None of the regulations has a direct impact on the Republic of Croatia and enterprises registered and operating in Croatia; however:

- international guidelines will definitely have an impact on the expectations of foreign investors and, consequently, may affect the future legal framework in Croatia;

- the penal provisions, currently effective under Croatian law, may be more frequently used in the future;

- investors tend to associate more and more low corporate governance standards with high investment risk;

- the interest of the broader public in the corporate governance standards may be increased.

As a result, it is in the best interests of the managing bodies of an enterprise to ensure:

- appropriate emphasis by management on a reliable accounting and internal controls system;

- appropriate audit arrangements to achieve efficient audits;

- adequate focus on the decision-making process and the segregation of duties;

- implementation of various committees by the management or supervisory boards (such as Audit Committee, Performance Appraisal Committee, Environmental Commission, and similar).

# 5.6

# Employment Law and Work Permits for Foreigners

*Adrian Hammer, Deloitte & Touche*

## Introduction

The labour market in Croatia is regulated by the Labour Act. The Act defines the key employment issues, such as terms of employment, leave, dismissals, workers' unions, health and safety in the workplace, and so forth.

The Act prescribes the mandatory content of an employment agreement. Such agreements should always contain sections on the parties, place of employment, the position with a short description, date of commencement of employment, duration of employment if the employment is for a fixed term, annual leave, termination notice periods, salary and the length of the working day or week. All of these terms should be within the limits prescribed by the Act.

The working week is a 40-hour one. If circumstances beyond the employer's control arise, the employer may require the employees to work overtime for up to 10 extra hours in one week.

## Mandatory leave

The Act defines the shortest period of leave for Croatian employees in the following way: generally, a holiday of 18 working days is mandatory. Minors (under the age of 18) are entitled to a minimum of 24 working days, and employees working under hazardous conditions are entitled to a minimum of 30 working days.

Please note that it is possible, for determining the employee's annual leave, to determine the working week as a six-day week. If the working week is not defined in the employment contract, it is treated as a six-day week by default.

Persons who enter an employment contract for the first time (eg as a trainee) and persons who take a break between two jobs that is longer than eight days, have a right to a holiday after six months of uninterrupted work. The schedule and calculation of duration of the holidays is determined by the employer's regulations. An employer who has 20 or more employees is obliged to consult the employees' council regarding the holiday plan. An employee has a right to use his or her leave in two parts, but in such a case, the first part of the leave must consist of at least 12 days and the second part of the leave must be used by 30 June of the following year.

## Maternity leave

The Labour Act defines two types of maternal leave: obligatory and additional. Obligatory maternal leave starts 28 days before the birth is expected and continues for six months after the birth. However, women are allowed to start using their leave 45 days before the birth is expected, and continue the leave until one year after the birth. Women can return to work before the end of the six-month period after the birth, but not earlier than 42 days after the birth.

## Dismissals

There are two main types of termination of an employment agreement in Croatia: ordinary and extraordinary termination. Ordinary termination happens in the following cases:

- if a position is no longer required due to economic, technical or organizational reasons (dismissal caused by business reasons);

- if the employee is not capable of fulfilling his or her work obligations because of his or her personal situation (dismissal caused by personal reasons); or

- if the employee breaks his contractual employment obligations (dismissal caused by the employee's behaviour).

In the cases of dismissal due to business or personal reasons, the employer is only entitled to dismiss in the case of the employer not being able to find a suitable replacement position and training the employee for that position. When making the decision on dismissal due to personal or business reasons, the employer must take into account the duration of the employment, age, family commitments of the employee, and so on.

Dismissal notice periods are determined on the basis of duration of employment with the employer. The notice periods are:

- two weeks if the employee has been employed for less than one year;

- one month if the employee has been employed for one year;

- one month and two weeks if the employee has been employed for two years;

- two months if the employee has been employed for five years;

- two months and two weeks if the employee has been employed for 10 years; and

- three months if the employee has been employed for 20 years or more.

The employee is entitled to give up to one month's notice.

Employers that plan to dismiss 20 or more employees within a 90-day period due to business reasons are required to create an outplacement programme.

## Severance payments

Employees are entitled to redundancy payments after two years, unless the dismissal is due to employee behaviour. The redundancy payment is calculated according to the length of employment with the employer, and should be no less than one third of the average monthly salary of that employee for each year of employment with the employer. The average salary, for the purpose of redundancy payments, is calculated as the average salary over the last three months before dismissal.

The redundancy payment can be no more than six average monthly salaries, unless otherwise stipulated by the contractual employment terms.

## Work permits for foreigners working in Croatia

The procedures necessary for investors and expatriates to enter Croatia and perform certain business activities are covered by the Foreign Persons Act. In order to work and reside in Croatia, foreign citizens need an appropriate permit.

Two types of permits are of particular concern to foreign investors and expatriates: the business permit and the work permit.

### Work permit

In order to have a foreign employee issued with a work permit, the foreign person's employer needs to submit an application for an issue of a work permit on behalf of the said person. The application is submitted to the police authority in the district where the employer is situated.

The following supporting documentation should be submitted with the application:

- general information on the employee;

- information on the position of employment;

- an excerpt from the Commercial Court Registry showing the employer is registered as a company in Croatia, or similar proof of registration of the employer;

- proof that the employer is solvent and that it has no outstanding liabilities towards the Tax Authority;

- a letter giving reasons for employing a foreign person.

If a previous work permit is being extended, the applicant is also required to submit copies of the previous work permit and the employee's work book. The extension of the work permit should be applied for no later than 45 days before the expiry of the current permit.

The employer must enter an employment agreement (in written form) with the foreign person no later than 15 days after the work permit is issued. A work permit is issued for the duration of the employment agreement, but for a period not longer than two years.

## Temporary residence

A person who applies for a work permit, or intends to stay in Croatia for more than 90 days needs to apply for temporary residence.

The first temporary residence application is to be submitted to the appropriate Croatian embassy or consulate, or, if the applicant does not need a visa to enter Croatia, at the police authority in Croatia.

An extension of the existing temporary residence permit should be applied for no later than 30 days before the expiry of the current permit. The application form should be accompanied by:

- two photos of the applicant (3 × 3.5 cm);

- a copy of the current and valid passport;

- a birth certificate;

- proof of means of support during the stay in Croatia;

- proof of having adequate health insurance;

- reason for residence in Croatia (a work permit is treated as an appropriate reason); and

- proof of no criminal record in the domicile country, not older than six months (first time applicants only).

## Business permit

A business permit is a permit that allows both residence and work in Croatia. It is issued to foreigners who have their own business, a majority share in a company, or who provide services on behalf of a foreign employer, in Croatia. The applicant should also fulfil the criteria for temporary residence.

An application for a business permit is submitted to the police authority at the place of residence. It should be accompanied with all the documents needed for a temporary residence permit, and proof of registration of the business or company he or she owns, or a consulting or service agreement with the company he or she is employed with.

An application for an extension of a business permit should be submitted at least 30 days before the expiry of the current permit.

## Registration of address in Croatia

Each foreign person has to register the address of his/her residence in Croatia within 24 hours of arriving in Croatia. If a foreign national stays at a hotel, the hotel will do the registration and the person should register (at the Ministry of Internal Affairs) his/her private residential address once the address is known.

The registration procedure requires the following documentation:

- registration form;

- passport (including visa);

- ID card of the landlord (owner of the rented flat/house) or the person authorized to represent the landlord;

- evidence of the landlord's ownership of the flat (purchase agreement or excerpt from the land registry); and

- rental agreement.

## Croatian ID number for foreign nationals

A Croatian ID number for foreign nationals (MBS) is allocated to each foreign national in possession of either a business or a work permit. In order to obtain a certificate with the ID number, an application should be submitted to the Ministry of Internal Affairs at the place of residence.

Documentation required for this procedure is the following:

- application form (obtained at the Ministry of Internal Affairs);

- passport;

- copy of the passport – ID side and extended residence permit;

- two passport size photographs – needed only in case where a foreign national wishes to obtain a Croatian ID card (not mandatory); and

- a letter requesting issuance of the ID number and of the ID card (if applicable) and stating the purpose of issuance.

The minimum fee is HRK40, and is higher if an ID card is requested.

## *Procedures after receiving a permit*

If a foreign national is working at a Croatian entity that he or she is employed with, that person should also obtain a 'workbook'. The workbook is endorsed by the City Economic Department and the following documentation needs to be submitted:

- application form;

- the company's request to employ the foreign national, with justifications;

- workbook (prepared by the employer);

- copy of foreign national ID card;

- copy of the work permit; and

- copy of the passport (containing extended residency permit).

Upon completing this procedure, the employee is in a position to sign a formal employment contract with his employer.

Finally, the foreign national must apply for a 'tax card'. Documents necessary to be submitted to the Tax Authority are the request for the tax card and the foreign national's ID (MBS) number.

The entire process of acquiring all the necessary work-related visas and permits generally takes around three months. In order to facilitate the procedure and further boost the foreign investment opportunities, government institutions are currently preparing a new set of regulations, which should simplify and shorten the procedure.

## 5.7

# Legal Regulations on Land/Real Estate Ownership in Croatia

*Marinko Mileta, Marković & Plišo Law Firm*

## General

Real estate in the Republic of Croatia may be owned by domestic physical and legal persons and foreign physical and legal persons under the condition of reciprocity regulated by international agreements between the Republic of Croatia and the domicile country of the foreign physical or natural person acquiring such real estate in Croatia (with certain exceptions).

For example, the foreign legal and physical persons may not acquire the title over the agricultural and forest land located in the regions of national parks and other zones pronounced to be of interest to the Republic of Croatia. Certain real estate, such as those located within the maritime well, whose borders were determined by the Maritime Code, cannot be subject to the legal transactions for any legal or physical person. The borders of the maritime well situated within the specific regions are determined by the Decisions on Establishment of Maritime Well. The foreign physical or legal person must obtain from the Ministry of Interior an approval of its acquisition of the real estate in the Republic of Croatia, after having previously obtained the opinion of the Ministry of Justice and Administration.

In the Republic of Croatia, real estate can be acquired on the principles of legal transactions (contracts), decisions passed by the court or Croatian administrative bodies and, in exceptional cases, based on maturity.

The domestic legal persons (companies) owned by foreign physical and/or legal persons may acquire real estate in Croatia without any special consents or approvals.

The essential regulation referring to the ownership over real estate in Croatia is the Property Law, which has been in force since 1 January

1997. Enactment of that Law allowed for the transformation of the previous regime of public ownership into one of private ownership of real estate.

Real estate owned by the Republic of Croatia (ie by cities, counties and municipalities, as well as the Croatian Privatization Fund that holds in its portfolio certain real estate, which had previously belonged in public ownership and which had not been thereafter transformed in the process of transformation of public ownership) can be sold only by means of a public tender, if being the subject of legal transactions.

# Construction

Real estate in Croatia, which is based on a physical plan representing the building land for a specific purpose, may be subject to the construction of buildings, the purpose of which is foreseen by such physical plans, on the basis of the documents on physical planning and permits issued by the authorized administrative bodies; those documents are the following: a) location permit (confirming the intended construction complies with the physical plan and town planning regulations) and b) building permit as the basis for construction. After the completion of construction of a building, it is necessary to obtain the certificate of inspection asserting that the building was built in compliance with the building permit as well as with technical and construction aspects.

A special building regime and building controls were established in the region of the Protected Coast Belt, covering the territory from sea line to 1 km of inland area, according to the Law on Physical Planning and Decree on the protection of the coastal belt. Currently all physical plans in that area are being adjusted according to those new regulations. The target of these regulations is to restrain further devastation of the Adriatic Sea.

# Taxes

Real estate transactions in the Republic of Croatia are subject to payment of a basic five per cent real estate tax on the assessed value of the real estate (market value), which is determined by the competent Tax Administration Office. Physical persons are encumbered by an additional tax on profit from property and property rights, in other words the tax payable on the difference between the purchase and sale value of the real estate if such real estate is sold in the period of three years from the day of its acquisition. The payment of real estate tax is a legal obligation of the purchaser, who is liable to report the contract to the Tax Administration within 30 days of the day of conclusion of the contract, and pay the tax under the resolution of the Tax Administration within the final 45-day term from the day of receipt of the resolution.

Physical and legal persons engaged in the construction of marketable buildings (apartments, business premises, suits etc) are obliged to charge the purchaser with 22 per cent VAT on the price of the building (value of the building and profit), whereas the purchaser pays five per cent real estate tax on the basic amount, which includes the value of the land the building is constructed on and the payment of the charges collected on behalf of the building permit (communal contribution).

## Lien

Real estate in Croatia may serve as a lien for security of the payment of certain pecuniary obligations towards the creditors. Such lien is established by the Agreement on establishment of a lien (mortgage) over the real estate or Agreement on transfer of real property right for purpose of security (fiduciary transfer). To have the capacity of an execution document (the one based on which it is possible to directly perform execution over the real estate being the subject of the lien, for purpose of payment of the claim secured by that real estate), such agreements must be executed in the form of a notarial deed and they also have to be solemnized by the notary public and contain explicit execution clauses.

The execution over the pledged real estate is performed by the sale of the same real estate by public auction and payment of the creditors from the amount acquired through the sale of the same real estate.

The lien must be entered in the land registry. The holder of the pledge right can be both the domestic and foreign physical and legal person.

## Essential regulations referring to the pledge rights are Property Law, Execution Act and Land Registry Act

### Land Registry and Cadastre

The main problems in Croatia are the unsettled property relations referring to real estate, as well as the land registry status of real estate, which is not adjusted with the actual status of ownership and possession of real estate. Additional problems are the inefficacy in the system of the land registry files and the general inefficacy of the judicial system (long-term settlement of land registry cases and court proceedings in property disputes), despite the fact that the general regulations are mostly adjusted along the lines of Western European legislature. The worst situations are found in the courts in major Croatian cities, such as Zagreb and Split.

The situation has somewhat improved recently, after the initiative of the Ministry of Justice and after the attempt to reform the land registry and the courts.

The base records regarding the ownership over real estate and rights over the same are found in the land registry, which is kept by the Land Registry Departments of Municipal Courts for real estate situated in their regions. The main regulations are the Land Registry Law and the Land Registry Bylaw.

In the land registry, the buildings can be divided into their separate parts (apartments, business premises etc).

According to the Law, the real estate consists of the land and everything built on that land, and it is not possible to dispose legally with one of those parts separately, save in exceptional cases, ie when the building right is established on the land. In that case, the construction right and the building built on the land the construction right was founded on, or the building's separate parts, can individually participate in the legal transactions.

The land registry consists of the land registry records referring to individual land registry municipalities (of which more than one can be in the region of jurisdiction of a certain court). This land registry record consists of three sheets: the Census Sheet A, the Title Sheet B and the Encumbrance Sheet C.

The Census Sheet contains all essential data about the real estate – its nature (plow, meadow, house with yard, housing building and yard, business building and similar), land plot, area, entries on existence of the building permit and certificate of inspection etc.

The Title Sheet includes the data about the ownership over the real estate and/or its separate parts (apartments, business premises etc), including the transfers of ownership for security purposes.

The Encumbrance Sheet includes all the burdens entered into with respect to certain real estate – mortgages, servitudes and similar.

It is possible to register in the land registry (the titles, pledge rights and other rights over real estate), entries (real estate disputes, existence of certain relations relative to the real estate, execution proceedings, bankruptcy of the owner, appeals, injunctions banning the alienation or encumbrance of the real estate issued by the court etc) and subscriptions (of ownership, pledges).

The Excerpt from the Land Registry includes all three sheets and represents the only evidence of title over the real estate, and the title is acquired on the bases of legal transaction only upon its registration in the land books. The status in the land registry is considered to be the actual status of real estate title, and anyone who asserts differently is obliged to evidence such an assertion.

It is obligatory to make evident in the land registry, immediately upon the receipt of any proposal, the existence of such proposal by subscription of the so-called 'Seals' in the land registry record (records) of the particular real estate. The Seal contains the number of the case, a short description of the proposing party and the type of proposal.

Modifications of status in the land registry are performed on the principles of the proposals and valid documents; so, the resolution that is based on such proposal is passed by the land registry department judge or by an authorized administrator. There is the possibility of filing an appeal against the resolution within 15 days of the day of the receipt of the resolution. The appeal will then be subscribed in the land books and, until the settlement of that appeal, any further actions referring to the subject land registry record are prevented. The appeal will be resolved by the land registry judge and if the judge determines the appeal is grounded, the judge accepts the appeal and returns the case for the repeated proceeding to the authorized administrators. In the opposite scenario, if the judge pronounces the appeal to be ungrounded, the judge sends the same to the second instance court for its decision.

The land registry is still mostly kept manually but most of the courts have currently been subject to the computerization of the land registry.

Cadastre means the records on possession over the real estate and, in principle; it represents an actual situation of possession in practice. Cadastre also keeps records on cadastre plans of lands and buildings, including the ducts (power, water, gas, telephone etc). The intention is to adjust, as soon as possible, the cadastre and land registry data, which presently differ significantly.

The forming of building plots, plotting and re-plotting of the land is performed on the principle of location permits and geodesic elaborates verified by the Cadastre Institute and the competent administrative organ.

Registrations of constructed buildings are performed on the bases of application sheets certified by the Cadastre Institute, along with the attached construction permit and certificate of inspection. Exceptionally, the building can be registered without permits, but with subscription in the Land Registry that such permits do not exist, about which the construction inspection is to be reported.

Division of the building into its separate parts and thereto related co-owned proportions and accessories (parking lots, storerooms etc) is performed on the basis of condominium elaborates. Condominium elaborates must be verified by the competent administrative organs after the inspection of the commission and conclusion of the division agreement or signing of the owner's statement about such division, which should be made in compliance with the condominium elaborate. The building divided in such manner enables each of its separate parts, with the pertaining co-owned proportion, to independently appear in legal transactions.

## Conclusion

As a consequence of disparity between the land registry and actual situation regarding the possession and title over real estate, it is necessary when acquiring real estate in Croatia to be especially attentive and to engage expert legal and other assistance, and not to rely only upon the status provided in the land registry.

# 5.8

# Arbitration and Dispute Resolution

*Ante Glamuzina and Kristijan Galić,*
*Marković & Plišo Law Firm*

## General

Disputes in Croatia may be settled either before the Croatian courts or before a tribunal, where arbitration may be institutional or informal (ad hoc). Disputes in Croatia may also be resolved by an institution of conciliation in front of the special conciliation organizations (legal persons or their bodies having organized the conciliation proceeding). The provisions dealing with these matters are set out in Croatian legislation and in the applicable international conventions that Croatia is a party to. Needless to say, there are no obstacles for any clause that agrees on the jurisdiction of an Arbitral Tribunal seated outside of the Croatian territory.

The most notable domestic sources of law in this respect are the provisions of the Law on Civil Litigation (*Official Gazette,* nos. 53/91, 91/91, 112/99 and 117/0), the Law on Arbitration (*Official Gazette* no. 88/01), the Law on Conciliation *Official Gazette* no. 163/03), as well as the Ruler on Arbitration of the Permanent Arbitration Court attached to the Croatian Chamber of Commerce ('The Zagreb Rules') (*Official Gazette* no. 150/02) and the Rules of Conciliation (*Official Gazette* nos 81/02 and 65/04). Thus, following the provision of Article 34 of the Zagreb Rules, the Management Committee of the Croatian Chamber of Commerce is authorized to enact the bylaws related to the reimbursement of arbitration costs.

According to the Constitutional Resolution on Sovereignty and Independence that was enacted on 25 June 1991, all international conventions that were in force in former Yugoslavia also apply in Croatia, provided that they do not contravene the Constitution or the general provisions of its legal system. Consequently, almost all important multilateral treaties on arbitration that former Yugoslavia was a party to, were taken over or adopted by the Republic of Croatia. The most important of these are:

- the 1958 New York Convention on the Recognition and Enforcement of Foreign Arbitral Awards;

- the 1923 Geneva Protocol on Arbitration Clauses;

- the 1927 Geneva Convention on the Execution of Foreign Arbitral Awards;

- the 1961 (Geneva) European Convention on International Commercial Arbitration;

- the 1965 Washington Convention on Settlement of Investment Disputes between States and Nationals of Other States.

An awaited novelty in the Croatian legal system with respect to this is the adoption of the Conciliation Law (NN 163/03). This Law, in line with the Conciliation Rules (NN 81/02) being applicable since 2002, has been regulating by means of the law, an alternative manner of dispute settlement – that of conciliation. Pursuant to this law, conciliation is possible in cases of civil disputes, including the disputes arising from the trade, labour and other property-law relations with respect to the issues the parties may freely dispose in (requests that do not oppose the Constitution of the Republic of Croatia, mandatory regulations and public edicts), provided that in the case of such disputes, it has not been otherwise foreseen by a special regulation.

Pursuant to the legal provision, the conciliation is performed by a conciliation organization – the legal persons or legal person's bodies organizing the conciliation procedures. The conciliation proceedings may end either through settlement, thereby finally resolving the case (unless certain claims remained resolved by the conciliation), or by a Decree on adjournment of the proceedings if it is established that the conciliation proceedings may not be successfully pursued further. It is interesting that the law itself does not define the conciliation organizations. Therefore, in the current situation, the provisions of the Conciliation Law necessarily rely on the provisions of the Conciliation Rules (NN 81/02), ie the Rules on Modifications and Amendments of the Conciliation Rules (NN 65/04). Namely, these Rules institutionalized the body in charge of the conciliation procedure – the Conciliation Centre at the Croatian Chamber of Commerce, with its seat in Zagreb. The Rules also foresee the possibility of founding regional centres of conciliation in Split, Osijek, Rijeka and Varaždin, as the centres of other county chambers of the Croatian Chamber of Commerce.

# Enforcement

The Croatian Law on Arbitration expressly provides Article 40, Paragraphs 1 and 2, that any foreign arbitral award shall be recognized and executed in the Republic of Croatia, unless the court finds upon the other part's objection that certain criteria have not been met. These are cases where a) certain obstacles defined in provisions of Paragraph 2 of Article 36 exist, or b) where the award did not become legally binding, or c) where the court of jurisdiction where it was rendered has annulled or postponed the legal effects.

According to the provision of Paragraph 2 of Article 36, the application for recognition and/or execution of a foreign award shall be dismissed if the court establishes: a) that the matter in dispute may not be subject to arbitration pursuant to the laws of the Republic of Croatia, or b) that the recognition of enforcement of the award would be contrary to the public order (*ordre public*) of the Republic of Croatia.

Since according to the Law on Arbitration, an arbitral award originates in the state on whose territory it was rendered, foreign arbitral awards are executed in the same manner as domestic awards. In other words, that is by adhering to the procedural provisions of the Law on Arbitration and attaching the original or a certified translation of the award, the agreement, containing the arbitration clause and the eventual translation thereof. However, foreign awards have to be first recognized in separate court proceedings, where the court shall explicitly examine whether any of the aforementioned negative presumptions exists. Interestingly, the Law explicitly allows the parties bound by the arbitral award to request the court to rule that there are no grounds for challenging the award, thereby effectively preventing the other party from doing so (provided, however, that the pertinent applicant possesses adequate legal grounds for such a motion).

Thus, the Law explicitly allows the court to informally re-examine the merits of the case and to request clarification from the arbitral tribunal itself or the parties involved in the proceedings. It is also entitled, at its own discretion, to postpone the proceedings at either the stage of recognition or enforcement, should separate annulment proceedings or an application for stoppage of recognition be initiated or filed.

When the matter comes to the stage where the recognition or even execution measures are to be made by the court, the Law imposes an obligation on the court to grant the parties an opportunity to respond with their own views on the merits of the case, thereby somehow starting the process again. This is due to the fact that the arbitral award differs slightly in its legal nature from the court judgement, and has a duty to apply special enforcement rules contained in the Law on

Arbitration – namely, pertinent Decrees on recognition and execution of the arbitral award have to contain a legal argumentation.

As regards jurisdiction, to resolve on the jurisdiction of the arbitral tribunal itself, the deposition of the award, a complaint on annulment of the arbitral award and a request to recognize and/or execute the award, the Commercial Court in Zagreb is entitled to deal with these issues where they fall within its competence, and the District Court in Zagreb deals with all other issues. A court whose competence relates to the subject matter is defined by special Laws (Law on Courts, *Official Gazette* nos 3/94, 100/96, 131/97 and 129/00 and Law on Civil Litigation, *Official Gazette* nos 53/91, 91/91, 112/99 and 117/03) and shall have the jurisdiction to pursue the execution proceedings, as well as to resolve any interim measure. Consequently, in certain cases, provisions of the Law on Arbitration shall derogate and overlap the application of the provisions of the Law on Execution during the enforcement of an arbitral award (*Official Gazette* nos 57/96, 29/99, 173/03, 194/03 and 151/04).

# 5.9

# Intellectual Property

*Nikolina Staničić and Josip Grošeta,*
*Marković & Plišo Law Firm*

## General

According to Croatian legislation, intellectual property is divided into
'industrial property', covering the patents, trade marks, industrial
design, appellation of origin of products and services and integrated
circuit layouts, and 'copyright and other congenial rights'.

This field experienced significant reform in Croatia at the end of
2003, when the following new laws were adopted: Law on Copyright
and other Congenial Rights, Patent Law, Law on Protection of
Topography of Semi-Conducting Products, Law on Industrial Design,
Trade Mark Law, Law on Geographical Indications of Origin and
Appellation of Origin of Products and Services. The reasons for the
adoption of the new laws primarily lie in the necessity of adjusting
Croatian legislation to the guidelines brought by the EU authorities
and to the provisions of international conventions to which the
Republic of Croatia belongs.

As the main state institution in the field of intellectual property, the
Croatian State Intellectual Property Office (CISPO) was originally
founded on 31 December 1991 under the name of the Republic Office
for Industrial Property. The State Patent Office then assumed
authority for copyright protection and changed its name to CSIPO.
CSIPO is in charge of all administrative and expert matters in relation
to protection of copyright and industrial property. It also carries out all
activities concerning collecting, administrating and publishing
relevant data. On the international level, it cooperates with the World
Intellectual Property Organization (WIPO) and related offices in other
countries, and participates in the preparation and conclusion of multilateral and bilateral treaties and agreements.

Here we provide the basic provisions of the law that determine
single fields of intellectual property.

# Copyright

The Law on Copyright and Other Congenial Rights (NN 167/03) was passed on 1 October 2003, and from its coming into force the Copyright Law (NN 53791, 58/93, 9/99, 76/99, 127/99 and 67/01 and the Publishing Law ceased to be valid (NN 28/83). The stated law determines:

- copyright – authors' right over their works from literary, scientific and artistic fields; congenial rights – rights of artists and performers over their performances, rights of phonogram producers over their phonograms, rights of film producers (and video producers) over their videos, rights of organizations for radio transmission over their broadcasting, rights of publishers over their editions, rights of producers of databases over their databases;

- realization (individual and collective) of copyright and congenial rights;

- protection of copyrights and congenial rights in case of their infringement; and

- the field of application of the Law.

The Law is drafted in line with the guidelines set forth by the Copyright Law of the WIPO, and its provisions protect foreign physical and legal persons in the framework of liabilities that the Republic of Croatia took over on the principles of international agreements or on the basis of effective reciprocity.

# Patents

Patent Law (NN173/03) was adopted on 15 October 2003 and it has been applied since 1 December 2004. As of the date of its application, the provisions of the Patent Law (NN 78/99 and 32/02) ceased to apply, except for the provision of article 95, the section referring to the representation that will apply until the adoption of a special law.

The Patent Law established the system of protection of inventions by means of patent and consensual patent. The foreign legal and physical person enjoys the protection foreseen by this law, if such protection ensues from the international agreements obliging the Republic of Croatia or if it ensues from the application of the principles of reciprocity.

The process of acknowledgement of a patent is performed by the State Intellectual Property Institute. The duration of protection of a patent, based on the complete examination, is 20 years as from the day of submission of the application of the patent. Such patent protection in the case of a consensual patent lasts for 10 years. The Patent Law also determines the European patent application and European patent, the provisions of which shall apply from the coming into force of the Agreement between the Croatian government and the European Patent Organization regarding their cooperation in the field of patent.

## Trade marks

The Trade Mark Law (NN 173/03) adopted on 15 October 2003 applies as of 1 January 2004. From the day of its application, the provisions of the Trade Mark Law (NN 78/99 I 127/9) ceased to be valid, except for the provision of article 59 in the part referring to the representation, which shall apply until the adoption of a special law.

The Trade Mark Law applies to the individual, joint and warranty trade marks being the subject of registration or application for registration of the trade mark submitted to the CSIPO. The Law defines as an object of trade mark protection a mark that can be shown graphically, in particular words, including personal names, drawings, letters, numbers, product shapes or their packaging, three-dimensional shapes and colours, as well as the combination of all the aforementioned marks, provided that they are suitable for distinguishing the goods and services of one merchant from those originating from another merchant.

The holder of registered trade mark, or the submitter of an application for registration of the trade mark, can be a physical or legal person. A foreign physical or legal person has the rights pursuant to the provisions of the law, if that ensues from the obligations of an international agreement with Croatia, or if it ensues from the application of the principles of reciprocity. The protection period of the registered trade mark lasts for 10 years, starting from the date of the submission of the application to register. The international registration of trade marks, the protection of which has expanded to the Republic of Croatia (based on the Madrid Agreement Concerning the International Registration of Marks and the Protocol referring the Madrid Agreement), is subject to the provision of the Trade Mark Law and Trade Mark Rules with respect to other questions that have not been regulated by the aforementioned Madrid agreement.

## Industrial designs

The Industrial Design Law (NN 173/03) passed on 15 October 2003 applies from 1 January 2004. As of the day of its application, the provisions of the Industrial Design Law (NN 78/99 and 127/99) ceased to be valid, except from the provision of Article 59 in the part referring to representation, which shall apply until the adoption of a special law.

This Law prescribes the conditions necessary for the protection of design. It established the right of protection, acquisition of industrial design, exclusive rights resulting from industrial design, procedure of industrial design registration, modifications of industrial design, cessation of validity and annulment of industrial design, international filing of industrial design, legal civil protection and breaching provisions.

Protection of industrial design lasts for five years starting from the date of submission of the industrial design application. The protection of industrial design may be extended each time for an additional five-year period, to a maximum of 25 years starting from the day of submission of the application.

The international filing of industrial design is performed in line with the provisions of the Hague Agreement on International Filing of Industrial Design adopted on 6 November 1925, revised in the Hague on 28 November 1960, amended in Stockholm on 14 July 1967 and modified further on 28 September 1979 in the text of the Hague Agreement.

International filing may be directly performed by the WIPO's International Office.

# Appellations of origin

The Law on Appellations of Origin and Geographical Indications of Goods and Services (NN 173/03 and 186/03) was adopted on 15 October 2003 and has applied since 1 January 2004. As from the day of its application, the provisions of the Law on Geographical Indications of Goods and Services (NN 78/99) ceased to be valid, except for the provision of Article 14 in the part referring to representation, which will apply until the adoption of a special law.

This Law determines the manner of acquisition, system of protection and realization of rights to use the geographical indication and appellation of origin of products and services.

The geographical indication refers to the name of the region, certain place or, on certain occasions, the indication of the country that is used for marking of the product or service that originates from that region, place or country and which possess a special quality, reputation or other feature that is ascribed to that geographical origin and whose production and/or processing takes place in a certain geographical region. The appellation of origin is the name of the region, certain place or, in special cases, country used for marking of the product or service originating from that area, certain place or certain country, whose quality and whose features significantly or specifically occurred under influence of the special nature of human-related factors that belong to certain geographical region, and its production, processing and preparation takes place completely in that geographical region.

The rights and obligation prescribed by this Law refer to domestic legal and physical persons as well as foreign physical and legal persons, under the following prescribed limitations for foreign persons.

The foreign persons may request the protection of its geographical indication of appellation of origin and the subscription of authorized users if such rights have been acknowledged to them in the country of origin and if they fulfil the conditions of this Law.

Relating to this Law, the expression 'state of origin' covers the regional system in which the registration of the geographical indication and appellation of origin was made for the products originating from the territory of one or more member states.

The rights from Section 2 of this Article may be used by a foreign person when they have ensued from bilateral or international agreements on reciprocal protection of geographical indications of origin concluded or ratified by the Republic of Croatia.

The right to use the indication of geographical origin lasts for 10 years as from the day of subscription of authorized user in the registry of authorized users of geographical origin indication or in the registry of authorized users of appellation of origin.

## Integrated circuit layouts

The Law on Protection of Topography of Semi-Conducting Products (NN 173/03) adopted on 15 October 2003 has applied since 1 January 2004. As from the day of application of this Law, the provisions of the Law on Protection of Integrated Circuit Layouts (NN 78/99 and 127/99) ceased to be valid.

This Law regulates the protection of topography of semi-conducting products. A semi-conducting product indicates the final or transitional form of any product:

a) containing the material that includes a layer of semi-conducting material; and

b) having one or more other layers made from a conducting, isolation or semi-conducting material positioned in line with the three-dimensional sample determined in advance; and

c) intended for the performance of an electronic function, exclusively or jointly with other functions.

The topography of semi-conducting products (hereinafter: topography) indicates a sequence of certain pictures, which has a fixed form or is coded in any manner whatsoever, and:

a) which represents a three-dimensional sample of the layers the semi-conducting product is made of, and

b) in whose sequence every picture shows a sample or a part of the sample of the semi-conducting product's surface at any stage of its manufacturing process.

The commercial utilization of the topography designates the sale, renting, lease or any other manner of commercial distribution of the topography, including the offering with the same purpose. The first commercial utilization of topography does not include its utilization under conditions of confidentiality, provided that its further distribution will not be towards third persons (persons not being parties to the agreement).

The foreign legal and physical persons without their registered seat, domicile or regular residence being in the territory of the Republic of Croatia enjoy the protection covered by this Law, if such protection ensues from the obligations of international agreements on the Republic of Croatia or if such protection ensues from the application of the principle of reciprocity.

The provisions of the Law on Patent (which refer to the representation, holders of the joint right, procedure for nullity announcement, terms for filing of the claim due to breach of right, transfer of rights, licence agreements) apply in an adequate manner to the topography of semi-conducting products that are subject this Law.

# 5.10

# The Regulation of Investment Funds

*Josip Grošeta, Marković & Plišo Law Firm*

## Legislative system

The Investment Funds Laws (NN 107/95, 12/96 114/01) regulate the incorporation of the investment funds and investment funds management companies.

The first Croatian investment fund management company obtained approval for business operations in 1997, and according to the data received from the Croatian Chamber of Commerce (October 2004), there were 17 companies in the Republic of Croatia registered for investment fund management. Those 17 companies are managing 41 closed-end and four open-end funds.

The Croatian Securities and Exchange Commission issued its approval for business operations to the investment funds and it supervises the funds' transactions. Within the framework of the Croatian Chamber of Commerce an Association for Management of Investment Funds was founded to promote and protect the mutual interests of the stated companies in the Republic of Croatia.

## Definition and types

An investment fund can be incorporated in the form of an open-end or closed-end fund.

An open-end fund is a separate property, having no legal personality, incorporated by a company for the management of funds upon the Securities and Exchange Commission's (hereinafter: the Commission) approval. Its scope of business is strictly the collection of pecuniary devices through issuance and public sale of the documents related to the share in a certain fund, the devices of which are invested in compliance with the appropriate application of the principles of security, profitability, liquidity and division of risk and whose owners are entitled, besides their right to a proportional part of fund's profit, to require at any time whatsoever to receive the payment of the documents related to the share, including its return, and thus also to step out of the fund.

A closed-end fund is a joint stock company, incorporated upon the approval of the Commission by the company for the management of funds, whose scope of business is strictly collection of pecuniary devices and property items, through the sale of its unlimitedly transferable shares and investment of such devices. The minimal nominal amount of the share capital of a closed-end fund amounts HRK4 million.

Depending on the investment structure, the funds can be divided into:

- pecuniary funds;

- share related funds;

- bond related funds;

- mixed funds.

## Fund management company

The fund management company (hereinafter the Company) is a company in the sense of Company Law, incorporated in the legal form of a joint stock company or a limited liability company, with scope of business being strictly the incorporation of investment funds and the management of same (ie the investment of pecuniary devices in its own name in favour of the joint account of the shareholders opened for management of the same devices in conformity with the principles of security, profitability, liquidity and division of risk). In practice, all such companies in Croatia are incorporated in the form of a limited liability company.

The Company is allowed to start its business only after it has received the Commission's approval. The Commission issues its approval to the management, if the Company enclosed with its request for issuance of the approval for operating the business, the documents proving the fulfilment of the following conditions:

1. that the share capital at the moment of submission of the request for issuance of the approval amounted to at least HRK1 million;

2. that the Company employs at least two members of the Board (directors) who possess expert knowledge needed for the management of the company, as well as the experience in management of companies of the same size and the same kind of business;

3. that the provisions of the Company's Articles of Association (ie Memorandum of Association) referring to the scope of business contain only the activity of incorporation and management of investment funds.

4. that the authorized auditor has been appointed.

The Commission shall decide on the request within 60 days of the date of its filing. If the Commission fails to bring its decision on the request for the approval of the business within this period, the same will be considered as approved.

If the stated conditions no longer exist, the Commission is allowed to deprive the Company of its approval to perform the business. If the Company within one year of the issuance of the approval for business operation in the management of funds, fails to incorporate a fund, it shall no longer be entitled to run its business.

The Company acts in legal transactions in its own name and for the joint account of the owners of the share documents in an open-ended fund, as well as in the name and for the joint account of the closed-ended fund. Thereby, the Company is not allowed, either directly or indirectly, to acquire the documents of share in the fund it manages, whereas a shareholder or a member of the Company is allowed to acquire the documents of share in the fund it manages, but only during the incorporation of such a fund.

The compensation for the management of the Company may amount annually up to 3.5 per cent of the total value of the fund's assets, whereas the cost of issuance of the share documents and the costs of the return of the share documents and their payment can amount to no more than five per cent of such document's value. If the payment of the pecuniary devices of the person investing in the purchase of the fund share has been agreed in instalments and for a period of several years, with regard to covering the costs related to the issuance of the share document, at most 25 per cent of the agreed first year single payment may be deducted, whereas the rest of the costs, up to the full amount of the issuance costs, can be divided over the remaining number of instalments. In such case the Company, itself, is liable to organize the sale of the share in the fund.

## Open-end fund

The Company will incorporate an open-ended fund as soon as it has prepared the fund's bylaws and the prospectus of the fund and enters the agreement with the depositary bank and submits to the Commission a request for approval.

The property items of the fund can be transferable security papers registered to the bearer or to the name of those enlisted or non-enlisted in the stock exchange, the real estate subscribed in the land books to the name of the fund or the shares in the company whose scope of business is exclusively, or mostly, the acquisition and sale, renting, lease and management of real estate, if the voting right referring to the share enables at any time the prevailing influence on the business and ceasing of the company whose shares it holds, as well as the pecuniary deposits. The Company shall determine the value of the fund's assets.

## Closed-end fund

The closed-end fund shall be established by an investment company when it adopts the closed-end fund's bylaws and prospectus, takes over shares, appoints members of the management board and the first supervisory board, and files application with the Commission for approval of establishment.

## Depository bank

A depository bank is a bank selected by the Company, which, on the principles of the Agreement and upon the Company's order, performs all activities determined by the Investment Law. The selection of the depository bank, and every change of same, must be approved by the Commission. The Agreement concluded between the Company and the depository bank enters into force as from the day of its approval by the Commission. If the request of the law is fulfilled, the approval of the depository bank can be withheld only if, according to the preliminary obtained opinion of the Croatian National Bank, there are facts indicating that the selected depository bank is not able to fulfil its obligations in conformity with the Law. The depository banks of the investment funds must be banks seated in the Republic of Croatia. The same company cannot perform the obligations and the activities of the Company and a depository bank. The Company and the depository bank must execute their obligations independently and exclusively in the interest of the owners of the shares.

## Investment and investment limitations

The security papers of an investment fund consist of:

- security papers enlisted in the official (regular) quotation for sale of security papers on the stock exchange in the Republic of Croatia or on the stock exchanges and other organized markets of EU member states and OECD states;

- security papers enlisted for sale on other stock exchange official (regular) quotation outside the states stated above, if the selection of other stock exchanges is foreseen by the prospectus or statute of the fund;

- security papers originating from the new issues, if the conditions of the issue contain the obligation to submit the request for the official (regular) sale quotation on the some other stock exchange in one of the above stated countries.

The security papers that are not enlisted in the official (regular) quotation for sale on some other securities stock exchange or are not being sold on some other organized market can be acquired in an amount of up to 10 per cent of the fund's property value, whereas the debt security papers issued by the Republic of Croatia, the local administration or regional self-administration unit, which are not enlisted in the official (regular) quotation for sale on the securities stock exchange or which are not intended for sale on some other organized market, can be acquired without limitation.

It is not permissible to invest more than five per cent of the investment fund's value in the security papers of one issuer. Exceptionally, it is possible to invest up to 10 per cent of the investment fund's value in the security papers of one issuer, under condition that the total value of such other issuers' security papers does not exceed 40 per cent of the investment fund's value. The bonds issued by the EU member states or member states of OECD, are calculated, with respect to the mentioned limitation of investments, at only half of the value.

The open-end investment fund can acquire the bonds of the same issue only if their total nominal amount does not exceed 10 per cent of the total nominal amount of all bonds of the same issue, if such are in circulation.

The shares of the same issue can be acquired for an open-end investment fund only if the voting right of the company related to the shares of the same issue does not exceed 10 per cent of all voting rights related to the shares of that issuer.

The deposits in the financial institution and other pecuniary devices of an investment fund may amount to, at most, 49 per cent of the investment fund's value, whereas the limitation does not refer to an investment fund whose activity is disposal with pecuniary deposits. It is allowed to keep in the depository bank at most 50 per cent of pecuniary devices.

The debt security papers issued by the Republic of Croatia or which the Republic of Croatian guarantees, can be acquired by the fund without limitation.

The funds must not acquire:

- securities issued by a member or a shareholder of the company whose share in the company exceeds 10 per cent;

- securities of the issuer with whom such member or shareholder is related by holding a share in that issuer exceeding 10 per cent;

- securities of the issuer that hold a share exceeding 10 per cent in the member or the shareholder of the company.

Such limitations do not refer to the security papers enlisted in the official (regular) quotation of the stock exchange.

The Company is allowed, under certain conditions, to acquire real estate for the investment fund. An investment fund for real estate, according to its statute, is allowed to acquire in Croatia and abroad, on the basis of reciprocity.

With respect to the optional and term affairs and other instruments and techniques, it should be mentioned that they are allowed only for purpose of security of the claims and fund's assets.

# Part Six

# Appendices

# Appendix I

# Business Organizations

With its network of 20 county chambers, the Croatian Chamber of Economy (CCE) is the key national organization connecting the Croatian and global economies.

The CCE is a non-profit, professional public institution serving the business community with the aim of strengthening and promoting economic growth in Croatia, and thereby contributing to overall social prosperity. The CCE was established in Zagreb in 1852, with the mission to protect and represent the economic interests of its members.

The improvement of economic cooperation with the international business community is a primary task of the CCE. For this purpose, various activities, focused on increasing the exchange of goods and services as well as other forms of economic cooperation with foreign business entities, are in place.

Special attention is given to promotional activities, presenting the Croatian economy in individual countries by informing business partners about Croatian laws and regulations as well as about investment opportunities and incentives. The CCE organizes visits of foreign business partners to Croatia and arranges meetings of Croatian delegations with international business partners, in which specific forms of cooperation are discussed. In this context, the promotion of Croatian export-oriented industries at various distinguished international exhibitions and fairs is an important part of CCE activities.

The CCE, as the principal promoter and organizer of joint participation at fairs and exhibitions, makes it possible for its members to get insight into a particular market, both in financial and organizational terms. This level of service is the result of very good relationships between the CCE and international chambers of commerce and/or other economic institutions, which help Croatian firms establish bilateral relationships with those in a particular country or region. These activities are carried out in cooperation with 20 county chambers, trade associations and other institutions.

The CCE also puts substantial effort into Croatia's global trade liberalization trends and in the process of European integration in order to ensure fair market competition in an export-oriented economy. The CCE is actively and directly involved in these processes, such as joining the WTO and all activities related to further trade liberalization resulting from membership, signing of the Stabilization and

Association Agreement (SAA), joining the EU, free trade negotiations with CEFTA countries, including Croatia's membership of this association, and negotiations with EFTA members and other countries. On the level of multilateral cooperation, the focus is on the EU, Croatia's most important foreign trade partner, owing to the fact that full membership of the Union is the country's long-term strategic goal. The enlargement of the single European Market is being systematically monitored. Its integration is being closely followed, as well as its trade policies and customs regulations, which directly affect the export conditions for Croatia. The CCE is participating in the practical implementation of the Agreement on Trade in Textile Products between Croatia and the EU as well as in a number of regional initiatives, – the Stability Pact, the Central European Initiative (CEI), the Adriatic-Ionian Initiative (AII), the Alps-Adriatic Working Community, the SECI and others. So far, the CCE has signed about 40 cooperation agreements with chambers of economy from all over the world.

The CCE exercises public authority, eg issuance and verification of various certificates of the Croatian origin of goods (non-preferential origin of goods, Form A certificates of Croatian origin of goods required for preferential treatment – General Scheme of Preference). Other documents required for the export or import of goods are also issued and verified, such as export licences and non-preferential certificates for textile goods, ATA Carnet, documents facilitating customs clearance of temporary import or export of goods intended for personal or professional use, especially for commercial samples, professional equipment, fair exhibits and exhibition objects, fair samples, etc.

In 2000, the CEE became the 34th member of the Eurochambres – the Association of European Chambers of Commerce and Industry. Even though it is an affiliated member, the CCE has been included in several initiatives. The European Business Panel (EBP) is a joint initiative of European economic chambers (coordinated by the Eurochambres), involved in opinion polling of member companies on various hot issues. The results are used to strengthen the influence of the European chambers network. The ChamberPass is an initiative of Eurochambres for internet services to chambers, which has been launched as a response to the need for a higher level of services provided to companies by chambers, both in qualitative and quantitative terms, using new technologies. The Eurochambres Survey provides an overview of the economic situation in Croatia as a separate section in the European Economic Report.

The CCE has been member of the International Chamber of Commerce in Paris (ICC) since 1995, where it participates in the work of several committees and specialized groups. Within the ICC, chambers from all over the world exchange views and experiences to improve their activities and further develop services relevant to their members. Cooperation with the International Trade Centre – UNCTAD (ICT) in Geneva – plays a prominent role in the promotion of the effects of WTO rules on trade and business systems in general, particularly in transition and developing countries. The CCE is a member of other international organizations such as:

- ASCAME – the Association of the Chambers of Commerce and Industry of the Mediterranean, UEAPME – European Association of Crafts, Small and Medium-sized Enterprises;

- ECSB – the European Council For Small Business, affiliation of ICSB – the International Council For Small Business, Halmstad;

- TII – the European Association for Technology Transfer, Innovation and Business Information, exchange of technology tenders of EBEN, TRN, CORDIS networks, Brussels;

- FIATA – the International Federation of Freight Forwarders Associations, Zurich;

- OICA – the International Organization of Motor Vehicle Manufacturers, Paris; and

- EMEC – the European Marine Equipment Council, London.

With the aim of better promoting the interests of the Croatian economy internationally, the leaders of the CCE have decided to establish representative offices abroad, whose main task is to facilitate access to, and the competetiveness of CCE members, especially of SMEs, in the international market, by providing timely and high-quality information, finding potential partners and helping them to establish contacts.

The first representative office of the CCE was founded in Sarajevo, Bosnia and Herzegovina, in 1996, and the first civil aircraft to land in Sarajevo was Croatia Airline's plane with Croatian businessmen on board, who were interested in the revival of business relationships with Bosnia and Herzegovina. Shortly after, in 1997, an office in Mostar was opened, and the office in Banja Luka, which was established in 1996, began operations in 2001.

Since some 80 per cent of the total commodity exchange involves EU countries, the CCE established its office in Brussels, the capital of the EU, in 2000. Due to the fact that the members of the Chamber expressed great interest in expanding business cooperation with Kosovo and in its reconstruction, the CCE founded an office in Priètina in 2000. In early 2002, its Belgrade office started operations. The office in Kotor, Montenegro, was opened in the first quarter of 2003 and an office in Serbia also now exists.

Since 1 January 2002, Croatia has been member of a large free trade zone, the CCE plans to establish offices in Italy, Austria and Germany.

# Appendix II

# Useful Websites

## Government

President of the Republic
http://www.predsjednik.hr/

Government of the Republic of Croatia
http://www.vlada.hr/

Parliament of the Republic of Croatia
http://www.sabor.hr/

Ministry of Economy and Foreign Affairs
http://www.mingo.hr/
http://www.mvp.hr/

Ministry of Finance
http://www.mfin.hr/

Ministry of Labour and Social Welfare
http://www.mrss.hr/

Ministry of European Integration
http://www.mei.hr/

## Government agencies

Croatian Information Documentation Referral Agency
http://www.hidra.hr/

Croatian Guarantee Agency
http://www.hga.hr/

State Bureau of Intellectual Property
http://www.dziv.hr/

Croatian Privatization Fund
http://www.hfp.hr/

## Others

Croatian Chamber of Commerce
http://www.hgk.hr/komora/eng/eng.htm

Zagreb Stock Exchange
http://www.zse.hr/

Croatian National Bank
http://www.hnb.hr/eindex.htm

## Croatian Embassies Overseas

### *Austria*

Joanneumring 18/3
8010 Graz
Austria
Tel: (316) 33 82 50
Fax: (316) 33 82 50 14

### *Belgium*

Kunstlaan 50
8ste verdiep – bus 14, 1050
Brussels
Belgium
Tel: 2 500 09 20
Fax No: 2 512 03 38

### *Canada*

229 Chapel St
Ottawa
Ontario K1N 7Y6
Canada
Tel: (613) 562 7820
Fax: (613) 562 7821
Email: info@croatiaemb.net

## *France*

39, avenue Georges Mandel
75116 Paris
France
Tel: (01) 53 70 02 80
Fax: (01) 53 70 02 90
Email: secretariat@amb-croatie.fr

## *United Kingdom*

21 Conway Street
London
W1P 5HL
Tel: (020) 7387 2022
Email: political@croatianembassy.co.uk Political
economic@croatianembassy.co.uk Economic Section
cultural@croatianembassy.co.uk Cultural Section
consular-dept@croatianembassy.co.uk Consular Department
info-press@croatianembassy.co.uk Information & Press Section
amboffice@croationembassy.co.uk

## *United States of America*

2343 Massachusetts Avenue NW
Washington DC 20008
USA
Tel: (202) 588 5899
Fax: (202) 588 8936
Email: webmaster@croatiaemb.org

# Embassies in Croatia

## *Australia*

Intercontinental Hotel, 6th Floor
Krsnjavoga 1
Zagreb
Tel: (385 1) 489 1200
Fax: (385 1) 483 1216

## *Belgium*

Pantovchak 125 B1
10000 Zagreb
Tel: (385 1) 45 78 901, 45 78 903
Fax: (385 1) 45 78 902
Email: Zagreb@diplobel.org

## *France*

5 Schlosserove Stube – BP 466
10000 Zagreb
Tel: (385 1) 455 77 67/68/68
Fax: (385 1) 455 77 65

## *India*

Boskoviceva 7A
10000 Zagreb
Tel: (385 1) 487 3239, 487 3240, 487 3241
Fax: (385 1) 4817907
Email: embassy.india@zg.tel.hr

## *United Kingdom*

Ul Ivana Lucica 4
Zagreb
Tel: (385 1) 6009 100 (Switchboard)
Email: british.embassyzagreb@fco.gov.uk
commercial.section@zg.htnet.hr

## *United States of America*

Andrije Hebranga 2
Zagreb 10000
Tel: (385 1) 661 2200
Fax: (385 1) 661 2373

# Appendix III

# Contributor contact details

**American Chamber of Commerce in Croatia**
Mr Damir Vucić, Executive Director
Krsnjavoga 1
10000 Zagreb, Croatia
Tel: +385 (0) 1 4836 777
Fax: +385 (0) 1 4836 776
Email: info@amcham.hr
Please visit us at: www.amcham.hr

**Wade Channell**
Former President, American Chamber of Commerce in Croatia
Av. Gevaert 217
1332 Genval
Belgium
Email: wade.channell@earthlink.net

**Civilitas Research**
Samos Street 10/2
PO Box 16183
CY-2086 Nicosia
Cyprus
Tel: +357 22 44 68 40
Fax: +357 22 44 68 35

**Croatian Chamber of Economy**
Headquarters
Rooseveltov trg 2
HR-10 000 Zagreb, Croatia
P.O. Box 630
Tel: +385 (0) 1 4561 555
Fax: +385 (0) 1 4828 380
Email: hgk@hgk.hr
Website: hgk.hr

**Deloitte d.o.o.**
Heinzelova 33
10000 Zagreb, Croatia
Contacts: Artur Gedike
Corporate Communication & Marketing Regional Manager
Adriatic Region
Tel: +385 (0) 1 2351 900
Fax: +385 (0) 1 2351 999
Email: agedike@deloittece.com
Adrian Hammer, Consultant
Tax and Regulatory Services
Tel: +385 (0) 1 2351 900
Fax: +385 (0) 1 2351 999
E-mail: ahammer@deloittece.com
Website: www.deloitte.com

**Dr Anamarija Frankic**
Assistant Professor, University of Massachusetts Boston
Research Faculty Associate, College of William & Mary/VIMS
USA
Tel: +1 804 684 7807
Fax: +1 804 684 7179
Mobile: 757 897 0779
Email: afrankic@vims.edu
Website: http://ccrm.vims.edu/staff/frankic_a.html

**Michael Glazer**
Director
Auctor Advisors
Palmoticeva 2
10000 Zagreb, Croatia
Mobile: +385 98 310 771
Tel: +385 (0) 1 4814 139
Fax: +385 (0) 1 4814 143
Email: mglazer@auctor.hr

**The Institute of Economics, Zagreb**
Iva Condic-Jurkic
Trg J. F . Kennedy 7
10000 Zagreb
Tel: +385 (0) 1 2335 700
Fax: +385 (0) 1 2335 165
Email: icondic@eizg.hr

**Professor Dr. Sc. Josip Kregar**
Pravni Fakultet
Sveučilišata u Zagrebu
(School of Law)
Trg maršaala Tita 3
Tel: +385 1 4597522
Email: josip.kregar@zg.htnet.hr

**Markovic & Pliso Law Firm**
Smiciklasova 21
Tel: +385 (0) 1 4699 400
Fax: +385 (0) 1 4699 499
Email: zmarkovic@markovicpliso.hr

**Ministry of Foreign Affairs and European Integration of the Republic of Croatia**
Trg N. S. Zrinskog 7–8
1000 Zagreb
Croatia
Tel: +385 1 4569 964
Fax: +385 1 4551 795/4920 149
Email: mvp@mvp.hr

**Raiffeisenbank Austria d.d. Zagreb**
Petrinjska 59
10000 Zagreb
Croatia

**Professor Velimir Scrica**
Tel: +385 1 2383 333
Email: delfin-razvoj-managementa@zg.tel.hr

**Trade & Investment Promotion Agency**
Vukovarska 78
10000 Zagreb
Croatia
Website: www.apiu.hr
Contact: Igor Maricic, Managing Director
Tel. +385 (0) 1 6109 860
Fax: +385 (0) 1 6109 868
Email: igor.maricic@mingorp.hr

**VIPnet Corporate Communications**
Tel: +385 (0) 1 4691 182
Fax. +385 (0) 1 4691 189
GSM: +385 91 4691 182
Contact: Nina Kulaš

# Index

accommodation capacity   147
accounting requirements   306–12
  audit   309–12
  entrepreneur definition and
    classification   306–07
  financial statements   309
  legal framework   306
  records   308
  representative offices   275
  standards   308–09
    Dalekovod   224–25
    Piramida   241
*acquis comunautaire*, harmonization
  with   34
acquisitions   286–87
  food industry   131–32
  of shares   285–86
Action Plan for Fighting Corruption
  (National Strategy)   90–91
administration charges, real estate
  purchase   192
Adriatic area   97–101, *99*
adriatica.net   181
adventure tourism   151
age structure   116–18, *116, 117, 118*
agricultural land purchase   193
agriculture sector   102–04, *103, 104*
Agrokor group   128–29, 131, 132
annual leave   313
annual reports   310
Anti-Money Laundering Office   93
apartment property market, Zagreb
  197–98
apparel industry *see* textile and
  apparel industry
appellations of origin   332–33
Appellations of Origin Law   332
aquaculture   104–05
arbitration   325–28
Arbitration Law   327–28
areas of special national concern, tax
  relief   292

ascribed merit, emphasis on   44
assessment for tax   293, 303
audit firms   310
audit requirements   309–12
  availability of information   311
  corporate management trends
    311–12
  financial statements   309–10
  indemnification   311
  report content   311
  responsibilities of auditors   310
Austria, FDI level   25, *26*, 51, 52, 53
Avis questionnaire   30

bank accounts, representative offices
  276
Bank Rehabilitation Act   70, 71
Banking Act   70
banking sector   68–75
  Croatian National Bank   68
  current developments   73–75, *74*
  ICT implementation   181
  privatization   50, 71–72
  regulations and standards   69–70
  rehabilitation programme   70–72
  SME use   144
Belupo   121, *122*, 123–24
beverages industry *see* food and
  beverages industry
BICRO (Business and Innovation
  Centre)   187
'Big Bonds Scheme'   71
biodiversity   97–98
birth rates   117, *118*
biscuit production *see* Koestlin
bond types, securities market   76–77
Bosnia, historical background   6
Bosnia-Herzegovina, relations with
  8
branch offices   276–77
brands, food industry   132
brewing industry   132

building industry *see* construction
  industry
Business and Innovation Centre
  (BICRO)   187
business-enabling environment
  142–44
business entities   273–87
  acquisition of shares   285
  branch offices   276–77
  dividend payments   287
  entrepreneurial contracts   287
  mergers and acquisitions   286–87
  representative offices   274–76
  types of organization   277–85
business permits   317
business professional organizations
  343–45

cable TV (CATV) operators   163, 186
Cadastre   323–24
café culture   43
campsites   151–52
CARDS *see* Community Assistance for
  Reconstruction, Development and
  Stabilization
cargo services   233
CARNet (Croatian Academic and
  Research Network)   184
CCA *see* Croatian Chamber of
  Economy
CDA (Central Depositary Agency)   78
CEB   28
CEFTA membership   27
Census Sheet A, land registry records
  322
Central Depositary Agency (CDA)   78
central heating appliances production
  *see* Centrometal
Centrometal   249–53
  business development   251–52
  corporate form   250
  labour   252–53
  organizational history   249–50
  product lines   251
Chamber of Commerce   144
ChamberPass initiative   344
charts of accounts   308
closed-end investment funds   336,
  338

clothing industry *see* Emka; MTC;
  textiles and apparel industry
CNB *see* Croatian National Bank
Commercial Court Registry   278
commercial relations, legal rules of
  268
Community Assistance for
  Reconstruction, Development and
  Stabilization (CARDS) 38–39
companies   280–84
Companies Act   273, 277, 279
  acquisitions   285, 286
competition   65
  ability of Croatia to withstand
    33–34
concessions   270–71
  telecommunications services
    174–76
Conciliation Law and Rules   326
Conditions for Formation and
  Operation of Foreign
  Representative Offices in Croatia,
  Decree on   274–75
Constitution   267, 274
Constitutional Court   4
Constitutional Resolution on
  Sovereignty and Independence
  325
construction industry   110–15, *112*
  companies by size   113, *113*
  international markets   114, *114*
  residential construction   111–12,
    *112*
  road construction   114–15
  *see also* Konstruktor-Inženjering
construction of buildings, real estate
  320
Consumer Price Index (CPI), food
  industry share   133, *133*
contractual rules   268
contributor contact details   350–53
coastal area   97–101
confectionery production *see* Koestlin
conference tourism   152
Constitutional Court   268
contractual joint ventures   280
Convention on Biological Diversity
  97
Conventions on arbitration   326

copyright   330
Copyright and other Congenial Rights
   Law   330
corporate governance   63, 66, 311–12
corporate income tax   269–70, 288,
   290–94
   assessment   293
   calculations   290
   rate reductions   291
   relief, exemptions and incentives
      291–92
   transfer pricing   290–91
corporate management see corporate
   governance
Corporate Profit Act   288
corporations   280–84
correction, taking and giving   45–46
corruption   83–94
   barrier to development   88–93, 89
   political trends   83–88
Corruption Perception Index (CPI)
   89, 89
corruption rating   8–9
county courts   268
courts   268
CPI see Consumer Price Index;
   Corruption Perception Index
credit rating   76
criticism, taking and giving   45–46
Croatian Chamber of Economy (CCE)
   343–45
   textiles industry   137
   tourist industry   154–56
Croatian Democratic Union (HDZ)
   party   5–6, 7, 9, 12, 83, 84–85,
      86
Croatian Equity Market Index
   (CROEMI)   78
Croatian Institute for Health
   insurance (HZZO)   119
Croatian National Bank (CNB)
   19–20, 68
Croatian Peasant Party (HSS)   8
Croatian People's Party (HNS)   8
Croatian Securities Commission
   (CROSEC)   78–79
Croatian Social Liberal Party (HSLS)
   8, 9
'Croatian Spring' movement   5

Croatian State Intellectual Property
   Office (CSIPO)   329
Croatian Telecommunications Agency
   173–74
CROEMI see Croatian Equity Market
   Index
Crosco Integrated Drilling & Well
   Services Ltd   204
CROSEC (Croatian Securities
   Commission)   78–79
CSIPO (Croatian State Intellectual
   Property Office)   329
cultural factors   42–46
currency, key points   65

DAB see State Agency for Deposit
   Insurance and Bank
   Rehabilitation
Dalcom Ltd   220
Dalekovod   217–27
   affiliated companies   220–21
   business development   222–23,
      224–25
   core products and services
      218–19
   effect of EU accession   225
   foreign markets   223–24
   future   226
   history   217–18
   organization   219–21, 220
   product design   221–22
Dalekovod-Cinčonica   221–22
Dalen Ltd   220
data communications services   187
democratization   9
demographic data   116–18, 116, 117,
   118
depository banks   338
Deutsche Telekom   158, 159
direct investments   81
dismissals   314–15
dispute resolution   325–28
dividend payments   287
domestic equity market   77–79
domestic vs multinational food
   producers   133–34
donors, relationship with   27–28
double taxation treaties   294, 304
Dubrovacka banka   72

EBP (European Business Panel)   344
EBRD *see* European Bank for
    Reconstruction and Development
e-commerce   185–86
economic activity, FDI classification
    50–53, *52*
economic classification, foreign trade
    21–23, *23*
economic indicators   *13–14*
economic overview   11–28, 143
    adjustment for EU accession   31–34
    environment for FDI   53–55, 64
    foreign trade and investment
        21–27, *22, 23, 24, 25, 26*
    history and nature of transition
        11–12, *13–14, 15*
    international institutions and
        donors   27–28
    recent performance   16–18
    structural reforms   18–20
EDGE (Enhanced Data Rates for
    Global Evolution)   166, 168
education, ICT   188
EIGs (European Interest Groupings)
    279
electric power transmission projects
    *see* Dalekovod
embassy websites   347–49
Emka   254–58
    business development   256–57
    organizational history   254–55
    product lines   255–56
Employee Stock Ownership Plans
    (ESOPs), Dalekovod   218
employment incentives   292
employment law   313–18
    dismissals   314–15
    leave   313–14
    work permits   315–18
Encumbrance Sheet, land registry
    records   322
energy industry *see* Dalekovod; INA
    Industrija nadte
engineering services *see* Dalekovod
Enhanced Data Rates for Global
    Evolution (EDGE)   166, 168
'entrepreneur' definition and
    classification   306–07
entrepreneurial contracts   287

equity joint ventures   280
Ericsson   187
ESOPs *see* Employee Stock
    Ownership Plans
EU *see* European Union accession
Eurochambres   344
European Bank for Reconstruction
    and Development (EBRD)
    18–19, 28
    Transition Report   33
European Business Panel (EBP)   344
European Interest Groupings (EIGs)
    279
European Partnership for Croatia
    30
European Union (EU) accession   8,
    10, 27, 29–41, 53–55
    economic adjustment   31–34, 87–88
    effect on securities market   76
    impact on Dalekovod   225
    investment key points   63–64, 67
    legal harmonization   34
    National Programme for the
        Integration   34–37
    political criteria   87
    technical assistance   38–41
exchange *see* foreign exchange
exemptions
    corporate income tax   291–92
    VAT   297–99
exhibitions, textiles industry   137
expenses, reimbursement   304
exports *see* foreign trade
extradition of war crime suspects   9
extraordinary terminations   314

fairs, textiles industry   137
FDI *see* foreign direct investment
financial institutions, ICT
    implementation   181
financial statements   309–10
financial system growth   73–74, *74*
fish processing industry   105
fisheries industry   104–06, *105, 106*
fixed-line operators   157, 158–60,
    176, 177
food and beverages industry   107–09,
    *108*, 126–34, *127*
    foreign trade   108–09, *109*, 133, *133*

latest trends   130–34, *133*
most important companies   *128,*
   128–30
*see also* Koestlin
foreign debt levels   17
foreign direct investments (FDI)
   49–57, *50*
   by economic activity   50–53, *52*
   economic and political environment
      53–55
   foreign trade   17, 24–27, *25, 26*
   incentives   55–56, 61
   investment climate and future FDI
      flows   58–61
   methodology   49–50
foreign exchange market   18
foreign exchange regulations   19,
   80–82
Foreign Exchange Transactions Act
   80
foreign trade
   agricultural products   104, *104*
   Dalekovod products   223–24
   Emka products   256
   FDI   17, 21–27, *22, 23, 24, 25, 26*
   fish and fish products   106, *106*
   food, beverages and tobacco
      108–09, *109*, 133, *133*
   Koestlin products   246–47
   liberalization   32
   Piramida products   240
   VAT   297, 299–300
Framework agreement   40
free trade agreements   27
free zones   271–72
   tax relief   292
fund management companies,
   investments   336–37

Gallup research on corruption   90
gas and oil industry *see* INA
   Industrija nadte
GDP *see* gross domestic product
general partnerships   278
General Tax Act   289
geographical indications, appellates of
   origin   332–33
geographical overview   3, 61
Germanic background   44

Germany, FDI levels   25, *26*, 51, 52,
   53
glass pharmaceutical packaging *see*
   Piramida
*Global Information Technology Report*
   182
Globalnet   163, 185
government and government agency
   websites   346–47
government consumption levels   16
government debt levels   18
government policy, structural reforms
   18–20
gross domestic product (GDP) levels
   11–12, *13, 15*, 16, 17
group tax registration   289
GSM operators   167, 175, 176

HACCP (hazard analysis critical
   control point) system   131
Hague Tribunal   9, 10
HAMAG agency   142, 144
hazard analysis critical control point
   (HACCP) system   131
HDZ *see* Croatian Democratic Union
   party
health insurance   305
health tourism   150
healthcare system   20, 116–25
   demographic data   116–18, *116,*
      *117, 118*
   pharmaceutical market   121–25,
      *122, 125*
   pharmaceutical pricing   118–19
   reform project   120–21
high-rises, construction of   212
historical overview   3–10
HITRA programme   187
HNS (Croatian People's Party)   8
holidays   313–14
hotel industry   149
hours of work   313
house property market, Zagreb
   197–98
housing savings banks   69
HT-Hrvatske telekomunikacije   180,
   186
HTmobile *see* T-mobile
HTnet (HThinet)   183

humour, need for sense of   46
Hungary, FDI inflows from   51
Hrvatska postanska banka   72
HSLS (Croatian Social Liberal Party)
    8, 9
HSS (Croatian Peasant Party)   8
human resource management *see*
    employment law; labour
HZZO *see* Croatian Institute for
    Health insurance

ICC (International Chamber of
    Commerce)   344–45
ICT *see* information and
    communication technology
ICTY *see* International Criminal
    Tribunal for the Former
    Yugoslavia
identity (ID) numbers   317–18
IDS (Istrian Democratic Assembly)   8
image of Croatia abroad   58–59
IMF *see* International Monetary Fund
Implementation Plan   30
imports *see* foreign trade
INA Industrija nadte   51, 201–06
    core businesses   201–03
    key subsidiaries   204–05
    management   203–04
incentives
    investment   269
    tax   291–92
income tax *see* corporate income tax;
    personal income tax
independence, war for   5–7
industrial activity levels   17
Industrial Design Law   331–32
industrial designs   331–32
industry sectors, FDI by   25, *26*
inflation rates   18, 65, 66–67
information and communication
    technology (ICT)   179–89
    education   188
    international ranking   181–82, *182*
    legislative and infrastructural
        environment   182–87
infrastructure development   55
    *see also* Dalekovod
inheritance, acquiring property
    through   194

inherited merit, emphasis on   44–45
insurance *see* Zagreb Insurance
    Company
integrated circuit layouts   333–34
intellectual property   329–34
    appellations of origin   332–33
    copyright   330
    industrial designs   331–32
    integrated circuit layouts   333–34
    patents   330–31
    trade marks   331
Inter-banking Services Institute
    (MBU)   185
Interim Agreement on Trade and
    Trade Related Matters   30
International Chamber of Commerce
    (ICC)   344–45
International Criminal Tribunal for
    the Former Yugoslavia (ICTY)   6,
    9, 10
international institutions, relations
    with   27–28
International Monetary Fund (IMF)
    FDI methodological requirements
        49
    membership   27
international organizations, CCE
    membership of   344–45
international ranking, ICT   181–82,
    *182*
international standards, food industry
    130–31
internet service providers (ISPs)
    161–62, 163, 181, 183–85
INTERREG programmes   40
investment climate, and FDI flows
    58–61
investment fund regulation   335–40
    definition and types   335–36
    depository banks   338
    fund management company
        336–37
    limitations   338–40
    open-end and closed-end funds
        337–38
investment incentives   169–70
investment levels   16–17
Investment Promotion Law   269
investment strategies   62–67

key points    62–65
strategic principles    65–67
IPA (pre-accession instrument)
        39–40
IskonInternet    162, 184–85
ISO standards
    Koestlin    247
    Piramida    239, 242
ISPs *see* internet service providers
ISPA programme    39
Istrian Democratic Assembly (IDS)    8

Jadranska pivovara    132
Jadranski Pomorski Servis (JPS)
        231–35
    business development    233–34
    history and structure    231–32
    maritime services provision
            232–33
Jamnica    128
JANAF oil pipeline system    205
joint stock companies    283–84
    legal structure    284
joint ventures    280
    Dalekovod    224
joke-telling    46
JPS *see* Jadranski Pomorski Servis

Karlovacka pivovara    132
Koestlin    244–48
    business development    246–47
    labour    247
    organizational history    244–45
    product lines    245–46
Konstruktor-Inženjering    207–13
    current position    208
    future    212–13
    high-rises    212
    organization    209
    road infrastructure    209–11
    utilities and marine structures
            211
Konzum    129, 131, 132
Kraš    129, 130, 132

La Divina fashion wear    256–57
labour
    Centrometal    252–53
    costs key points    65, 66

Emka    257–58
    JPS    234
    Koestlin    247
    Piramida    241–42
    *see also* employment law
Labour Act    313
Land Registry    192, 321–24
Land Registry Law and Bylaw    322
large entrepreneurs    307
leave (holidays)    313–14
Ledo    128, 131, 132
legacies of the past    43–45
legal framework    267–72
    auditing and accounting    306
    concessions    270–71
    corruption    90–91
    dispute resolution    325
    free zones    271–72
    intellectual property    329
    investment funds    335
    investment incentives    269–70
    key points    63, 66
    SMEs    143
legal harmonization with EU    34
    supporting institutional
            mechanisms    37–38
legal institutes    268
legal transaction method of property
        acquisition    194–95
lending regulations    82
Liberal party (LS)    8
lien, real estate as    321
life expectancy    116–17, *117*
life insurance    262
LIFE III programme    40
limited liability companies    281–83
    documentation required    282–83
    formation    282
limited partnerships    278–79
living conditions    42–46, 61
loan regulations    82
LS (Liberal party)    8
lubricant plants    202
Lura    129, 131, 132

macroeconomic situation    11–12,
        *13–14*
management boards, limited liability
        companies    281–82

maps   xx, xxi
marine fishery industry   104
marine protected areas   98–101
marine structures, construction of
    211
maritime services *see* Jadranski
    Pomorski Servis
market economy, existence of
    functioning   32–33
maternity leave   314
Maziva Rijeka   202
Maziva Zagreb   202
MBU (Inter-banking Services
    Institute)   185
medium-sized entrepreneurs   307
mergers and acquisitions   286–87
Mesić, Stipe   8, 10, 86
Ministry for European Integration
    37–38, 41
Ministry for SMEs   142
Ministry of Finance   289
Ministry of Foreign Affairs   191, 195
Ministry of the Sea, Tourism,
    Transport and Development   172
Mlaka lubricants plant   202
Mobile Communications Association
    165
mobile telecommunications   157–58,
    164–70
    operators   160–61, 166–69, *167–70,*
        176, 178, 180
    services   166
modernization of food industry   130
MOL (Hungarian oil company)   205
monetary developments   17–18
mortality rates   117, *118*
MOST trading system   78
MTC   228–30
    business development   229–30
    core business   229
    history   228
    organization   228–29
municipal courts   268

Naftaplin   201
National Council of Public
    Prosecutions   92
National Programme for the Fight
    against Corruption   90

National Programme for Integration
    (NPIEU)   30, 34–37
National Strategy (Action Plan for
    Fighting Corruption)   90
NATO membership   8, 10
natural heritage   97–101
Nature Protection Law   190–91
nautical tourism   150
new chemical entities (NCE) projects
    125, *125*
non-life insurance   262–63
notice periods   314–15
NPIEU *see* National Programme for
    Integration

Office for the Prevention of
    Corruption and Organized Crime
    (USKOK)   9, 92–93
office space, Zagreb   196–97
oil and gas industry *see* INA
    Industrija nadte
Ombudsman   4
online market   185–86
open-end investment funds   335–36,
    337–38
Opinion on Croatia's Application
    (Avis)   30, 32
Optima Telekom   157, 159–60, 176, 177
ordinary terminations   314
over-the counter (OTC)
    pharmaceuticals market   122

Panonaska pivovara   132
Parliament   4
partnerships   278–80
PAs (protected areas)   98–101
patents   330–31
Patents Law   330
payments of tax   303
'pedigree', emphasis on   44
pension insurance   305
PEP (Pre-accession Economic
    Programme)   31–32
personal consumption levels   16
personal income tax   302–04
petrol stations   203
Phare programme   39
pharmaceuticals industry   121–25,
    *122*

distribution channels   121
main producers   123–25, *125*
over-the-counter market   122
packaging *see* Piramida
pricing and reimbursement
    118–19
Rx trends   123
Physical Planning Law   320
Piramida   237–43
    business development   239–41
    labour   241–42
    location   239
    organizational history   237–38
    privatization   238–39
'place of supply', VAT   294–95
Pliva   121, *122*
Podravka Group   129, 130, 131
police, role in fighting corruption   92
political overview   3–10, 83–88
    for FDI   53–55
population data   116–18, *116*, *117*,
    *118*
Portus   157, 160, 176, 177
power supply structures, construction
    of   211
Pre-accession Economic Programme
    (PEP)   31–32
Pre-accession Strategy for Croatia
    31, 39
president   4
privatization   50
    banks   71–72
    Emka   254–55
    Piramida   238–39
    telecommunications   186
product design, Dalekovod   221–22
Property Law   319
property ownership *see* real estate
Proplin Ltd   204
protected areas (PAs)   98–101
Protected Coastal Belt   320
Protection of Topography of Semi-
    Conducting Products Law   333–34
public prosecutor   92

quality of life   46

Racan, Ivica   8, 9
real estate   190–98, 319–24

company purchase   194
construction   320
investments   81
lien   321
major obstacles   63, 143, 144,
    195–96, 321–22
old vs new property   193–94
other ways of acquiring ownership
    194–95
procedure for acquiring   191–93
regulations   321–24
taxes   320–21
VAT   301
Zagreb market   196–98
reciprocity agreements   192
recovery of VAT   299
redundancy payments   315
refineries   201–02
refunds, VAT   297, 301
regional government   20
registration for VAT   296
registration of address, foreign
    persons   317
Registry of Representative Offices of
    Foreign Entities   276
Rehabilitation Act   70, 71
rehabilitation programme, banks
    70–72
relational culture   43
relief on tax   291
representative offices   274–75
research and development
    ICT sector   187
    pharmaceuticals market   125
research strategy principle   66
reservation deposits, real estate
    purchase   191
residence regulations   80–81, 302
    work permits   316–17
resident investments abroad   81–82
residential construction   111–12, *112*,
    212
retail loans levels   74
retail operations, oil industry   203
retail property market, Zagreb   197
retraining costs   292
Rijecka banka   72
Rijeka Gateway Project   211
Rijeka refinery   202

Rijeka-Zagreb Highway   210
road construction   114–15, 209–11,
    219
Rulebook on drug pricing   118
rural tourism   151
Rx (prescription drug) trends,
    pharmaceutical market   123

SAA *see* Stabilization and Association
    Agreement
Sabor (Parliament)   4
Sanader, Ivo   9, 85, 86
SARs (Serb Autonomous Regions)   6
satellite communications   186–87
SDP (Social Democratic Party)   7–8,
    83–84
Seals, land registry   323
securities market   76–82
  Stock Exchanges   77–79
security papers, investment funds
    338–40
Serb Autonomous Regions (SARs)   6
Serbia and Montenegro (SMN),
    relations with   8
Serbian refugees   9, 10
severance payments   315
share acquisition   285–86
Siemens   187
'significant market power' (SMP),
    telecoms operators   176–77
silent partnerships   279–80
Sisak refinery   202
Slavonska Banka   72
small and medium-sized enterprises
    (SMEs)   19, 141–45
  business enabling environment
    142–44
  environment for   64, 65
  key sectors   144–45
  relevance to foreign investors
    141–42
small entrepreneurs   307
'small town feeling' of Zagreb   42–43
SMEs *see* small and medium-sized
    enterprises
SMN *see* Serbia and Montenegro
SMP *see* 'significant market power'
Social Democratic Party (SDP)   7–8,
    83–84

social programmes, key points   65, 66
social security contributions   305,
    *305*
Split Bypass Road   210
Splitska Banka   72
Stabilization and Association
    Agreement (SAA)   8, 27, 29, 30,
    53, 268
Standard & Poor's credit rating   76
State Agency for Deposit Insurance
    and Bank Rehabilitation (DAB)
    70, 71, 72
State Audit Office   93
state prosecution service   92
statute of limitations   293
Stimulating Investments Act   55–56
Stock Exchanges   77–79
structural reforms   18–20
STSI – Interirani tehnički servisi
    204–05
supervisory boards of corporations
    281
  taxation of members   304
Supreme Court   268
sustainable economic development
    97–101, *99*

TAIEX (Technical Assistance
    Information Exchange Unit)   38
Takeovers Act   285–86
tanker services   232–33
Tax Administration, Ministry of
    Finance   289
tax losses   293
tax rates   290, 303–04
tax returns   289, 303
taxable bases and calculations   290
taxable income, personal   302–03
taxation   288–301
  administration   289
  corporate income tax   290–94
  investment incentives   269
  personal income tax   302–04
  real estate purchase   192–93,
    320–21
  representative offices   275
  social security contributions   305,
    *305*
VAT   294–301

taxpayers   290
T-Com   157, 159, 162, 176, 177
Technical Assistance Information
    Exchange Unit (TAIEX)   38
Telecommunications Act   172–73
Telecommunications Agency
    173–74
telecommunications sector   157–63,
    *159*, 171–78, *174*, 180–81
  fixed   158–60, *159*
  Globalnet   163
  government bodies   172
  internet providers   161–62, 163
  market liberalization   177–78,
    186–87
  mobile   157–58, 160–61, 164–70,
    *167–170*
  privatization   50
  regulatory framework   172–76, *174*
  service providers   176–77
  *see also* Dalekovod
telemedicine project   188
temporary residence   316–17
TEMPUS programme   40
termination of employment   314–15
textile and apparel industry   135–40,
    *139, 140*
  current situation   136–37
  fairs and exhibitions   137
  top ten companies   138, *138*
  *see also* Emka; MTC
T-Havratski Telekom   158–59, 177
'think small' principle   66
'time of supply', VAT   295–96
Title Sheet, land registry records
    322
T-Mobile (formerly HTmobile)   158,
    160, 164, 166–67, 180
  ownership *167*
  services   165, 176, 177, 178
tobacco industry   107–09, *108, 109*
tour operators   149
tourism   55, 61, 64, 146–56, *153, 154*
  Croatian Chamber of Economy
    154
  importance   148
  key factors   148–49
  regions   146
  role of SMEs   144–45

sustainable natural resource
    management   99–100
  types   150–52
tourists   147
Trade Mark Law   331
trade marks   331
traffic infrastructure projects *see*
    Dalekovod
transfer pricing   290–91
transition, history and nature of
    11–12, *13–14, 15*, 63
Transparency International   90
  CPI index   89, *89*
transport, tourist use   147
travel agencies   149, 181
Treća sreća   157, 161, 164, 165, 169
  services   165, 176, 178
Tudjman, Franjo   5, 6, 7, 83
tugboat services   233

UMTS networks   165, 167, 175, 176
unemployment levels   17, 20
UNIDAL   224
UNIOR   224
United States, FDI levels   25, *26*
university education, ICT   188
USAID   28
USKOK (Office for the Prevention of
    Corruption and Organized Crime)
    9, 92–93
utilities structures, construction of
    211

value added tax (VAT)   294–301
  exemptions   297–99
  foreign trade   299–300
  place of supply   294–95
  real estate   193, 321
  recovery   301
  refunds   299
  registration   296
  returns   297
  scope and rates   294
  time and value of supply   295–96
  tourism   149
Value Added Tax Act   288
'value of supply', VAT   296
Varazdin Stock Exchange (VSE)
    77–79

VAT *see* value added tax
Voice over Internet Protocol (VoIP)
    162
Vindija company   129, 130, 132
VIPnet   158, 160–61, 164, 167–68, 180
    growt   *168, 169*
    internet services   183–84
    mobile services   165, 166, 176, 177,
        178
VIP.parking   181
VSE *see* Varazdin Stock Exchange
Vukovar, tax relief/exemptions for
    people in   292

war crime extraditions   9
warehouse property sector, Zagreb
    197
water supply appliance production *see*
    Centrometal
websites   346–49
Western ways, learning   63
withholding tax   293–94
work permits   315–18
'workbooks'   318
working conditions   42–46
World Bank group   27–28
World Economic Forum Report   33
world tourism industry, place of
        Croatian tourism in   152

World Trade Organization (WTO)
    accession   32
World Wildlife Fund (WWF)   98, *99*
WTO *see* World Trade Organization
WWF *see* World Wildlife Fund

Yugoslavia, history of   4–5

Zagreb   42–43
    real estate market   196–98
Zagreb-Gorièan Highway   210
Zagreb Insurance Company   259–63,
        *260*
    life and non-life   262–63
    performance   261
    plans   263
    products   261–63, *261*
Zagreb lubricant plant   202
Zagreb-Macelj Highway   210
Zagreb-Split (Dubrovnik) Highway
    209–10
Zagreb Stock Exchange (ZSE)
    77–79
    Dalekovod   224–25
Zagreb University, as ISP provider
    184
Zagrebacka banka   72
Zagrebacka pivovara   130, 132
Zvijezda   128–29